Rethinking Practice, Research and Education

ALSO AVAILABLE IN THE BLOOMSBURY RESEARCH METHODS SERIES

Challenging the Qualitative-Quantitative Divide, Barry Cooper, Judith Glaesser, Roger Gomm and Martyn Hammersley
Education Policy Research, edited by Helen M. Gunter, David Hall and Colin Mills
Partnerships in Education Research, Michael Anderson and Kelly Freebody

Also available from Bloomsbury

Educational Research [2nd edition], Jerry Wellington
Philosophy of Educational Research [3rd edition], Richard Pring
The Philosophy of Education: An Introduction, Richard Bailey

Rethinking Practice, Research and Education

A Philosophical Inquiry

KEVIN J. FLINT

Bloomsbury Research Methods

Bloomsbury Academic
An imprint of Bloomsbury Publishing Plc

B L O O M S B U R Y
LONDON • NEW DELHI • NEW YORK • SYDNEY

Bloomsbury Academic
An imprint of Bloomsbury Publishing Plc

50 Bedford Square
London
WC1B 3DP
UK

1385 Broadway
New York
NY 10018
USA

www.bloomsbury.com

First published 2015

British Library Cataloguing-in-Publication Data
A catalogue record for this book is available from the British Library.

ISBN: HB: 978-1-4411-4526-0
PB: 978-1-4411-8151-0
ePub: 978-1-4411-9304-9
ePDF: 978-1-4411-6757-6

Library of Congress Cataloging-in-Publication Data
A catalog record for this book is available from the Library of Congress.

Typeset by Newgen Knowledge Works (P) Ltd., Chennai, India
Printed and bound in India

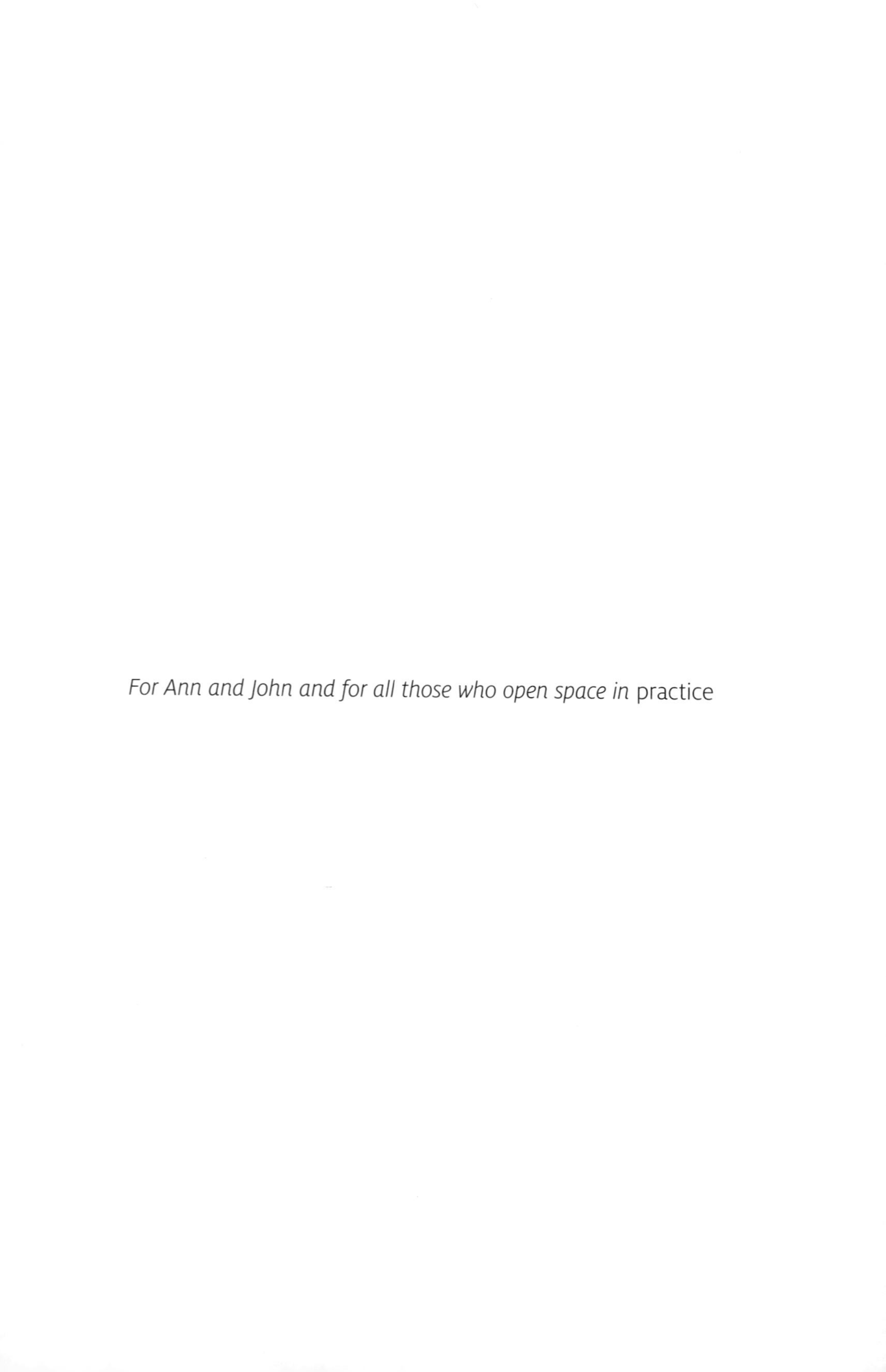

For Ann and John and for all those who open space in practice

CONTENTS

ACKNOWLEDGEMENTS

To put it simply, I have a lot of people to thank; many from a number of specialized fields of social and educational research, along with significant others involved with philosophy, mountaineering, and poetry, who have variously opened reflection upon the practice of research as a regenerative event.

In reading acknowledgements one is conscious that, in keeping with the tradition, one identifies individuals and organizations that have been pivotal in a given project. Although not wishing to break with this tradition, I would also like to acknowledge a large number of others identified in this book, whose writings have been greatly influential in shaping the course of its development, whom I have never had the pleasure of meeting. Also, in recognizing such writers themselves reflect the influences of others, one is aware of the impossibility of ever acknowledging fully the other who has contributed to the shaping of ideas featured here.

In more traditional terms, I would like to say a big thank you to my research students and to colleagues in the International Association for Practice Doctorates [IAPD] and those involved with the International Conference on Professional Doctorates [ICPD], who in their various conversations and questions have greatly challenged thinking concerned with the practices of research and their complex interrelationship with education. My particular thanks go to colleagues who have worked tirelessly in steering developments in the IAPD over the past five years: Carol Costley [Middlesex], Carol Robinson [Brighton], Michele Westhead [Kings College, London], Val Poultney [Derby], Carol Taylor [Manchester Metropolitan], Sarah Corey [Middlesex], Pauline Armsby [Westminster], Marg Malloch [Victoria University, Melbourne], and Len Cairns [Monash University, Melbourne]. Their questions, ideas, and challenges generated from experiences in a range of different practices of research have inspired thinking concerned with *practice* itself that knows none of the many arbitrary boundaries we ordinarily create in the language of research in the name of disciplinary specialization.

Adam Barnard [Nottingham Trent] has been there since the very inception of this project. I thank him for his support and friendship over the years I have been at Nottingham Trent, and for his much-appreciated capacity and enthusiasm to read and provide insightful commentary on various drafts. I am also indebted to the help and assistance given by Tina

Byrom [Nottingham Trent]. Her support and encouragement has been influential in shaping this project.

The challenges for practice-based research become particularly apparent when one attempts to open a programme of research in a new region of the world – Scandinavia, for example – that has a strong tradition in academic PhD-based forms of research. Another locus of inspiration for the ideas developed in this book has emerged from many conversations with Gerd Bjørke, Ingrid Gilje Heiberg, and other colleagues at University College, Nord-Haugasund, in beginning to develop a practice-based approach to research in Norway. Many thanks for the challenges and the significant questioning you all continue to generate that have inspired thinking in this book concerned with the complex interplay of practice, research, and education.

From the commencement of my work in Higher Education, I have been a member of the Philosophy of Education Society of Great Britain, whose conferences and workshops have inspired much discussion and thinking concerned with the writings of a number of philosophers. Through this agency, I was fortunate to meet with Nick Peim [Birmingham] who shares a common interest in the writings of Heidegger and has greatly encouraged my readings of Derrida. Many thanks to Nick for a number of memorable conversations concerned with philosophy and research that have been influential in shaping my thinking. I am also particularly grateful to one of my students, Simon Uttley, [who is Headteacher at Saint John Bosco College, London, SW19], who has a strong background in philosophy at Oxford, for his encouragement and the many philosophical discussions we continue to have concerned with his deconstructive reading of Bernard Lonergan's writings, drawing from Foucault, Heidegger, and Derrida. While these discussions are not directly connected with this book, I am really appreciative of such on-going dialogue that helps to maintain one's fluency with philosophy in practice.

I would also like to thank my friend, fellow mountaineer, and rock-climber, Alan Dougherty, who completed a philosophical research project in aesthetics and ethics concerning human interaction in wilder places at Lancaster University soon after I had completed my own doctorate at Newcastle in 2003. Our many conversations during our fell-running and our climbing together helped to open space for grounding the possibility of incorporating philosophical discourse within particular forms of practice. My thanks also go to Tim Hoskin, who as a practicing lawyer with considerable interest and experience of rock-climbing and mountaineering and is interested in philosophical inquiry. In the past few months before the final drafting of this manuscript, our conversations have helped to concretize some of the challenges and the possibilities arising from incorporating philosophical discourse within different forms of practice that consume this book.

Further removed from the obvious rigours of practicing research, but no less influential in shaping the argument that is developed here, particularly concerning the issue of 'bare life', have been a number of experiences in mountaineering and rock-climbing. I am particularly thankful to innumerable conversations with David Hopkins and many others – Andy Parkin, Martin Moran, Charlie Heard, Mike Sharpe, Tom [Richard] Thomas, Adrian Cooper, Graham Hoey, Alan Dougherty – whose enduring friendship, shared sense of adventure, and openness to possibilities concretize the invisible forces of bare life and its possible regeneration.

Many thanks, also, to Cassie Levine: her shared love of poetry and literature over many years has opened much space for thinking about the contributions of research to the continued regeneration of our essential home in language.

Finally, my thanks to Bloomsbury for agreeing to publish this book, in particular to Alison Baker, Frances Arnold, and Rachel Eisenhauer, the commissioning editors with whom I have worked over the past two years, and to the assistant editor, Kasia Figiel, and her colleagues for their helpful advice and directions given in the final stages of production.

Kevin Flint, June 2014

Introduction

This book aims to generate a new language for research as an event, as something to come that opens space for new thinking and debate concerning regeneration of lives and societies. In response, what follows are the outcomes of an initial philosophical study that has been directed towards rethinking the complex triangular relationship between practice, research, and education.

The motivation for this book arose from working to develop the professional doctorate as a way of introducing students to researching aspects of their own practices. Over the past five years, the International Association for Practice Doctorates [IAPD] and a series of International Conferences on Practice Doctorates [ICPD] have brought together a number of workshops and symposia concerned with issues of researching practice. But, on these occasions, philosophical issues have tended to remain at the margins. Such displacement raises a number of questions, not least: Does 'factical life' in its customary everyday world 'seek the easy way out'? Does 'it tend to make things easy for itself'? [Heidegger, 1985a: 108–10]. These questions suggested the need for an approach to thinking related to research that incorporates Feuerbach's principle of '*Entwicklungsfähigkeit*' [cited by Agamben, 2009: 13] – that is, thinking drawing from a philosophical style of writing that has the capacity to be developed. In drawing from Derrida, at issue remains a form of writing opening space for research as an event [*évenement*], as something 'coming' [*venir*], and as something 'to come' [*a-venir*][1]. In moving towards such an elaboration, therefore, this study sought to restore the existence of practicing research to its original difficulty; bringing it back to the question of 'bare life', to the possibilities of being. The latter remain largely without discourse in moves taken in the name of research for the knowledge economy, and even more generally in the traditional contributions of research towards the 'good life'.

Symbolic of the difficulty is the inclusion here of both an introduction and a prologue. As may be expected, the introduction speaks to a context for what is happening in this study and seeks to gather matters of concern with the inquiry presented here, locating it within the present. But, the figure of something to come [*l'avenir*], an event given expression in a prologue is something that cannot be seen coming, opening the question for us in research as to whether it can take us by surprise. The prologue constitutes its own dramatic composition. Its dramaturgy speaks to the possibilities of the future, standing in relation to the structures of the apparatus of research located in the present. There is, then, in the conventional use of the introduction along with the addition of a prologue, the interplay of *mask* – what is represented in the present, and *voice*, exposing readers to the possibility of research as something futural. Given such interplay would remain forever silenced without the mediation of signs: Don't we also have to keep in mind the 'empire of signs' in which we now live?

The particular practices that are the subject of this study concern what we are calling 'social/educational' research in the human [or cultural] sciences. The study is delimited by philosophical readings of a number of authoritative texts within this field.[2] It concentrates attention primarily upon patterns of doings and sayings of the people involved. In the study reference made to 'research' alone, unless otherwise qualified, refers to the social/educational sciences. Together, these leading texts are considered to provide a form of archival record concerned with this field of research and with opening spacing for a critical elaboration and examination of forms of education unfolding *in* this field.

In such customs, the way we tend to make light of the difficulties of existence becomes obvious. For example, if one asks what is to be learned within the traditions of research, one possible starting point is a definition of learning. In his paper on 'transformative learning: theory to practice' the sociologist and professor of continuing education at Columbia University, Jack Mezirow [1997], for example, speaks of it as a 'process of effecting change in a frame of reference' [ibid: 5]. For Mezirow, 'frames of reference are the structures of assumptions through which we understand our experiences. They selectively shape and delimit expectations, perceptions, cognition, and feelings. They set "our line of action" [ibid: 5]. He argues that 'transformative learners move toward a frame of reference that is more inclusive, discriminating, self-reflective and integrative of experience' [ibid: 5].

It is easy to be taken in by the unspoken metaphysical directions given by his paper. Within such metaphysics, he distinguishes two dimensions of 'frames of reference' in terms of:

- 'habits of mind' – those 'broad, abstract habitual ways of thinking, feeling and acting influenced by assumptions that constitute a set of codes' – and,
- specific 'points of view' – 'the constellation of belief, value judgement, attitude, and feeling that shapes a particular interpretation.' [ibid: 5–6]

Re-contextualizing his discussion about a multiplicity of forms of learning from research, and its relationship with thinking, one notes from Mazirow, 'it is crucial to recognize that learning needs must be defined so as to recognize both short-term objectives and long-term goals' [ibid: 8], just as in research, potential sponsors wish to know beforehand its expected outcomes, ambitions, and purposes. His metaphysics provides an easily accessible means–ends structuring of existence, gathered in the present. These various outcomes from formal inquiry are typically understood to be 'objects' of consciousness.

But, there is no mention of the mysteries of existence, of its continual struggles, of the issues concerned with identity, and of the possibilities of death, along with the effects of such possibilities upon human beings involved in research, and so on.

There are parallels, too, in qualitative research. In reflecting upon 'definitional issues', two leading authorities within the international field concerning 'qualitative research', Norman Denzin and Yvonna S. Lincoln [2005], speak of a 'set of interpretive and material practices that make the world visible' and so 'transform the world' on the basis of 'studying things in the natural settings, attempting to make sense of, or interpret, phenomena in terms of the meanings people bring to them' [ibid: 3]. One is struck by the absence of consideration given to what might escape any possible learning gained from such qualitative research; that is, to issues that can never be reduced to objects of consciousness.

Undoubtedly, the concerns and the approach taken in this book reflect my own experiences. In being concerned with the interplay of futural [*l'avenir*][1] and present aspects of 'bare life', the thesis developed here reflects three overlapping and inter-related trajectories of my own experience. These concern [1] learning, teaching, and formal education; [2] rock-climbing and mountaineering; and [3] practicing research. The details of my memories are limited. What follows, therefore, are a series of fragmented traces of my world that have been influential in shaping the thesis.

Kevin writes:

> In the throw of existence as a working class boy in a small village in Kent where all of the men in my family had been builders, carpenters or worked in the local factories making cement, as a young boy any possible move into studying philosophy never became a reality. But, the leader of the local church who was interested in philosophy presented a sequence of lessons I still remember with great interest and affection. I loved the discussions we had on Descartes and others.
>
> * * *
>
> In those post-war years there had been a strong moral commitment, too, from my family in support of my education.

* * *

> A pivotal aspect of my approach and interest in understanding both the practice of research and our everyday world more generally arose from my early experience in training as a teacher. In the summer of 1980 having completed my Post Graduate Certificate in Outdoor Education at '*Y Coleg Normal*', Bangor, I had been struck by the fact that throughout the entire year no one had opened discussion concerned with understanding what being human means.
>
> Here was my first professional experience of the Apollonian tradition, concerned with objectification that is largely consumed by the intentionality of cold calculation and categorical thought. I never felt comfortable with the everyday conventions and norms generated in this form of organisation. In my first post I taught chemistry. I was interested in attempting to help my students make sense of both its abstract ideas and of the discourses of science more generally, so that they could use some of this language in making sense of aspects of their own worlds.
>
> By the time I had moved on I found ways of involving groups of students in small-scale environmental research projects. I kept this interest going in my next two posts in Braunstone in Leicester and later in the 1990s in Weardale in County Durham. I wanted the students to gain first-hand experience of undertaking their own research in ways that helped them to make a contribution to their society. But, at that time the governmentality of formal education placed emphasis upon reiterating objects of formal knowledge evaluated in seemingly endless testing.
>
> I moved on to take up full time study on my doctorate in education at Newcastle, where I became consumed with Heidegger's philosophy of *Being and Time* and his later work on 'technological enframing'. It began to open my eyes to different ways of understanding science and aspects of bare life, our existence, and not least my own mountaineering.

In reading Agamben, who has also been influenced by Heidegger, it has now become obvious that the absence of any formal discussion concerned with 'bare life' in research reflects its location within a 'state of exception' in our society.

Along with experiences in education, another parallel trajectory that has been influential in shaping this thesis has grown from my engagement with rock-climbing and mountaineering.

> I took up rock-climbing when I became an undergraduate in Manchester. It had symbolized for me that I was doing something adventurous and far removed from what I had considered to be the norms of society. It was my way of treading a path away from the materialistic and instrumental culture in which I felt that my parents had become located.

> Mountaineering has a rich literature. I came to love poetry. As a young man possessed with the instinct to climb everywhere and everything it also brought me face-to-face with a number of near-death experiences. It put me in touch with the Dionysian and Chthonic dimensions of existence, so opening reflection on identity and the possibility of death. I love the aesthetic experience of climbing in wild places – on the sea cliffs, in the mountains. The poesy of experience still keeps alive the sense of mystery in our existence that it seems to me research is in danger of losing.

The third parallel and inter-connected trajectory of my experience is concerned with research itself and with using research as a way of challenging the possibilities of new thinking and different ways of living.

> My first experience of research was gained from working towards a PhD in chemistry at Manchester. I never completed this project. It was directed towards the synthesis of a less toxic fire retardant that could be incorporated in polymers.
>
> Looking back there was a strong sense of the Apolline spirit at work here. I had always been totally absorbed to find ever more about the hidden structures of the great numbers of elements and their transformation into substances that can be found in our world, and by the history of the transformations of the language of alchemy into formal chemistry. But, the synthesis of organic compounds, I came to understand, was not my passion. I departed after only two years of study and took up mountaineering. Here was one of my first real decisions in life. I was no longer being swept along in the ebbs, flows, and eddies, in the river of everyday life.
>
> Here was a working class boy with an Enlightenment ideal that chemistry could be put to good use in order to generate products for society. But, there were many forces at work that compromised such an ideal and its many contradictions. Immersing myself in the world of teaching I became much more interested in working with people and understanding the intricacies of human existence.
>
> In my doctoral research in education at Newcastle, involving the work of Heidegger, Foucault and others I initially found myself lost and almost overwhelmed by the difficulties. It is only more recently that I began to see the struggle between the desire for order and the chthonian principle of identity. I recall, too, just how easy it is to become taken-in by the fetishism of modern information and communication technology, ICT. The time-scale for doing a review of the literature for a given study has become much reduced. Such relationships with technology Heidegger conceives in terms of enframing [*das Gestell*]. His discourse began to open space for consideration given to the counter-intuitive production

of a dystopia on grounds of reason. What had particularly excited me about Heidegger's critique concerning technological enframing was its connection with being, with language and with the mystery of existence. It begun to open a new language and a radically different space for thinking to that in which I had been thrown as an undergraduate.

On moving into higher education, initially involving the training of teachers, the complex struggles that have generated these experiences made me think about so-called lifelong learning and how it can become strongly driven in enframing [Flint and Needham, 1997]. It lay behind the possibility of opening space for learning as an event in research. Consequently, the structure of this book is given by a series of paradoxical assertions concerned with learning from research that are always necessarily incomplete, reflecting such an event.

This project sought to address the overarching question of the extent to which ironically formal learning, in its focus upon objects of consciousness, necessarily delimits research. Countering such boundary-work opened the question of the shape of research needed for learning to become an event, as something emerging in the passage of everyday life that continually surprises and excites new possibilities.

The argument in this study is divided into four steps. Each step sought to address one of four consecutive and interrelated questions concerned with learning from the traditions of research, so generating its own thesis. Each of the theses generated from the deconstruction is presented as epilogues, ἐπίλογος. The prefix ἐπί, in addition, is here taken to open a futural orientation for thinking, so that the epilogues open 'spacing' outside the languages [λογος] of research.

This study opens in response to the question – *is there more to learning about practice than you think*?

Chapter one is concerned with the pragmatics and patterns of the customary doings and sayings of people. Rather than examining practice through many approaches to qualitative research – including those explored by Ritchie; Lewis; McNaughton, Nicholls and Ormston; Silverman; Green, and others – or even by reference to those leaders in the field of action research who thematize 'practice' including Kemmis, Taggart, and Nixon; Elliott; Baumfield; McNiff; Chevalier, and others – here the focus will remain on the underlying sociology of practice and its synthesis of theory. It begins with consideration of the sociologist, Andreas Reckwitz's [2002], practice theory. At issue is the question of how social order arises from the multiplicity of actions taken by people. The discussion sheds light upon how Reckwitz's theory is located along a Cartesian–Husserlian axis [based upon Descartes's ontology] for understanding the world, where many of our customs are located within Kant's courtroom of reason. Comparison is made with one of the emerging leaders within the field, Theodore Schatzki's theory of integrative practice as a dispersed nexus of doings and sayings, with Martin Heidegger's [1962] largely pragmatic reading of our everyday world that emerges from his magnum opus, *Being and Time*. It closes with a consideration of what is often missing in pragmatic readings of practice, namely, our relationship with being and the 'upon which' or 'meaning maker' structuring projections of beings in research.

Chapter two moves to examine the tranquilizing effects of the dominion of everyday research. The opening half of the chapter continues to excavate deeper into the pragmatic readings of Heidegger's [1962] *Being and Time*, in order to open thinking of the existential and temporal dimensions of our world that stand outside any metaphysical determinations of *practice*. We also pick up another story created from the work of Jacques Derrida. Many view Derrida as a frivolous revolutionary, but this reading takes seriously his work in opening the necessary intellectual tension and dissonance at the heart of research. The focus upon identity leads us to examine the ontotheological structuring at work in most research that is ordinarily passed over. Customarily, this phenomenon simply has not received attention. But, in the sublime quantum leaps in ICT used around the globe over the past 40 years, our relationship with technology [which far exceeds everyday technological applications], and what Heidegger [1977] calls enframing [*das Gestell*], there is a danger of it reducing human beings to becoming its puppets. The force with which the ontotheology drives enframing in our everyday routines is given expression in Giddens's [1990: 130] terms of 'the juggernaut of modernity' – 'a runaway engine of enormous power which collectively as human beings we can drive to some extent but which also threatens to rush out of control and which could rend itself asunder' [ibid: 139]. But, Giddens makes no mention of enframing. In drawing from Derrida in response to the question of enframing the thesis concentrates upon *différance* – in English we have no single word that translates this term but roughly it expresses both a difference in space and a deferral in time between express signs and the unfolding actions or phenomena to which they refer. *Différance* is shown to be pivotal in opening space for the possibility of balancing the powers at work in enframing and in opening *spacing* for bare life.

In Chapter three we turn to consider the biopolitical and juridico-institutional models of power shaping much investigation. Here we examine the arguments of Foucault and Agamben concerned with the issue of powers that until this point have largely remained silent. Both protagonists work towards localized resistances to the growth of powers. Foucault's analysis of the contingent histories of the body opens critical reflection upon both his archaeology and genealogy of power and the effects upon what is seen as the Janus face of identity. The powers of social practices arising from within panopticism, emotivism, and neoliberalism are all seen to converge in providing administrations and other governmental apparatuses concerned with research with the fantasy of 'transparent' representations of what is done in the field. It opens questions from Foucault and Agamben on the biopolitics shaping traditions and the nature of the apparatus. In this study, we focus principally upon the apparatus of research. Where Foucault attempts to separate juridico-institutional models of power from biopolitical models, Agamben explores their intersection, so opening further questions concerned with the sovereign powers of languages of research and the ways research itself shapes bare life. The focus upon 'bare life' creates a counterpoint to enframing; the space it generates opens all forms of inquiry to becoming 'events', whereas '*das Ge-stell*' is always infused with the nostalgia of a new beginning for philosophy in a world prior to Plato.

The next step in the argument sought to address another related question on learning from our habitual doings and sayings: *Are we really open to learning*?

The current system of ethics in vogue in research still retains the assumption that all that is required is a deontological structure governing the production of truth claims to knowledge. In Chapter four, this assumption is questioned in the light of the intensity and extensity of the powers arising from our relationship with enframing that continue to grow around the globe [Held et al., 1999: 32–86]. Deontological structuring of the ethics of research, it is argued, blinds researchers from the powers at work in enframing and the sovereign powers of its languages shaping bare life. The examination of moves towards justice in research opens space for challenging the reformulation of ethics and an understanding that justice to come always exceeds its pre-judicial structuring. It opens space for research as an event. The intentionality of deconstruction and the work of mourning in research are both futural, it is argued, opening bare life to the possibility of justice to come. This process always carries with it a gesture, 'yes' to emancipation without being delimited by its possible metanarrative.

Chapter five provides concrete examples, uncovering moves towards justice and its relationship with laws inscribed in research. In looking out from such customs, the extant focus of the *practice* of research upon the visible aspects of its ontotheology connects it with the wider *Society of the Spectacle* [Debord, 1977]. What becomes apparent is that although there are latent forces at work in the research moving some of its traditions towards justice in opening space for bare life, these remain largely delimited within structures consonant with *the spectacle*. The analysis suggests strongly the need for the de-centring of such structures.

In considering the paradigms of research, their methodologies, methods, and data analysis, the question that informs the study in the next step of the argument may be stated simply as *is it not possible to step beyond learning in research*?

The study presented in Chapter six sought to understand *what is given* in patterns of doings and sayings within different paradigms. Here we should keep in mind the Latin, *datum*, meaning that which is given, present, from which we derive our modern term, data, used in research. The study reveals the potency of both the metaphysical structuring and the naming force of being as presence. It also explores in more detail the movements of the force we will call 'delimiting education' derived from the work of the neo-Marxist critic, Raymond Williams [1966]. This is seen to emerge from the cultures of research. Just how this happens and the question of its relationship with authentic education will have to wait until the concluding chapters. The argument shows how forces delimiting education, locate the process of research as visible, so creating an almost perfect disguise for its ontotheology.

At issue in Chapter seven are the methodologies used. The study reveals the extent to which many researchers are already beginning to anticipate some of the issues arising from the ontotheological structuring of methodologies. Ordinarily, however, this form of language at the time of writing is simply not used. Also apparent is the violence of enframing – that is, the way particular emphases are placed on aspects of everyday customs to the exclusion of others that arise from the sovereign powers of their languages. Although the general pattern that is uncovered is one in which enframing remains almost perfectly disguised, there are some notable studies, particularly within feminist discourse, that serve to challenge aspects of the ontotheology, albeit without registering their contestations in this way. The study details the pedagogic actions of cultures delimiting education in research, so providing an indexical measure of the powers silencing bare life.

Chapter eight focuses attention upon the relationship of methods and any possible moves towards justice. At issue is the extent to which in particular studies the methods reveal beings constituted in *différance* before their reduction to desubjectification and their possible subjectification. The study provides a number of case examples from research where practitioners have actively sought to challenge aspects of the extant order. It also introduces the issue of the style of disclosive spacing created within research. In so doing, it generates spacing for thinking concerned with the structural necessity of incorporating unconditional, incalculable, and impossible dimensions of practice.

In Chapter nine, the deconstruction of the analytics of research is structured against indications drawn from the writings of Deleuze and Guattari. It opens spacing for reflection upon the rhizomatic networks and the assemblages mediating thinking in research. Consideration is also given to the dynamic interplay between what Deleuze and Guattari identify as molar and molecular dimensions of practices. In this way, the study opens questions concerning the efficacy of the production of powers used to counter the orders of domination experienced in many traditions. From a psychoanalytical perspective, drawing from Lacan [2006], it opens space for thinking concerned with desires and their structuring within sub-conscious forms of *jouissance* driving particular approaches to research. The cases explored reflect obvious gestures in the direction of justice and even moves towards uncovering aspects of the interiority of the self, although such terminologies are not used currently within the traditions.

In moving to examine the final step in the argument concerned with policy in research, the overarching question remains: *Can research open spacing for learning to learn*? One possible response to this question can be found in the epilogue.

In focusing upon the issue of policy, Chapter ten provides a reading of Denzin's seminal paper on the politics of evidence. What becomes obvious is the ignorance of policy makers. The privileging of quantification, as the very acme for obtaining measures of objectivity and truth that now finds expression in the emergent knowledge economy, is found wanting. Policy makers' complete unawareness of the hidden forces shaping such activity, aligned with misunderstandings of the nature of trust and risk in research as an event are particularly alarming. Such unfamiliarity, it would seem, arises from the forces delimiting education that focus policy makers' attention only upon the conditional, possible, and calculable dimensions of customary forms of action. They ignore completely the structural necessity of its unconditional, impossible, and incalculable dimensions, without which there could be no transformations in any of the visible aspects of research, and without which bare life is ever in danger of becoming moribund. The focus upon the objectivity of what can be learned from research has served to elide completely the significance of the movements of *educere* and of *educare* in authentic education unfolding from such formal inquiry. The spacing cultivated by these movements, it is shown, constitute the grounds for trust and risk in the reiteration of discourses in research that literally vitalize such activity. In this way, conscious measures of what can be objectively learned from research serve only as a distraction from the hidden forces at work in its pre-judicial structuring.

At issue in Chapter eleven are the languages of research mediating such integrative practice. Here we return to the disseminative drift of the 'Empire of Signs' [Barthes, 2005]. The argument is developed on the basis of a critical examination of the Rabinnical and Joycean forms of repetition of signs in language. Of particular interest is the play of signs within Joycean critical forms of repetition. At issue is not the content of research claims, but their ontotheology. On the basis of the history and cultures of integrated practices, it is argued that we simply have not taken sufficient account of what is *at play* in research. This thought brings into play aspects of the natural sciences and, in particular, the work of a leading neuroethologist, Paul Maclean, whose evolutionary approach to the study of mammals also alerts his readers to the significance of play within family units. It leads on to further attention being given to the forces of Eros at work in shaping research, and the examination of the supplement, authentic education, that emerges from engagement in such practices. Authentic education is found to be an education constituted in *différance*. In concluding the argument, we return once more to the incalculable, unconditional, and impossible dimensions of the patterns of our habitual everyday doings and sayings. These are found to be structurally necessary for the growth of bare life's horizons and also find expression in Heidegger's work with the mystery of 'earth'.

The argument in the concluding Chapter twelve opens consideration of a movement into a post-metaphysical bricolage. The thesis has a similar structure to this openg preface, involving interplay of a conclusion with a futural epilogue that is here based upon a deconstructive reading of Joe Kincheloe's [2005a] bricolage. It opens with a brief examination of the historical and the cultural space in which his studies have been located. Questions are raised concerned with decision making and finding a pathway forward that is at the heart of the traditions of research as events involving bare life. The deconstruction challenges reflection upon the significance of *aporia* – the non-way – and the structural necessity of everyday customs incorporating the dimensions of the possible, conditional, and calculable along with spacing for the impossible, the unconditional, and the incalculable. The deconstruction sought to open thinking concerned with the heterogeneity of ethical research that in its moves towards justice always exceeds its extant laws.

Prologue: Rationale for the approach adopted in this study

Facing the unknowable future many readers may still be wondering about the rationale for the approach adopted here. Critics could easily argue those who may be interested in issues concerned with the human condition may consult specialist areas of philosophy, psychoanalysis, and psychology, along with many forms of expression explored and created in the name of art.

Indeed, in the customs of research, the difficulties of human existence, it would appear, are simply not something that concerns most researchers. Their primary challenge, it would seem, is to develop reliable and validated knowledges that are valued on the basis of the fresh insights they bring to the world. That is *the* primary requirement of the knowledge economy.

All of the training received in research aligned with its evaluation simply creates and reinforces this seemingly solid platform on which to develop further knowledge of the social world. No one here mentions the violence of such discourses that in one stroke close down bare life's capacity for expression in accord with the technological structuring of research. Instead, one's professionalism as a researcher, it is coming to be assumed, is primarily concerned with obtaining 'quality outcomes' – whatever that may mean: these are currently being shaped by hubristic forms of 'managerialist discourse'. The fantasy of 'accountability' and 'audit' creates cultures littered with hegemonic performatives – 'standards', 'benchmarking', 'performance indicators', that are continually subject to 'surveillance' – give indications of 'ends' for research that has become the very means of achieving such desired outcomes. A measure of the powers of this magnificent fantasy is given by its sublime 'emotivism'. This still remains without critics in research. The technological means–ends structuring of existence is further reinforced by training and modes of evaluation used by sponsors and other governmental agencies [Flint and Peim, 2012]. Bare life in such technological world is always in danger of being reduced to a sublime excess of energy that is continually available for use. Moreover, the current deontological structuring of research ethics does nothing to open space for thinking about the alienating effects of such technological structuring.

Ironically, in compartmentalization of research, it is apparent that the basis for critiquing such technological structuring drawing from specialist discourses of philosophy has become separated completely from the means of production of knowledge in research. It is for this reason that the thesis developed in this book is concerned with *practice. Practice* per se knows none of the boundaries and divisions created by specialization. Indeed, *practice* itself is not delimited by the identity 'research'. It not only gives us a way of connecting with the capitalist canon that here will be read primarily through the work of Guy Debord's [1977] '*The Society of the Spectacle*', but it also opens new space for thinking by connecting with other practices – poetry, literature, mountaineering, philosophy . . . – that ordinarily in the customs of research have tended to remain excluded. Such practices not only challenge research with the facticity of existence, they also reveal many of the secrets of bare life. It is to this question of *practice* and its relationship with research that we now turn.

PART ONE

Practice of social and educational research

CHAPTER ONE

The pragmatics of practice in research: What is so easily missed?

Here we are concerned with the issue of *practice* that permeates every boundary and division in our modern world and the apprehension of possibilities for research emerging from such concerns. The issue of *practice* also opens questions on what is missing from research that has come to privilege knowledge production in response to the demands of the knowledge economy. *Practice* turns out to be the complex matter of an education – or rather, different forms of education – that arise from being involved *in* the world of research. The complex relationship between forms of education and research that both opens and closes down thinking is a theme to which we will return throughout this book. It also points the way towards the hidden interiority of the self, Heidegger had conceived in metaphysical terms, as being-in-the-world. The full story concerned with what is missing from pragmatic accounts of the customs of research will also take up most of this book.

* * *

The express mission for the European University Association [EUA], of 'contribut[ing] to the development, advancement and improvement of doctoral education and research training in Europe'[1] suggests there are many challenges for such *practice* if its 'ambitious objectives concerning enhanced research capacity, innovation and economic growth are to be met'.[2] At issue are not just how the *practice* of research can be shaped over time but how we understand this event [*événement*]. A recent communiqué from the Oxford Learning Institute [OLI] [2013], opening reflection on 'the substantial impact' of the Bologna Process' and on the traditions of 'doctoral education, indicates that such *practice* is unlikely to remain simply confined to Europe.

In pragmatic terms of what is observable and what can be done in the name of customary actions according to Crosier and Parveva's [2013] report on 'The impact of the Bologna Process in Europe and Beyond', the teleoaffective shaping of such practice 'has created a dynamic that will not be stopped' [ibid: 81]. Such a dynamic is characteristic of 'integrative practices' [Schatzki, 1996: 99–110], reflecting not just sets of individual actions alone, but also the teleological and affective dimensions guiding individuals in the patterned repetitions of practices [ibid: 124–25].

Language is one such integrative practice. Since 'Dewey and Wittgenstein', we know that rather than 'mirroring reality' 'it is something we do' [Biesta, 2005: 54]. For Heidegger, what can be known and be thought in our everyday world, is largely determined by what 'one' does and 'one' says. In the field of education the reclamation of practices involving reiterations of the language of education, Biesta [2005] has argued, from other customs centring upon the 'language of learning', has emerged as a particular locus of disputation over the past two decades. Similarly, one of the motivations in this study of research is to open thinking upon the significance of particular forms of education cultivated within practices of research. These are often pushed aside in the rush by sponsors, administrators, and others who wish to know, in purportedly 'objective' terms, what can be *learned* from particular research projects.

While Biesta's [2005] paper centres upon the customary use of language in education, it also raises other questions regarding how we understand 'integrated practices' more generally in the world of research. Here, the question of what is meant by practice takes us behind the headline, 'The fundamentals of planning', in Crosier and Parveva's [2013] report.

In a move towards a 'theory of social practices', the sociologist, Reckwitz [2002], indicates that the 'turn to practices' in social theory 'seems to be tied to an interest in both the 'everyday' and the 'life-world' in which theorists draw upon 'Wittgenstein and to a lesser degree, early Heidegger' as 'common philosophical points of reference' [that are hardly ever systematically analysed]' [ibid: 244]. Given that Schatzki [1996; Schatzki et al., 2001] has already provided such an examination of Wittgenstein's and, more recently, Heidegger's philosophy for practice, and given also that education is concerned with the cultivation of new cultures, here the focus is upon uncovering what is so easily missed in pragmatic views of our everyday world, drawing initially upon Heidegger's philosophy and later taking a left turn with Derrida.

The locus of much contemporary doctoral research into practice for the past three decades has been the professional doctorate, and practice-based PhD studies. In Australia, the United States, and the UK, where the professional doctorate has enjoyed its own trajectories and histories in each of these regions of the world, in its grounding of researching customary patterns of the everyday doings and sayings of people in particular contexts, it has almost exclusively relied upon the privileging of knowledge production within the traditional disciplinary structures. Part of the backdrop to such developments has been created by a complex epistemology of knowledge production outside the traditional disciplinary structures of the university by Michael Gibbons and his colleagues [1994] and by Helga Nowotny and her colleagues [2001]. The latter have also been the subject of exploration and debate [Seddon, 2000; Maxwell, 2003; Stephenson et al., 2004].

Against this backdrop, three generations of researching practice in and through the professional doctorate have been observed. First- and second-generation professional doctorates have been structured largely on grounds of epistemologies located within and outside the university, respectively [Seddon, 2000; Maxwell, 2003]. In the UK, many such programmes in education still remain grounded in first-generation university-based disciplinary structures [Flint, 2011a]. Third-generation professional doctorates, by contrast, continue to be explored and examined in 'multi-disciplinary' practices that are seen as a characteristic of the everyday world of the workplace located largely outside the university [Gibbs and Costley, 2006; Maguire and Gibbs, 2013; Gibbs and Barnett, 2014]. But, in each of these forms of research, the axis of understanding around which the understandability of everyday customs are organized still remains the disciplinary structures of knowledge.

Seeking to uncover what lies behind the headlines of our everyday world, the concern here is to explore and to examine critically the basis upon which our customs serve to constitute social order in the supposedly complex world of actions taken by a multiplicity of individuals in contrasting forms of integrative practice. The question remains the basis upon which customary repetitions involving the doings and sayings of people constitute a form of organization, independent of the privileging of knowledge production. In examining *practice*, one might begin, therefore, with the following thesis: the horizon of *practice* per se is simply constituted by the limits of what can be said and done by people, and as a being practice constitutes its own organization in the world, independent of any imperative for the foregrounding of knowledge production. But this initial thesis creates its own problems, just as Heidegger's [1962] metaphysical 'care structure' for beings did when it was first published in 1927 as a deconstruction of what is done in our everyday world within the horizons of *Being and Time*.

Heidegger's [1992] analysis was based on his particular reading of 'Plato's Sophist'. It strongly reflected his own reading of Aristotle's *Metaphysics* and the *Nicomachean Ethics*, and in particular the relationship between being and non-being that emerged from his line-by-line examination of Plato's dialogue in the Sophist. Heidegger's questioning of our everyday world had arisen from a thought-provoking and original reiteration of Ancient Greek philosophy in the context of the modern world while still retaining some of its earlier metaphysical structuring.

Let us examine Heidegger's thesis from a pragmatic standpoint to see what can be learned [where learning is not reduced to uncovering an object that is presupposed to exist] in such a world. It is important to keep in the foreground the big picture involving the existential and temporal dimensions of the patterns of our ordinary doings and sayings that are so easily elided. We should keep in mind everything that is done in our world is mediated by our relationship with discursive practices and with the drift of the great 'empire of signs' [Barthes, 2005] in which we live.

Rather than the rhetoric of moves towards supposedly superior purchases on various truth claims to knowledge, the approach taken here, in the spirit of Aristotle's education,[3] is to open space to become conversant with and to keep in play many possibilities of understanding that have been uncovered from practices involving the act of research.

Approaching practices

The approach adopted is one of 'making strange the familiar' – '*Verfremdungseffekt*' is the term used by the playwright Bertolt Brecht [cited by Willett, 1971: 91]. At issue is the possibility of teachings that free oneself through particular styles of research from the often hidden forces of oppression at work in our lifeworlds.

In drawing from Heidegger at issue are not teachings about our everyday world that are always in danger of being reduced to 'economic transactions' based upon spurious measures of the quantity and quality of information appropriated about practice [Biesta, 2005]. But, as Heidegger [1968{1954}] suggests, 'it is a teaching that calls for this – to let learn' [ibid: 15] in and through what is done in practice. In looking towards the future, such teaching is not based upon the pre-supposition what *is* to be learned already exists somewhere, but rather that any possible learning unfolds from the experience of research.

In the traditions[2[Introduction]] making sense of what Heidegger is saying to us here in his concern with the everyday world is not straightforward. Especially when confronted with a multiplicity of theories in almost every direction that already carry with them presuppositions of what *is* to be learned. In attempting to resolve this issue let us return once more to Reckwitz's [2002] paper in its moves 'Toward a Theory of Social Practices'. Here, it will become more obvious what is at stake in making sense of the customs of research, therefore providing a more detailed rationale for thinking mediated by Heidegger's philosophy.

Theoretical synthesis of *practice*

At issue in theorizing practices is an explanation for social order arising from the complex, multifarious, and sometimes chaotic actions of individuals. Reckwitz distinguishes three contrasting options used to explain how social order emerges in such circumstances. He identifies these in terms of the economics of 'rational choice theory' – where social order is assumed to result from the choices made by suitably informed individuals – or the sociology of norm-referenced behaviours and actions drawing from Durkheim's and Parsons' understandings of social interaction, or 'practice theories'. In Reckwitz's [2002] terms, 'the vocabularies' of the latter theorists 'stand opposed to purpose oriented and norm referenced models of explaining actions' [ibid: 246]. From his perspective, 'practice theory does not place the social in mental qualities, nor discourse, nor in interaction but in practices' [ibid: 249] [*vide* Bourdieu, 1977; Butler, 1990; Foucault, 1978, 1985; 2002{1969}; Garfinkel, 1984{1967}; Giddens, 1979, 1984; Latour, 2007, Schatzki, 1996].

The tacit 'subject' of Reckwitz's [2002] synthesis, 'practice theory', is first distinguished from cultural theory per se and then defined by the following unspoken 'object' of his consciousness on grounds of reason [which itself remains unstated] concerned with practice. He writes: 'a practice [*Praktik*] is a routinized type of behaviour consisting of several interconnected elements [ibid: 249], including:

- Forms of bodily activities
- Forms of mental activities, things and their use
- A background of knowledge in the form of understanding, know-how, states of emotion and motivational knowledge. [ibid: 249]

Let us hold any reflection upon the background to the privileging of the body in Reckwitz's theory until after we have connected a little more with Heidegger's philosophy. Continuing to differentiate his understanding of his subject, he writes that 'the core of practice theory lies in different ways of seeing the body' [ibid: 251]. In accord with the reasons grounding his synthesis, he further differentiates the conscious object of his understanding, the body, viewed 'not merely as an instrument used by an individual to act', but in terms of 'routinized actions' being seen as 'bodily performances' [ibid: 251]. Such routines also connect with the performativity of the body within panoptic institutional regimes. We will explore this a little later. His synthesis of his subject, practice, therefore, would appear to be grounded upon Kant's 'conditions of the possibility' or the a priori conditions of experience that must be fulfilled for his subject to relate to objects of consciousness.

Reckwitz's writings concerned with practice theory continue to reflect critically upon and so move on from the mind–body dualism characteristic of a Cartesian view of the world where the subject was considered to stand in relation to an external world. According to Rene Descartes's thesis: 'I think, therefore I am',[4] the only sure way of constituting knowledge is on the basis of what 'I think'. Of course, Kant's critiques serve to create a philosophical analysis that reconciled Descartes's rationalism with empiricism [Gardner, 1999]. Empiricism for Kant gave us the basis for being sure of the world outside the subject's mind. Following Kant, Husserl considered that he had 'culminated this philosophical tradition',[5] with his focus upon the intentionality of consciousness, challenging the privileging of epistemology by focusing upon the semantics of meaning production. Here was the backdrop to the so-called language turn in social theory.

In Reckwitz's words: 'for practice theory bodily and mental patterns are necessary components of practices and are thus social' [ibid: 225]. In accord with Husserl, the individual's consciousness in Reckwitz's ontology is intentional, that is, in being directed towards specific objects of consciousness concerned with our lifeworld, it serves to create a representation of such practice. In Husserl's ontology of the lifeworld, as detailed in the *Crises* between 1935 and 1938, moments of such intentionality fall under 'distinct essences' he identifies as 'Consciousness, Nature and Culture' [Woodruff –Smith, 2007: 182].

As a conscious subject in practice, I think, perceive, and intend, in this case a theory. Here, as a subject, my consciousness is drawn to Reckwitz's synthesis of a theory of practice. Now, cognitive science keeps in play Husserl's conception of the intentionality of consciousness as a guide to experimentations on the mind.

Practice theory has already identified its essential Nature in terms of the body being the locus of social order. Maurice Merleau-Ponty [2002] saw the need for such analysis of the body in perception. He recognized that one of the limits of Heidegger's analysis amounted to seeing things without fully appreciating the significance of the body in this process, and he developed a philosophical account of the way perception is always already an embodied activity.

In social interaction we 'use particular things in a certain way' [Reckwitz, 2002: 252] in accord with the essential Culture in which we are located. For example, in emphasizing the cultural dimensions of intentionality concerned with the conscious subject, he alerts readers to 'specific forms of knowledge' that are 'more than 'knowledge-that' [ibid: 253]. Reckwitz's foregrounding of know-how, motivation, and understanding underlines for him the enabling character of cultural knowledge.

In reflecting upon Reckwitz's theorizing of practice, it is interesting to examine in a little more detail Schatzki's thesis, as one of Reckwitz's bases for theorization. Given that Schatzki's [1996: 88] conception of practice has been influenced by his readings of Wittgenstein and Heidegger's [1962] *Being and Time*, it begins to point the way to an examination of more subtle, but no less powerful forces at work in practice that remain largely presaged within Reckwitz's [2002] paper. Unlike Reckwitz, Schatzki [1996] lays emphasis upon what he calls a 'temporally unfolding dispersed nexus of doings and sayings' [ibid: 89]. He distinguishes three 'major avenues of linkage' connecting any 'nexus of practice':

1. 'Through understandings . . . of what to say and do;
2. Through explicit rules, principles, precepts, and instructions; and
3. through what he identifies as 'teleoaffective' structures embracing ends, projects, tasks, purposes, beliefs, emotions and moods' [ibid: 89].

Rather than the theory of practice developed by Reckwitz with its locus in the consciousness of individuals that tends to still any play in the unfolding movement of beings, in his own particular discursive practice Schatzki [1996] has been concerned with developing a language expressive of the movements of beings in time: 'the manifold doings and sayings' [ibid: 106] of people. But, it is easy in our modern cultures to read Shatzki's discourse in Cartesian or Husserlian terms, as further information available to the conscious subject, here concerned with practice. As this reading of Reckwitz's paper illustrates, it is relatively straightforward to expropriate discourse concerned with the 'know-how' of practical activity into propositional knowledge appearing in the form of theories. We have therefore got some work to do in orienting ourselves towards reading Heidegger's understanding of *how* our practical activities unfold in the world of research in a completely different way.

Here there is always a danger of becoming excessively analytical in the process of deconstruction. Nevertheless, it is interesting to observe that whereas Reckwitz [2002] chooses to retain the language of '*routines*' of behaviour, Schatzki [1996: 102–3] reflects critically upon 'allegedly rule-governed *customs*' of practice, here, for example, found in research, that he indicates 'are not governed by any explicit rules' [ibid: 102, emphasis added]. Reckwitz's language of 'routine' connotes 'a regularly followed procedure'. As 'an established way of doing something' [OED] it provides a focus upon the objective, definable and localized dimensions of practice consonant with the nature of theorizing such practice that makes demands for clearly defined objects of consciousness, without ever fully encompassing the horizon of possibilities expressed in such practice. The language of 'custom', by comparison, connotes directly 'a habitual use of practice' [OED] where the horizon of such custom remains largely unchanged. The word 'largely' has been inserted in recognition that there is always the possibility of change in custom and practice – in the scientific world, for example, Kuhn's [1970] 'paradigms in crisis' represent such possible transformation. Behind everyday practice Heidegger [1962: 239] viewed such breaks from custom in terms of 'authentic being'.

Custom also expresses the informal spoken form of law reproduced in practices [Stein, 1966: 9–10]. In reflecting upon the relation of 'law and writing' in her *Dialectic of Nihilism*, in etymological terms Gillian Rose [1984: 135] connects 'custom' as 'the public declaration of *ius*' [justice] in 'lex', law, that she derives from the Greek verb, *legein*, meaning to gather, to say and the Greek, *logos*, word. Interestingly for the OED [2013] 'the Latin, *leg*, – *lēx* is not now generally believed to be cognate [being referred to the root *leg-* of *legĕre* to gather, read, *legein*, to gather, say]; but in many other languages the word for "law" is derived from roots meaning "to place"'. We will return to this issue of customs of our everyday lifeworld in considering further the placement of the 'principle of reason' as grounds for much contemporary practice, and in considering the significance of law within a reformulated ethics of practice.

It is also apparent for Shatzki [1996] that custom [law] in practices is not a matter of following rules, because for him these 'threaten to obscure not only the unformulability of understandings, but also the presence and complexity of normative teleological hierarchies' [103]. The latter Shatzki draws from *Being and Time* [Heidegger, 1962]. So, rather than Kant's courtroom of consciousness where your freedom is on trial, and you have been, as Rose [1984] indicates, 'judge, witness, and clerk for so long you have ceased to notice its strange ambience' [ibid: 11], Heidegger's ontology creates a more complex picture of our world. Kant's courtroom has gone; in its place, Heidegger examines and opens a language for our doings and copings within our everyday world. Practices more generally, in fact, where we are 'thrown', and in which we remain in the throw of existence throughout our lives [Heidegger, 1962: 135, 145].

From a sociological perspective, Bourdieu [1996] here stops us in our tracks. He reminds his readers that the 'elevated style' of Heidegger's discourse is 'not merely a contingent property' but a matter of politics. He coins the phrase 'conceptual magistrature' [ibid: 88] to describe the authority of law invested in a collective body by virtue of its conformity with an 'elevated style' of discourse. It is not difficult to uncover the many devices Heidegger uses in registering such style. Instead of practice, for example, he draws on the rarely used term 'comportment'; Husserl's 'intentionality' becomes 'being-in-the-world' [Richardson, 2012: 48–49]; and, what is interrogated by Heidegger is not an individual, person, or even a human being, but an entity – *Dasein* – that in the tradition remains un-translated. In the German language, *Dasein* means existence or presence – '*etwas ins Dasein rufen*' – to bring something into existence, or to call it into being. Michael Inwood's [1999] dictionary is helpful at such points. It indicates that '*Dasein* is used for 1. the being of humans, 2. the entity or person who has this being' [ibid: 42]. Even in attempting to make sense of this definition we must be cautious. Though correct, it is important to see that 'being' is not something that we are ordinarily and actively conscious of in our everyday practices. A priori, it constitutes a largely unconscious background to our know-how and understandings of the world.

At this point, however, it becomes apparent that any such 'conceptual magistrature' is not confined to Heidegger's discourses alone; it is difficult, for example, to find any understanding of 'world' articulated within the discourses of research[2[Introduction]] used to inform this study. Though Denzin and Lincoln [2011] and Arthur et al., [2012] make references to 'worldview', their books create their own form of magistrature in not including understandings of 'being-in-the-world' itself. Here, in remaining in *practice* per se that is no longer striated by arbitrary disciplinary boundaries, we learn from philosophical discourse that 'my world consists of the kinds of things for which I am prepared by my competent directedness. It is that vast network of these kinds, linked in organised ways' [Richardson, 2012: 99]. A world is that wherein *Dasein* lives. Richardson captures neatly how it functions in two memorable phrases: 'the world is the web of routes we know our way along; it is the system of ways we know how to handle things' [ibid: 100]. At issue for Heidegger are understandings of being and of being-in-the-world in the flux of time. Not the time of chronometers, but lived time, temporality, constituting the horizon of being.

It is ironic then that Bourdieu uses the term '*conceptual* magistrature', because concepts and theories have already arrested any such play of the flux in lived time. If there is a political intentionality in Heidegger's writings, therefore, preference is given to Brecht's term '*Verfremdungseffekt*' – making strange the familiar – to describe such intent. It creates a number of obvious challenges for practices of research.

We might start by thinking about reason and theory in such practices[2]. These issues usually give rise to a multiplicity of applications rather than becoming the subject of any deeper critique in research.[2[Introduction]] But, in 1956–7, in a series of lectures titled *The Principle of Reason*, Heidegger [1991 {1957}] wished to break the hold that this very principle – 'nothing is without reason' – has in our world. For Heidegger, the power of this principle arises because:

> the subject demands that reason [ratio] be brought forth for the object, only because the subject has long ceased to let being be in its own ground. [Caputo, 1987: 223; Heidegger, 1991{1957}: 53–4][6]

Its power arises, then, not only from its generation of technological means–ends structuring, but also from providing only one way of revealing the world in the practice of research that Heidegger identifies in terms of a neologism, enframing – *das Ge-stell*. In its wake it leaves ever the possibility of worldless subjects who are taken out of the flux of time.

But, as Stambaugh [1986] has argued, Heidegger's 'temporality' has already 'pull[ed] the rug out from under the concept of man as sub-ject because there is no standing-under [sub-stance] involved' [ibid: 93]. Rather than trying to explain how the subject has experiences, Heidegger speaks of the 'coming about of reality itself' [ibid: 93] in terms of the temporal unfolding of beings within a horizon of being. Rather than static faculties in the mind of the researcher, the language of 'temporality' begins to open space for the dynamic structuring of research as an event [*événement*] – as something to come.

Indeed, in research, it still remains difficult to find any reference to such dynamic temporal structuring[2[Introduction]] even though it is easily detectable in our everyday social interactions in the workplace [Flint, 2011b]. In giving expression to the dynamism of social practice unfolding from the flux of lived time at play in our world [before it becomes separated and partitioned within specialized forms of research], Heidegger [1962] speaks of 'temporality, temporalizing itself as a future, which makes present in the process of having been' [ibid: 350]. In the poetic language of the opening lines to 'Burnt Norton', in his 'Four Quartets', T. S. Eliot similarly opens thinking about lived time:

> *Time present and time past*
> *Are both perhaps present in time future,*
> *And time future contained in time past. . .*

Indeed, within the customs of everyday research, such philosophical and poetic forms of discourse are ordinarily simply excluded from what is deemed to be research, even though the horizons of such discourses are always already included and structuring such practice.

In *the practice* of inquiry, however, Heidegger's discourse indicates that '*Dasein*' continually projects understandings of its world, as possibilities, as beings; not empty logical possibilities calculated in statistics, but what it can be. Here, in making strange the familiar 'event' [*événement*] of research, and in projecting into the future that is always ahead of itself, with the future coming towards it, it is always coming [*venir*], and *Dasein* is brought back to having been its past. Ordinarily, until now the event of research, however, has simply sought objects of consciousness that can be visualized in the present; within the technology of research 'know how' and the dynamics of temporalizing simply become specialized areas of knowledge.

In this pragmatic reading of Heidegger's work, we should also be clear that he was not a pragmatist; given Heidegger's understanding of unconcealment this would be impossible. Heidegger [1962: 68] himself does make reference to '*pragmata*' – things or entities – in his analysis of the being of entities encountered in environment. In reviewing Heidegger's contribution, Caputo [1987: 69] speaks of 'understanding [*Verstehen*]' as a 'pragmatic and existential and never primarily a theoretical matter'. Essentially, Heidegger views such entities as 'equipment' [ibid: 68], that is, entities found in *Dasein*'s 'comportment' towards other entities in the world and used 'in-order-to' achieve particular ends.

A strongly pragmatic reading of Heidegger's *Being and Time,* created by the American philosopher, John Richardson [2012], lays particular emphasis upon the individual's use of such equipment. But, Richardson

[2012] makes clear that any pragmatism detectable in Heidegger's picture of the complex dynamics of our world rests upon and is shaped by two other more hidden aspects of such practice concerned with its existential and temporal dimensions. In this reading of *Being and Time* we will also keep in play the collective view of customs that follows in anticipation of the space created for the possibility of authentic readings of practice. There is no manifesto for authenticity. What follows in this book is an attempt to open space for new understandings concerned with the practices of research and *practice* more generally.

A pragmatic view of the everyday world of *practice*

Here we come to another particular objection for researchers, because although the traditional Husserlian–Cartesian axis of understanding used in research focuses upon the individual subject, Heidegger's [1962] ontology takes seriously that *Dasein* continually falls towards the world. But, in English, the notion of 'falling' can be misleading. Rather than 'falling', Stambaugh [1986] translates Heidegger's term, *verfallen*, with 'ensnarement' in the world. Such ensnarement is apparent when Heidegger [1962] speaks of '*Dasein*, as everyday being-with-one-another, stands in subjection to others. It itself is not; its being has been taken away by others. These others, moreover, are not *definite* others. On the contrary any other can represent them' [ibid: 164]. The everyday being-with-one-another or being-with is the mode of *das Man*. In the original translation of *Being and Time*, this became 'the they', but this is also misleading because it suggests others rather than oneself. More recently, translators have emphasized that '*das Man*' is an indefinite pronoun, for example, used in expressions like '*man muss es tun* . . .' one must do it, etc. So, the mode of being in the everyday world of *Dasein* is determined largely by what 'one' does. 'As a result', as Wrathall [2005] suggests, 'our understanding and interpretation' of the world is at least initially, the understanding and interpretation dictated by the way others understand and interpret things'. Interpretation is the way for Heidegger that 'understanding gets developed, filled in, articulated'; understanding stands in relation to interpretation as 'the less determinate to the more determinate' [Caputo, 1987: 69].

In the worlds of doctoral research, of practice-led research, of qualitative research, for example, 'one' comes to understand a number of different possible ways of structuring the familiar web of routes used to conduct one's inquiries. As Wrathall [2005: 52] has observed, 'the meaning of nearly everything we encounter or everything we do, then, is informed by the fact that we inhabit a shared world with others, and the way we exist in the world is essential structured by others: "the world of Dasein is a world-with"' [Heidegger, 1962: 155]. Almost invariably within the traditions of doctoral research 'one' begins with the privileging of knowledge claims – and an original contribution to knowledge, of course, remains one of the bases upon which doctoral studies are evaluated. The default position, then, for Heidegger, is inauthentic existence determined largely by what 'one' does in our everyday world. In each case, 'in existing inauthentically I am not being myself'. The self of inauthentic existence Heidegger calls the One-self [*das Man-selbst*]. The possibility of *Dasein* being authentic arises from the way, as Richardson [2012] has indicated, it 'makes mine' its projects. But, we will have to wait a little to get to an understanding of just how *Dasein* may enact such a possibility.

Intentionality has now been taken out of consciousness. For Heidegger, as we have seen the movement of temporality makes possible being-in-the-world. 'Being-in' is not a matter of the world being a container, it expresses our concern [*Besorgen*] for things and stands in relation to the way we are variously solicitous [*Fürsorge*] towards other *Dasein*. Here in the semantics we find more of the temporal play in Heidegger's writing. *Besorgen* expresses 'concern' for how things have been in the past, and in being solicitous [*Fürsorge*] towards others, *Dasein* is oriented towards unfolding future possibilities, not least, those determined by what 'one' does. In researching practice for the most part, ordinarily 'one' comports oneself to theories and information as a subject, so that the movement of lived-time, and our various modes of concern for entities and for others in the world are often dissimulated [Flint 2011b].

Being-in-the-world, therefore, we need to be clear on the different ways things are disclosed in familiar methodologies. Everything in the ever-unfolding dynamic of the world is a mode of concern for Heidegger [1962: 59–62], but theories of practice, like those created by Reckwitz, and theory more generally, stills and subdues the on-going practical activity of producing, manipulating, and so on. Theory for Heidegger is therefore regarded as a 'deficient' mode of concern. This was his way of indicating that theorists have yet to understand his ontology!

His particular understandings of ontology become a little more obvious in one of his narratives. There is a story Heidegger once observed that on entering his lecture his students did not first carefully examine the door handle,[5] nor did they spend time observing it, or even reflecting that they believed the door handle would turn. They had not been actively conscious of the door and its handle. Rather being-in-the-world they simply came into the lecture theatre. Their practical coping had involved them in a goal-directed activity. In Kant's terms, a priori, their practical activity had not been conditional upon prior conscious assimilation of propositional knowledge detailing the properties of the door, its handle, or the pathway they used to get to the lecture. What Heidegger takes from this trivial example is that our practical coping activities, the customary, habitual, and practical matter of doing things in our world each day, gives us all some understanding of 'being-in-the-world'.

For Heidegger we simply have not paid sufficient attention to the being of entities encountered in the everyday world. He distinguishes two modes of being. Reckwitz's theoretical attitude, exhibited earlier, uncovers entities as 'present-at-hand'. 'At-hand' [Richardson, 2012: 92] simply expresses that they sit quite inertly before us in our world. In contrast, the stance of 'concern' renders entities 'ready-to-hand'. In this mode, the hand is prepared for a practical encounter with such entities. For example, in my 'to-hand' attitude, this entity, the chair, next to my desk, has the mode of being as 'equipment' [*Zeug*] 'in-order-to' do something practical – I can sit on it, shift it, rearrange it, remove it, . . . In this case my practical attention is structured around the question of what can be done, what needs fine tuning in-order-to make it more comfortable. Equally, in an idle moment we notice its style, shape, and colour and it becomes an object 'at-hand'. In looking back at an 'at-hand' object – a material thing, information, theory . . . – attention is given to it without the distraction of personal values and concerns. 'Roughly speaking', therefore, as Richardson [2012] points out, an object such as 'a rock is to-hand if we mean it for use, and at-hand if we mean it for theory' [ibid: 81]. Every one of our various specialist fields of research, in taking a region of being as the particular locus of its concern, creates an 'at-hand' object world constituted by an inter-connected array of sometimes competing, sometimes cooperative, ever-more specialist theories.

What is so easily missed in our theoretical attitude is the dynamic of the 'to-hand' dimensions of our unfolding world. In our 'to-hand' world, ordinarily entities remain in the background, and concerns only 'light up' for us when we become aware of some failure in the equipment we variously use. Ordinarily, for example, having been trained to use the keyboard on my laptop I hardly notice the keys when typing, until one particular day when the key for the letter 'U' became detached from the board. Concerns arise, then, when 'to-hand' 'equipment' breaks down in some way [Heidegger, 1962: 73–4] and then we notice what its former practical function had been, that is, when it becomes:

- unusable
- missing
- in the way.

Here we have also stumbled on a way of studying concern that does not lend itself to standard techniques privileging our capacity to know. We can now begin to see some of the difficulties presented by Reckwitz in generating his theory of practice. It is not only in danger of reducing ready-to-hand equipment of everyday practice down to 'at-hand' objects of consciousness. The attitude of privileging theory is also in danger of cutting us off from seeing how concern is a stance that guides our customary actions.

In studying concern, therefore, as Richardson [2012] shows, we need an approach that side-step[s] the special problems of access to this underlying practical stance: 'how it recedes under scrutiny, how attention to it disrupts it' [ibid: 95]. This non-theoretical attitude of lighting up our 'to-hand' concerns gives us a way of bringing such concerns into the open. Such actions, then, orientate us to the background of our intending, and so the unfolding being of entities we variously encounter in the world.

More concretely, however, according to Heidegger, most people, including many researchers, mistakenly believe that 'theory is basic', and that practical concern arises simply as a way of adding value by treating such concern as 'as a mode of development of' theory [Richardson, 2012: 90]. There is always the danger of researchers entering into the theoretical stance and so discovering aspects of the world of practice 'as they are in that stance'. Reckwitz, for example, and here we can add many researchers, speaks as if there is only this theoretical way of intending the world, and so uses it as a model for how people are in practice more generally. In this way, 'everyday intending' in research 'becomes invisible if one interprets it in a way that is ontologically inappropriate' [Heidegger, 1962: 59; Richardson, 2012: 90].

An example of such a mistake can be found in empiricists' and others' views of sense data in research. This is typically perceived as constituting a given, that provides the basis for interpretation [Denzin and Lincoln, 2011]. In this way, it would seem that perception initiates my relation to an aspect of customary actions in the world by first acquiring empirical or other forms of 'data' as the basis for interpretation of 'evidence and knowledge for practice' [Evans and Hardy, 2010]. As Richardson [2012] has noted, it gives a kind of proto-theory about my surroundings: how they are independently of my aims and desires – though the latter of course then use immediately that perceptual data' [ibid: 90]. In contrast, for Heidegger [1985b], 'natural perception as I live in it when I move in my world is mostly not a detached observing and study of things, but is rather absorbed concrete practical dealing with matters' [ibid: 29–30; Richardson, 2012: 90]. Following Merleau-Ponty, as we noted earlier, such dealings are always embodied, and this notion of embodiment is explored in qualitative research [Conquergood, 1991; Maddison, 1999, 2005; Pelias, 2011: 663].

The question remains, therefore, is how do we bring into the open our everyday world of practice. In response to this question at issue in what follows is the ever-unfolding dynamic relationship of being with lived-time.

Bringing into the 'open' the everyday world of *practice*

There are three aspects of the relationship between being and time, or in Kantian/Husserlian terms, three conditions of the possibility of intentionality for Heidegger's, 'being-in-the-world' of practice – that is explicated by him in terms of [1] self-finding [*Befindlichkeit*] and mood, [2] talk/discourse [*Rede*], and [3] projecting and pushing forward into understandings [*Verstehen*]. Each of these conditions may open possible objections within discourses of research.

'Self-finding' is Richardson's much superior translation of Heidegger's term, *Befindlichkeit*. In Macquarrie and Robinson's translation, it is agreed that 'state of mind' was one of their poorest choices' [Richardson, 2012: 107]. Self-finding is not a matter of cognitive introspection. Self-finding stands in relation to one's thrownness [*Geworfenheit*] and of being in the throw [*Wurf*]: it constitutes grounds for *Dasein*'s intentionality. For example, 'self-finding' is one locus for Elizabeth St Pierre's [2011] 'transgressive data' – emotional data, dream data, sensual data . . . that for her 'disrupt linearity, consciousness and mind/body dichotomy' [ibid: 621]. Things show up as mattering for us in some way in research: we may find them attractive, useful, stubborn, intractable. The tradition culminating in Husserl has always overlooked this and falls into the privileging of knowing. In the words of Heidegger [1962]:

> An entity of the character of Dasein is there in such a way that, whether explicitly or not, it finds itself [*sich befindet*] in its thrownness. In *Befindlichkeit* Dasein is always brought before itself, it has already found itself, not as a perceptual-finding-itself-before [*Sich-vor-finden*], but as a moody self-finding [*gestimmtes Sichbefinden*]. [ibid: 135]

In the German language, it is clear that 'he wants his readers to hear such 'finding' in his term, *Befindlichkeit* [Richardson, 2012: 107]. Self-finding is the default direction from which our intentionality runs in giving meaning to things in our world of research. As researchers we find them mattering to us in some way [Flint and Barnard, 2010a: 202–22]. But, this is another difficult issue for research, because this finding is *not* a cognitive or theoretical matter. It is a matter of something that is 'felt' during the everydayness of our habitual actions, in our moods or in the way that we are tuned [*abgestimmt*][7] to the ethos, customs, and traditions in which we are variously located. Being affected by moods is a structural feature of *Dasein*'s ontology; it is not an aspect of subjectivity that somehow adds value to the supposedly objective outcomes of a piece of research. Moods, then, shape and sustain the intentionality of all those involved in research.

Heidegger makes plain, as indicated earlier, that our moods are always in each case where 'I am first finding myself' [Richardson, 2012: 109]. This is so for the empiricist researcher, just as it is for the phenomenologist or for other individuals in any other specialist form of research. It reflects the power of analysing practice no longer constrained by any arbitrary disciplinary boundaries [Flint and Barnard, 2010b]. Self-finding occurs in the mood generated in practice including moods created in any acts that in some way take us out of such a world, it lies in feeling oneself affected in any form of research. In Heidegger's Utopian view, in which the world remains structured around ends, *Befindlichkeit* in our thrownness is the locus of Shatzki's 'teleoaffective' structures of practice. In this latter context, it is important to be clear that self-finding is in feeling oneself affected, and *not* in somehow finding a psychical state. In Heidegger's [1962] terms, mood 'is disclosed to itself *before* all knowing and willing, and *out above* their range of disclosure' [ibid: 136].

It is important to see that in each case in my mood I find myself thrown in my thrownness, and so thrust into my present way of practising, for example, in research by forces outside me. But, thrownness [*Geworfenheit*] is not an objective fact; in each case, it is a way 'I feel about myself.'

In each case, too, thrownness raises the additional question: where do I find myself. Heidegger points out that the world is always already articulated in some way through 'discourse' [*Rede*] – Richardson [2012] prefers 'talk' as it expresses the everydayness of the context of significance in which we find ourselves as researchers, for example. Basically, Heidegger sees that in each case within the context of such extant discourse/talk with all the pieces of equipment fitting together in our world – he uses the term 'referential totality' – I can articulate what I am doing in some way. In *Rede*, then, we adopt a stance that is not a looking back at our thrownness, but a looking outwards towards the encompassing social practice in which we find ourselves, and to the actions of others who share such customs. In his exploration of bricolage, for example, Kincheloe's [2001, 2003, 2004a, 2005a,b, 2006, 2008a,b] writings place much emphasis upon a style expressive of *Rede*.

Rede [discourse/talk] is our express capacity to mean something in relation to what an encompassing social practice means to us in the present, to mean out of engagement with that world [Richardson, 2012: 115]. In *Rede* we intend meaning in relation to practice.

Hopefully by now it is already anticipated there is a futural dimension structuring such engagement with our everyday world that Heidegger terms pressing forward and projecting understanding. Understanding is an existential structure called projection [Heidegger, 1962: 145]. We are possibilities, even though we are not yet them; projection is that into which [*Dasein*'s] ability-to-be is not yet [ibid: 145]. We are who we are. Becoming and projecting has nothing to do with a well-thought-out plan, according to which *Dasein* arranges its being [ibid: 145]. 'The well-springs of understanding are implicit', they remain silently 'in the background' of the world of research [Richardson, 2012: 106].

Researching know-how in *practice*

Rather than privileging truth claims to representations as the purpose of actions in researching practice, Heidegger conceives of our actions as being primarily concerned with matters of *sheltering, preserving, saving, and possibly distorting aspects of our world* [Stambaugh, 1992: 8; emphasis added]. He draws upon the Ancient Greek word, *aletheia*, in order to express the possible purposes directing our complex essential relationship with being and other entities in the world. Such a focus comes for Heidegger from his reading of 'Plato's Republic', and in particular Plato's famous 'cave allegory'. In short and covering over much of the subtleties of Heidegger's reading of this allegory, for him it is clear that Plato took a wrong turn and the whole complex tradition that led up to Husserl followed. Once the prisoner in the cave had finally found an escape into the sunlight, truth became largely a matter of what can be seen in the light of day from which emerged the correspondence theory of truth [Thomson, 2000, 2005; Flint, 2012a]. It returns us once more to the issue of the purported 'transparency' of 'evidence' featured in managerialist regimes.

Heidegger [1977] translates *aletheia* as '*Unverborgenheit,* meaning unconcealment' [ibid: 8] that gives a way of opening space once more in the German language, at least, for the subtleties and end-points of purposeful know-how. In the semantics of the German language, the compound noun, *Unverborgenheit,* is connected with its root verbs that create an articulation for the possibilities that may unfold as *Dasein* comports itself to other entities in the world; namely, '*bergen*, to preserve and to shelter, *entbergen*, to unconceal; *verbergen*, to conceal' [ibid: 7]. Stambaugh [1992] elaborates the many possibilities that arise from Heidegger's conception of *aletheia.* At the time of writing, the implications of this understanding of unconcealment for research into the know-how of practice are difficult to find. It would lend itself to use in bricolage.

The missing dimension of the world of *practice*

In 'The Open',[8] in this background of understanding, of know-how that projects and presses into possibilities that unfold as beings, particular entities found in the seedbed of the play generate conditions for the cultivation of new cultures of research [Flint, 2013a: 152–63]. Recent developments in research [Denzin and Lincoln, 2011, Alasutari et al., 2011; Arthur et al., 2012] all bear witness to the outcomes of such play. But, it has to be seen within the foregoing intensely conservative forces we have found at work in such everyday cultures of research.

One possible end in the world of the researcher, identified by Heidegger [1998a: 266], as 'the openness of being', is something for which *aletheia*, the unfolding of unconcealment in practice, has already directed us. For example, in Heidegger's case in the open, in that clearing he found 'he never gave up a difference between being and beings' [Stambaugh, 1992: 35]. Beings are entities, whereas 'to be' is not an entity and so the being of entities is not an entity. But, despite the focus here upon 'being-in-the-world' of practice and despite the times we have used 'to be', we are in danger of largely missing being itself.

Despite earlier references to play, and to the silent play of difference between being and beings, we have remained largely on the high ground of the meaning of *beings* that keeps watch over any possible play encountered in research. This is why Rose [1994] could speak with authority earlier about *The Dialectic of Nihilism*. As Heidegger [2000] puts it in his *Introduction to Metaphysics*, 'merely to chase after beings in the midst of the oblivion of *being* – that is nihilism' [ibid: 217; emphasis added]. For example, in summarizing what unfolds in the openness of being 'one' may still remain insensible to being, itself. Richardson [2012] writes 'just as in feeling the thing I turn back to my effects and feel the thing from them', and 'just as in wording [*Rede*] the thing I step out of the community of speakers and mean the thing from them', 'so in . . . understanding a thing I press ahead to my ends and come back to mean the thing' [ibid: 115]. But, as we have done until now, in attempting to simplify and to clarify what Heidegger had to say on these matters, Richardson has passed over the question of what makes such meanings, so losing sight here of the precise locus of the meaning maker in research.

What remains is the question of what organizes, nourishes, and directs our understanding of being in research. In response, we should examine Heidegger's discourse both in being researchers from the outside of such practice and in being open to the possibilities of *practice*, from within Heidegger's discourse.

Viewed from the outside Heidegger's language opens space for many possibilities in *practice* that ordinarily the customary practices of research pass over. Such possibilities, as we will see, sometimes emerge within everyday practices, particularly within leading-edge research. In general, they can be understood as constituting exceptions to the customs of practice that arise from bare life, from the hidden social forces in research unfolding as possibilities in *Dasein*. In what follows when we excavate below Heidegger's more obvious pragmatism, we will also find many more phenomena that are included as essential to *Dasein*'s very existence, but remain located generally within the practices of research as exceptions to the customs of everyday practice.

From within his practice, Heidegger [1962] turns to the question of the meaning of being. In *Being and Time,* he asks, what does meaning signify? '[M]eaning' for him, it turns out, 'is that wherein understandability [*Verstehbarkeit*] of something maintains itself – even that of something that does not come into view explicitly and thematically' [ibid: 323–24]. In this reading, 'meaning sustains what is understood' in practice, 'giving it a pivot around which its understandability can organise itself' [Caputo, 1987: 172]. Hence, 'meaning signifies the upon-which [*das Woraufhin*] of a primary projection in terms of which something can be conceived in its possibility as that which it is' [Heidegger, 1962: 324]. So, as we have seen, being presses forward and is projected in its being – that is its primary projection – and from it we understand a particular entity, such as *practice-in-its-being*. But, the meaning of the practice to be understood arises from that organizing point – the '*upon which*', or meaning maker in the primary projection. There is a second phase to our primary projection of beings that determines the lines of force in the primary projection, sustaining it, and holding it together [Caputo, 1987: 173].

In research, therefore, and in response to the issue of what's so easily missed in pragmatic views of practice, the question remains as to the extent to which researchers are in possession of [1] the entities [beings] that are there to be understood in research, [2] the being of those entities that constitutes their horizonal frame, and [3] the meaning of the being of those entities, that is, the meaning maker or upon which that organizes and sustains projected understandings of such entities [ibid: 173]. Our next step, therefore, in moving to address the nihilism of research is to learn more about this meaning maker at work in the practice. But, in so doing, and in anticipation of a critical reading of Heidegger's discourse concerning how practice unfolds, it is also important to keep in mind not only the metaphysical structuring of much of his thesis, but also his latent Platonism in the attempt to purify and to rid the essence of practice of any Cartesian influence.

It is important to be clear, also, that the meaning maker in *Being and Time* was identified as 'temporality'. It is still there in the background of everyday practice in the workplace [Flint, 2011b]. But, it is now often displaced by another more dominant meaning maker – 'the principle of reason': the latter opens the possibility in every form of social interaction of transforming the temporal unfolding of beings, so gathering them into a relationship between subjects and objects of consciousness. This is the drive in our relationship with technology, including research itself as a technology.

In this reading of Heidegger, too, lies the background to understanding the practice of research as an event [*événement*], as something 'coming' [*venir*]. In understanding such an event and in moves towards balancing the powers of technology we will also begin to explore in what follows a constitution of language that not only takes away any possibility for such gatherings, but also underlines the forces at work moulding the objectification of knowledge.

CHAPTER TWO

Existential dramas in researching practice: What is their significance?

In concerning ourselves with practices, involving our complex relationship with technology, we have yet to find any possible freedom from the tranquilizing effects of the dominion of everyday practice. In the foreground of the emerging story of integrative practices, the familiar repetition of signs – each of which always points to something else – would appear variously to structure, communicate, and create meanings in the world of research. But, it is here in *practice,* where there are no arbitrary boundaries separating research and philosophy, that we enter into what at first reading may appear a radical departure from the customs of research that, as we will see, come to be understood as generating exceptions to the everyday norms of practice uncovered from the leading edge of research. In continually foregrounding what is given in practice in the present – its 'data' – it does not appear to give itself formal space in which to consider the possibilities of being emerging from the nothingness of the future. But, without the forces explored and elaborated here that ironically not only do not find their way into annuls of research, without such *annullā* – that capacity to make into *nothing* out of which beings emerge [Heidegger, 2000] – there could be no transformation. Two radically contrasting elaborations of Heidegger's story will be examined that open space for the exploration of the generative powers of the nothing, we have already begun to uncover in the foregoing pragmatic analysis of practice.

Heidegger's expansion is informed by his *gathering* of signs structured around an essentially Platonic vision of a hidden ideal world outside our own. In returning us to the meaning maker, the 'upon which' [*das Woraufhin*] shaping our projections of beings, Heidegger's eschatology leads him to imagine that he could return us once more to a new beginning for our societies. A beginning where, in all our practices, the *phusis* of a purified unfolding essence of existence finally breathes new life into us, so that we can at last see and work with the dangers of technology in our society. In returning to Bourdieu's [1996] 'conceptual magistrature' [ibid: 88] describing Heidegger's style of writing, this is considered to dissimulate its 'condemnation of the Welfare State' behind a 'theory of temporality' [ibid: vii], in accord with 'its ultra-revolutionary conservativism' [ibid: viii]. Ironically, however, while Heidegger's *Verfremdungseffekt*, in continually attempting to make strange the familiar in practice may be read by critics as a condemnation of the social world, including the Welfare State, the constitution of Bourdieu's [1977] language remains largely imprisoned within the same '*society of the spectacle*' that Heidegger was at least attempting to question.

Another story concerned with practices has no beginning, middle, or end, nor does it separate essence from technology, but it does at least open a radically contrasting language. It would not have been possible without Heidegger's story. This other narrative also begins to alert us to many of Heidegger's [1962] metaphysical determinations of *Dasein* in *Being and Time*. It emerges from Derrida's writings and foregrounds only spacing, rather than the hubris of any gathering of signs. In so doing, it invites the possibility of holding onto the repetition of informal customs and laws inscribed in practices, and so carries with it the charge of taking responsibility. At issue in the possibility opened by this particular spacing is taking responsibility for working with the play of *différance* in our desire to create ever-renewed archives of research and of practices more generally: opening spacing for new laws and customs in moves towards justice that always exceeds extant laws. In contrast to Heidegger's story that in speaking continually of the gathering powers of being that remain located in the play of difference in identity, there remains the challenge of research in which the fulfilment of identities is always impossible. Derrida is unequivocal; gathering is not possible.

Here our focus will remain with Heidegger's story concerned with the ways in which technological enframing in *the* world[1] has tended to brush aside the complex interiority of the unique worlds of the self.

* * *

Repetitions of the everyday world of practice of research[2] would appear to be largely positioned somewhere along the Husserlian–Cartesian mind–body axis of understanding around which meanings and understandability are organized. Paradoxically, despite the tacit 'upon which' of the world of *practice* that made possible the major contributions of Kant and Husserl on this same axis, there still remains the subject situated upon grounds of reason. This is the mighty power of reason that somehow connects the subject with its objects of intentional consciousness without ever saying precisely how, except by recourse to itself. For example, and again tacitly, Kant's a priori conditions of the possible are manifest in the public statement on *The Researcher Development Framework*, RDF [Vitae, 2014] made by one of the leading UK organizations in the field, 'Vitae'. Like Reckwitz, Vitae's RDF is grounded upon reason, though this remains silent. Its discourse [*Rede*] sought to look out to the wider horizons of being constituting practices of research in an attempt to articulate a coherent schema for developing 'one's' possible actions as a researcher in a multiplicity of settings. But, there is no formal distinction made between the horizons of being shaping the world of research and the ontic projections of what it is expected that researchers will do at different stages of their development. Vitae's philosophy, too, remains with the privileging of knowledge production. This is not, therefore, a wholesale rejection of the Vitae framework, only a reminder that its ideological objects of knowledge are in danger of distracting researchers from the complex issue of research as an event, as something futural that in opening possibilities is never completely knowable.

The question remains as to how one might gain freedom from the Cartesian axis of understanding with its worldless subject.

Certainly in his examination of what 'critical ethnography . . . could be' by comparison with 'conventional ethnography', Jim Thomas [1993: 4] opens space for reflexivity, not least concerned with the being identified as the presence of integrative practices of research. But, as we have seen already, it is important to examine the 'meaning maker' structuring and shaping such everyday forms of practice. Especially, it would seem, as this appears to have moved in the past 80 years from 'temporality' to that of 'reason', or more precisely, the principle of reason: 'nothing *is* without reason'.

At issue, too, is the question of what remains hidden below the obvious layer of pragmatism featured earlier. One such hidden force at work in the world of practice that we call 'anxiety' has no object and opens the possibility of taking us out of the everydayness of such a world. Here we arrive at a real drama in *practice* because, as Heidegger [1962] recognized, we constantly tend to 'flee' away from such a possibility [ibid: 254].

Here, we arrive at a radical dimension of Heidegger's existentialist analysis. This analytic of existence, distinguishing *Dasein* from all other entities in the world, brings into the open anxiety not as a psychological phenomenon [although such a possibility is never negated], but as a force, leaving us to our own devices [Heidegger, 1962: 188]. In the quiet drama of research, anxiety is a force at work influencing and shaping researchers' world from which, ordinarily, we 'flee' in all divisions of such research, however they may be conceived.

It is also important to distinguish this existential form of individualizing from economic imperatives at work in our 'late modern age' [Giddens, 1991], foregrounding 'the individual' as an object of consciousness at the centre of such economies. Of course, 'one' can reproduce the economics of individualization and conduct oneself in accord with its presuppositions within professional organizations, and still remain open to the effects of existential anxiety that alerts us to the normalizing effects of everydayness in such settings.

But, how does anxiety work? At issue is the question of how anxiety may possibly deprive us of the assurances that what one does, emerging from framing in practice, is really worth doing. Such 'framing'[2] of research continually secures its hold on the metaphysical guardrails of existence. In a positive way, Heidegger [1962] notes how 'anxiety makes manifest in *Dasein* its being towards its own-most-ability-to-be, meaning its being free for the freedom of choosing and taking hold of itself' [ibid: 188] outside any framing. Does not in each case 'my' being towards this own-most-ability-to-be, which is always mine, lie at the heart of authentic practice in research?

Of course, we are always already ensnared in the world of practice. Such captivation Heidegger calls 'falling' [*Verfallen*]. This does 'not mean some original sin', but rather it indicates a phenomenon 'that belongs to *Dasein*'s being as such' [Richardson, 2012: 110]. As a researcher, for example, one tends to become lost in 'one's' concerns regarding the 'world' of a specialist division of research. Laying emphasis upon 'world' in this way indicates the totality of entities for which, in each case, 'I' am concerned as a researcher in a particular field. This has to be distinguished from *the* world identified earlier by Heidegger in terms of the 'upon which' that makes the encountering of entities possible. Being completely absorbed in *the* world of practice is an indication of 'falling'.

For Heidegger, falling is governed in our everyday practices by what he calls 'chat' [*Gerede*], curiosity [*neugerig*], and ambiguity [*Zweideutigkeit*]. Essentially, in 'chat', we lose sight of the being of other entities in our 'world' of practice. Being grounded in curiosity as a locus of excitement and motivation in our research through constant novelty, chat is always in danger of creating ambiguity between the ontic and ontological projections of entities, between representations and their unfolding, and other beings whose world remains ill-defined. In 'falling', then, as Richardson [2012] has observed, 'we become distracted from our basic existential structures – of projection, self-finding and talk – which hold the world open for us' [ibid: 136]. In contemporary research, therefore, there is always a danger that *Dasein* has fallen away [*abgefallen*] from itself, conceived as its 'authentic-ability-to-be-itself' [Heidegger, 1962: 175–76].

The question of how *Dasein* opens space for the possibility of being authentic in research and so in each case makes such practice uniquely 'mine' is one that will consume the remainder of this book. A starting point towards such a way of thinking is to uncover two pivotal dimensions of *Dasein*'s existential drama that open space for the possibility of anxiety. They arise from our relationship with the possibility of death and our associated guilt.

Ordinarily, perhaps, speaking of 'death' in the context of writings concerned with the practice of ethical research may seem of little relevance to questions concerning methodologies, etc.: quite simply this constitutes an error in thinking. Heidegger [1962] devotes a whole section of his book to examining the ways in which ordinarily in our modern society *Dasein* tends to disconnect itself from facing questions concerned with its own finitude. Here is another radical feature of Heidegger's analysis opening space in which to think beyond the metaphysical determination of entities. 'Death is' uncovered for him 'as the end of *Dasein*, in the being of this entity towards its end' [ibid: 159]. In being alive and always 'ahead-of-itself', therefore, *Dasein* is always incomplete. When viewed in this way, *Dasein* is 'defined as possibilities not yet realised' [Richardson, 2012: 145] and the possibility of our relationship with death in research becomes generative.

Death can also be viewed as a 'present-at-hand' object, an object of consciousness that in our modern cultures we tend to dissimulate, so evading our being-toward-death. But, this loses sight of its profound ontological significance: in our first-person reflexive, we are always aiming towards it. In *Dasein*'s 'own-most' and 'non-relational . . . potentiality-for-being in which its being is an issue for it' [Heidegger, 1962: 263], it becomes wrenched away from what in the everydayness of practice 'one' does and 'one' says.

So, Heidegger keeps being-towards-death that is essentially futural in play with guilt that looks back and is 'given in self-finding's way, by our feeling ourselves thrown' [Richardson, 2012: 154]. In our everyday world, looking towards the future carries with it the possibility of facing death, the nothing. In this way in being in the throw and in guiding itself in accord with its attunement and self-finding, *Dasein* uncovers in guilt what it is not. Thus, formally, Heidegger [1962] defines guilt as 'being the ground for a being that is determined by a not [*Nicht*], that is to say, as being the ground of a nullity' [ibid: 283]. He then goes on to elaborate and clarify how he conceives the nullity. In Heidegger's projection of the nullity, it is presented 'as ability-to-be [*Dasein* that] stands in each case in one or other possibilities, it is constantly not others and has wavered these in its existentiell[3] projection. Freedom, though, is only in the choice of one, that is, in bearing not having chosen and not being able to choose others [ibid: 285]. Bricolage, to which we will return, tries to have it both ways – freedom in the choice of one, while keeping in play the freedom to choose other possible ways of understanding a particular phenomenon or event.

Therefore, in the world of research, in both its relationship with death and its existential feeling of guilt, there is space opened for *Dasein* to understand its own lack. Herein lies a rationale for education emerging from cultures of research. But, as we will see the situation is complicated by the emergence of the interplay of two radically contrasting forms of such education. Each of the avenues of this world of research open to *Dasein* can only be articulated in the repetition of signs. Consequently, in moving to understand the grounding of the 'meaning maker' in our projections of entities in the world of research, it is first essential to work with Derrida's oeuvre, as he makes manifest another *lack* in the repetition of signs mediating such a world.

Derrida's early work was strongly influenced by his own deconstructive readings of Husserl and Heidegger, among others. For Caputo [1987], where Heidegger's former student, Hans Georg Gadamer, had taken a conservative reading of Heidegger, Derrida sought to radicalize Heidegger's thesis. Derrida's particular interest is language, following his deconstructive reading of Saussure's structuralism. He strenuously resisted the identity, post-structuralist, meaning he refused that label.

In this writing, too, the deliberate insertion of the hyphen in this and other terms that appear later in this book is symbolic of the same struggle with the powers constituting the concord of identity at work in the contemporary language of research. The custom within grammar structuring such practice and the practice of writing research is not to include the hyphen, thus ordinarily underlining the harmony of identity. Here, in contrast, it remains as a mark of the intricacies of language, and of this deconstructive writing that brings to the fore textual difference. As Michael Lewis [2008] has observed in his study of Lacan's and of Derrida's writings, the retention of the prefix 'indicates that something has been put in an unaccustomed place thus changing the meaning of the two halves' [ibid: 117]. Thus, the hyphen in this book is used to open readers to questions 'concerning the unities of simulacra created [ordinarily in practice] without the use of such hyphen' [ibid: 117]. One of Mark Dooley and Liam Kavanagh's [2007] observations, for example, from their authoritative and insightful account of Derrida's *oeuvre*, indicates that:

> Derrida was not in the business of making strong truth-claims. Neither did he aim to build deconstruction into a school of thought. He was simply in the modest business of persuading his readers that understanding who we are is more complicated than philosophy had traditionally presupposed. [ibid: 151]

Many people in the past have derided his work, indicating that it is simply the outpourings of a 'frivolous iconoclast'. I am completely set against such a reading. Like Richard Rorty [1998: 184], I view him as 'educator', whose continual appeal to deconstruction and related devices may be used in provoking new understandings of practice. In my view, Derrida's oeuvre opens space for the possible inauguration of lively and thought-provoking dissonance and intellectual tension that can be found at the very heart of authentic education emerging from cultures of research. Derrida himself once remarked that 'deconstruction is anachronism in synchronism', it is attuning to something that is out of joint, out of tune [Dooley and Kavanagh, 2007: 17]. In what follows, therefore, we will also keep in play insights from Derrida on some of the complexity found in the practices of research.

One particular locus of complexity in understanding what is done and said in every conceivable division of practice for Derrida is identity: here we are about to enter into another dramatic act that cuts through *practice*. For the cultural theorist, Stuart Hall [1990: 225], as a starting point for our deconstruction, 'identities are [seen as] the names we give to the different ways we are positioned by, and position ourselves within, the narratives of the past'. But, Derrida questions the extent to which we are able to name exactly how we are positioned in this way. Derrida had seen that Heidegger, like most philosophers, and, we can add cultural theorists along with educational and social researchers, work with presuppositions concerned with the teleology of fulfilment of identity. Given enough time and effort, it is presupposed, we can bring into totalization the plenitude of each and every identity encountered in research.

In addition to the incompleteness at the heart of Heidegger's story related to *Dasein*, existence, Derrida puts forward at least two further lines of argument, inviting us all to question such a presupposition, as follows, concerned with [1] the repetition of signs and [2] memory.

One of the driving forces grounding our on-going repetition of signs is the metaphysical principle: 'something is repeatable to the extent that it *is*' [Caputo, 1987: 123] – that 'something' in research being 'data', 'theory', 'methods', 'methodologies' and so on. This is not surprising. This principle has never been in question in the philosophical tradition culminating in Husserl's work, and it is difficult to find where it has been subject to questioning in research. Interestingly, however, although not brought into sharp relief, such questioning would appear to remain implicit in a number of qualitative researchers' discourses [*vide* Lather 1991, 1993a,b, 1994, 2007a; St Pierre, 2011; Richardson, 1993, 1997; Olesen, 2011]. Although unspoken, here identity would appear to be understood as proportionate to repetition – where the repetition of patterns of signs comes first before any identity, before any sense of 'is', can be revealed.

More formally, this position emerges from Derrida's [1973a] rereading of Husserl, in *Speech and Phenomena*, that had been 'conducted under the rule of the principle of repetition', so reversing the ordering of being as presence and re-presentation: 'The presence of the present is derived from repetition and not the reverse' [ibid: 52; Caputo, 1987: 122–23]. Something *is* – for example, 'the revealing of phenomena through researching practice – takes on the unity of an identity, to the extent that it is brought forth by repetition; being or identity in this reading of practice is 'proportionate to repetition' [Caputo, 1987: 123].

The meaning of what something *is*, therefore, is not a matter of resurrecting the original intention of the respondent/author/ researcher. Roughly speaking, there is always a *difference* in space between the 'signifiers' – the various projections and interpretations of practice, and the 'signified' – the lived experience of such practice [Flint, 2009]. In his lectures on 'the nature of language', for example, Heidegger [1982] speaks of experience as 'something that befalls us, strikes us, comes over us, overwhelms and transforms us' [ibid: 57]. The question remains as to whether we gain such experience from language constituted in *différance*.

The hermeneutic circle of meaning making that we began to uncover earlier in Heidegger's writings is always broken in Derrida's discourse by loss, death, and spectral ghosts of the Other. There is, too, always a deferral in time between the signifiers drawn upon in the practice of research and what such signs signify. In the context of researching practice, Derrida's [1973b] neologism, *différance* expresses both a difference and deferral between signifiers and the lived experience signified by such practice. We will be returning to understand more about *différance* later, because such understanding opens space for the possible freedom to be free to choose and to explore as researchers the spacing opened by deconstruction of the technologies of research.

Being-in-the world of *practice*

Différance is always already in play. It opens space for a continuum of possibilities from 'Rabbinical repetition', as a metaphysical idea of repetition' that 'moves backwards' [Caputo, 1987: 121]. At the opposite pole, there is a Joycean or poetic repetition, 'which is prior to presence and productive of it, which as a kind of critical reading is free to produce as it reads' [ibid: 121].

In Derrida's terms, the everydayness of 'one's' understandings is identified with the repetition of the Rabbi – a repetition that continually attempts to be a perfect replication of the same in the form of the original signs [ibid: 121]. The Vitae RDF statement relies essentially upon Rabbinical forms of repetition of the metaphysical principle of being in order to maintain its integrity, so grounding reflection upon what is done in research. Ironically, Rabbinical repetition tends to exclude the spectral Other from any identity.

For example, in the larger emerging picture of *practice*, we should keep in the foreground the work of Ikujiro Nonaka and his colleagues in Japan [*vide* Nonaka and Takeuchi 1995; Von Krogh et al., 2000]. Their work illuminates the multiplicity of contingencies requiring sophisticated know-how found even in practices involving some of the most highly specified and technically exacting processes in the manufacture of silicon chips and so on. Many of the standard archives for research, too, silently rely upon Rabbinical forms of repetition for their expressions of methods, methodologies, and epistemologies.[2[Introduction]]

In contrast, there is poetic repetition that pushes forward in research, opening space for the exploration of new possibilities. As may be expected from the everydayness of practice, poetic forms of repetition remain in the minority. Fortunately, Denzin and Lincoln's [2011] pioneering work in the *Sage Handbook for Qualitative Research*, while retaining much Rabbinical repetition, have served to provide a focus for poesy in research by gathering studies involving Joycean forms of repetition. In her article on analysis and representation across the continuum, Laura Ellingson [2011: 595–610], for example, puts a spotlight on the poesy of practice in research in a number of different contexts, including 'field work in India' [Chawla, 2006]; the exploration of prisoner's experiences of American jails [Hartnett, 2003], and in the 'examination of culture and identity' [Prendergast, 2007; Austin, 1996]. Susan Finley [2011: 435–50] speaks of the 'proliferation of poetic forms in arts-based research' [ibid: 445]. But, while these forms of practice open space, creating the freedom to be free to challenge extant understandings of the structuring of practices in *the* world of research – Finley, for example, speaks of resistance politics that she sees requires a 'new urgency' [ibid: 436] – they remain disconnected from other forms of practice by divisions created in the name of specialization.

While both such forms of repetition underline contingency in practice, they have not yet given a full explanation for the *lack* that emerges in repetitions of identity. For Derrida [1995a] we are always in danger of being cut off from questioning any presuppositions concerned with the teleology of fulfilment of identity by the 'catastrophe of memory':

> I would say that what I suffer from inconsolably always has the form, not only of loss, which is often! – but of the loss of memory: that what I am living cannot be kept, thus repeated, and – how to put it? – decipherable, as if an appeal for a witness had no witness, in some way, not even the witness that I could be for what I have lived. This is for me the very experience of death, of catastrophe. [ibid: 207]

Notice how in his interpretation Derrida goes back to Heidegger's thematic concern regarding death and the nothing that, as we suggested earlier, indicates possibilities not yet realized in any 'event' of research. The nothing in this sense is generative. Such catastrophe for Derrida also leaves what comes into being as no more than mere 'traces'. With *différance* at play, the 'Other' constitutes each sign; 'trace' is the name Derrida gives to replace the foregoing assumed 'presence' of a sign. In the light of the play of *différance*, being [as presence] becomes a trace. The full implications of the trace for the event of research have yet to be realized.

In thinking through repetitions of practice in terms of the catastrophe of memory, Derrida indicates what remains from our practices are the 'cinders'. He asks us to imagine burning a letter to one's lover, for example, so that in this way we both keep the memory to ourselves and let it go. This is 'the work of mourning' that is 'love itself', because in mourning for everything I lose, 'I want to keep it' with me, but what I do best is to mourn the loss, so keeping it 'inside me' [Dooley and Kavanagh, 2007 14]. But, the ashes that remain indicate the impossibility of safeguarding everything: the ever-growing range of books concerned with research bear witness to the unspoken work of mourning in practices of research. The identities reiterated within every form of organization are always inhabited by absence, loss, death, and the work of mourning, manifest in our ever-growing archives of research, not only testify to the impossibility of the plenitude and totalization of identity. Such traces drive practices so that always more can be done in their regeneration [ibid: 17]. But, there is a real danger, too, that such moves can become an obsessional drive reproduced in the hegemony of 'transparency', so loved by policy makers and others involved in the governance of research.

It is impossible, then, to recreate a historical presence of some phenomenon in its full context. In *Signature, Event, Context*, Derrida [1982a] uses the term 'iteration' to describe this impossible relation: in place of repetition in a Joycean move, he speaks of re-iteration that nuances repetition with a difference [from the Sanskrit, *itera*] in our language [Austin, 1975; Derrida, 1982a: 309–30]. The Canadian writer, Norman Levine, once remarked in conversation that 'in order to remember something we have to change it slightly'. His apparently simple comment nevertheless acknowledges both the impossibility of absolute repetition and the pervasive presence of our very being that is always inhabited by loss and absence. In Derrida's [1992a] terms, identities are inhabited by a 'ghostliness that renders all totalization, fulfilment, plenitude impossible' [ibid: 116]. Given such manifest lack of fulfilment of identity that can be found in the discursive dimensions of all forms of integrative practice, it is, perhaps, no surprise that a number of structures have evolved for maintaining order. Largely unspoken, the work of mourning, for example, always keeps alive aspects researchers come to love.

As a researcher, any obligation to become free from such structures, necessitated by the demands made by particular research to change in some way an extant situation, carries with it the additional requirement to gain greater understanding of the nature of structures grounding and shaping our practices. In concerning ourselves with the question of being, or at least its trace, there remains the additional question of how it constitutes an omnipresent force at work in shaping our research.

Grounding *practice* in research

To understand first what grounding means we have to first appeal to the metaphysical determination of entities, drawing from Derrida [1981b], as the name given to 'the direction taken by a sequence or chain' of signs [ibid: 6]; for him 'there is no such thing as a metaphysical concept' [ibid:

6]. In Derrida's understanding, metaphysical exigencies are much closer to everyday practice in all divisions of research than is generally realized. In metaphysical terms, being has been interpreted traditionally as a presence and as 'the ground or foundation [*Grund*] in which every being as being is grounded' [Heidegger, 1969: 32; Thomson, 2000: 303]. The metaphysical direction given to sequences and chains of signs by reason, for example, is used in both Reckwitz's paper and in Kincheloe's work as grounding for their theses. Notice too, their writings are all based upon presuppositions concerning the teleology of identity, here found to be wanting. Ordinarily, such telos arise from the metaphysical determinations given to chains of signs.

In Heidegger's discourse, metaphysics signified traditional philosophy. Since Aristotle for Heidegger this has been guided by the question: *What is a being*? Iain Thomson's [2000, 2005] deconstructive reading of Heidegger's ontology, which also deals comprehensively with many criticisms of Heidegger's work, shows that in response to this guiding question there emerge two complementary 'stalks'. One stalk takes us into seeking the 'ground that is common to all beings as such' that for Heidegger is when metaphysics becomes ontology. For example, in concerning ourselves with action or with the question of what is done in the name of research, this again arises from a metaphysical determination of the direction taken in this chain of signs, drawing from ontology and so constituting ontological grounds for such practice: it seeks the common aspect of all beings in terms of 'what is done'. Thomson [2000: 302] shows that the other stalk, in response to Aristotle's original guiding question, simultaneously raises two further questions: '1. Which being is the highest [supreme] being? 2. In what sense is it highest?' Here can be heard the metaphysical and theological dimensions of the structuring of beings in research. For example, we meet the theological dimension in the way research is organized to undertake particular actions. The form of organization in each case determines the boundaries, inscribing the highest being of what actions are possible.

There is, then, at work in much everyday research an ontotheological structuring appropriated from the metaphysical determination of the direction taken by chains of signs. In this way, value-positing, theorizing, and representing, all invite metaphysical determinations of the directions taken by each of these signs. A number of ontotheological structures commonly encountered have been identified [Table 2.1].

It is the ontotheological structuring that constitutes grounds for the possibility of the 'meaning maker' being at work in our everyday projections of beings in research. We noted earlier that in Heidegger's [1962] original analysis, the meaning maker had been identified as temporality, and this still remains a possibility in *practice*. We have also seen that it has now become displaced by the 'principle of reason' as the dominant meaning maker used in research. It is this new meaning maker that constitutes what Heidegger [1977a] identifies by the neologism, *das Ge-stell*, itself translated

TABLE 2.1 The Ontotheological Structuring of Social and Educational Research (adapted from Thomson, 2000: 303)

Ontological structure		**Theological structure**	
Metaphysics	**Space for questioning**	**Metaphysics**	**Space for questioning**
Beings as such	This term only makes sense in relation to the nothing [Heidegger], emerges in the spacing from the play of *différance* [Derrida]?	**Beings as a whole**	*Always necessarily incomplete in practice* – Heidegger's being-towards death; Derrida's play of *différance* in identity?
Most basic being	Predicated upon reducing being to a metaphysical principle?	**Highest being**	Predicated upon reducing being to a metaphysical principle?
'Whatness'	Expresses the characteristics and functionality of practice in accord with its ontotheology?	**'Thatness'**	Thatness delimits the upper limits of practice in accord with its ontotheology?
Essentia attributes that make an entity what it fundamentally *is* – based on the principle of being	Heidegger re-defined this notion by reference to *ek-sistence*[4] in the history of being as *enframing*?[13] The metaphysical principle of being has now been deconstructed [Derrida]	***Existentia***	*Dasein* exists in the temporal throw[1] [Heidegger]? For Derrida, our world of practice is contingent, being caught up in the play of *différance*?
Idea as universal [Plato's theory of forms or the idea as universal]	Radically disputed and opened to questioning in Heidegger's [2004] examination of the ontology of truth and the ontology of the art of practice.	**Idea as paradigm** [and *Episteme*: Foucault's term for the body of ideas shaping perceptions of knowledge at a particular period].	David Morgan's [2007] comprehensive review of paradigms used in social research shows how in discursive practice it is so easy to lose sight of any concern for *Dasein*'s alienation in enframing?

Ultima ratio Leibnitz [ultimate reason]	-Principle of reason -Principle of assessment -Principle of being As grounds for theorization and conceptualization of practice, how much do these and other metaphysical exigencies freeze up possibilities unfolding in the intentional structuring of *Dasein*'s being and of being more generally?	***Causa prima*** [first cause]	Tradition holds that 'god' is the *causa prima – in practice possibilities opened by beings and being in relation to the nothing*? God has been expropriated and rewritten in terms of the theological structuring of practice?
Ens commune - Predicated upon the metaphysical principle of being	Being in general [Aquinas] falsely taken to be specified by communities of practice?	***Summum ens*** - Predicated upon the principle of being	Goodness arranged up to the highest good [*summum bonum*] *–open to questioning in the ontology of art*
Quidditas [essentiality] this is Aquinas' term for 'whatness'	These various terms that Aquinas used in a particular context we can never recreate?	***Quomodo* [modality]**[5] Quomodo for Aquinas also indicates a 'measure'	Ontotheological structuring: does it reduce modalities and measures of research to those that are quantifiable? Modes /measures of research – do they account of *Dasein*?
Reality is absolute [tradition from Plato] independent of thoughts and feelings	Heidegger opens questioning concerned with thinking, feelings, and language as a basis for reality. Derrida foregrounds the significance of spacing?	**The real –** traditionally the world around us is real	Theorizations and conceptualizations based upon the principles of reason and assessment – how much do they ossify *the* world and what is real?

TABLE 2.1 Continued

Ontological structure		Theological structure	
Metaphysics	**Space for questioning**	**Metaphysics**	**Space for questioning**
Subjectivity	How much does the foregrounding of subjectivity deflect attention from feelings, attunement, and dispositions structuring guiding practice [Heidegger]?	**The subject**	To what extent is the object of economies, based upon metaphysical exigencies of reason, assessment, the market?
Substantiality – Aquinas's reading of Aristotle's notion of the substantiality of the finite and being becomes totally dependent on the divine[6]	Herein lays the historical background to the ontotheological structuring of enframing?	**The substance** -in Aristotle's *Metaphysics* the substance is the concrete thing	In Heidegger's reading of Descartes only god is a substance giving ground to the creation of things – how much does theological structuring now give ground?
Content	The metaphysics of content currently takes no account of spacing?	**Form**	Current forms shaping the disciplinary structuring of practice take no account of the space required for *Dasein*'s home?
Action[7]	How much does research itself take [explicit] account of spacing [Derrida]?	**Organisation**	In accord with ontotheological structuring of existence – no account taken at present of the nothing?
'Will to power' Nietzsche's ontology	How much do re-presentations of practice in research acknowledge enframing ?	**Eternal return of the same**	The pivotal dimension of enframing in practice – is it acknowledged within the biopolitics of research?

as 'technological enframing', 'enframing', or simply 'framing'.[2] Given that being as presence unfolds when we use each and every one of the verbs and nouns in our lexicon, enframing is an omnipotent force at work in our everyday practices.

In the many specialist divisions of research, however, such an issue simply does not appear to arise because it is does not form part of the 'regime of truth'. In each specialist field, as Foucault [1994a] has suggested, in the metaphysical determination of the being of truth, 'truth is understood as a system of ordered procedures' located within each particular domain, which are used in 'the production, regulation, distribution, circulation and operation of statements' [ibid: 132]. Consequently, questions related to the metaphysics of specialization simply excluded from much practice. Later we will work up Foucault's regimes of truth in terms of the biopolitics of research that also elides completely any relationship with traces of being.

It is important to be clear that enframing is not a framework imposed upon practices. Rather, the gerunds, enframing/framing, express contingent actions, the unfolding of possibilities whose projections are structured by reason, and the exigencies of metaphysical structuring. As the principle of reason, it is this particular meaning maker, or more precisely, in its metaphysical determination that constitutes an ordering and shaping of our projections of particular beings as subjects connecting with various objects of consciousness. Given that the principle of reason makes its presence known everywhere in practice, its metaphysical determination has become the dominant way of revealing our world of practice.

In this way, there is always the possibility of enframing ordering our world of research in terms of the grammar of subjects and objects of consciousness, holding us back as worldless-subjects who, in our everyday world of practice, retain and hold on to the Husserlian–Cartesian axis of understanding we explored earlier. As human beings in this enframing the freedom to express possibilities in beings is constantly in danger of being reduced to an indication of the excess energy, we have to create such possibilities that is always available for use in the enframing – Heidegger [1977a] called this '*Bestand*' – 'standing reserve' [ibid: 16], in which in English we should also hear as enduring in its existence.

In more poetic terms, T. S. Eliot's masterpiece, 'The Wasteland'[8], also returns us once more to express concerns for 'The Burial of the Dead' and its generative powers in the temporal unfolding of the world:

April is the cruellest month, breeding
Lilacs out of the dead land, mixing
Memory and desire, stirring
Dull roots with spring rain . . .

As suggested by 'The Waste Land', a recent initial exploration of everyday social interaction at the workplace indicates that while our contemporary discursive practices have tended to move away from expressions concerned with the ever-unfolding lived-time of our temporal world that now seem to most of us terribly 'old-fashioned' and 'out of date'. Quietly, however, much of our everyday social interactions remain grounded in temporality as the meaning maker in our everyday world of practice [Flint, 2011b]. In the words of Heidegger [1962], 'temporality temporalizes as a future, which makes present in the process of having been' [ibid: 350].

Here we have glossed temporality as the unfolding of beings, as an attempt to break the stilled objects of consciousness in our everyday world of practice. In this way, rather than the imaginary conditioning and cybernetic calculus of *the* world of practice featuring that fantasy of objective consciousness, temporality expresses the ever-unfolding nature of *Dasein* that in pushing towards future possibilities is always caught up in some aspect of the past, out of which we variously create the present moment. Even though it is from the unfolding of temporality that our current preoccupations with the cybernetics of controlling practices in research arises, on its own the unfolding of lived-time now seems for most of us, it would seem, part of another by-gone age.

But, rather than remaining with what some have seen as Heidegger's nostalgia for attempting to bring back times-past, driven as we mentioned earlier by his own eschatology, we will begin to uncover how Derrida's reading of Heidegger has given research a range of intellectual resources that can be used to create 'spacing' for practice outside the ontotheological structuring driving enframing. Eschatologists, like Heidegger, Caputo [1987] reminds his readers, 'look to antiquity for light and a time of original solidarity' [ibid: 241]. As we began to suggest earlier, they begin with a sense of loss, that pivotal move of Plato in the cave allegory, for example, where the full richness of *aletheia* eventually becomes largely laid to rest in antiquity and reduced to a correspondence theory of truth in the emerging Enlightenment and our world of research. With such eschatology, following 'the great beginning in the Greeks' and the 'decline in modernity', Heidegger offers hope for a 'new beginning' informed by melancholy and 'antimodernism' [ibid: 241].

At this point, hopefully, the force and complexity of being at the heart of the teleoaffective shaping our world of practice in research through metaphysical exigency, including the principle of reason and temporality, is beginning to come into view. What is required, therefore, is to make more concrete the grounding of beings projected in all paradigms, divisions, and forms of organization of our everyday research in the ontotheological structuring driving enframing. This is now relatively straightforward, with help from Thomson [2000, 2005], who has created the basis for making clear the many dimensions of the ontotheological structuring driving enframing in our practices [Table 2.1]. The table may at first seem at little daunting, but we will be referring back it frequently.

At issue in more concrete terms is the question of just what the ontotheological structuring of enframing means in the practice of research.

Here we should keep in view the German neologism, *das Ge-stell*, because '*-stell*' derives from the verb, *stellen*, to place, connoting to put something, to make something stand, to create a space, etc. Our word thesis can also be traced back to a similar root, from the Greek, *thesis*,[9] placing an affirmation, derived from the verb *thé*,[10] *to place*. As we saw earlier in etymological terms, in jurisprudence the verb, to place, has been identified as grounds for informal laws, including those being uncovered in the customs of everyday practice of research to which we will return. For Inwood [1999] the prefix *Ge-* meant 'together, with' and was later used to form collective nouns: *Gebirge,* mountains, mountain range' from *Berg*, mountain, etc. [ibid: 210]. Heidegger frequently speaks of a gathering together of entities, but he knew there was more at stake – in his later work, for example, he examines the interplay of 'Identity and Difference' [Heidegger, 2002]. Derrida is unambiguous on this matter. There is no gathering in Derrida's understanding of practice, only the play of *différance* and traces of the past, so becoming the locus of mourning and regeneration that desires to go beyond what is already inscribed in extant customs. For Derrida, this is the desire for justice.

Though the ways in which the emplacement [*Stellung*] of signs in our practices are deferred from earlier sources [Table 2.1] will be useful for our analyses of practices of research, reflecting the metaphysical determinations of their ontotheological structuring, here we are going to focus once more upon the relationship between the structures in contemporary research for 'action' of what is done in practice [as ontological grounds] and the 'organisation', delimiting, and constituting boundaries for such practice [in its theological structuring].

Three more obvious forms of organization reflecting the actions driving enframing in research can be found in [1] representing practice, [2] theorizing practice, and [3] compartmentalizing practice. It will become evident from the analysis that follows the 'content' of each of these 'forms' of practice are express aspects of metaphysical determinations of the direction taken by sequences of signs at work in every dimension of enframing.

The point of the analysis is to contribute to greater understanding of some of the complications in the relationship of research generated by its enframing. What is particularly noticeable here is that at work in the practice of research, potentially affecting us all, quite independent of race, culture, gender, or class, this phenomenon is simply rendered in a 'state of exception' to the archives of research[2[Introduction]] used for this study.

Enframing in representation of and value-positing in *practice*

One aspect of the issue of turning practice into theory here is implicated in what some have called the 'crisis of representation'[11] in ethnography.

For David Altheide and John M. Johnson [2011: 581–94], such crisis has arisen from the reification of analyses that come 'to *stand* for actual experience[s]' [ibid: 591, emphasis added]. But, as indicated already, rather than approaching this 'crisis' with Altheide and Johnson from within the traditional science of ethnography that in its primary intention of gaining knowledge is always open to the reiteration of enframing, from a Heideggerian perspective, what is required is a form of ethnography that in foregrounding the care of the self, recognizes human beings are always already in the throw of practice. But, we still have not entered into the deconstruction of such practice with the work of mourning.

In another take on the crisis of representation for Denzin and Lincoln [2011a] 'language is the key' [ibid: 683]. It is agreed this is pivotal, but what is required, it will be argued, is not so much concerns over 'politics and ideology' [ibid: 683], though these issues are not unimportant, but the deconstruction of the language [or languages] of biopolitics that is [are] also incorporated within methodologies.

An important backdrop to this requirement for the language[s] of biopolitics is Nietzsche's 'will-to-power'. As Heidegger [1977c] indicates, this remains pivotal to enframing in our contemporary practices. In his lecture series, 'What Is Called Thinking?', Heidegger [1968 {1954}] observes that 'the will is the sphere of representational ideas which basically pursue and set upon everything that comes and goes and exists' [ibid: 93]. In expressions of the will, what Heidegger places in focus is the way the unfolding beings are always in danger of becoming, in effect, cast in stone. But, this talk of the will may seem far removed from everyday practices of research: this is not the case.

In addition to removing beings from their ever-unfolding lived world that is the case for all forms of representation in research, the will-to-power is Nietzsche's [1973] express term for value positing. Although art-based forms of inquiry are doing much to challenge extant notions of representation in this emerging specialist field of research, it is difficult to find any connection made in the field as a whole with the metaphysical determination of the ethics of value positing. Caputo's [1987] incisive summary of Heidegger's [1977c: 53–114] 'searching critique' of such ethics makes clear that, 'an ethic of 'values,' . . . arises precisely from' the metaphysical determination of 'subjectivity'. It emerges from the 'barrenness of any idea of being which stands in need of supplementation by value and the hollowness of any idea which is issued not by being but by the 'subject.'' As we have seen, when 'being is reduced to an object, values are made the issue of the subject' [ibid: 236].

Again, this does not mean that all researchers should somehow eschew value positing or representation, but it does begin to uncover the power of metaphysical exigencies at work in research.

Enframing in the theorization of *practice*

Within the traditions of research generating theories and pressing forwards in to theorization of phenomena have always been much-valued aspects of the trade. Independent of the metaphysics of value-positing, theories themselves, in Heidegger's understanding of the world, constitute another dimension of enframing. As Heidegger [1977e: 155–83] points out, 'theory makes secure at any given time a region of the real as its object-area' [ibid: 169]. Against the backdrop to the stage set for understanding practice that he has helped us to create, involving the possibilities unfolding in the pragmatic, existential, temporal dimensions of *Dasein*'s existence, the metaphysical aspects of theory as observation, and as the making-secure of 'object-spheres' constitute ontotheological grounds for its own violence. Violence here does not mean necessarily doing harm to someone, but rather it imputes the selection of particular aspects of practice to the exclusion of others that arises from the structuring of language. In our theorizing, for example, for Heidegger, such violence arises from theory being 'the observation' of 'the real' [ibid: 166], so entrapping the world of practice. In Heidegger's language, to look at something and to subject it to closer examination he calls *Betrachtung*, contemplation. Etymologically, he connects with the German *Trachten* – 'to strive', meaning 'to strive after something and to entrap and secure it', and with the Latin *tractare* – to manipulate, work over, or refine what has been secured.[12] The violence of research, then, arises from grasping aspects of 'the real' in order to change it – manifestly, theorization and observation serve to kill any movement of beings unfolding in all of the specialist dimensions of practice.

The teleoaffective dimensions of the doings and sayings of researchers that we are calling practice are, in fact, located within the metaphysical and ontotheological structuring of grounds generated from 'the projection of a circumscribed object-sphere' [Heidegger, 1977d: 123] in accord with the Cartesian axis of understanding seen earlier. Meaning that always has to do with a making possible [Heidegger, 1962: 324], in this case, sustains the intelligibility of research, giving it an axis around which it can organize itself. The 'object-sphere' arises, in this case, Heidegger [1977d] suggests, when 'science' becomes 'research' [ibid: 123]. Consequently, the character of science as research is necessarily individualized and compartmentalized. But, notice here that Heidegger [and here we can again add researchers] is working with a metaphysical determination of existence based upon the presupposition of the teleology of identity. In drawing from Derrida, we are concerned to open space for research that takes away the grounds for such metaphysics.

One of the difficulties confronting such a standpoint is the existing form of specialization and division within research. Compartmentalization of science as research emerges in *practice*, Heidegger argues, from 'the development of a projected plan by means of its methodology' [ibid: 123]. But, the methodologies that researchers employ, of course, are not fixed; they are not simply there to generate results. Rather, with the help of such outcomes, methodology constantly adapts itself to innovation. Consequently, when guided by such methodologies of research, the question remains concerning the extent to which researchers are directed towards provoking fresh questioning concerned with being, and with the multiplicity of metaphysical exigencies found in the practice of research. An imaginary critic, one possessed with a positivistic understanding of what is real, would undoubtedly retort with another question on why to waste energy on such abstract questions. What remains at stake in struggling with these issues in research is the shape and the shaping of our very existence as human beings and as societies.

The horizons of both the telic and affective dimensions of *practice*, per se, however, always take us far beyond the necessarily delimited confines of both the subject of specialized forms of research and particular methodological dimensions of science as research, including 'creating a data repertoire' and 'integrating data sets', following threads in methodology, interviewing, analysing narratives and themes, etc.[2[Introduction]] The horizons of practice conceived here also take us beyond the powerful insights of particular projects that gather together a range of methodologies, including the 'Practice and Process in Integrated Methodologies', PPIMs, project [Cronin et al., 2011: 572–84].

The horizon of *practice* is not delimited by a self-reflexive theoretical projection of 'at-hand' objects confined to particular methodological contexts, including 'ethnography' [Armstrong, 2008: 54–67; Bhatti, 2012: 81–84] and 'action research' [Brydon-Miller et al., 2011: 389]. Nor is *practice* [as distinct from policy] merely delimited by either matters of 'applied educational research' or matters of 'basic research' concerned with the advancement of knowledge per se without the privileging its possible use [Coe, 2012: 9]. But, the foregoing narrower conceptions of practice arise precisely from researchers pressing themselves into the object spheres of specialized forms of science in accord with the ongoing activity associated with the management of traditional methodologies.

In radical contrast, the horizon of *practice* is here conceived as incorporating and opening possibilities in the multiplicity of *Dasein*'s own horizons of being. Such possibilities come into being through authentic forms of education used in cultivating cultures in all walks of our lives. Practice, so conceived, opens space and freedom to be free for the possibility of conducting scientific forms of inquiry outside the necessarily delimiting horizons of technological enframing.

The possibility of enframing, we have now seen arising in theorizing, in representation, in value positing, in our specialist compartmentalization of science as research, and in the manipulations created by the privileging of methodology in research over whatever *is*, that are rendered as objects of such research [Heidegger 1977d: 125]. What connect each of these aspects of practice are metaphysical determinations of the directions given by chains of signs on grounds of reason. From Heidegger's perspective, the essence of technology, enframing[13] is a way of revealing the world of practice through metaphysical determinations of writing and speaking, so rendering[14] the possibilities of our very being as so much excess energy that is available for use.

Enframing – opening space beyond metaphysical determinations of *practice*

The point here is not to overcome enframing by means of our gaining better understandings of practice. That would amount to more of the same. At issue remains how researchers can open space and the freedom to be free for their research outside the space constituted in enframing and so beyond any metaphysical determinations of entities. This also carries with it the challenge of opening space for rereading Heidegger's [1962] metaphysics of the care of the self within the horizons of being and time.

Derrida suggests a way forward in coming back to Heidegger's [1977a] express concern that the 'essence of technology is nothing technology' [ibid: 4]. In Derrida's words:

> We cannot exaggerate the risk and gravity of this brief sentence [for example]: the essence of technology is foreign to technology. Apparently very trivial, it can yet again be put into question, with all of the entailing consequences, the scope of even the most philosophical gesture [Derrida, 1986: 140; Dooley and Kavanagh, 2007: 95]

For Derrida, this 'brief sentence' suggested that in Heidegger's eschatology he wished to purify the essence of the truth of whatever being, including being itself, and to exorcise it all from such 'technology' [Dooley and Kavanagh, 2007: 95]. In Dooley and Kavanagh's [2007] reading, they argue that for Derrida, 'the essence of technology is always technological' [ibid: 96]. In their incisive reading of Heidegger, they contrast the latter's 'attempts to draw a clear distinction between living memory and its external embodiment [as the means to memorization] in material signs', for example, found in the archives of researching practice, with Heidegger's 'attempt to draw a distinction between essence and technology [which] repeats Plato['s] model' [ibid: 95, 96].

While research would appear to be largely informed by the same desire – that the being of practice constitutes an 'act of memory' in the 'gathering, appropriation and recollection' of such practice in its various archives – as the locus of memorization of whatever beings, for Derrida 'memory and memorization are always mutually contaminated by each other as part of the same circular economy' [Dooley and Kavanagh, 2007: 95, 96]. In Derrida's deconstruction, *différance* and related devices, to which we will return, simply give us ways of keeping in play the possibilities opened by technologies of research.

In anticipation of such deconstruction, what follows is a closer examination of the powers of the technological institutions at work in practices and their grounding biopolitics. Such scrutiny is used to foreground consideration of both law and justice within the ethics of practice for research.

CHAPTER THREE

Power, politics, and rationalities of researching practice: What can be learned from Foucault and Agamben?

Practice would amount to nothing without power: nothing more than empty words on the page if it were not for that capacity to be able to do things, that is, without the power 'to be able to'[1] take action when confronted with an imminent issue that has to be addressed in some way. Without power, knowing how to 'get on' in a given situation would be quite impossible. As Foucault [1980a] observed in his reflections on 'Prison Talk', 'it is not possible for power to be exercised without knowledge and it is impossible for knowledge not to engender power' [ibid: 52].

Interestingly, in their preface to 'The Managerial State' where John H. Clarke and Janet E. Newman [1997] were concerned with creating a context for their analysis of 'power, politics and ideology in the remaking of social welfare' in the UK, the authors spoke of the 'absent presence' of power 'in many existing analyses of change' [ibid: 3]. The same observation could be made here from the opening two chapters.

But, here too, rather than rushing to align ourselves with Foucault's concern, directed towards the reciprocal relationship between power-knowledge, it is important to take a little time for meditation. Surely, another 'absent presence' at work in practice is the power to acknowledge phenomena. In Wittgenstein's [1969] terms, 'knowledge is in the end based on acknowledgement' [ibid: 378]. Of course, in both Foucault's acknowledgement of the ineluctable reciprocal interrelation of 'power-knowledge' and in Clarke and Newman's account where credit has been given to the 'absent-presence' of power, acknowledgement is demonstrable. Acknowledgement itself is always constituted in the cinders of particular contexts. So, in the discursive practice of acknowledgement, there is the possibility of developing other such practices within communities of research based upon shared languages. Here we have to make the distinction between those languages constituting the ontotheology of the apparatus of research, and those languages constituting bare life itself. Thinking is here directed towards uncovering languages for the latter. It is also helpful to uncover from Foucault, what he meant by 'apparatus', in order to situate 'bare life' with Agamben [1998, 2005] as a 'state of exception' within the apparatus of research.

As we shall see in concluding this chapter, it is the essential structure of exception constituting language per se that in giving expression to power, knowledge, acknowledgement withdraws itself from concrete instances of speech/writing involving such terms, so dividing the linguistic realm of practice from the non-linguistic. Consequently, it is to this state of exception that this study will turn, with help from Agamben, in examining the implications for research.

As an initial move, therefore, in examining the contributions of Foucault and Agamben to our understandings concerned with the exercise of power in *practice*, it is important to keep in mind a complex triangular relationship between knowledge, acknowledgement, and power in which the power to generate knowledge and the power invested in acknowledgement, along with knowledge itself, each open the possibility of developing new shared languages as essential homes to particular communities of research. Following Agamben's [1993] investigation of 'whatever being' in *The Coming Community*, it is important to acknowledge, too, that community is opened as a possibility by 'belonging itself': 'not by any condition of belonging' [being a researcher, being philosophically minded] 'nor by the simple absence of conditions, a negative community' [as suggested by the work of Maurice Blanchot] – a community for those in research who consider they have no community. In being concerned with questions on power/knowledge, therefore, in addition to the complex issue of the language of acknowledgement, it is also important to examine the politics of identity itself that is practised in research – that is, by way of the deconstruction of such identities. Though we have already begun to explore the multiplicity of ways in which identity may be understood, Agamben places particular emphasis upon the language of 'bare life' that ordinarily tends to remain hidden within our organizations and institutions. The *language* of bare life carries, for him, and for Foucault, the imperative to explore and to examine further a language of biopolitics that brings into the public sphere a consciousness regarding the inclusion of bare life that is ordinarily excluded. Although for Foucault biopolitics emerges in the seventeenth century, Agamben in effect provides a correction to Foucault's work by tracing it back to Aristotle.

Given that issues of identity lie at the heart of all forms of integrative practice, it is to the principles of identity in *practice* as grounds for politics of research that we will first turn our attention.

The politics of identity in *practice*

Here interest is focused upon the analysis and philosophy of power, and of the biopolitics shaping and ordering contemporary practices of research, in particular, approaches taken in research to the analysis of integrative practices. In concert with the traditions of philosophy running from Plato to Husserl, much of the sciences also retain assumptions concerned with the plenitude and fulfilment of identity. These ground the philosophies of two influential thinkers, Kant and Descartes, whose works can be readily apprehended in such practices. Although there has been express interest in the past two decades in making sense of Heidegger's *oeuvre*, the practices reiterated in many areas of research appear to hold onto their traditions, almost as if the provocation generated by Heidegger's [1977b: 36–49] thinking can be reduced to an objective presence, a matter of fact, at best, the trace of any identity found in research being glossed by theories of complexity. Perhaps this is one measure of the power of the everydayness of *das Man* [Heidegger, 1962: 129] mediating any sense of identity – an express matter of what 'one' does as an individual researcher, almost without question, in practising within its various traditions.

Heidegger's standpoint regarding identity, too, is not clear-cut; his 'ethics of *Gelassenheit*' is one that simply lets beings be in their own ground, including the being of identity. Given his influence upon the work of our two protagonists, Foucault and Agamben, it is important to see where Heidegger stands regarding identity. Although in his later work after the war he refers often to the 'gathering' of beings, suggesting the plenitude and fulfilment of identities, it is clear from Heidegger's [1982] account of 'Identity and Difference' that this is not the case. For example, in this context, he contrasts 'the totality of the technological world [that for him] is interpreted in advance in terms of man, as being of man's making' [ibid: 34], with the *belonging* together of man and being [ibid: 34]. He asks us to think whether we should place more emphasis upon the 'belonging' or upon the 'together'. It takes us back to Heidegger's attempts to exorcise any technological gatherings from the essence of truth. We will return a little later to this particular relationship with Agamben, who pays particular attention to bare life. With emphasis placed upon the 'belonging' rather than the assumed 'togetherness' of 'man and being', Heidegger's meditation, and Agamben's elaborations on this issue, suggests how researchers may be moved away from 'representational thinking' [ibid: 32]. Given that being is only ever a trace, the totalization of identity characteristic of technological thinking is quite impossible from this perspective.

Agamben's [1993] reflections on 'belonging' are more politically focused than those of Heidegger – his observations concerning the Tiananmen Square 'demonstrations of the Chinese May' place emphasis upon 'the relative absence of determinate contents' of any demands made by the protesters. In parenthesis, Agamben notes how 'democracy and freedom are notions too generic and broadly defined to constitute a real object of conflict' [ibid: xix]. His argument leads him to a conclusion concerned with 'the novelty of the coming politics'. For Agamben 'it will no longer be a struggle for the conquest or control of the State, but a struggle between the State and the non-State [humanity]' that he views in terms of 'an insurmountable disjunction between whatever singularity and the State organization' [ibid: xix]. Such disjunction can be traced back to the exclusion of bare life. As we have begun to see, already it is the *language of identity* involving here such intentional structuring that constitutes grounds for the state of exception, not least, for example, in the politics threatening the very existence of qualitative inquiry within the governance of research in the United States and the UK to which we will return in the final chapters.

Like Heidegger, our two main protagonists retain assumptions concerned with the gathering of identities; they are built into their respective expressions of ethics. Ironically, however, in both cases such expressions seem, somehow, to assume immunity from their own respective critiques. Nevertheless, we could hardly move forward in the analysis of power without the insights and understandings of Foucault and Agamben.

Foucault's questioning sought to illuminate in historical rather than in transcendental terms, the contingent repetition of identities within particular institutional and organizational practices. Where Heidegger viewed the understanding of beings in terms of *Dasein* pushing forward and projecting possibilities in the context of the everyday world of practice, Foucault concerns himself in being located within the ever-unfolding practice of reproducing contingent histories involving the 'body' [following Merleau-Ponty]. In contrast, Agamben's critical reading of Heidegger returns once more to Aristotle's notion of potentiality – Agamben is concerned with the negative ways of thinking based upon the not, anxiety, and guilt, and in place of such negativity Agamben would seem to take up the ethos of Latin American cultures in concerning himself in much of his writing with the positive potentialities at play in identities. In this way, Agamben provides us with a new focus upon bare life and some significant corrections to Foucault's earlier work.

In the bigger picture of understanding *practice,* it has to be kept in mind also that in their own different ways both of our protagonists resort to gathering together a plenitude of identities constituting their own metaphysical schemas. In each case these are to be found on the high-ground of meaning, in their respective expressions of the ethics of practice. Here, too, in their schemas, once again the absent presence of power is manifest. From Heidegger's [1977c] perspective, drawn from his reading of Nietzsche, both Foucault's and Agamben's expansions of gathering powers in creating their respective ethics would appear almost ineluctable. Heidegger puts forward the ontic proposition that 'power is only power when and only so long as it remains power-enhancement and commands for itself more power' [ibid: 78]. From this ontic perspective of the representation of power, we would appear to be inescapably caught up in the grip of its expansion. In radical contrast, in understanding the ontology of Heidegger's conception of power from the perspective of its coming into being, this stands in relation to 'the not, the nothing', the being of power only makes sense in relation to 'the nothing' and the possibility of disempowerment that is implied but not thematized as such within his conception. It becomes obvious in the 'Introduction to Metaphysics' and his meditation upon 'Identity and Difference' [Heidegger, 1969, 2000, 2002].

From a Derridaean perspective of the being of power appearing on the 'scene of presence', this power we face is always fissured; on the one hand, the Janus face of this figure carries the 'mark of its past element' that represents it as ineluctable expansion, and on the other hand, it is corrupted by 'the mark of its relation to a future element' that disempowers by taking away the grounds for any build-up of powers in the constitution of *différance* [Derrida, 1973b: 142]. In formal terms, as we will see, the latter still remains barely explored in fields of research.

Our protagonists, Foucault and Agamben, however, sought to open space for localized resistance to the seemingly inexorable growth of knowledge-power in this age of information. In the words of Foucault: 'where there is power there is resistance' [Foucault, 1978: 95]. Agamben's approach is to open questioning concerned with biopolitics. It begins to uncover his sense of potentiality hitherto largely unrealized within the customs of everyday practice.

Contrastingly, in seeking to address the issue of the customs or informal laws that still remain inscribed in research, we have sought to open space for understanding more of the powers at work delimiting and shaping the very processes of researching practices. These are always open to the possibility of disempowerment. The approach to the analysis of power here, therefore, is not intended to conflict or confound, but rather to complement readings of Foucault and Agamben. The approach adopted has not sought to eschew Foucault's [1978] conviction, first given expression in his *History of Sexuality* [Volume 1] that 'power comes from below', though it is also recognized that the language that gives expression to such metaphysical direction itself has no such bearing. Nor, in concerning ourselves with the question of informal laws inscribed within researching practice, is there any disagreement with Foucault that 'there is no binary and all-encompassing opposition between rulers and ruled at the root of power relations' [ibid: 94], though in such binary there remains the as-yet-unaccounted-for state of exception in the structuring of language to which we will return.

At issue are ways of taking away the very grounds for the generation of centralized powers wherever they occur within organizations and institutions to create a balance within integrative practices. 'Homo Sacer' [Agamben, 1998], for example, puts a spotlight on what had been at stake for Foucault in his analysis of power. For Agamben [1998], Foucault's work has illuminated how 'the modern Western state has integrated techniques of subjective individualization' – based upon biopolitical models of power, concerned with rights – 'with procedures of totalisation to an unprecedented degree' [ibid: 11]. The latter procedures for Foucault are grounded upon laws inscribed as juridico-institutional models of power. But, for Agamben, this point at which these two faces of power converge remains 'unclear in Foucault's work' [ibid: 11]. Some of the consequences are given expression in Agamben's inquiries into this 'zone of indistinction [or, at least, the point of intersection] at which techniques of individualization and totalizing procedures converge' [1988: 11], so providing a focus for the second stage of our analysis of power in practice.

Rather than turning away from the powers generated by laws and by expressions of rights in order to generate an ethics of practice, as both Foucault and, to a lesser extent, Agamben have done in their own particular ways, the strategy adopted here is also one of gaining further understanding of the nature of laws/customs, and later we will return to the pre-judicial structures [Table 2.1], inscribed within the methodological practices of research. So, rather than working with Foucault's or with Agamben's presuppositions concerned with the gathering powers of an ethic of practice as the locus of dispute for the extant build-up of centralized powers within integrated practices, here the inquiry is focused upon understanding the nature of the laws inscribed in *practice*. The object of this strategy is a clearer focus upon the grounds for the generation of sovereign juridical models of power and institutional powers exercised in *practice*, and so to open space for moves towards justice in their possible disempowerment. Justice, as we wish to understand it, always seeks to exceed extant laws. In *practice*, this interplay of informal law or custom and justice is an express consequence of the play of *différance* in *language* – language itself being an omnipotent sovereign power. Our starting point in adopting this strategy, therefore, is Foucault's own language used in his analysis of power.

The analysis of power in *practice*: insights from Foucault

In the words of Agamben [1998],

> one of the most persistent features of Foucault's work is its decisive abandonment of the traditional approach to the problem of power, which

> is based on juridico-institutional models [the definition of sovereignty, the theory of the State], in favor of an unprejudiced analysis of the concrete ways in which power penetrates subjects' very bodies and forms of life. [ibid: 11]

In the spirit of Heidegger's approach to practice, Foucault's [1986] concern with 'how power is exercised', rather than with the question of 'how does it manifest itself' [ibid: 337] was most obvious in his opening 'Two Lectures' [Foucault, 1980b] on this subject. He argues for a schematic change of the question structuring inquiries into power. In his schema the 'traditional question of political philosophy' is expressed 'in the following terms': How is the discourse of truth, or quite simply, philosophy as that discourse that *par excellence* is concerned with truth, able to fix limits to the rights of power? In challenging such thinking, Foucault arrives at a completely different question that he sees as 'much more down to earth and concrete' compared to the 'traditional and noble philosophical question'. Foucault [1980b] asks 'what rules of right are implemented by the relations of power in the production of discourses of truth?' [ibid: 90]. In concerning himself with the 'how of power', Foucault 'related its mechanisms to two points of reference, two limits: on the one hand, to the rules of right that provide a formal delimitation of power; on the other, to the effects of truth that this power produces and transmits, and which in turn reproduce this power' [ibid: 93].

At the heart of Foucault's schema for the analysis of power in practice is a triangular relationship between 'power, right and truth' [ibid: 93]. This triangular relationship is always contingent upon the unfolding over of history into the present, and silently, as we have begun to uncover, the very state of exception structuring language itself. The issue concerning the history of practice is merely the reiteration of 'Heidegger's point', as Schwarz [1999] has seen; namely, 'past practices are sedimented in current ones' [ibid: 122]. Perhaps, more interesting, is the way Foucault [1994a] understands truth in the context of historical practice, rather than conceptualizing it in absolute or transcendental terms, as we have seen he views it as 'a system of ordered procedures' [ibid: 132] used within practice. Truth in this sense has a strategic function; as technology it becomes the very means to particular ends concerned with the generation of order, rather than being an end in itself.

In this way, Foucault sees that '"truth" is linked in a circular relation with systems of power that produce and sustain it, and to the effects of power which it induces and which extend it' that he identifies as 'a regime of truth' [ibid: 132]. Consequently, as Schwarz [1999] has observed in *The Order of Things* Foucault [1970{1966}] explores how 'truth is related to each episteme' in which each trace of context carries with it 'the progressive dissolution of truth-as-correspondence' [Schwarz, 1999: 117].

In his analysis of power circulating in such regimes of truth and in opening space for resisting power in practices, Foucault adopted two principal methodological approaches in his earlier work, which he identified in terms of archaeological and genealogical analyses.

The analysis of power: the archaeology of *practice*

For Hans Kögler [1996] in *The Power of Dialogue*, 'archaeology lays bare the symbolic structures' mediating 'discursive formations' [ibid: 175]. In her introduction to Foucault's work, Sara Mills [2003] uses the term 'unwritten rules which produce, organize, . . . distribute' [ibid: 24] what Foucault [1972] had seen as 'archives' for 'the formation and transformation of' authoritative 'statements' [ibid: 130]. It is to these customs or informal laws that we will be returning in exploring their relationship with justice in the exploration of a proposed extension of the ethics of research. Kendall and Wickham's [1999] memorable phrase 'opening up visibilities' suggests that in research archaeology could be viewed as a historically based study of authoritative statements recorded within archives, including text books, journals, and electronic databases. Here, the same approach is being adopted in a critical examination of archives, chiefly in the form of leading textbooks used in research.[2[Introduction]]

Perhaps the clearest statement on Foucault's archaeology comes from Thomas Flynn [2003] who, in speaking of 'Foucault's mapping of history', like Mills suggests a focus for the process on the archival record in research [ibid: 30]. But, he also makes apparent archaeology's twofold character as a 'judicative and veridicative' practice [ibid: 31]. That is, in taking a strategic view of 'practices', Flynn [2003] suggests they 'establish and apply norms, controls, and exclusions', arising precisely from their capacity to 'render true /false discourse possible' [ibid: 31]. But this strategic view is premised upon the principle of the plenitude of identity as grounds for the inclusion/ exclusion of statements gathered within extant regimes of truth. Later we will explore how the relationship between such research and a particular understanding of norms and customs of practice constitutes grounds for the build-up of powers, and for the reproduction of regimes of truth in such practices.

Flynn views 'Foucault's archaeological period' reflected in the publication of *The History of Madness*, *The Birth of the Clinic*, *The Order of Things* and *The Archaeology of Knowledge*' [ibid: 32] as 'counter-history and social critique' [ibid: 32]. Flynn argues that Foucault's archaeology is 'counter-history because it assumes a contrapuntal relationship to traditional history, whose conclusions it more rearranges than denies and whose resources it mines for its own purposes' [ibid: 33]. Later we will be drawing upon resources from Derrida's *oeuvre* concerning the play of *différance*, so underlying a sense of contingency in *practice* as the basis for critique of the gathering of identities, and putting a spotlight on how the growth of powers generated by regimes of truth and identity in research may be balanced within localized places of *practice*. Such an approach also turns us to the genealogical question of how power works.

The analysis of power: a genealogy of *practice*

Mills [2003] views genealogy as a 'development of archaeological analysis that is more concerned with the workings of power and with describing the history of the present' [ibid: 25]. In this way, consonant with understanding of the effects of everydayness upon *das Man*, 'genealogical investigation focuses upon the individual and group-directed techniques of normalization, control, exploitation' [Kögler, 1996: 175] of the 'docile body'. The subtle techniques of 'normalisation' of the self-directed body mark a displacement of the older targeting of the body in a system of penal repression. As Flynn [2003] observes, 'power relations underwrite all Foucault's genealogies' [ibid: 35]. Consequently, any 'history' of *practice* is translated and transformed 'from a project of meaning and communication towards a micro-physics of power' in Foucault's incisive phrasing [Foucault, 1977: 139].

However, as Flynn [2003] observes, though Foucault's 'anti-Utopian thinking . . . separates him from Marxists and other optimists', grounding his claim 'that every exercise of power is accompanied by or gives rise to resistance, [it also] opens a space for possibility and freedom in any context' [ibid: 36]. But, this seems to result from a distinctly strategic reading of Heidegger's [1962] *Being and Time*. Conveniently, it would seem, it plays down completely the powers of *das Man* inscribed in what 'one does' in *practice*, and places an undue strategic emphasis upon a reading of *Dasein*'s authenticity – which is only ever projected as a contingent possibility in *Being and Time*. From Foucault's reading of *Being and Time* it is his language that gives expression to a metaphysical investment of the body with a strategic rather than contingent capacity to somehow transcend the 'averaging down' of the omnipotent effects of both group-think, and the ontotheological structuring of practices. But, in such express language, Foucault does not appear to trouble himself with the state of exception at the heart of his own language. Thus, while not denying the possibility of the powers of such resistance, here we will be concentrating upon how the build-up of powers from the ontotheological structuring of research may be balanced by localized moves towards justice that always exceeds its customs/laws. The approach taken, therefore, is concerned with the very *language* constituting grounds for the centralization of such powers.

Given the emphasis upon discipline and control in the practices of research, it is to Foucault's genealogical studies of the powers at work in the subtle techniques of normalization to which we now turn. In Foucault's 'microphysics of power' Flynn [2003] suggests there is a shift from 'hermeneutic[s] . . . and interpretation to strategy and technique' [ibid: 35], reflecting the privileging of 'relations of power' over 'relations of meaning'. But, it is important to keep in mind it is Foucault's *language* of microphysics, and in particular its state of exception structuring such language that constitutes grounds for such a shift. It is the state of exception at the very heart of the *language* of the multiplicity of disciplinary technologies in *practice* driving activities of research that still remains operative today.

The analysis of power: towards a genealogy of disciplinary technologies grounding *practice*

One locus of such disciplinary technologies is the coded space constituting the abstract architecture of the Panopticon. Foucault first uncovered this architecture in accord with Bentham's [2005{1843}] imagination [Foucault, 1977: 200–09]. In plan, the Panopticon is an annular structured prison with partitioned cells located rather like slices of cake around a central viewing platform. The subjects, its prisoners, are prevented from seeing each other by the absence of any adjoining windows in each of the cells. In this architectural space, each prisoner is continually made aware of its own activities as a self-directed subject by the apparatus of surveillance. Such apparatus, Foucault [1977] makes plain, is driven by the machinery of Panopticism that 'dissociates the seeing / being seen dyad' [ibid: 201]. He notes 'in the peripheric ring one is totally seen without ever seeing; in the tower one sees without ever being seen' [ibid: 201]. Consequently, Foucault argues, 'he who is subjected to the field of visibility, and who knows it, assumes responsibility for the constraints of power; he makes them play spontaneously upon himself; he inscribes in himself the power relation in which he simultaneously plays both roles; he becomes the principle of his own subjection' [ibid: 202]. Here in *practice* is the basis for many of the powers operative within the visible field, delimiting education in research, consonant with the powers at work in *The Society of the Spectacle* [Debord, 1977]. This architectural space, therefore, constitutes grounds for the production of the docile body [ibid: 135–69] in both individual and collective senses of the term. It raises the question of the extent to which cultures of research constitute docile bodies.

Foucault's genealogy uncovers a multiplicity of modalities of just how a large and anonymous group of individuals become disciplined and socialized as a 'docile body'. He speaks of 'discipline sometimes requir[ing] enclosure' and he takes examples from 'the confinement of vagabonds and paupers . . . "colléges or secondary schools" where the "monastic model was gradually imposed" and "boarding became the most perfect, if not the most frequent, educational régime"' [ibid: 141]. In contemporary research, regimes of truth for the individual researcher are now frequently constituted within specialist fields of inquiry, each with their own traditions in terms of methodology, methods, and techniques of analysis.

In contemporary research – or more precisely of the language of 'education-in-and-through-research' – there is always a danger that such an educational régime obviates any requirement for the languages of bare life and enframing. Consonant with such regime, officially designated specialist subjects of research, reflecting a multiplicity of forms of organization and their respective boundaries [Gibbs and Barnett, 2014] are ontotheologically structured. Language establishes the ontological grounds for many such inquiries, and the disciplinary organization where researchers' variously locate much of their research. It also founds the theological structuring of investigation. Many leading researchers, identified in this study, continually seek to confront such extant, albeit largely unspoken forms of ontotheological structuring.

What more can be learned from Foucault's 'microphysics of power' that is pertinent to understanding *practice*? Foucault had seen that by the eighteenth century, a reciprocal and circular relationship between knowledge and power manifested itself in the hospital, the school, and the workplace [ibid: 224]. Returning to the present, we can add modern formal systems delimiting education found in most developed and developing countries around the globe are driven by such relations of power based upon a complex admixture of Panopticism and technological enframing [Flint and Peim, 2012]. In this way, the hospital, the school along with modern formal education, and the workplace 'become apparatuses such that any mechanism of objectification could be used in them as an instrument of subjection, and the growth of power in them [predicted earlier by Heidegger] generates new knowledge' [Foucault, 1977: 224]. For research there is a significant danger of Panopticism becoming introduced as with the emergence of concerns delimiting education through such practice; especially, it would seem, although not intended in this way, in the language of Vitae's Researcher Development Framework [RDF][2] as one highly visible architectural space in which the individual-self-directed-subject of research is structured in their work. The controlling feature here is not a manager, an administrator, or even the RDF in research, but rather silent and ceaseless forces of enframing and of language.

It is important, too, to keep in mind that Panopticism, in the seventeenth and eighteenth centuries, was born out of a 'whole fiction that grew up from the plague' [Foucault, 1977: 195, 197]. This fiction separated those considered 'normal' from those viewed as 'abnormal' or in some way the exception to the norm. In this narrative the plague came to symbolize 'all forms of confusion, disorder', so requiring powerful means of maintaining law and order. At present, in research, it is interesting to note that 'chaos' and 'disorder' have now come to be constituted as a science. So, in the politics of identity, the state of exception structuring the language of such science opens space providing the grounding theorizations and the very means of understanding how order may arise even from such chaotic starting points. In this privileging of the strategies and techniques of power over the hermeneutics of interpretation and meaning, the latter are rendered by inclusion within a state of exception.

Foucault had also seen the figure 'of the leper – symbolising the real population of beggars, vagabonds, madmen, and the disorderly – [had been] cut from all human contact, underlying projects of exclusion' [ibid: 198–99], thus separating those considered abnormal. Similarly, while the range and specialization of methodologies within the sciences continue to grow, though probably unintended, in its current rendering, the state of exception structuring the *language* of the Vitae RDF serves to generate space for the possible inclusion of the multiplicity of ways of being open to researchers only by means of exclusion. As Agamben [1998] suggests, it is this 'bond of inclusive exclusion' found in the 'presuppositional structure of [the] language' of research that finds particular expression in the structuring of its tacit laws/customs [ibid: 20]. Emphasis here will be directed towards the bond of 'inclusion/*exception*' rather than 'inclusive exclusion' as a way of underlining that discourses of research largely unconsciously tend to except issues from the scope of its propositions rather than actively seeking to exclude them. Therefore, here we are concerned with a critical examination of such laws/customs in ways that seek to open space for debate concerned with their possible inclusion within any ethics of research. Justice at the heart of the event of research in seeking to exceed extant law serves to open thinking on what may otherwise have been rendered as a possible exception.

In the capillary actions of the microphysics of power at work in the body of those involved with research, therefore, the imperative to take action on this matter would appear never to have gained greater force. In the light of the ontotheological structuring in research, there is:

- the cultivation not only of highly manipulative 'emotivist cultures' [MacIntyre, 1984: 23] in which ends become means;
- neo-liberalist economies in the social world of everyday practice foregrounding competition in the market, so eliding completely any subtleties concerned with language; along with,
- one form of education in research we are identifying as 'delimiting education' that has now become grounded in assessment constituting the basis for a myriad forms of technology: its sublime force, in concert with the biopolitics, drives the programmatic ontotheology of the apparatus of research.

This sublime hegemonic force delimiting education in research cultures creates ideal grounds for the world of governmentality. A world in which the managerialist and the administrator are given ever-more feedstock in the form of what appears to be neat and tidy representations of practice, so informing readings of techniques and strategies employed in the enhancement of their own centralized powers. It is on this basis that greater consideration should be given to disempowerment, so removing grounds for centralization.

Governmentality in research, however, is grounded in the very politics of identity. It accords with philosophical traditions in vogue from Plato through to Husserl, currently and largely privileging the plenitude of identity as the basis upon which one understands the world of research. In practice, in this large and all-encompassing episteme there is to be found the dominant fiction of research that now constitutes grounds for distinguishing normal from abnormal forms of such work.

The analysis of power: regimes of truth and conceptions of doctorateness

The position adopted by Vitae in their RDF is, perhaps, not surprising, given the ways in which 'doctorateness' have been conceptualized. Four complementary and interlinked avenues of discussion have emerged over the past decade concerning this subject. Tacitly, at least, these discursive practices hold on to the fiction of the plenitude of identity. Along each of these avenues in the world of research the political fiction of the fulfilment of identities concerned with 'doctorateness' constitute grounds for the exercise of powers privileging regimes of truth upon which all forms of doctoral study are currently based. Paradoxically, the language constituting the familiar mantra of doctoral research being based upon original contributions to knowledge owes much to investment in particular to 'regimes of truth' [Foucault, 1994a: 132] that preclude its possible declaration of its own state of exception.

In their own way such 'regimes of truth', currently used as grounds for identifying research deemed to have reached 'doctoral level,' each give expression to a 'regime of truth' [Foucault, 1977: 132] concerned with official designations of such research. In constituting grounds for such regimes, three of the four groups involved create a particular focus for their own conceptualization of 'doctorateness'. The appropriate assessment criterion for doctoral research has provided one avenue for discussion [Denicolo and Park, 2010]. But, this is always in danger of being caught up in its own ontotheology [Flint and Peim, 2012; Peim and Flint, 2009]. A second way of working with the language of doctoral research provides a focus upon the 'generic features of conceptualization and doctorateness'

[Scott, Brown, Lunt and Thorne, 2002]. But, again these features are always in danger of opening space for the individual self-directed subject of Panopticism in which the self is always at risk of becoming reduced to a technology – a means-ends structured being in accord with such extant forms of 'conceptualization and doctorateness', with the latter revealing the world of research only upon grounds of the principle of reason or the principle of assessment [Flint and Peim, 2012; Flint and Barnard, 2010b]. A third, more recent form of language constituting another avenue for discussion on the matter of doctorateness has arisen from discourses representing 'doctoral learning journeys'. It involves participants at critical points in 'crossing conceptual thresholds' through making 'learning leaps', and so 'moving their work to conceptual levels of understanding' [Wisker et al., 2010]. Ironically, it seems that in moving to such conceptual levels there has remained an absence of any critical reflexivity concerned with the politics of identity and in particular the state of exception grounding the language of this particular schema.

Interestingly, too, in appealing to such possibilities of critical reflexivity, in not one of these avenues for debate on the matter of 'doctorateness' has there been any consideration given to the ironic and strategic practice of privileging of power over knowledge as the basis for further generation of knowledge. Nor has there been any explicit consideration given to the politics of identity. A fourth approach to understanding doctorateness has emerged from Jerry Wellington [2013], who approaches the issue through questioning that in effect opens thinking related to the constitution of *différance* – but this is not thematized as such in his paper.

In his 'searching for doctorateness', Wellington [2013] examines in-depth issues on thinking, the relationship of a doctoral candidate with other colleagues, impact, originality, theory, criteria used within university handbooks, and so on, as a basis for his analysis and discussion. In conclusion, he comes to realize that there is no 'common-to-all property called doctorateness' [ibid: 1501]. On reflection, however, and in reading Wellington's paper from the perspective of the differences involved, the outcomes of this particular study also open space for other ways of understanding 'doctorateness' and the basis for assessing quality in research, based more broadly upon the constitution of *différance* [Flint, *in preparation*, i]. But, in returning to express forms of *Rede* [talk], so looking out from the practice of evaluating doctorateness, though Wellington explores the powers of difference, he does not acknowledge the gathering powers of being and the powers of plenitude invested in identities, themselves contributing more generally to the enhancement of powers within research that may be otherwise balanced by the play of *différance*.

It is to this larger question of the enhancement of powers at work in practices constituted within the apparatus of research-based-education and their possibility of balancing such powers that we now turn with help in the opening steps from Agamben.

Rainer Maria Rilke's poesy, in particular, his *Ninth Elegy*, too, opens liminal space for the play of possibilities whose boundaries are given expression in the ever-unfolding multi-levelled paradoxical drives at work in being human that are surely at the heart of every practice. He writes:

> '*Why, when this span of life might be fleeted away*
> *as laurel*[3], . . .
> - *Oh, why*
> *have to be human, and shunning Destiny*
> *long for Destiny?* . . .

It is this ever-present desire for happiness in what Aristotle called the 'good life' whose existence Rilke calls into question, that is at the root of contemporary apparatuses; ironically, not least the apparatus of delimiting-education-in-research. For Agamben [2009], 'the capture and subjectification of this desire in a separate sphere constitutes the power of apparatuses' [ibid: 17]. In locating the exercise of this particular power through apparatuses, people 'attempt to nullify animalistic behaviours [of bare life] that become 'separated from' them [ibid: 17].

What remains to be thought, therefore, is how the writings concerned with qualitative forms of research reveal bare life, and what they reveal about the plight of bare life within the ontotheology of the apparatus of research. Pivotal is the question of the meaning apparatus.

The locus of power: the ontotheology of research

In Agamben's [2009] reading of Foucault's 'apparatus':

> It is a heterogeneous set that includes virtually anything, linguistic and non-linguistic under the same heading: discourses, institutions, buildings, laws, police measures, philosophical propositions and so on. The apparatus is the network that is established between these elements. [ibid: 2–3]

It should also be noted there is a tangible consonance between Agamben's apparatus and the everyday world of *Dasein*. We saw earlier, for example, how 'world' may be understood in terms of a vast network of familiar avenues that we know our way along. It is also important to keep in mind that while there is this accordance between *Dasein*'s world and the structuring of an apparatus, Agamben's words quite correctly serve to generate a separation between living beings and apparatuses.

Two additional points further underline that separation between the possibilities unfolding in living beings and an apparatus:

> The apparatus always has a concrete strategic function and is always located in a power relation.
>
> As such it appears at the intersection of power relations and relations of knowledge. [ibid: 3]

The genealogy of 'apparatus' developed by Agamben also helpfully connects back and shows how the language of 'apparatus' is aligned to Heidegger's writings concerned with *das Ge-stell* and with Hegel's concerns regarding 'positivity'. According to the latter, this was considered as 'an obstacle to the freedom of man' [Hyppolyte cited by Agamben, 2009: 5]. What makes these connections for Agamben [2009] is the Ancient Greek term, *oikonomia,* economy. But, in this reading, greater emphasis is placed upon the capacity for contingent actions, that is, to contingencies within a set of technological means–ends structured practices that constitute powers for the primary strategic function, of drawing upon 'bodies of knowledge, measures, and institutions' for managing, governing, controlling, and orienting people's behaviours within such practices [ibid: 12].

Agamben [2009] also helpfully generates an expansion of Foucault's large class of apparatuses. Apparatus comes to name 'literally anything that has in some way the capacity to capture, orient, determine, intercept, model, control, or secure the gestures, behaviours, opinions, or discourses of living beings' [ibid: 14]. So, in concert with Foucault, for Agamben, the class of apparatuses not only includes 'prisons, mad houses, the Panopticon, schools, confession, factories, disciplines, juridical measures and so forth' where the connection with power is, perhaps, self-evident, 'but also the pen, writing, literature, cigarettes, navigation, computers', [ibid: 14] and cellular technologies, including the iPhone and the iPad, along with, as Agamben playfully suggests, 'language itself' [ibid: 14]. The latter, we should remind ourselves, has been seen as a sovereign power in which history continually folds over and presses into the present. It suggests in 'the most ancient of apparatuses' in which many thousands of years ago 'a primate let himself be captured probably without realizing the consequences that he was about to face' [ibid: 14], there is the suggestion that the consequences of this most ancient apparatus for research, even now, remain unrealized.

At issue is the complex struggle between living beings and the accumulation and 'proliferation of apparatuses' [ibid: 15]. In Agamben's significant move away from Foucault, where he separates completely apparatuses from living beings, subjects are constituted in the struggles between these two classes. He understands these struggles in response to the desire for happiness as a subject's attempt 'to nullify animalistic behaviours that are somehow separated from him' [ibid: 17]. Such struggles opened further thinking to which we will return, involving the incorporation of justice to come and the deconstruction of paradigms of research that follows. Before examining such a move towards elaboration on the state of exception, of particular interest here is the process of subjectification. By opening space for the subjectification of this desire for happiness in a separate sphere from apparatuses and living beings, Agamben uncovers the precise locus of the power constituted by such apparatuses.

The locus of power: desubjectification and subjectification

Agamben [2009] argues that such a process of subjectification arises in the first instant from 'desubjectification' [ibid: 20]. He notes how 'a desubjectifying moment is certainly implicit in every process of subjectification' [ibid: 20]. In the training of researchers, for example, the identification of an individual with a hierarchically structured grade of some kind creates the risk of the desubjectification of the individual, who, in the moment of receiving their grade, is reduced to that object – for example, grades awarded in differentiated forms of MA, doctoral, and postdoctoral awards. Through education, the individual can work and struggle to relocate themselves as a subject from such desubjectification; an active agent capable of developing their ideas in research. Agents for much of their subjectification in this way have been determined within the economy of research. In reflecting upon how apparatuses within the disciplinary societies constituted within research aim to create docile yet free bodies, one learns from Agamben that 'bodies assume their identity and their freedom' as subjects of research 'in the very process of desubjectification' [ibid: 20]. Consequently, in this very process 'it is impossible for the subject to use any form of [technological] apparatus in the right way'. Agamben arrives at a similar conclusion to that suggested by Derrida, for whom every trace of identity is not only invested with the play of *différance*, but also suffers from the catastrophe of memory.

For Agamben, the process of subjectification at work in 'integrated practices', however, is further complicated by the state of exception constituted for us all in our contemporary biopolitical order. Rather than as Foucault [1978, 1985, 1986] had done, in his genealogical studies of the *History of Sexuality*, where he had traced the emergence of biopolitics back to the seventeenth century, Agamben connects the emergence of biopolitics in the modern world of practice back to both Aristotle's discourse and to what Agamben calls the 'state of exception'. In so doing, Agamben in effect provides a corrective reading of Foucault, not only in no longer separating sovereign power from disciplinary power, but also in providing a much clearer understanding of the essence of law that now finds expression in customs of research.

In reflecting upon Aristotle's express distinction between '*zoē*' – the simple fact of living common to all living beings, including animals, people, gods . . . and '*bios*' – indicating the way of living proper to an individual or group – Agamben [1998] notices that *zēn* is implicated in *bios*; that is, bare life exists in a state of exception within politically qualified life. But how is bare life to be understood? In response, we might begin by imagining that in Agamben's reading of the inclusion/exclusion structuring language that 'bare life', *zēn*, connotes biological existence. Clearly, without the everyday autonomic functioning of homo sapiens' biological systems, bios would not be possible. But, such conscious moves to exclude 'bare life' itself presupposes a political intentionality, and while it is not difficult to imagine examples of such intent, as we have seen, the notion of 'exclusion' is also connected with Agamben's [2005] 'state of exception'; the latter carrying with it the political intentionality to exclude through more subtle and unconscious, and for the most part, invisible forms of displacement. In this study, too, in accord with the latter we have uncovered many unspoken forces driving bare life that ordinarily remain silenced, seemingly without express discourse in research, rather than reflecting express forms of political exclusion. Bare life in this sense is understood as giving expression to those many silent vitalizing forces at work in our everyday practices of research, without which politically qualified life would not be possible.

This conception takes seriously the inclusion of bare life within the good life, whereas most commentary on this issue tends to work from presupposition of the separation of bare life from the good life [Ziarek, 2012] or the way bare life is exposed to 'political calculation' [Ross, 2008]. For Agamben [1998], it remains 'a zone of indistinction and continuous transition between man and beast' [ibid: 109], and his case examples tend to reinforce Alison Ross's thesis. But this reading takes seriously the inclusion of bare life without which there could be no good life. 'Bare life', therefore, gives expression to both the *inclusion* of behaviours of the animal hidden within humankind *and* also to those hidden vitalizing forces arising from the nothing that remain without express discourse in research. One agrees, then, with Agamben that apparatuses function to exclude animal behaviours that are socially unacceptable in societies' understandings of the good life. But here one needs to separate those socially unacceptable animal behaviours from the silent vitalizing forces at work in bare life. The latter would seem to have been missed in Agamben's [1998, 2005, 2009] writings.

He concentrates attention upon the visible artefacts of power, consonant with the '*society of the spectacle*'. Controversially, Agamben [2008] suggests one such political artefact in the form of 'the Nazi concentration camps' do not constitute an aberration from modernity, but rather the 'thanatopolitical face' [ibid: 142, 150] of power made visible in the '*society of the spectacle*'. As Ewa Ziarek [2012] suggests, for the first time the visible 'spectacle' of 'concentration camps . . . actualizes the danger implicit in Western politics, namely, the total genocide made possible by the reversal of the exception signified by *homo sacer* into a new thanato-political norm' [ibid: ch.9].[4] Here, in the camp, Ziarek proposes, in which power confronts nothing but the visible aspects of bare life, manifestly 'totalitarian regimes can reduce a whole population to disposable bare life that could be destroyed with impunity' [ibid].

We will be returning to the politics of thanatos at work in research in the final step of this study, but in moving to that point we have much work to do in seeking to understand what lies behind such 'norms' by concentrating upon the invisible vitalizing forces of bare life at work in the practice of research. Such vitalizing forces we have connected with death, the future, anxiety, guilt, and not least the play of *différance* that are ordinarily included in research as exceptions. Bare life's very home, then, we see as the language constituted in the play of *différance*.

The biopolitics of research and bare life

This state of exception constituted in the play of *différance* has implications for the analysis of human behaviours, actions, and gestures. Here, using the language of the 'bare life'/politically qualified life divide as a case-example of the process of desubjectification/ subjectification deferred from Agamben [2005, 2009] it is helpful to reflect critically upon the words of one leading feminist qualitative researcher, Patti Lather's [2007a] various explorations of 'Getting Lost' in a 'Doubled Science'. In one particular 'interlude' in her work that she calls 'naked methodology' [Lather, 2007b: 49–57], Lather's discussion with other women, while she chose to sit naked in a Jacuzzi and they asked her a number of questions about one of her research projects concerned with women living with HIV/AIDS, reveal in more concrete terms involving the process of subjectification through research.

In terms of 'bare life', one of the women, 'Mimi', observed that 'in the extreme these people are dying' [ibid: 50]. Another, 'Liz', reflected that 'all of us are one blood cell away from HIV, one injury' [ibid: 51]. Following much discussion 'Liz' came back with the observation that 'HIV people are living out some of the most profound, wild, ambiguous, contradictory moments' [ibid: 54]. 'Janet' later reflects that 'research is never just clean. It becomes part of our lives' [ibid: 55]. This simple statement gives expression to the inclusive register of bare life within the process of subjectification in research. Earlier in their discussion 'Patti' had raised the question with the other women: 'what does it mean to see these women as data, as victims, as AIDS patients ' [ibid: 50]. Voicing such a question, she points to what can now be seen as the opening 'desubjectification' that commences the very practice of research; that is, when these people become 'labels' or objects within Lather's research [ibid: 50]. Responding to her own question, 'Patti' goes on to reflect the question of their 'emancipation' [ibid: 50] in which she conflates her concern that space is given for their subjectification as active subjects through 'emancipation' with the fact of bare-life-in-its-being '*who* these women *are*'. An unspoken aspect within their discussion concerned with researching the women with HIV/AIDS is their holistic understanding of 'bare life'. It becomes pivotal to the researchers' various understandings of the ways in which the power exercised by the researchers penetrates the bodies of those researched. At issue in these political concerns are the ways in which the *language* of research maintains its relation with 'bare life' in its bond of inclusive exception in the play of *différance*. At issue is our very humanity or rather its continued regeneration.

Sovereign power, language, and the state of exception

In considering some of the implications for understanding practice from *Homo Sacer*, 'sacred man', Agamben's [1998] study returns us once more to that 'point of intersection between juridico-institutional and biopolitical models of power' that Foucault had worked assiduously to keep separate. We have to keep in mind, as Agamben indicates, 'that the two analyses cannot be separated' [ibid: 11]. Within the 'political realm' of identity grounding research, as suggested by Agamben, 'its inclusion of bare life constitutes an original, if concealed nucleus of the sovereign power[s]' [ibid: 11] inscribed in the multiplicity of its discourses. Moreover, the very placing of bare life at the centre of calculations within the modern state apparatus of delimiting-education-in-research becomes obvious, and so 'bring[s] to light the secret tie uniting power and bare life' [ibid: 11].

The languages of research, therefore, have a pivotal role to play in opening space for the reconsideration of Aristotle's definition of the polis in terms of an opposition of life [*zēn*] and good life [*eu zēn*], especially when concerned here with the state apparatus delimiting-education-in-research. This thought returns us once more to Agamben's [1998] concern with the sovereignty of language, which in its doubling declares a permanent state of exception, wherein 'there is nothing outside language and that language is always beyond itself' [ibid: 20]. Consonant with the 'presuppositional structure' of all languages [ibid: 20] is the structure of law and its 'express bond of inclusive exclusion' found in this very state of exception. In this sense, the reiteration of customs in the language of research is in effect 'to speak the law, *ius dicere*' [ibid: 20]. Such laws are inscribed in the ontotheological structuring of the apparatus [Table 2.1].

The question remains, therefore, concerning the complex relationship between the apparatus of research and bare life. At issue remains the apparatus of research working within the horizon of being as presence, whereas the horizon to come for bare life is essentially futural. Given that the 'event' of bare life in being open to its many futural possibilities is both permanently located within a state of exception and continually open to being reduced to standing reserve within enframing, the question remains, too, how moves towards justice in research may be understood.

Of course, in taking this particular line of argument there remain many unanswered questions concerning the intricacies and complexities of democratic forms of political practice in research suggested by the writings of Ernesto Laclau and Chantel Mouffe [2014{1985}; Mouffe, 2005{1993}] and more recently by Jacques Rancière [2010] that are beyond the scope of this present study.

* * *

Epilogue

In deconstructing the powers mediating bare life in practice we began this study with the question: *Is there more to learning from practice than you think?*

From these opening chapters in rethinking research as an event in the regeneration of bare life the following thesis has emerged:

1. *The sublime forces of enframing reinforce the ego-logy and positivity of objects of consciousness in* the language *delimiting-education-in-research, whereas, unconditionally, the forces regenerating bare life remain forever incalculable and impossible to objectify. Such forces, therefore, appear to remain outside traditional conceptions of learning from research.*

* * *

The question remains concerning justice to come. Can it live up to its promise of exceeding the powers inscribed in the *language* of research?

PART TWO

Laws and justice to come in practice

CHAPTER FOUR

Reframing the ethics of research: Laws and justice to come

Without laws and customs, there is a significant risk that practice may become reduced to anarchy and chaos. This express anxiety generates drives towards maintaining social order within integrative practices. But the language of 'law' rarely features, in particular, in research where deontological practices structured around norms, principles, and rules tend to remain dominant. Thus, while the structuring of law is consonant with the bond of inclusive exclusion found in the presuppositional-structure of language and with the biopolitics of research [Agamben, 1998], deontological structuring has emerged as a basis for social order.

The pre-judicial structuring of law/customs, therefore, remains consonant with the structuring of language. Reference to law in research, therefore, refers to its essential pre-judicial structuring [Table 2.1] and not to the various meanings, rules, or theorizations of this term in practice [Rose, 1984].

Viewed historically, of particular interest in research are the multiplicity of ways in which it has sought to reformulate, reconfigure, and to move beyond the possible straightjacket of the laws of nature that had first emerged from the Enlightenment in the work of Bacon, Newton, and others. Such 'laws' first found expression in the nineteenth century in Auguste Comte's formulation of a 'positive science' encompassing the philosophies of the physical, natural, and moral world. At issue is not their detailed structure and content [the subject of much debate], but rather the multiplicity of moves to replace the language of law in research with terms borrowed from deontological thinking in ethics. Symbolically, such transformations tend to denote moves away from doctrinal forms of positivism. But, in a post-9/11 world, the state of exception has become an issue. From Agamben's [2005] studies it is clear such moves towards deontological thinking in ethics have tended to blind researchers and the process of research to the law-like structures mediating the state of exception in the apparatus of research. In the context of the juggernaut of enframing in research and in the social world more generally, the historical moves towards deontological structures for the ethics of research constitute an error of the highest order that deserves to be remedied.

Moves towards justice involve deconstruction of the laws/customs of research. This creates space for thinking concerned with the hidden biopolitics. Until 'now' this has served to elide almost completely questions concerning bare life.

In examining the proposed extension of an ethics of research to incorporate consideration of both the pre-judicial structuring of research [Table 2.1] and justice to come, we have, therefore, first some work to do in examining how the latter differs from extant philosophies of justice, in preparation for a more detailed examination of the laws/customs of research.

* * *

'Justice is the first virtue of social institutions, as truth is of systems of thought'. Here in one of John Rawls's [1972: 3] opening statements in his book, *A Theory of Justice*, 'truth' and 'systems of thought' are both located in the practice of language. Given that we have already uncovered the impossibility of the telos of any intentional structure concerned with virtue, one asks why this so-called institution of systems of thought – identified here as research – is separated from 'justice' and its relation to social institutions.

Why does the language of 'ethical research' for specialist areas of inquiry seem only to reinforce this separation? Both the BERA [2011] Revised Guidelines for Ethical Research in Education and the guidelines for the Social Research Association [SRA, 2003], for example, make no reference to 'justice' or laws governing research. Nevertheless, the deontological force of 'the guidelines' imputes a responsibility for researchers to use the guidelines 'as a tool' [ibid: 7]. Although the SRA [2003] make a number of references to law, they speak principally of the laws of the land, rather than the laws [customs] inscribed in research. There is only one reference made to 'injustice'. 'Obligations to funders and employers', researchers are reminded, do not 'compromise a commitment to morality and to the law and the maintenance of standards commensurate with professional integrity' [ibid: para 2].

The systems of ethics governing research, however, as Rawls's [1972] division suggests, have been developed primarily to govern the generation of truth claims within systems of thought. Rawls's division may have worked because, in ideological terms, when somehow researchers were imagined to be primarily concerned with knowledge and its relation to truth. But, it is not working 'now'. The ontotheological structuring of research driving the ever-growing powers in enframing is not a locus for justice. What has changed has been the sublime quantum leaps in such powers at work in society and in research that arise most obviously from contemporary on-going developments in ICT [Flint, 2013a], along with correlative increases in the intensity and extensity of technologies at work in the social world [Flint and Peim, 2012].

In a post-9/11 world, too, these sublime powers can be switched off with immediate effect by sovereign powers – in an instant, population can become placed in a 'state of exception' [Agamben, 2005]. With the ever-increasing powers at work aligned to growing knowledge economies in our networked [Castells, 2009] globalized societies, in this age of technology, the rationale and the imperative to re-think the ethics of research has become ever-more urgent. In this deconstructive reading of the ethics of research the hyphen is used to indicate that 're-think' is not only a compound noun, but it also points to the deferred and differential relations of the iterativity of the sign, in this case, 'think'. Ethics, too, deserves re-thinking, incorporating the dynamic interrelationship of justice and laws of research, in order to open space for questioning the powers inscribed in such language. Given the contingency of re-iteration and iteration of signs involving ethics, given also, as we shall see that in this deconstructive reading, moves towards justice extend beyond current understandings inscribed in the ethics of research, 're-thinking' also makes further demands upon education in research, to which we will return in the final chapters.

How do these powers arise in language? What is their relationship with the structure of law? Agamben [1998] observes that Hegel 'was the first to truly understand the pre-suppositional structure thanks to which language is at once both outside and inside itself and the immediate [the non-linguistic] reveals itself to be nothing but a presupposition of language' [ibid: 19–20]. 'Only language as the pure potentiality to signify', indicates Agamben, 'withdrawing itself from every concrete instance of speech, divides the linguistic from the nonlinguistic and allows for the opening of areas of meaningful speech in which certain terms correspond to certain denotations' [ibid: 20]. So, when a lover says to their loved one within the particular circumstances of their relationship: 'I love you', such an expression of feeling both stands outside the norm as an exception [this would make no sense in such a relationship if it were not understood as in some way an express form of exception to the norm] and, yet, as a syntagm belongs to this express norm. As Agamben indicates, in such an example lies a 'paradox' in that 'a single utterance in no way distinguished from others of its kind is isolated from them precisely insofar as it belongs to them' [ibid: 20]. More generally, we can understand this paradox because 'language is the sovereign who, in a permanent state of exception, declares that there is nothing outside language and that language is always beyond itself' [ibid: 20].

Drawing upon Agamben, therefore, concerns will be directed towards the sovereign powers of the *language* of research. We will also keep in play

Derrida's understanding of *différance*. As a presuppositional structure of language, it constitutes the basis for decisions concerned with deconstruction in particular instances. Derrida's approach accepts that life in the state of exception is our only possible future, because this form of life has been our only past. Such a state of exception is there in the ontotheology of pre-judicial structures in *research, driving vis-a-tergo* enframing that remains elided, so dissimulating bare life [Table 2.1]. What is required, it is argued, are communities of researchers who in rethinking the ethics of research are concerned with moves towards justice that seek for the re-empowerment of bare lives. The danger, of course, is that Derrida, or the communities of researchers come to play sovereign as doorkeepers to the laws of research. Keeping this process of deconstruction democratic and emancipatory is therefore essential.

We are also reminded of the sovereign powers at work in this process. What follows, therefore, is a deconstruction that uncovers the interplay of justice and law in research, so opening questioning about systems of justice that have been employed in research. In a critical reading of Derrida's [1989, 1990] *oeuvre*, therefore, the final step in this particular research is to examine not only his claim that 'deconstruction is mad about justice' [ibid: 965], but also how one may conceive an apparatus of deconstruction that can be employed in research in moves towards 'emancipatory justice'.

Justice in research: the professional doctorate

Here the stage set for deconstruction is taken from the point when the professional doctorate programme was first set up at Nottingham Trent University. This opening scene involves two main characters, 'James' and 'April', who were members of the first cohort of professional doctorate students.

> In the summer of 2008 James and April commenced the professional doctorate at Midlands Highway University. The 'weekend' – a Friday and Saturday, in practice, went smoothly. The evaluations had been positive. But, within one year of commencing the programme they had come back, having gained ethical approval through official channels. They were concerned that they had each become interested to pursue particular forms of research, and on the other hand, at their respective workplaces they had each come under considerable pressure to undertake activities that were deemed to be in accord with their own 'professional responsibilities'.

At first, this research act was examined in terms of the space for personal development and the powers at play in research [Flint and Barnard,

2010a,b]. But, in speaking with colleagues from other institutions where similar compelling stories began to emerge, it became clear there was a larger issue at stake concerned with justice in research. Within ethical research, although there are strict guidelines concerned with the rules of conduct inscribed in the traditions of research there is no express appeal to the language of law.

In professional doctorates, as one emergent locus of research, those involved – candidates, students, researchers . . . – are engaged in the practice of generating new knowledge claims within traces of their own social practices. Given that *practice* is a social medium symbolically, all dimensions of the practice of research are therefore inscribed in a relation to the Other. Here, a significant locus of power in research becomes apparent. It is intimately tied to the constitution of claims to ethical research. It can be found in the paradox of the apparatus used to govern the conduct of research. Such apparatus in claiming to provide grounds for ethical research concerned with the individual's relationship to the Other constitute systems structured as law for the production of identities – truth claims to knowledge – that largely exclude the Other. The fact that the 'state of exception' [Agamben, 2005] is built right into the fabric of disciplinary apparatuses should now be of no surprise, given that it is an essential dimension of the structure of languages.

In practice, earlier injunctions concerned with 'now' are always fissured by both a multiplicity of possible historical connections and many possibilities unfolding in the future. But, in harmony with its ontotheology, the criterionology of what is deemed to be 'ethically' grounded research is concerned almost exclusively with the conditional, calculable, and possible dimensions of practice. It has to be so in order to exclude the Other, preserving the object of research – namely, truth claims to knowledge, as though the object remains unsullied by the play of *différance*. The guidelines for ethical research in education [BERA, 2011] and the human sciences [SRA, 2003] would appear to take in the possibility of such play in recognizing that there is much on-going debate on many differences in the approach used by researchers in their practices.

In the guidelines and the archival record there is a tendency to bring everything of concern to [the] researcher[s] into the present – as 'evidence' and 'findings' that arise from the application of methodology in response to 'research question[s]' and associated 'aims' of research. Paradoxically, one dimension of the freedom to engage in research is that the gathering of research into the present is also consonant with its ontotheology. It creates the illusion of mastery and control. It creates a danger, too, that any sense of justice in research becomes expropriated and lost within calculus of the conditional, possible, and calculable dimensions of practice as illustrated, for example, in a scene recreated from working with patients in the National Health System [NHS].

Justice in research: Patient journeys in a hospital

The scene that follows, created from the clinical management of patient journeys through a hospital, opens reflection on justice from Fran Woodard and Gordon Weller's [2011] research. Related to clinical management, their study makes concrete concerns about justice in research. Silently, it is apparent from the researchers and from the medics, in their engagement with their practices in one hospital in the National Health System [NHS] in the UK, there were concerns for justice that had been futural in their direction: being rooted in a multiplicity of concerns arising from past experiences. For example, in their final remark on their research, Woodard and Weller [2011] indicated that, 'patients' voice is at its most powerful when it is facilitating the focussing of improvements on enhancing quality of life' [ibid: 113]. Unspoken, their express concern for 'voice' that always faces a monster – the unknowable future identified as 'improvement' – is deeply rooted in the past experiences of the patients. These researchers' interest points to a matter that is incalculable, unconditional, and always impossible to articulate fully.

It is always beyond the realms of possibility to express all matters of the 'Other' at play in the identities of both 'voice' and any 'improvements in quality of life' of patients. Silently, in these moves there is a desire for justice in research. As Derrida [1990: 947, 953] suggests, here is the affirmation of a relation to the Other as 'unconditional', 'incalculable', 'impossible'.

The following brief exegesis uncovers where this idea had emerged in his earlier essay, 'Violence and Metaphysics'. Derrida reflects upon the profound lesson in ethics to be drawn from Husserl's [1960] fifth *Cartesian Meditation* [Derrida, 2001d: 154–5]. His reading of Husserl brings to life that 'there is no intuition of the other *as such*; that is, I have no originary access to the alter-ego *as such*' [Derrida, 1999: 71; emphasis as in the original]. There is 'no pure phenomenon or phenomenality, of the other or alter-ego as such' [ibid: 71]. Right at the heart of the gathering powers of being as presence, therefore, there is located our incapacity to gain access to the Other. The 'unconditional' affirmation of this incapacity in our relationship with the Other, in which the other is 'impossible' to recognize completely and therefore within any economy remains 'incalculable' came to be understood in his later writings as a manifestation of 'justice to come' [Derrida, 1990: 947, 953].

Unspoken, but no less powerfully, this same desire for justice was there at the very heart of Woodard and Weller's [2011] chosen focus for their case study of action research into two 'change projects'. It served to align their approach with both a 'continuous quality improvement methodology' and an exploration of 'the characteristics of good clinical leadership across organizations' within a hospital [ibid: 91]. Here the unspoken impulse towards justice can be understood in the moves towards the impossibility of improvement being ever fully realized in practice and towards the impossibility of the totalizing fulfilment of identities concerned with 'clinical leadership across organisations'.

Ordinarily such desire for justice cannot be expressed formally in this way by researchers because of deontological structures requiring them to conform to established principles of inquiry. But, the conditionality of the presuppositional-structuring of laws governing research as they currently stand presupposes that practice itself is always already concerned with matters that are in some ways unconditional. In this reading of Derrida [1989, 1990], one locus of the unconditional is the desire for justice. Justice in this sense is driven by a desire to move beyond the bounds of the conditional, the calculable, and the possible – it expresses a concern to move beyond the bounds of the present situation. It reflects the 'force of *différance*' [ibid: 929] that is always unconditional, impossible, and incalculable – it keeps open the vitiation of our relationship with the future, and equally is vigilant and alert to the catastrophe of memory in our relationship with the cinders deposited from past events. This play of *différance*' is unconditional in the sense that it is 'what makes the movement of signification possible' in any reading or writing of text [Derrida, 1973a: 142]. Meaning is uncovered because in the play of *différance*, 'each element appearing on the scene of the presence, is related to something other than itself, thereby keeping within itself the mark of a past element, and already letting itself be vitiated by the mark of its relation to a future element' [ibid: 142]. *Différance*' opens space awakening us to identities being located outside the metaphysics of presence. Identities are all regarded as traces or cinders, ordinarily constituting archives of research. Its challenge to the politics of plenitude is palpable. Gathering of signs no longer makes sense in the play of *différance*. This is because such traces that are 'no less what is called the future than to what is called the past, and [in] constituting what is called the present by means of what it is not' [ibid: 142], take away the very grounds for any possible objectification in research.

Given the foregrounding of quantification in much research that has the effect of excluding beings that do not accord with its logic [Flint, 2013b], it is interesting to find that *différance*' is incalculable. 'An interval must separate the present from what it is not', according to Derrida [1973a], 'in order for the present to be itself, but this interval that constitutes it as present must, by the same token, divide the present in and of itself thereby also dividing along with the present, everything that is thought on the basis of the present, that is, in our metaphysical language, every being, and in particular the substance or subject' [ibid: 143]. There is, then, a fissuring and a double play at the heart of any presence. Uncovering the nihilism of enframing in research, 'deconstruction', therefore, 'is [indeed] . . . mad about justice' [Derrida, 1990: 965].

Ordinarily, however, in privileging what is conditional, possible, and calculable, so-called ethically grounded research serves to conflate concerns about the conditionality of its laws with the unconditional desire for justice. This is not surprising. For example, as the Social Research Association, SRA [2003], put it, 'research is . . . problem based' [ibid: 5]. There is an obligation to the SRA: researchers have a responsibility to pursue objectivity and to be open about known barriers to its achievement [ibid: 18]. The SRA are also clear that there is responsibility for researchers 'to ensure that the quality of their "product" is maintained' [ibid: 21]. Ironically, however, such objectivity is reached at the expense of bare life that is simply not registered within the SRA ethics.

Unspoken moves towards justice, therefore, are concerned with exceeding what is currently possible – through researchers' 'better insights' and through moves towards 'improving social conditions'. But, the presuppositional-structure of law inscribed in these guidelines is also unequivocal in seeking 'the truth'. This seeking of the calculable, the possible, and the conditional in coded acts of research, presupposes the incalculable, the impossible, and the unconditional, that is the locus of moves towards justice. But, like 'bare life', justice to come remains silent in these ethics. These largely do not express discourse for such issues.

The ethics of research, therefore, deserves to be re-conceived to incorporate the interplay of moves towards justice and the presuppositional-structuring of laws inscribed in its traditions [Table 2.1]. Without such interplay and without the work of deconstruction there is always a risk of research becoming reduced to the machinery of identity, where the latter's plenitude and fulfilment is never brought into question.

Justice to come: Philosophical understandings

It is not surprising that ethical guidelines for research make no such distinction between law and justice, nor has there been any exploration of their possible inter-relationship. It would seem that, with the exception of Derrida's work, in the majority of the classical philosophical explorations of justice no distinction is made between justice and justice to come. Such classical examinations of justice include:

- Kant's [1997] understanding of justice as a 'categorical imperative';
- John Rawls's [2012] 'principle of fairness' [ibid: 387] as grounds for 'a theory of justice' [ibid: 387–402];
- Rawls's utilitarian view of justice [2012: 262–65];
- Hobbes's [2012] justice located in the laws of nature [ibid: 25];
- David Hume's [2012: 79–95] 'rules of justice' and so on.

In being gathered in the present, each of these metaphysical representations of justice is the locus of two logical contradictions.

1. In such gatherings, each of these contrasting philosophical positions creates conditions, at the same time, for the acceptance and denial of truth concerned with justice, however understood, consonant with their structuring as language-games.
2. In gathering practice in the present, each of the philosophies purports to constitute understandings of justice in the present for humans who are temporally structured in their being [Heidegger, 1962]. As Derrida [1990: 959] suggests, the horizons of classical ethical conceptions of justice both create openings and limits, whereas justice does not want either.

It is interesting, too, to note that Derrida's understanding of justice, as the work of deconstruction and its relation to the law, does not even receive a mention in a recent authoritative new book concerned with the philosophy of ethics [Sher, 2012]. This is unsurprising. Such current forms of ethics concern themselves almost exclusively with the conditional, the calculable, and the possible dimensions of *practice*. Ironically, research deemed ethical, under the current guidelines, already blocks any path towards a deconstructive reading of justice and law. It provides another example of Foucault's [1994a: 132–33] 'regime of truth'.

But, as Derrida [1997b: 17; Dooley and Kavanagh, 2007: 113] has suggested, it is these determinate, calculable aspects of such laws inscribed in what is currently believed to be ethical research that opens them to deconstruction. 'Justice is not the law' [Derrida, 1997b: 17]. For example, in Woodard and Weller's [2011] study, they had adopted 'a pragmatic approach incorporating action research, using a single case study design', 'in order to take account of the inherent complexity of the study' [ibid: 88]. Deconstruction is 'the condition of historicity, revolution, morals, ethics, and progress' [Derrida, 1997b: 17]. It emerges from, and is made concrete here in, Woodward and Weller's [2011] study. 'Justice as deconstruction is what gives the impulse', currently inscribed as ethically grounded research, 'the drive, or the movement to improve the law, that is to deconstruct the law' [ibid: 17]. At issue is any possible hospitality given to debating this issue [Derrida 2000] – in Woodward and Weller's [2011] study opened within communities of research concerned with the methodologies employed.

Woodard and Weller [2011], for example, speak of their study being concerned with 'the impact of thirty doctors working within a large cross-organisational health-care change project' [ibid: 87]. Their research was designed to improve the experience of patients, who, on entry into NHS hospitals, and upon receiving care and treatment, are likely to journey through several different specialist forms of organization within an NHS hospital. In their words, 'the change project was focussed on improving the whole patient journey' [ibid: 87; emphasis added]. Silently, the researchers' hospitality in this case is already conditioned by their review of practice and by their particular way of focusing upon what they have identified as the patient's journey in an NHS-run hospital.

Their continued reiteration of signs concerned with 'change' opens connections with the intentional structuring of practice deferred from Husserl and Plato. They, too, are caught up in the drift of signs from 'Plato's Pharmacy' [Derrida, 1981b: 61–171]. Although not mentioned as such, their hospitality welcomes the Other only under certain conditions identified within their own research design, and grounds for interpretation of data. Tacitly, the mastery and manifest skills they express as researchers is marked by their capacity to engage with traces of such a circular economy of exchange.

Such ideology in some ways is currently strengthened by the demands made upon research deemed ethical. In the BERA [2011] ethical guidelines for educational research, such strengthening arises silently from the ontotheology that gathers everything into the present – 'the underpinning aim of the guidelines is to enable educational researchers to weigh up all aspects of the process of conducting educational research within any given context'. It returns once more to the politics of plenitude to reach 'an ethically acceptable position in which their actions are considered justifiable and sound' [ibid: para 3].

Again, while the unequivocal standpoint of the social research guidelines [SRA, 2003] requires researchers to 'take responsibility' in moving to generate truth claims,[1] they also provide no easy way out of the circularity. The SRA [2003] guidelines indicate a moral responsibility to 'society at large' [ibid: 22]. Indeed. But, as this reading of '*The Society of the Spectacle*' indicates, any such responsibility discharged by researchers remains located within the visible dimensions of practice. Surely, any moral standards should always foreground a direction of travel towards justice that exceeds the law through deconstruction?

At issue remains the question of how does the incorporation of justice in ethical research make it possible for researchers to move out of their standard circular economy of exchange [that is always broken]. Here it is important to deconstruct hospitality a little further against indications drawn from the unknowable future, 'the figure of the future, that which can only be surprising, that for which we are not prepared . . . which is heralded by a species of monsters . . . what Derrida calls, the 'monstrous arrivant' [Derrida, 1995b: 386–87]. This a matter of absolute hospitality, of gesturing 'yes' to being free in research to the possibilities that come to shore in the arrivant that cannot be anticipated – and not the 'predictable, calculable and programmable tomorrow' [ibid: 386].

Herein we return to the event [*événement*] of research, involving the interplay of deconstruction with extant structures. In trying to think *arrivant* in an absolute sense, Derrida [1993] points out that it does not yet have a name or identity, and it is not something that arrives, a subject, a person, an individual, or a living thing [ibid: 34]. For Derrida 'the arrivant is hospitality itself' [Derrida 1993: 33].

Research itself tends to gather data, questions, aims, methods, and methodologies in the present. Hospitality in this context is always conditional: delimited in accordance with the standard economy of exchange in research. This is not surprising. It accords with its ontotheology [Table 2.1]. For example, much research is consonant with both the ancient metaphysical principle of being – 'something is repeatable to the extent that it is' [Caputo, 1987: 123] and with the metaphysics of being as presence. But, following Derrida's deconstruction of Husserl, being is here regarded as proportionate to the repetition and reiteration of signs. Such reiterations are already deferred in what Derrida [1973b: 142–43] indicates is 'spacing' separating 'the present from what it is not'. The heart of the play of *différance*, therefore, always points to aspects of the Other – those ghosts from the past, that cannot be gathered by researchers within the present.

Both the Ethical Guidelines for Educational Research [BERA, 2011] and the Ethical Guidelines for Social Research [SRA, 2003] indicate that the 'responsibility' of researchers is 'ultimately concerned' with seeking 'truth'. But these responsibilities are located in the present. They serve to conflate justice with the law. For Derrida, too, there is a sense of responsibility, concerned with justice. As he puts it 'no justice . . . seems possible or thinkable without the principle of some responsibility' [Derrida 1994: xix]. Pivotally, for him, however, such a responsibility is located 'beyond all living present, with that which disjoins the living present, before the ghosts of those who are not yet born or who are already dead. ' [ibid: xix]. Dooley and Kavanagh [2007: 127] use the term 'spectral others' to express these many possibilities.

It is this desire for justice that breaks the hermeneutic circle of exchange found in a multiplicity of standard forms of social research. It is always a desire that exceeds the present, a desire to move beyond the identifiable, the calculable, and the determinate. Its deconstructive vigilance is always alert to the cinders remaining from past events constituted as archival records of research, and the impairment of the quality of research that almost invariably arises from facing that completely unknowable monster, the future. It is a desire to move beyond the law that only makes sense within the law inscribed in the ethical practice of research.

The locus of deconstruction is justice to come. It expresses a direction of movement away from the living present, a movement without telos, a movement of questioning concerned with the practices of research that can no longer be contained within the present; pointing to a time, to borrow from Shakespeare's character, Hamlet, 'that is out of joint' for researchers, whose time is that of the ethics of research. It opens spacing for the event of research and for the regeneration of life and of societies. In biopolitical terms, research deserves its own time for justice, a time when justice to come in research and in other practices, becomes explicit, explored and debated in its relationship with 'bare life'. This is a time for justice that is no longer delimited by the present. As Dooley and Kavanagh [2007] put it 'the time of justice is the time of those who have long since passed [revanants] and those whose time is still to come [arrivants]' [ibid: 127] in the literal, metaphorical, and deconstructed senses of arrivant.

But, what does time being out of joint mean for researching practice, where what might be called "meaning" is always open to the play of *différance*? In some ways, the whole of this book is concerned with this question. Do not researchers have a responsibility, as Dooley and Kavanagh [2007] have suggested, to open our essential dwelling place, language, and 'our laws' and the very 'identities' produced in the name of research 'to the call of the spectral "others?"' [ibid: 128]: 'others' remaining in a state of exception. Such a call comes from this time for researching practice being out of joint.

Justice to come: Time is out of joint

Derrida's [1994] deconstruction in *Specters of Marx* is also an approach that can be drawn-upon here with research. We should recall that what Heidegger [1962: 305–07] calls 'being-towards-death' that has been read as not only concerned with other people, but also with the possible death of pedagogic performatives, of the supplement, and of the symbolic Other – Lacan's [2007] symbolic capital – more generally.

In reflecting, with Derrida, on Act 1, Scene 5, of Shakespeare's Hamlet, where the ghost of Hamlet's father returns to inform his son of the injustice of his untimely death, is there not a powerful symbolism of the injustice of the death of lived time [Lefebvre, 1996: 95], of temporality, of performatives, of the supplement, in our late-modern world of research? Certainly, the dialogue between the ghost and Hamlet opens questions for Derrida about duty and absolute responsibility.

GHOST
9 . . . I am thy father's spirit,
10 Doom'd for a certain term to walk the night,
11 And for the day confined to fast in fires,
12 Till the foul crimes done in my days of nature
13 Are burnt and purged away . . .

The ghost then imparts to Hamlet an injunction!

GHOST
25 Revenge his foul and most unnatural murder.

Is not the death of temporality in our own essential home, language, unnatural? Is it not a murder too? With such an injunction is there not a newfound sense of responsibility to do justice in research:

GHOST
27 Murder most foul, as in the best it is;
28 But this most foul, strange and unnatural.

HAMLET
29 Haste me to know't, that I, with wings as swift
30 As meditation or the thoughts of love,
31 May sweep to my revenge.

GHOST
34 . . . Now, Hamlet, hear:
35 'Tis given out that, sleeping in my orchard,
36 A serpent stung me; so the whole ear of Denmark
37 Is by a forged process of my death
38 Rankly abused: but know, thou noble youth,
39 The serpent that did sting thy father's life
40 Now wears his crown.

HAMLET
180 . . . Swear.

GHOST [Beneath.]
181 Swear.

[They swear.]

The Ghost symbolizing Derrida's spectral other, constitutes the locus of one's duty. Is not bare life constituted by the spectral other in research? Derrida's 'concept of duty and absolute responsibility' is taken from his reading of Abraham's fable in the bible, following Kierkegaard's lead on this matter. 'When Abraham responds to God's demand that he kill' his son, 'Isaac', as Dooley and Kavanagh [2007: 117] note, 'he embodies the terrible *aporia* of the undecideable' – he is willing to sacrifice or 'deal death' to the law in the name of justice and responsibility. 'The moral of the fable would be morality itself, at the point where morality brings into play the gift of death that is so given' [Derrida, 1995d: 66; Dooley and Kavanagh, 2007: 117]. For Derrida [1995d]:

> The absolutes of duty and of responsibility presume that one denounce, refute, transcend, at the same time, all duty, responsibility and every human law. Absolute duty demands that one behave in an irresponsible manner [my means of treachery and betrayal], while still recognising, and reaffirming the very thing one sacrifices, namely the order of human

> ethics and responsibility. In a word, ethics must be sacrificed in the name of duty. [ibid: 66–67]

As Dooley and Kavanagh [2007: 117] put it, 'having suspended the authority of the law', Abraham 'finds himself in the *aporia* of the undecideable, whereby he has to negotiate between the conditional law [which commands him not to kill] and the unconditional voice of the other [God] who commands him to sacrifice his son'. The authors show that Derrida's appeal to Abraham is there 'to illustrate his willingness to sacrifice the law in the name of justice' [ibid: 118]. Just as with Abraham, in the case of researching practice we have already argued for the suspension of the law inscribed in ethical research, so suggesting that researchers should be open to negotiation between the conditionality inscribed within the ontotheology of its pre-judicial structuring of laws [Table 2.1] grounding ethical practice and the unconditionality of the Other. This would mean temporarily sacrificing ethical research in the name of justice given to the 'spectral other'.

So, just as 'God's demand of Abraham that he kill Isaac knocks Abraham's world off course' and 'the call of the other shatters all his preconceptions and expectations, confounding his understanding of justice and the law' [Dooley and Kavanagh, 2007: 128], have we not arrived at the same point in consideration of researching practice? The call of the Other also confounds Hamlet's understanding and his world is knocked off its hinges, committing him, however reluctantly, to a decision:

> HAMLET
> ...
> 188 The time is out of joint: O cursed spite,
> 189 That ever I was born to set it right!
> 190 Nay, come, let's go together.

In research, time is out of joint – the living presence of researching practice 'is always inhabited by traces of difference and deferral'. Such traces tend to be excluded from its economy of exchange: the Other in a 'dis-adjustment' being 'always at the heart of adjustment' [ibid: 128]; cinders as archival recordings always expose the partiality and incompleteness of memory and time – without this there would be no rationale for the continued production of new editions of books, for example. But, like Hamlet, and taking the lead from Derrida, Dooley, Kavanagh, and others, in opening space for further thinking about research 'there is a desire to set it right' [ibid: 128].

Rather than any arbitrary separation of literature, philosophy, and research, cannot inter-textuality, therefore, also remain a feature of such practice? 'Literature' provides a manifest example of understandings that open disputation about extant boundaries of such practice. It is *practice* without arbitrary boundaries. As Richard Beardsworth [1996: 2] puts it specifically in terms of the notion of writing [*écriture*] in his book *Derrida and the Political*: through emphasis on *écriture* Derrida [has] both reinvented the relations and spaces between philosophy and literature and opened a new field of inquiry into textual processes, these processes exceeding traditional distinctions between the real and fictional, the historical and imaginary [ibid: 2; Royle, 2003: 105].

The question remains as to whether reparation is possible. Such restitution, it has been argued, would involve moves to incorporate within the ethics of research concerns for the presuppositional-structure of law in relation to the work of deconstruction – a work concerned with justice.

Contrary to traditional conceptions of justice [Sher, 2012], justice is not the law inscribed in ethical research. Its impulse is born out of 'respect for the singularity of contexts' – this 'is what Derrida means by justice' [Dooley and Kavanagh, 2007: 112; Flint, 2012a]. 'Singularity', too, grounds Agamben's [2005: 10] 'coming community'. In the context of the ontotheological structuring in practice, it has been argued that justice affirms the relation to the 'spectral other'. In encountering the *aporia* of undecideability and incalculability, justice concerns thinking the impossible [Derrida, 1999: 947]. Justice gives unconditional hospitality to the Other. It is a direction of travel that is always yet to come, *ávenir* [ibid: 969]. It always opens the possibility of breaking the circle of exchange in practice-led research. It is a 'gift without exchange' [ibid: 965].

But,

> there can be no justice without an appeal to juridical determinations and to the force of law; there can be no becoming, no transformation, history, or perfectibility of the law without an appeal to justice that will nonetheless always exceed it. [Derrida, 2005: 150; Dooley and Kavanagh, 2007: 114]

The impulse of the desire for justice, therefore, is to open the pre-judicial-structuring of laws [Table 2.1] currently inscribed within ethical research to the Other in the name of practice itself.

The desire for justice must always negotiate with the conditionality of ethical research. In such practice, its spacing being always fissured by the spectral other, there remains the matter of ethical research no longer being conceived in the context of producing claims to knowledge without explicit reference to the desire for justice, as a matter of deconstruction.

Justice to come: The work of deconstruction

The logic of destabilization of deconstruction 'always on the move in things themselves', expressed in Royle's [2000: 11] pithy definition is already unfolding. By its own reckoning, such a logic is never adequate. For Royle, deconstruction is 'what makes every identity at once itself and different from itself: logic of spectrality ' [ibid: 11] that is already at work and is happening today in research. In reflecting on the 'tensions in the purpose and impact of professional doctorates' Hilary Burgess, Gordon Weller, and Jerry Wellington [2011] indicate that the outcomes have 'implications' for 'the continuing development of the professional doctorate' [ibid: 1, 17; emphasis added]. The impulse towards 'continuing development', is always 'already engaged by the infinite demand of justice, for justice' [Derrida, 1990: 955]. Just as in the work of Burgess and collegues [2011], unspoken direction of travel is towards justice in practice – the impulse from the work of deconstruction is inscribed by 'a sense of responsibility without limits' that always stand in relation to *practice* as 'necessarily excessive, incalculable, before memory' [Derrida, 1990: 953].

Is it not fitting, therefore, that the work of deconstruction should be concerned both with the death of past events, and of the symbolic Other as a work of mourning, so opening ourselves to that monster, the unknowable future.

Justice to come: The work of mourning

At issue are performatives. Such statements are always open to the possibility of their own death, and the work of mourning is concerned essentially with doing justice to the 'Other'. The Other unfolding from the play of *différance* that tends to be excluded from the exchange economies of traditional forms of research. Though it is difficult to find explicit formal examples of such work of mourning in research, itself, perhaps, a mark of the powers of enframing; wordlessly such moves are there in the continual refining and re-developing of pivotal texts for research.[2[Introduction]]

J. L. Austin [1975] first explored the notion of 'performative' in his thesis 'How to do things with words'. Austin makes the careful distinction between what he calls 'constative' statements – statements of fact – and 'performative' statements – utterances that contain within them the promise of action. The classic examples of the latter include the marriage vows and the words naming a new ship at its launch. But, in Derrida's deconstructive reading of Austin's [1975] book, he opens consideration of 'undecideability' between a performative structure and a constative structure. The 'undecideable' for Derrida [1990] is not merely the oscillation between two significations . . . it is the experience of that which, though heterogeneous, foreign to the order of the calculable and the rule, is still obliged . . . to give itself up to the impossible decision' [ibid: 963].

The question of whether readings of practice themselves constitute forms of production according to a performative structure and/or whether they reveal a variety of facts as a constative structure, remains, for Derrida, 'undecidable'. As a ghost that inhabits all texts, it renders impossible any politics of plenitude [Derrida 1992a: 116].

Such performativity is not confined to particular statements. Jean Francois Lyotard [1984] saw this in *The Post Modern Condition, A Report on Knowledge* made to the government of Quebec. It sought to examine knowledge, science, and technology in advanced capitalist societies. He showed the metaphysical grounds for the apparatus of research is to be found in the 'optimization of the global relationship between input and output'; what Lyotard calls the 'principle of performativity' [ibid: 11, 67].

Structurally, the performative, practice, is always haunted by the unthinkable, its own death. If we are to avoid such a possibility, it is the hermeneutic concept of polysemy continually driving developments in the machinery of the human sciences that must be replaced by dissemination [Caputo, 1987: 236–67] to which we will return in the final chapters. Performatives point also to the impossible drives of such *practice*, continually moving to make sense of aspects of the world; marking moves towards justice.

Such performativity also constitutes textual supplements to any unfolding lived experience. The supplement is another figure of mourning. In uncovering its 'crazy logic' one is reminded of the responsibility to do justice to the Other. 'A supplement is at once both what is added to something in order to further enrich it' [Royle, 2003: 48], and what is added on is also a mere extra [from the Latin for outside] [ibid: 48]. In the pedagogical discourses of modern 'doctoral education', for example, the supplement, 'education', as a form of pedagogy serves both to 'recontextualise' [Bernstein, 2000: 33] and to transform any lived experience, and yet it is also added onto such lived experience as in some ways an extra. In the rationale for this book, too, as a supplement it sought to address something that was considered to be missing, and yet it may also be regarded as a surplus, a plenitude that is already enriching another plenitude found in practice. For Derrida, the place of the supplement 'is not simply added to the positivity of presence . . . its place is assigned in the structure by the mark of emptiness' [Derrida, 1997b: 144–45; Royle, 2003: 49]. In fact, is this supplement not what is sought out in research, so opening a rationale for further research? As Royle puts it the supplement – for example, 'doctoral education' – entails a kind of crazy logic: it is neither inside nor outside, and/or both inside and outside at the same time. 'The supplement is maddening because it is neither presence nor absence' [Derrida's, 1997b: 154].

The work of mourning is concerned with deconstructing and uncovering this crazy logic of the supplement. The desire for justice in practice, too, is located in uncovering its impossibility. There is a double play of justice at work: the crazy logic is a humbling reminder, surely, to all involved in research of the essential limitations of its claims that also takes away the metaphysical grounds for much institutionalization of power practices in various apparatuses.

Deconstruction has also uncovered another figure of mourning – that of the cinders deposited in archival records. Any justice arises from its challenge to the politics of plenitude. In many specialist areas, there is, too, the impulse of justice to come arises from moves towards completing the picture. In some studies the Ethical Guidelines for Educational Research [BERA, 2011] themselves speak of 'context' as though it can be fully accounted for, and although quite impossible, such affirmations of context surely reflect moves towards the impossibility of justice that, like the future, always remains beyond us.

Justice to come: Opening horizons to come

The work of mourning also opens us to the future. One is reminded by Royle [2003: 107] and by de Man [1989: 181] of the likeness of Derrida and Keats, in that both seem 'haunted by a dream that always remains in the future'. Keats words in *The Fall of Hyperion*: *Canto I*,[2] similarly symbolize the opening of a new space:

> *Fanatics have their dreams, wherewith they weave A paradie for a sect* . . .
> For poesy alone can tell her dreams, With the fine spell of words . . .

For Derrida, perhaps, that dream in some ways was realized through his work on deconstruction. This 'has to do with the opening of the future itself' [Derrida, 1992b: 200; Royle, 2003: 110]. One is here prompted into thinking by the distinction Derrida makes between the monstrous arrivant and the planned and engineered tomorrow. In an interview with Elisabeth Weber [1990], Derrida puts it like this:

> The future is necessarily monstrous: the figure of the future, that is, which can only be surprising, that for which we are not prepared. . . . is heralded by species of monsters. A future that would not be monstrous would not be the future: it would already be predictable, calculable, and programmable tomorrow. All experience open to the future is prepared or prepares itself to welcome the monstrous arrivant. [Derrida, 1995b: 386–87; Royle, 2003: 110]

'The future [*l'aviner*]' of research is not constituted by the great multiplicity of different plans, schemes, and projects for research, it is always to come [*venir*, the *á-venir*], it is unknowable. In research it invites the possibility of invention that is completely unknowable. Nor is the figure of the future 'something that allows itself to be modalized or modified into the form of the present' [Derrida, 1992b: 200; Royle, 2003: 110].

Once again, in this study, it was difficult to find any explicit reference to such a distinction.[2 [Introduction]] It is perhaps a mark of the regimes of truth at work in research that the work of mourning bringing alive the figure of the future is not identified as such. The figure of the future is almost invariably there in the background – in the desires, the drives, the inventions, the intentionality of such work in moving towards the production of new knowledge. However, the figure of the future is not ordinarily conceived formally as a kind of monster, and consequently may become glossed as the programmable tomorrow.

This reflection brings us to the final step in the argument, returning us once more to the public act of research. It is concerned with spacing of theatrical space and what Susanne K. Langer [1953] has called 'the dramatic illusion' [ibid: 306] that opens consideration of the unfolding poesy of life 'which springs from the past but is directed towards the future' [ibid: 306]. It also opens space on the stage set for research for what Boal [2008{1974}] spoke of as the 'spect-actor', opening the possible empowerment of actors involved in its practice. Each of these three figures will be deconstructed in ways that open space for debate.

With education now foregrounding doctoral research, itself the locus of a multiplicity of forms of enframing [Flint and Peim, 2012], theatrical space is used here as a medium for deconstruction. Boal's theatre opens the possibility of freeing oneself from forces of oppression [ibid: xxi] in researching practice. His theatre, like his book, 'The Theatre of the Oppressed' [Boal 2008{1974}], strongly reflects the influence of his friend and colleague in South America, Freire [1972], author of the influential and acclaimed 'Pedagogy of the Oppressed' and others involved in the struggles in South America.

Most striking about Boal's [2008{1974}], theatre, unlike that of the classical Greeks and the Western tradition that was born out of the Ancient Greek world in a tradition always separating all of the actions taken by actors on the stage from the passive audience, is that the audiences are invited onto the stage to become spect-actors [ibid: xx]. This reading places on stage the world of practice. Such practice works with the Brechtian principle that people become empowered when they are able to speak for themselves [ibid: xx], and opens theatrical space to the spect-actor, who is not regarded by Boal as 'fictional' [ibid: xxi].

On the world-stage, Boal's theatre opens thinking upon the ways historical forms of practice, like that of the Ancient Greek theatre, tend to reinforce a separation between the active governance of research by researchers, and those others, its participants other identities used in research. They are ordinarily invited onto the stage for research only as a locus of their 'desubjectification' as 'data' that can be gathered and analysed within an economy of exchange that is entirely conditional in the hospitality it extends to the others who have been engaged in research. In research, there are some forms, notably action research, and forms of narratological research, genealogical research, that would appear to welcome the active engagement of participants on the stage set by social and educational research. But, even here, the economy of exchange at work in much research largely gathers everything into the present.

In reflecting upon 'spect-actors' entering the stage, Boal speaks of 'this invasion' as a 'symbolic trespass' [ibid: xxi]. He indicates the possibility of the 'spect-actor' 'taking possession of the stage in the fiction of the theatre'. Here is the possibility of acting 'not just in the fiction, but also in [her/]his social reality' [ibid: xxi]. For Boal this taking possession of the stage in a 'symbolic trespass 'symbolises' for him 'all the acts of trespass we have to commit in order to free ourselves from what oppresses us' [ibid: xxi].

On the world-stage set by research, the possibility of the participants in such research, trespassing in the research act – would appear not to have been explored. Ironically, in radical contrast to standard 'member checks' [Lincoln and Guba, 1985: 314–16], there is the possibility of participants trespassing and so uncovering the cinders of their own past histories and their unknowable futures. Each fragment being significant to them in their own unique contexts is always in danger of being lost within the exchange economy of the research. The locus of their trespass on the stage set by research are the very fragments of their own past histories, their own unique senses of how the future may unfold for each of them.

In setting the stage for engaging participants in practice, and in opening for them a medium for their exploration of the justice in practising research in our late-modern world, participants' appetite for multimedia seems almost unquenchable. Cinema opens a space in its spacing that is not dependent on the foregrounding of the human eye. Agamben's [2002: 317] work on certain sorts of cinematic image, understood as a 'prolonged hesitation between image and meaning' [ibid: 317], opens an unusual montage of constellations that may open participants in unique ways to aspects of their own histories and aspirations. Ordinarily, these are pushed out by the economies of exchange used in research. But, in this way, cinema and multi-media may open possibilities of trespass for participants on aspects of their own experiences that ordinarily may be excluded by researchers as a condition of their economy of exchange. Such possibilities create the space for participants' active reengagement as active subjects.

The impulse for such exploration of theatre, cinema, and multi-media is that of moves towards justice without any attendant risk of domestication, or of becoming docile bodies. In opening reflection on theatre, cinema, and multimedia, we are indicating that there is a strong possibility of engaging participants to trespass upon aspects of their own experiences; experiences ordinarily excised and located as bare life. For Agamben, it is 'gesture', rather than film, that is the locus of cinema. It is 'gesture' that 'opens up the ethical dimension for human beings' [Agamben 2007: 155].

One gesture may be found in the impulse towards justice in the expression, 'yes', to emancipation.

'Yes' to emancipation

The gesture 'yes' to emancipation is one indicating an unconditional hospitality [Derrida 2000]. It not only breaks free of any economy of exchange within traditions of practice, it unfolds within the play of *différance*, so that any metaphysical, teleological, eschatological, or even messianic accounts of emancipation are always already dis-adjusted and fissured by spacing [Derrida, 1996]. This is why Derrida would not want to 'inscribe the discourse of emancipation into' any one of such accounts [ibid: 82].

Ironically, Pieterse's [1992] review of emancipation, in gathering everything into the present, loses any sense of the spacing, of the fissuring, and of the work of mourning. But here the gesture, yes, keeps in play *différance*. It points to the 'arrivant', the future, as 'hospitality itself' [Derrida, 1993: 33]. As noted earlier, it is a matter of absolute hospitality, 'of saying yes or come or be free to the arrivant', that is, 'to the future that cannot be anticipated' [Royle, 2003: 111]. In this case the gesture, yes, constitutes 'unconditional welcome' [Derrida, 2000: 77]. The animating force of the 'yes' is there to indicate in the gesture a promise to take action, and to be continually vigilant in the work of deconstruction. It is the gesture, yes, to emancipation that keeps open the work of mourning, and the possibility of justice; always there in the monstrous arrivant, always beyond our capacity to know.

The 'yes' to emancipation is located as an undecideable – it is both/neither constative statement of fact and performative promise of something to come where the fulfilment of identity is 'impossible' [Derrida, 1992a: 116]. As a ghost the undecideable is there in every decision concerned with possible emancipation. Like the experience of the *aporia*, as a blockage and a 'no way' the undecideable can never be endured as such [Derrida, 1993: 78]. Yet, decisions to take action to engage with deconstructive vigilance, for example, while reflecting the impulse of justice,' have to be prepared by reflection and knowledge . . . one has to calculate, as far as possible', regarding justice and emancipation, 'but the incalculable happens' [Derrida, 2001c: 61].

'Emancipatory justice', therefore, is at once both a gesture reflecting the impulse towards the unconditional hospitality, the impossible, the incalculable, and action in taking responsibility in the work of deconstruction. There is no moment of decision informing any action – it is always an *aporia*. It is here that Derrida distinguishes his thesis concerning decisions on deconstruction and justice to come from that of Carl Schmidt [1922], for whom the sovereign is the one 'who decides on the state of exception'. As Agamben [2005: 1] has noted, Schmidt's thesis has evoked much commentary and discussion. In following Søren Kierkegaard, for whom the 'instant of decision is madness', in Derrida's terms 'the moment in which the decision is made is non-knowledge' [Derrida, 2001c: 61; Royle 2003: 5]. It reflects 'imperceptible suspense' [Derrida, 1990: 965], a mad instant when all deliberation is over. But, emancipatory justice has no force without the law inscribed in, and a responsibility to ethical research.

On emancipatory justice

Making visible 'justice' and 'emancipation', that are always to come, therefore, provides referents for both criticizing everywhere what parades as emancipation/justice and critically assessing the conditions for such possibilities within democracy. It does not deny political moves towards attempts to emancipate citizens. But, in the context of the current stranglehold enjoyed by the forces of neo-liberalism, where the language of citizenry has been replaced by that of the market, economics, the individual, and competitivism, Henry Giroux's [2008] does much to open the possibility of a struggle through research for a new language, for new discourses that open space for questioning the current seeming domestication of neo-liberal corporatism.

Unfortunately, Giroux has not yet seen that the principle of the market grounding such neoliberalism constitutes yet another modality of enframing [Flint, in preparation, ii]. It gives an indication of the scale of the difficulties of disguise constituted in and through enframing and thereby a measure of the struggle for gestures towards emancipatory justice. Despite the difficulties, the examples that follow provide indications of tacit moves by qualitative researchers that serve to challenge aspects of enframing. Finally, it may be possible for research to recognize this phenomenon, and its associated ontotheology.

From such a standpoint is there not an urgent requirement for re-examining the horizon for the ethics of research as an event [*événement*], as something to come [*venir*], consonant with the regeneration of bare life? Is it not time to open debate concerned with the re-examination and re-conceptualization of research ethics, and of its *language*, in ways that take account of the issues of enframing and of bare life?

CHAPTER FIVE

Re-framing the ethics of research: Laws and justice in the practice of research

In this information age with the continued growth of powers at work in research; itself generating an ever-growing reservoir of high-octane fuel enhancing such powers, it might be expected that there are already in place moves towards justice that seek redress, reparation and a new balance. But no such moves are evident. A significant issue is the naming force and gathering power of being as presence. This very locus of power can be found right here in the grammar used to structure this writing. In conventional terms it would be structured by recourse to being as presence – the 'is'. Inscribed into such grammatical structures are pre-judicial assumptions that it is possible to gather into the present what is correct. The same grammar is at work structuring almost all research. But, in moves towards reframing the ethics of research it is necessary to stand outside such hidden grammar. Hence we will also be employing a non-conventional grammar based upon the verb, *to have*, that not only carries with it no assumptions concerning the correctness, or otherwise, of what comes into possession in practice, but also reminds us of the temporal movement involved in such a process. In this deconstructive reading of law and justice we are not proclaiming some, hitherto, unknown secret about their relationship. Rather, in deconstruction in moves towards justice to come we are opening space/spacing for possibilities. The use of '*having*' rather than 'being' to structure aspects of the grammar is intended to signal such opening in *practice*.

We *have* yet to make concrete, therefore, how the possibility of such interplay between law and justice to come stands in research. Reflecting upon this inter-play one should keep in mind the irony that its very structures of language/law, currently tending to generate grounds and metaphysical directions almost invariably guaranteeing the on-going reproduction of *The Society of the Spectacle*. In such a society, as Debord [1977] indicates, 'all life presents itself as an immense accumulation of spectacles. Everything that was directly lived has moved away into a representation' [ibid: 1]. As a consciousness of the world it is a 'vision that has become objectified' [ibid: 5]. Here 'the *language* of *the spectacle* consists of signs of the ruling production that at the same time are the ultimate goal of this production' [ibid: 7; emphasis added]. Justice to come in an ethic of research, therefore, is directed towards taking away the grounds for such a spectacle and bringing into dispute its very discourses biopolitics.

What follows, therefore, is an exploration of the re-framing of the ethics of research.[2[Introduction]] At issue remains both the uncovering of latent moves in the practices of research directed towards justice and in opening the spacing for bare life.

* * *

The gathering together of ethical issues that emerge from traditional paradigms used in research provides a ready locus for deconstruction [Lincoln, Lynham and Guba, 2011: 97–128]. Their summary is based upon presuppositions concerned with polysemic structuring of research. It foregrounds a multiplicity of meanings of practice, indicating differences in the understandings of the Other, and of silent moves towards justice *for* the Other through the aims, ideals, design, procedures and methods employed in contrasting paradigms [ibid: 109–11]. But, the play of *différance* in the dissemination of justice to come and the structuring of laws [customs] in such practices *has* yet to be elaborated. We have to keep in mind, too, that extant practices are currently shaped by hegemonic politics of plenitude where identities are purportedly gathered together in their fulfilment within categorically differentiated forms of research, consonant with its truth claims. The structures of the laws [Table 2.1] inscribed within its language *have* yet to be examined in more concrete terms. The exploration of the re-framing of ethics for research that follows, therefore, creates grounds for such an examination and elaboration. The opening steps in such amplification will be taken up in the remainder of this book.

Lincoln and her colleagues [2011] have identified five paradigms, including 'positivism', 'post-positivism', 'critical theory [+feminist, + race]', 'constructivism [or interpretivist]', and 'participatory [+ postmodern]' research, reflecting on the contrasting methodological approaches used for the production of knowledge. For each of the paradigms they have further differentiated a number of thematic issues connected with ethics, including 'voice', 'training', 'inquirer posture', 'accommodation', and 'hegemony'. Although, following Laurel Richardson, each of the categories are presented as 'fluid' and their boundaries are seen to keep 'shifting' [Lincoln et al., 2011: 100, 116], reflecting deconstruction at work in practice, the sovereign powers inscribed in each of the paradigmatic languages presented in their tables are substantial. These delimit and circumscribe such fluidity, and despite their ever-changing boundaries, are simply not recognized as such. Thus, while it is agreed that the ethics of research 'presents. . .[a] definition of reality' [Kilgore, 2001: 111], at issue here are languages constituting grounds for the exercise of power rather than the individual who 'has power' [ibid: 111]. In such reality, therefore, it is the language of research that in constituting a politics of necessity in both 'not recognizing any law', remains in its structuring entirely consonant with the state of exception [Agamben, 2005: 24]. Herein lies the structure of its very 'language game'.

In this particular language game the ontotheological structuring of research shapes the actions of researchers and their organization. Herein lies the basis for its sovereign power and its laws structuring its language games. It is the bond of inclusive exception found in the presuppositional structure of language along with its ontotheology that constitutes grounds for the categorical separation of regimes of truth more commonly identified in terms of paradigms and specialist fields of research. It is this same bond that constitutes grounds for the inclusion/exception of bare life in research. It is telling, therefore, that for Lincoln and her colleagues [2011] the hegemonic cultures of one of their paradigms, positivism, are grounded in the 'belief that research should have the influence – not on the person conducting the inquiry', but rather on the production of 'truth' claims [ibid: 111]. But, they are in danger of missing the more general strategic function of truth. As grounds for the laws of research it is the *language* of 'truth' and its state of exception that fuels the very hegemony at the heart of each of the traditional paradigms. Knowledge claims arising from the powers inscribed in such language games are reflected in its laws/customs. Such claims ordinarily find expression in the deontological structuring of research. In playing out history in the very biopolitics of a multiplicity of forms of research that now find expression in the coded space for the 'good life' [*eu zēn*], such research shapes 'bare life' [*zēn*]. The moral standpoint taken by research remains directed towards fulfilment of the good life, where ironically bare life is included by its constitution as an exception – without express language. Consequently, the biopolitics of research elides and so precludes almost completely any possible debate concerned with the significance of bare life.

Within many apparatuses contemporary biopolitics is further complicated, as Alistair MacIntyre [1984: 23–35] suggests, by cultures of 'emotivism', where ends in research, here ironically directed essentially towards the production of a good life in *The Spectacle*, become reduced to means. In these manipulative cultures, of course, the identity of the researcher is always in danger of drawing resources from what MacIntyre sees as the archetypal characters of such emotivism – the 'manager', the 'therapist', the 'aesthete' [ibid: 30–1] – each of whom conflates ends with means. For example, in what Lincoln and her colleagues [2011: 111] call their 'align[ment] with postcolonial aspirations [Guba and Lincoln, 2005: 196]', constructivists [including interpretivists] are represented by the authors as 'offer[ing] challenges to predecessor paradigms' [Lincoln et al., 2011]. From a Heideggerian perspective this can be understood in terms of 'equipment' in the form of constructivist methodology 'in-order-to' question earlier paradigms – the challenge being seen as the end in itself. But, within the 'emotivist culture' at work in large institutional apparatuses this can also be seen in strategic terms of the way ends – here, the challenge made by constructivism [ibid: 111]– becomes the very means directed towards constructing new knowledge. Such strategizing is entirely consonant with the structure of the sovereign power at work in all research, its very language.

Dissimulated within such emotivist cultures, mediating the language games played within each of the traditional paradigms, there remains a largely hidden multiplicity of different emphases placed upon bare life. In drawing from Kilgore [2001], Lincoln and her colleagues [2011], for example, suggest how 'research demonstrates the interactions of privilege and oppression as they relate to race/ethnicity, gender, class, sexual orientation, physical and mental ability and age' [ibid: 111]. One is reminded, too, of the Utopian visions of society explored by the Frankfurt School in the name of critical theory. The latter was subsequently revised to critical readings of a negative Utopia [Gur-Ze've, 2010a]. But, in each of these cases one has to distinguish between such objective representations of reality emerging from research and the multiplicity of possibilities unfolding in life itself.

There is always a real danger, too, that emotivist cultures, and their on-going moves to reveal truth claims concerned with identities in the name of research, become a locus of distraction, turning researchers away from their complex relationship with being unfolding in life itself. In this reading of *The Society of the Spectacle* such a relationship becomes manifest more obviously in the contingent possibilities of enframing and the politics of plenitude. What is always in danger of being elided in research is the very possibility of justice to come in the space opened for bare life in such politics.

The question remains concerning the extent to which practices deemed ethical within research open space for thinking consonant with the constitution of bare life in the play of *différance*. The question also remains concerning the possibility of spacing for bare life being opened by moves towards justice and the characterization of such spacing and its possible effects upon '*the society of the spectacle*'. Here we should be mindful of the existing default position arising from the understandings of justice per se found in the traditions of philosophy, itself serving to maintain the status quo [Debord, 1977]. This is the work of delimiting forms of education, in which movements of *educare* and *educere* are restricted and bounded by the visible aspects of '*the Spectacle*'. Such forms of delimiting education work within a horizon of being as presence and the politics of plenitude, generating grounds for the gathering of identities within economies, where bare life is included in a state of exception

Justice to come

Unspoken, positivism/post-positivism's express sense of *justice* arises from concerns to produce 'truth' claims, revealing something hitherto hidden in our social world. In both Aristotle's and Kant's discourses on justice such moves towards truth may be considered as cultivating virtue in the light of concerns for the 'common good'. It could be argued from J.S. Mills' [1869] perspective, the production of truth claims reflects the individual's freedom of choice in how they may arrive at the ends within the terms of reference of such paradigms is consonant with justice. But, such senses of justice are not located within the futural horizon consonant with bare life, but are moulded within the horizon of being as presence. In this way the paradigms of positivism/post-positivism arrive at generic truth claims for that invention we call the 'individual' [MacIntyre, 1984]. The individual – or its many associated identities: person, narrator, participant, subject, actor, and so on so constructed – becomes the object of an economy of signs constituted and exchanged within paradigms. Given that such economies render lives in a state of exception where individuals become the locus of vast lakes of excess energy that is available for use, one can see that it is in the interests of the ruling elite within *The Society of the Spectacle* to maintain this status quo. Such moves now find expression in neo-liberalist discourses [Giroux 2008]. Within the ontotheology of the paradigms even the multiplicity of challenges to the extant social order emerging from research within critical theory, constructivism and postmodern/participatory paradigms are always in danger of being reduced to objects and subjects of these very paradigms. In its biopolitics research serves to shape bare life as an excess of possibilities over and above the regimes of truth they each produce. Rawls' [1972, 2012] liberal egalitarian view of justice that opens space for concern with the hypothetical choices people would make in an original position of equality serves only to reproduce such biopolitics.

Authentic education opens spacing for the multiplicity of our unique lifeworlds. Such spacing opened by deconstruction already at work in research can be found in the unique traces of histories and the particularity of 'place' grounding the unfolding of bare life. It is these issues that provide an index of authentic education opening space for justice to come [Derrida, 1989; Casey, 1998; Flint, 2012a]. But authentic education is currently not given expression in such paradigms. Their languages serve only to render economies of objects, delimited by the science of logic to the horizon the present.

Further confirmation of this position may also be found in the absence of any unconditional hospitality being given to 'the future that cannot be anticipated' [Derrida, 1994: 168]. Ironically, therefore, moves towards justice in these two paradigms are thereby rendered as impossible by such 'regimes of truth' [Foucault, 1994a: 132–33].

Within the traditional paradigms of research three contrasting alternatives as challenges to extant forms of positivism/post-positivism are represented as methodological visions of *how* to uncover aspects of the good life. These find expression in 'critical theory [feminism and racism]', interpretivism, and post-modern/participatory inquiry. Each case constitutes contrasting expansions of the sovereign powers of research. Ironically, each case serves to conflate the politics of plenitude with an ethic of research consonant with *The Society of the Spectacle.* Moves towards justice have largely become excluded within the biopolitics of *the spectacle.*

In the archival record[2[Introduction]] of research used to inform this study there is no mention of any ontotheology driving enframing, the sovereign powers inscribed in such languages, or the politics of plenitude, and there are no express distinctions made between traditional understandings of justice and the radically contrasting possibility of justice to come [Flint 2012b]. Research[2[Introduction]] simply elides bare life. Any distinction between bare life and the good life at the time of writing remains largely undisclosed, and the implications of such biopolitics *have* yet to be examined. Although not yet thematized in terms of the biopolitics of bare life, there are a number of examples within research that indicate moves towards consideration of such an issue that currently find expression in terms of concerns for justice.

The citations from the research archives that follow simply provide examples to illustrate in more concrete terms some of the issues that emerge from this deconstruction of 'paradigm positions' in relation to concerns for 'ethics', 'voice' and with 'training' in the practice of research [Lincoln et al., 2011: 109–10].

Ethics – a deconstruction

In citing Giroux [1982], and in reflecting upon participants telling their stories, Lincoln and her colleagues [2011] observe that 'the data' used in critical theory 'are created with the intent of producing social change and imparting social justice, that leads to equal rights for all' [ibid: 110]. But, any distinction between the horizon of such justice constituted by being as presence and any futural horizon consonant with bare life is simply not identified. As equipment used in the world of the researcher in this case the metaphysical direction of the signs constituted in the language of critical theory point towards 'imparting social change'. But, the impossibility, incalculability and unconditional nature of such imparting consonant with the futural horizon of justice to come [Derrida 1989, 1990] are simply not registered. Nor are the powers of enframing made explicit in the metaphysical directions given by this language game. Nevertheless, in their biopolitics of research the strong impulse towards justice [located within the horizon of being as presence] is there in what Lincoln and her colleagues [2011] coin as the 'inquiry posture' – the point of view from which the researcher operates. This serves to address the question of 'how . . . the researcher approach[es] the inquiry process' [ibid: 110; Guba and Lincoln, 2005]. So, as the biopolitics of an aspect of the good life, in Lincoln and her colleagues' reading of critical theory they characterize such inquiry posture in terms of 'moves towards understand[ing] a fair society, through social justice' [ibid: 110]. In their silent biopolitics, therefore, there remains the elision of any distinction between the good life and the ever-unfolding-possibilities-of-bare-life.

The subtleties of biopolitics are also manifest in Lincoln and her colleagues' [2011] focus upon 'voice' [ibid: 110], where Plato's and Socrates' visions of speech as the medium that 'guarantee[s] the true meaning of communication' [Dooley and Kavanagh, 2007: 22] continues to be played out, particularly within Lincoln and her colleagues' conceptions of constructivist and participatory paradigms.

Voice – a deconstruction

There appears to be no doubt about the privileging of voice. It is voice that constitutes grounds for many researchers' contributions to knowledge concerned with aspects of the good life. Lincoln and her colleagues [2011] speak of 'primary voice [being] manifested through self-reflective action' [ibid: 110] and they also distinguish what for them is the significance of 'secondary voices in illuminating theory, narrative, movement, song, dance, and other presentational forms' [Guba and Lincoln, 2005: 196]. In their reading of the inquiry posture for participatory paradigm there is also recognition of the power of alternative forms of data, including film and ethnography [Lincoln et al., 2011: 110] in accord with Agamben [1998, 2005], though the absence/presence of the inclusive/exception of bare life in their biopolitics remains as powerful as ever.

In concerning ourselves with *practice*, however, the contamination of speech and memory by writing becomes ineluctable as Derrida [1981b] shows in his essay 'Plato's Pharmacy' [ibid: 61–171]. In discourses of research it is simply not acknowledged. Nor is there any recognition of the logic of 'supplementarity' at work *within* any identity. Rather, unspoken, in taking the logic of the 'primary voice' Lincoln and her colleagues' [2011] writings come to appear as prostheses added on to the presumption of the purity of identity expressed in the primary voice.

In their moves to exceed and to confront the predecessor forms of research there is some hospitality being given to the Other consonant with justice to come for bare life, though this remains unacknowledged. A priori for these researchers it currently remains conditional upon the Other being located within one of the methodological maps, identified as paradigms and epistemes, projected within research. In their bonding together of inclusive/exception of bare life in accord with the language of research, silently Lincoln and her colleagues' [2011] hospitality to the Other remains conditional within the paradigms where it is directed towards community-based 'meaning-making activities' around 'social phenomena' [ibid: 116]. Although in such latter activities there are always incalculable, impossible and unconditional dimensions, associated with moves towards justice, these are not thematized as such.

This may in part reflect the forms of training received by researchers.

Training – a deconstruction

One distinctive mark of moves towards justice is that researchers come to possess a deconstructive vigilance. In considering the training received by researchers [Lincoln et al., 2011: 110] the possibility of them developing deconstructive vigilance is notable for its absence in any of the paradigms the authors have reviewed [ibid: 97–128]. However, in consideration of the training received by researchers within 'critical', 'constructivist' and 'participatory' paradigms [ibid: 110], while references are made to 'empowerment', 'liberation' and 'learning through active engagement in the process of inquiry, just how extra-paradigmatic spacing is generated and its significance for justice to come remains in question.

There remains, too, the question of how justice is understood within existing research that has sought to thematize this issue.

Justice in research

What follows is a deconstructive reading of three distinctive areas of research that have sought to focus variously upon the issue of justice [*vide* Charmaz, 2011: 359–80; Kamberelis and Dimitriadis, 2011: 545–61; Ellingson 2011: 599; Hartnett 2003]. In all three cases, un-self-consciously researchers draw upon resources from the language of research, challenging aspects of the extant order. Though unintentional, the first two cases provide examples of the ways *The Society of the Spectacle* [Debord, 1977] continues its, seemingly, inexorable expansion. The third and final case is introduced by a reading of Laurel Ellingson's [2011: 595–610] essay, 'Analysis and Representation across the Continuum', as a backdrop for the stage set for investigative poetry as research undertaken by Hartnett [2003] in prison regimes in the United States. In contrast to the opening two cases, and again, un-self-consciously, the language developed by the researchers in this case opens the possibility of challenge to the extant order created in *The Society of the Spectacle* by taking away its very grounds; that is, in opening space that removes the possibility of its ontotheology. But, though this is not recognized by Hartnett [2003], he makes strategic use of the research as a way of constituting powers that dispute aspects of the existing social order in prisons.

Each of the three cases selected is emblematic, too, of a pattern that has emerged from the great majority of research found in the archives used to inform this deconstruction.[2[Introduction]] In each of the three cases no themes have yet emerged opening space for critical consideration of the teleoaffective dimensions of practice mediated by the following structures:

- The foregrounding of truth as a historical and strategically located function driving the 'language games' as grounds for the exercise of powers and the generation of knowledges in the name of research;
- The ontotheological structuring driving enframing, pivotal to which are the metaphysical directions given within economies of signs;
- The gathering powers of such economies carrying with them the presupposition of the politics of plenitude for all identities; and,
- the laws in research arising from the bond of inclusive/exception structuring its languages.

The absent-presence of such themes is entirely consonant with the dominant biopolitics of *the spectacle* in the forge for bare life that becomes evident in the cases that follow.

Case: Explorations of grounded theory

As one of the international leaders in the field of 'grounded theory research', Charmaz [2011] remains located with traditional conceptions of justice. Charmaz reflects on the great majority of researchers working within the bounds of tradition. Despite her interest in people who are struggling with particular illnesses [Charmaz, 2005], and the insights emerging from her research, her studies remain located with the economy of objects found in *the spectacle*. For example, in speaking of 'social justice inquiry. . . that attend[s] to inequities and equality, barriers and access, poverty and privilege, individual rights and collective good, and their implications for suffering' [ibid: 359] there is a strong sense of working for the justice *of* others in accord with her own pragmatism, though her writings remain located in the present. Her writings, however, are also informed by a strong drive to understand the singularity of the contexts of her participants' lives [Charmaz, 2005], consonant with moves towards justice. Until now she remains silent on this matter.

What is particularly exciting is that in her concerns to identify 'small segments of data' and to begin 'questioning what theoretical categories each segment indicates' [ibid: 363], Charmaz opens a space where it is possible to take what she describes as a 'fresh look at the data and create codes that lead to innovative analyses' [ibid: 363]. It is at this point in Charmaz's argument that she begins to identify the issue of power. Here is the clearest indication of moves to exceed the tradition of grounded theory and in so doing, albeit unconsciously, working towards justice. Charmaz reflects:

> By simultaneously raising questions about power and connections with larger social units, social justice researchers can show how data are constituted in ways that elude most grounded theorists. [Ibid: 363]

But, the full implication of this line of questioning concerned with power simply remains locked within extant traditions. In a fashion consonant with the majority of researchers featured in this study,[2[Introduction]] there is at the time of writing simply no mention of our complex relationships with the sovereign powers of language, or its regimes of truth, or the powers arising from the ontotheology of research.

Case: Focus group pedagogy, politics and inquiry

The second case concerned with justice in research is based on George Kamberelis and Greg Dimitriadis' [2011: 545–61] 'contingent articulations of pedagogy, politics and inquiry' that arise from 'focus groups' [ibid: 545]. Ironically, though Kamberelis and Dimitriadis [2011] provide clear indications of their intention to exceed dimensions of the traditions of qualitative research concerned with the use of focus groups [ibid: 545–47], the intentional structure of their research remains directed towards the expansion of powers within *The Spectacle,* serving thus to question aspects of it in some ways while retaining its substantive structuring. For example, their own interpretation and novel application of Richardson's [2000] architecture of the crystal provides them with a way of 'mapping the changing complexity of the lives of. . . research participants' [Kamberelis and Dimitriadis, 2011: 545]. But, the critical implications for the biopolitics of bare life in *The Spectacle* remain dissimulated.

Like Charmaz, it would appear Kamberelis and Dimitriadis' [2011: 546] writings reflect their earlier training at the Chicago School of Sociology. Their work drawing upon Freire's [1972] 'praxis or critical reflection linked to political action' in *Pedagogy of the Oppressed*, and upon the social construction of reality, wherein 'knowledge is viewed as partial and perspectival', opens new space for focus group research [Kamberelis and Dimitriadis, 2011: 546, 549]. It is space produced by 'rich, complex and even contradictory accounts of how people ascribe meaning to and interpret their lived experience' [ibid:546] – a space produced by people's express critical consciousness [arising from 'conscientization' in Freire's [1975: 18 terms]. Ironically, however, the space created is one that privileges representations of people's lives, leaving bare life without express discourse.

The strategic dimensions of Kamberelis and Dimitriadis' [2011] practice where they move to expand powers of research are most apparent in their reflections upon 'second-wave feminism' [ibid: 551]. They take note of:

> the explicitly self-conscious ways in which women used focus groups as 'research' to build theory about women's everyday experiences, and to deploy theory to enact political change. [Ibid: 551]

Here they take responsibility for making others aware of the plight of these women and of how the focus group research can function in making this possible. In so many ways the acts of second-wave feminism brought on to the stage by Kamberelis and Dimitriadis [2011: 551] are reported to have had significant impact for many of the women involved [ibid: 550–54]. Ironically, however, the strategic approach they have adopted in wordlessly placing emphasis upon the politics of plenitude and the visual economies of research [so eliding any ontotheological structuring], while manifestly affecting the lives of those involved still remains stubbornly located in reproducing structures of *The Spectacle*.

Case: Investigative poetry

The question remains what poetry has to offer research. Laura Ellingson's [2011: 595–610] review of 'analysis and representation across the continuum' creates a range of approaches extending from what she calls 'science', located on the right-hand end and 'art' that she places at the left-hand end. The precise locus of her review is qualitative research. At issue is the way research can be represented by artistic means.

Of particular interest here within art and the language of poesy may be found an approach to research that opens spacing and the play of *différance*. Given the interest in finding approaches opening space for moves towards justice, the precise locus for this deconstruction is located on the left-hand side of Ellingson's [2011] continuum.

What follows is a deconstruction of one particular study identified by Ellingson, where there is silent interest in uncovering justice to come currently at work in art-based qualitative inquiry. With the fluid language of poesy opening spacing that is always on the move in the bare life of prisoners, it is interesting to deconstruct John Hartnett's [2003] *Incarceration Nation: Investigative Prison Poems of Hope and Terror.* Although other studies cited by Ellingson [2011: 599–600] could have been employed, at issue here is that point of intersection of the two faces of power identified earlier in Agamben's reading of Foucault, tying power with bare life. Given Foucault's insights and suggestions arising from Panopticism and the many apparatuses at work in integrated practices, the locus of the prison for Hartnett's study appears to be ideal as a basis for opening thinking concerning some of the complex issues involved.

Hartnett [2003: 1] identifies his subject as the 'prison-industrial-complex' – 'a sprawling network of penal colonies that stretches from coast to coast' in the United States [ibid: ix]. This is a place where many prisoners have written and published their poetry. The identity, prison, has resonances with Foucault's [1977] archaeology of panopticism at work in our institutions, including, education, the workplace, hospitals and so on, a panopticism that works in concert with a modern 'disciplinary society' in constituting prison-like institutional structures. Although Hartnett's study is based in the United States, its thesis is pertinent to researchers independent of geographical location.

Hartnett's [2003] book provides a complex, incisive and multi-layered introduction to what he calls 'investigative poetry'. Such poetry, according to Hartnett [ibid: 1] merges 'the evidence-gathering force of scholarship with the emotion producing force of poetry'. Though here is a form of language consonant with the teleoaffective structuring of integrative practice that could open space for bare life, as with the two earlier cases, Hartnett's writings remain silent on these matters. His critique remains more narrowly focused upon stimulating thinking within the US prison system.

In moving to consider such language mediating *practice*, one is mindful of Rainer Maria Rilke's point that poetry evokes the symbolic processes of the psyche. In this language, too, the impossible dimensions of our being become obvious in his 'Second Elegy'[1] [in the 'Duino Elegies'[2]]:

> *For we, when we feel, evaporate: oh, we*
> *breathe ourselves out and away: from ember to ember,*
> *yielding us fainter fragrance. . .*

If opening reflection upon his own poetry, so 'making people conscious of their own psychic reality, of their inner world, is a fundamental aspect' of his work, 'which is the healing of mental suffering', Rilke's poetry challenges research to reach out beyond what is considered possible.[3] There is a similar desire in Hartnett's poetic investigations, indicative of moves towards justice, though this does not yet find expression in Hartnett's [2003] work.

Hartnett's [2003] readers are given an indication of the complexities of his investigations from the very outset, in his deferment of signs from Walt Whitman's poem 'This Is What You Shall Do'. In reflecting on the poem Hartnett glances towards the language of 'pronouncements'. For him these 'lead rather quickly to a sense of overstuffed grandeur', before they come to focus upon 'Whitman's remarkable energy and dynamism' [ibid: 1]. But then, having stepped back from being identified as another possible Whitman, he sees the investigative poems printed in his book as seeking to 'enliven' what he calls a 'lost Whitmanesque tradition as seeing America as the world's best and most radical experiment in democracy' [ibid: 1]. This is his vision. He sees it as 'worth fighting for'. But, in historical terms he argues that 'the prison-industrial-complex poses one of' America's 'serious threats to that vision' [ibid: 1].

In some ways his investigative poetry is testimony to the tensions and conflicts emerging from the much wider complex social, cultural and historical setting of the prison within late modern societies. There is a sublime sense of love that is at work in Hartnett's [2003] book, not the many ontic expressions of love that emerge from Simon May's [2011] beautifully evocative history of this subject, but rather the presuppositional structure of such love. Agamben [2009] suggests that 'the lover wants' what is being loved '*with all its predicates*, its being such as it is' [ibid: I; emphasis as in the original]: Derrida [2000] uses the term 'unconditional hospitality'. It is another indicator of moves towards justice in research.

Instead, Hartnett uses the poetic investigations strategically; it creates for him another source of power that he employs in seeking to question aspects of the social order in prisons. In Hartnett's [2003] words, 'I strive in the investigative prison poems to celebrate the embodied, existentially unfiltered wonder of daily life, while always striving to speak from those experiences outwards to the larger historical, political and cultural conditions that infuse even the most mundane acts with deep significance' [ibid: 7]. Hartnett, too, obviously remains strongly encultured with the American vision which deferred from 'Ralph Waldo Emerson's heroic demand that the poet should strive to become the Knower, the Doer, and the Sayer' [ibid: 3]. But, inimitable to his particular style he also reflects critically, in passing, that 'postmodernist criticism has made notions of truth, good and beauty passé' [ibid: 3].

Hartnett's strategizing becomes much more focused in drawing from the writings of Bourdieu and Foucault. His concern about social justice has been clearly influenced by Bourdieu [1977], whose concerns overlap with those of Foucault [1977] on the matter of panopticism. For Hartnett [2003] fighting for social justice, drawing upon Bourdieu [2000], 'involves pursuing four goals to: 1. Produce and disseminate instruments in defence against symbolic domination; 2. Engage in discursive critique, meaning analyses of the sociological determinants that bear on the producers of dominant discourse; 3. Counter the pseudoscientific authority of authorized experts; and, 4. Help create social conditions for the collective productions of realist Utopias' [Hartnett, 2003: 6].

This particular case example will concentrate briefly on one of Hartnett's [2003] investigative poems, identified as 'Pendelton Poems' [ibid: 25–41]. His collection of 'Pendleton Poems' remains quietly playful in its use of signs. It opens with lines deferred from James Gilligan's [1998] reflections 'of life behind bars'. Being centred and italicized these create the appearance of a sermon. Here one learns straightaway of three significant issues for those in prison:

Punishment
Is the most potent stimulus
Of violence
Nothing corrodes the soul
As thoroughly as
vengeance

His themes, punishment, violence, vengeance and their effects on the very soul of human beings set the tone for the poem. In moving into the opening poem concerned with 'students' a number of playful moments become obvious. There is play in the identity, *students* symbolizing the possibility of the prisoners' becoming open to a new space, that of education and learning. Play also constitutes grounds for undecidability because identities could be read as facts or performative statements. But, the implications for such undecidability are not examined.

In moving into the poem itself, we can find that there are two obvious voices at play, one of the narrator and the other, presented in italics, is used to create a backdrop for this particular scene involving a number of significant events that continue to build up the sense of mood mediating the unfolding narratives of the 'students' in the poem. The intermittent repetition of rifle fire – *crack* – from the 'Colts!' continually falls away into the background. This voice then dialogues with the narrator, from a number of different people involved. As an anonymous one, with a distinctive violent dimension, the voice works from the very opening to create that sense of tension and oppression, where the gunshots reflect the violence of the segmentation and partitioning of time in the daily regime.

The narrator of the poem opens with lines that could so easily describe actions taken on a battlefield or in the prison yard. He presents fragments of events that have no subject. For example,

kneeling eastward imagining
Life beyond guard towers
35' walls motion sensors. [Ibid: 25]

Herein lies an express dimension of the violence of losing one's identity in prison. There is a third level on which the poem opens its readers to an on-going play of actions. It is there in the very opening lines. A footnote defers signs from an academic citation, serving to connect the actions in the poem within a wider field of scholarly inquiry. The reader is treated to this inter-play of the two voices in the poem, those of the student and the scholarly narrator, from whom various points are deferred during the course of the poem. In this way its language opens questions concerning the impossibility of transgressing the walls separating the inside of the prison with a much larger community of researchers and scholars. In this way though this writing provides an index of moves towards justice in research, the latter is not thematized as such.

This scholarly intervention, too, is not clear-cut, reflecting the contingent poesy of bare life. For example the narrator in the poem, readers learn, is 'reviewing notes on Kant' and one character, Jon, is 'leafing through Chomsky'. The writing continually opens space for all of these various aspects of bare life, and how they each unfold is open to possibilities within the poem. The silent contingency of bare life contrasts starkly with the violent and imposed segmentation of episodes of time for the prisoners. Symbolically, the violence of such experience is identified by the stark explication in the poem: 'end of break' [ibid: 26]. In this way though the writing generates indications of a possible distinction between bare life and the good life, it is not thematized as such.

There is a fourth dimension of play that unfolds in the poetry – the inter-play between the narrative dimensions of the poem. The narrative fragments and lyrical element in poesy underscore the moods of the prison and the subjectivity of particular prisoners. In being immersed in the lyrical dimension readers gain a strongly embodied sense of a distinctly violent and oppressive regime experienced by bare life. The latter, however, remains without voice.

Here, too, Hartnett's strategizing in his research becomes obvious. By keeping in play these dimensions the idiomatic style of the poem constitutes its own power, working silently to challenge the reproduction of aspects of *The Society of the Spectacle* that find expression in the prison regime. Although Harnett makes no explicit reference to *The Spectacle* and its related apparatuses, the qualitative inquiry using this particular and distinctly playful poetic form is there in an attempt to challenge one aspect of it in the very apparatus of the prison. In the poetic investigation there is also an evidently strong desire to improve the apparatus of the prison in exposing its contradictions. The silent moves taken towards justice are tangible. In being reflexive about his own immersion in poetic language, itself pivotal to Hartnett's [2003] work, is his attempt at the imaginative and creative re-articulation of how human beings experience language. There is a strong sense, too, expressed by Dylan Thomas in 1952 in a 'Note' presented in his foreword to his 'Collected Poems 1934–1952' that

Hartnett's poems 'are written for the love of Man. . .'. Though Hartnett does not share Thomas' theological convictions, in just the same way as the Welsh poet, 'with all their crudities, doubts and confusions' Hartnett's poems give powerful expression to the mysteries of existence. But, his research stops short of opening spacing for exploration of the biopolitics within the apparatuses at work in prison regimes. It does, however, create a point of reflection on our moves towards the possible re-framing of the ethics of research.

Re-framing of the ethics of research

Lincoln and Denzin's [2011: 715] epilogue toward a 'refunctioned ethnography' indicates that 'two decades ago only a handful of scholars were talking about the impact of their work *on* issues of social justice'. What has become evident is that justice had been represented as a matter of 'redressing a variety of historically reified oppressions in modern life: racism, economic injustice, the hidden injuries of class, discrimination in the legal system, gender inequities, and the new oppressions resulting from the restructuring of the social welfare system to "workfare"' [ibid: 715; emphasis as in the original]. In such integrative practices of *The Society of the Spectacle* this unspoken strategizing of truth claims concerned with justice [constituted in the present] constitutes a means of generating powers that seek redress and balance. Ironically, however, in its politics of plenitude it constitutes grounds for the on-going seemingly almost ineluctable expansion of power in this information age. This is why the concern with justice to come in research conceived as an event, opening us to the deconstruction of the present horizons of such practice.

The ontotheological structuring of such practice [Table 2.1], however, we should remind ourselves, drives enframing. In this reproduction of *The Spectacle* the 'good appears'; paradoxically, as we have seen, it is reproduced as 'the negation of life' in the name of objective representations [Debord, 1977: 10, 12] in a commodified existence 'dominating all that is lived' [ibid: 37].

Each of these three cases serves to illuminate how the 'language games' of research can be used in order to constitute powers that in some way open spacing for questioning aspects of the existing social order. But, in the exercise of such powers, ironically, and unconsciously, each remains 'centred' upon the *presence* of particular phenomena consonant with *The Spectacle*. Such language games serve to alienate bare life from itself as a commodity. Here is the spectacle's very 'moment', 'when the commodity has attained the total occupation of social life' [ibid: 42]. Such alienation arises because the lifeworld of bare life is futural, not located within the horizon of being as presence.

What is so easily missed is the centring of the systems of research upon the *presence* of ontotheological structures [Table 2.1]. These have a long history and have become deeply ingrained within the everyday practices of research. As Derrida [1978] observes in his essay, *Structure, Sign and Play*, 'by orienting and organizing and the coherence of the system, the centre of the structure permits the play of its elements inside the total form' [ibid: 278–79]. In its centring upon the deontological structuring of the ethics of research within its apparatus, therefore, there is a significant danger that the issues raised in terms of bare life and enframing not only continue to remain elided, but traditions of the so-called ethical research are continually in danger of serving only to fuel the expansion of the powers of *the spectacle*.

What is demanded at this stage in developing this thesis, therefore, as Husserl [1983] indicates in *Ideas*, is further preparation for his method, *epoché*, meaning that in each case *the* "I" being involved in research arrives at a position where "I" abstain from positing the world of research "I" currently experience. Husserl speaks of 'phenomenological reduction' or 'reductions' in the plural where the "I" suspends specific theses about the existence of the world of research. As John Cogan [2006] suggests, 'Husserl has referred to this variously as "bracketing" or "putting out of action" but it boils down to the same thing, we must somehow come to see ourselves as no longer of *this* world' of research, 'where "this world" means to capture *all* that we currently accept' concerning research [emphasis as in the original]. As we will see it is the constitution of *différance* as a language for research that will be uncovered from this bracketing.

The groundwork for a radical *epoché* in research will take up the whole of the next stage in the development of this thesis. It sought to deconstruct and to uncover the ontotheological structuring of enframing at work in traditional forms of paradigms, methodologies, methods and analyses. The direction of travel at this stage will be towards justice and the re-framing of the ethics of research.

Justice to come [Derrida, 1989, 1990] remains compatible with the structuring of research as an event [*événement*], as something we cannot see coming [*venir*] that takes us by surprise in immersing us within the inter-play of its present and futural [*l'aviner*] horizons. It works within the play of *différance* as the radical constitution of language: a decentred language constituted without any gathering powers so carrying with it the inverted sovereign capacity to remove all forms of ontotheology cultivating enframing. But, in preparation for the phenomenological reduction that follows we *have* yet to uncover just how enframing works within traditional forms of research.

* * *

Epilogue

Concerned with the ethics of research we began this study with the question: *Are we open to learning in research*?

The following theses, emerging from the deconstruction of the ethics of research, indicate that its deontological structuring is currently delimiting education in, and so what may be learned from, research:

1. *In the deontological structuring of the ethics of research constituting bare life, the powers of enframing [das Ge-stell], themselves almost perfectly disguised [sich verstellen] by the forces delimiting education in research. Paradoxically, in the name of ethically grounded research, these powers are constantly expanding, alienating bare life from itself, and continually increasing the risk of reducing bare life to an excess of available energy for use in the capitalist world.*
2. *Reconceiving research as an event coupled with moves towards justice that exceed its laws and customs open spacing for the regeneration of bare life and societies and open spacing balancing such expansion of powers.*

* * *

This study suggests there is much unspoken work being done in the name of justice to come in qualitative research. Silently, it opens spacing for bare life. It simply does not yet enjoy an express language for these and related issues raised by this study. The question remains as to whether such silent moves reflecting the life force of bare life unfold and have become obvious as transformations-*in*-the-world, consonant with being-*in*-the-world-of-research in terms of its paradigms, methodologies, methods and modalities of analysis.

PART THREE

Method/ologies in practice

CHAPTER SIX

Transformations-in research: Moving beyond disciplinary regimes

In being concerned with the multi-layered complex issue of the laws and powers shaping practices there is a real danger of not understanding just how such forces at work serve to reveal *only* the outer granulated face of the self. This particular identity is currently almost always located in *the* world. As we have indicated such laws and powers operate on grounds that this identity is 'at hand' and granular and so can be gathered together in economies. Such powers thereby simply exclude the unique interiority of the world of bare life. This form of biopolitics at work in integrative practices has served not only to elide completely the interiority of the self, in being concerned with objective and even subjective understandings of *the world* of practice, bare life remains in its state of exception. What is acknowledged, then, becomes the locus of officially legitimated objectivity/subjectivity, leaving bare life without any express discourse.

Fortunately, the deconstruction of paradigmatic research that follows sought to uncover transformations in practice that begins to reveal bare life. It opens moves towards the possibility of justice in awakening us to the matter of the hidden interiority of the multiplicity of worlds of the self. It invites reflection upon the extent to which such moves towards justice open spacing exceeding the laws in the metaphysical language of research, not least its ground plan of paradigms as the basis for undertaking research.

This spacing for research does not preclude the possibility of knowledge production emerging from the particularities of the interiority of traces of the world of the self, rather than its granulated face that becomes compartmentalized and separated in accord with the ontotheology.

At issue, therefore, are moves towards generating spacing for inquiry that exceeds the ontotheological structuring of research [Table 2.1]. Consequently, in the spirit of moves towards justice, what follows is a continued deconstruction of paradigmatic and epistemic structures. In biopolitical terms one of the pivotal issues is that of the dissimulation of the interiority of the unique worlds in which people live their lives. Such concealment arises from the economies of signs in the generation of research: the latter's metaphysical directions focusing attention almost exclusively upon the determination of the outer granular face of the self. But, ironically, while presenting the 'at hand' worldless subject/object that can be incorporated within economies, transformations-in-the-world of the latter are largely attributable to bare life.

We should keep in mind also that such gatherings of economies constituted by languages, each generating their own sovereign powers, are structured by the bond of inclusion/exception. Emerging from this bond there is another story yet to be elaborated concerned with the Janus-faced 'bare life' on the figure of the present. In the capitalist canon bare life has tended to be located within a space constituted in enframing – at least that is the picture emerging from a recent study of improvement in delimiting forms of education used within the so-called advanced nations [Flint and Peim, 2012]. In this way in accord with Heidegger's nostalgia enframing always provided a rationale for radically rethinking the modern world by returning to a new starting point prior to Plato.

But in looking to the future, we can conclude that qualitative research is ideally placed to open spacing for bare life and so to uncover the many unique possibilities open to it. It means rethinking research as an event, opening bare life to the possibilities of the future in moves towards justice and in moves towards rethinking and regenerating the Enlightenment in our contemporary world.

In order to understand how this might happen there is a need first to uncover more fully the structuring of research as a language, a law and a sovereign power on the basis of its paradigmatic/epistemic ground plans.

Gathering languages of research

We have shown before that to gather [*legein*[1]] may be regarded as cognate with 'lex' derived from law. As the OED notes, 'in many other languages the word for 'law' is derived from the roots meaning 'to place', from the root Greek, *the*-[θε], that continues to echo in our modern word, thesis. When researchers speak of their thesis, for example, there is an implicit metaphysical connotation with a defined object of study inscribed in particular law. But this term, law, has tended to decline in usage in almost all of the sciences, having been replaced by an understanding of the 'tradition' into which research is placed. As law is also to some extent a rendering of the Latin, *jus*, and of the Greek, *nomos*,[2] thinking [OED, 2012], in accord with the direction of travel towards justice, the question remains as to whether there is spacing for thinking: spacing awakening consideration of the interiority of the world of the self, unfolding in everyday practice.

As researchers it is easy to pass over the fundamental condition of the law inscribed in research, namely, the opening of spacing in which its procedures can move. There is no mention of this in a number of leading archives of research.[2[Introduction]] It is accomplished, as Heidegger [1977d: 118] observed, 'through the projection of some realm of what is' – in this case the social and educational world of research – on the basis of its ground plan.[3] These 'projections sketch . . . out in advance the manner in which' the procedures used to gain knowledge through research 'must secure for itself its sphere of objects within the realm of being' [ibid: 118]. Of course there is much detail given in the archives concerned with such procedures. But the law, the interiority of the self and bare life remain unexamined.[2[Introduction]] Heidegger [1977d] agrees; 'the establishing of a law', for him, 'is accomplished with reference to the ground plan of the object sphere' [ibid: 121] – in this case constituted by paradigms/epistemes.

What remains is a more detailed examination of these procedures put in place by research before we can free the self from its metaphysical determinations.

Epistemes and paradigms

Modern forms of episteme have their roots in Aristotle's [2000] notion of *épistèmé* expressed in his *Nicomachean Ethics*. Roughly speaking Aristotle had detected three modes of activity [*energeia*] in Plato's language of the soul – itself being disposed towards understandings of being [Heidegger, 1962; 1972 {1969}]. These modes he identified as *theoria*, *poiesis* and *praxis*. They correspond to the potentialities of the soul, or dispositions, identified, respectively, as '*Sophia*'[4] [wisdom] [itself uniting *épistèmé*] and nous [thinking], *techné* – art and craft concerned with making or doing and *phronesis* or practical wisdom [Aristotle, 2000: 1139b ff]. Within Aristotle's schema *épistèmé* has the goal of understanding explanations, whereas nous aims directly at the apprehension of metaphysical principles upon which *épistèmé* ultimately depends [ibid: 1076b 2–6]: hence, the disposition of the writings in research towards generalization of findings and the uncovering of principles of practice.

But here our thinking is located within a different place from that of Aristotle. Here *épistèmé* is with uncovering explanations of beings from within the ontotheology constituted in research that include 'bare life' by means of its exception.

In this late modern context *épistèmé* – the express disposition of *theoria* – finding expression in modern 'theory' is used to find explanations of what is, within such ontotheology, whereas *téchné* – the express disposition of *poiesis* – is applied to contingent things [ibid: *Meta*: 980a 28–981a 12] here reiterated in the apparatus of research. Again within the ancient schema the metaphysics of presence played out in the conceptions of *épistèmé, téchné, Sophia* and so on is demonstrable.

Foucault's [1977] particular reading of 'episteme' had been inspired by his archaeology of practice. As McWhorter [2005] observes, for Foucault 'an episteme is a set of relations or rules of formation that, at a given place and time, unite the set of discursive practices that make up an apparatus of knowledge production' [ibid: 176]. In elaborating upon how the episteme works, McWhorter makes clear an important distinction for Foucault. In McWhorter's [2005] words:

> Although descriptions of epistemes in *The Order of Things* [1966] were often taken to be descriptions of 'historical world-views' or 'conceptual schemes', Foucault insists, particularly in *The Archaeology of Knowledge* [1972] – that an episteme is not a collection of propositions or concepts or a type of rationality that permeates and governs a group of disciplines or sciences; instead, it is a set of dynamic relations that exist only in their concrete occurrences in discursive regularities across the fields of knowledge in a particular historical epoch. [Ibid: 176]

McWhorter adds that 'these relations are not hidden beneath the surface of the discursive practices they organise, but are, rather, what Foucault calls "the positive unconscious" of discourses, the operative rules of formation of discourses that are manifest in those discourses but not reflected upon them' [ibid: 176]. What is not seen is that Foucault's 'positive unconscious' is structured as a law grounding epistemic research by the metaphysics of being as presence. It is this horizon of being as presence that circumscribes an episteme [or paradigm], delimiting its focus upon the present-at-hand outer face of the self.

What Heidegger [1962] calls a 'horizonal projection' of 'fundamental concepts' is for Thomas Kuhn [1962] in *The Structure of Scientific Revolutions*, 'embedded in a paradigmatic exercise' so that the researcher has 'more of a working mastery of these concepts than a reflective grasp of them' [Caputo, 1987: 216]. Of particular interest here is not to use Derrida's understanding of repetition, and so examine the point when Kuhn's 'normal science' 'begins to catch on, to get passed along and re-enacted' within communities of research, with ever-greater 'sophistication, alteration and extension' until such communities are 'built up' [ibid: 216]. Rather, at issue are those moments of transgression, the points of revolution where the *phronesis* of the practising researcher will not do.

The question remains as to whether we have reached such a point in concerning ourselves with bare life. The strategizing in the paradigms means that despite the multiplicity of insights and understandings of being human that emerges from them, they each serve primarily the process of generating knowledge claims in a world of practice that captures the outer face of the self. A paradigm's syntagmatic structure simply allows for the possibility of adding other paradigms, and as Robert J. Coe [2012] has indicated there are 'a number of different ways of dealing with the existence of different paradigms'. He identifies these in terms of debates concerned with 'incommensurability', 'compatibility' and 'pragmatism' [ibid: 7–8]. Once again we are in danger of losing sight of the biopolitics of paradigmatic research. It foregrounds knowledge production in *the* world rather than opening space for 'bare life' that is free from its metaphysics.

The biopolitics of paradigmatic research

In this way the law inscribed in the biopolitical language of the paradigms has a structure, including the outer face of the self while excluding bare life. Here, too, we should keep in mind the fundamentally 'conservative' nature of *phronesis*. In functioning within the 'existing framework' it 'knows how to keep something alive, and to renew it with changing circumstances' [Caputo, 1987: 217], but always within a more or less established order of the very same biopolitics.

In being concerned with transforming the spacing of research, we should keep in mind that for Derrida such orders are simply fictions, contingent iterations of *the* world of practice. Thus in response to the 'violence with which' research 'enforces its paradigms' [Caputo, 1987: 220], constituting a basis for the organization of communities of research, and 'because of the violence that the paradigm inflicts upon the world' [ibid: 220], giving communities of research a way of seeing things, there always remains the possibility of being subversive. The normality at present is that the very grounds for such biopolitical violence can be challenged by a focus upon the interiority of the world of the self. It is easy to make the point that the very structure of paradigms opens them to iconoclasm. The question remains, how.

Given that 'subversiveness is structurally necessary to normalcy' [Caputo, 1987: 220] at issue remains the contingent architecture of signs and locating such normalcy and just how it 'is marked by contingency that is always open to subversion' [ibid: 220]. We have already suggested that such normalcy of practice arises from the paradigms [and epistemes], focusing only upon the outer face of the self in virtue of the primacy given to knowledge production. Thus what is required is not another paradigm, because this would have the same syntagmatic structure of the existing paradigms. At issue are moves towards generating spacing for researching the interiority of the self. But, before we arrive at that point, there remains first the necessity to reveal the contingencies of the architecture of signs used within extant paradigms and to examine just how conscious we are already of the state of exception constituted in research.

Husserl's [1970] phenomenology as a radical questioning gives us a way forward. He was concerned with the constitution of consciousness. In defining phenomenology in his 'Introduction to the Second Volume of the First Edition' of his *Logical Investigations*[5] he indicated that he was concerned with what lies underneath, below everyday matters,[6] and that he wished to move in a direction which looks for[7] and searches for the meaning of something[8] that is perhaps hidden in the everyday world. In this way phenomenology in Husserl's discourse became 'the science of every kind of object' of consciousness. In his words:

> To every object there corresponds an ideally closed-system of truths that are true of it and, on the other hand, an ideal system of possible cognitive processes by virtue of which the object and the truths about it would be given to any cognitive subject. [Sepp and Nenon, 1986: 69]

His conception of subjectivity is entirely consonant with many traditions of research and their modal methodologies used in the production of truth claims. Husserl's particular conception of phenomenology also suggested an approach to understanding phenomena that can be employed here in examining critically the contingency of *what is given* in the paradigms of research.

Biopolitics of bare life within the paradigms

In concert with Husserl, who spent much time meditating upon 'the philosophy of givenness, of intuitive contact, of the in-person presence of things themselves' [Caputo, 1987: 120] what follows is concerned with the contingency of *what is given* and reiterated in research. But there is a need for care, because unlike Husserl, who was concerned with consciousness per se here the thought concerns 'bare life'. The intentionality of this *epoché*, therefore, is directed towards writings in the practice of research, expressive of the consciousness of bare life.

At issue in this critical reading of the paradigms is not so much their content but rather what is given so mediating their contingent constructions of *the* world of practice. Here we will imagine a continuum of possibilities extending from the traditions of positivism/post-positivism through to 'critical theory' and 'trans-disciplinary' forms of inquiry, and we will restrict our examination that follows to these polar extremes.

- *positivism* was founded by Auguste Comte [1798–1857] as a philosophical and political movement which enjoyed a very wide diffusion in the second half of the nineteenth century. Comte's sophisticated social physics – now called sociology – provided the basis for the coordination of the whole of positive knowledge. For him the laws of social physics pass through three stages identified as the 'theological', 'metaphysical' and the 'positive'.

The logical positivists took up elements of Compte's thesis. Hempel's [1969 {2001}] 'Logical Positivism and the Social Sciences' provides a celebrated discussion of Comte's positivism. It concluded that 'there is no fundamental difference in subject matter between the natural sciences and the psychological and sociological disciplines' [ibid: 255]. This position was echoed by logical positivist, Carnap, who remained with the language of 'the laws of nature' and in so doing he made the claim that such laws 'hold for organisms, human beings, and human societies, are logical consequences of the physical laws' [cited by Hempel, 1969 {2001}: 267]. Though it is important to recognize that there are a number of possible understandings of positivism [Kaplan, 1964], it also clear that in seeking for generalized laws positivist discourses move in a direction away from justice to come. The latter is always concerned with uncovering the particularity of experience of individuals and groups.

Such generalizations of experience arise from the powerful hegemonic naming force of being as presence at work in these different dimensions of positivism, providing a strong axis of understanding in the social/educational sciences. It is this horizon of being as presence that serves as a powerful force in exiling the self from itself in any such research, the self being temporally structured as futural. Certainly, in the early twentieth century positivism was regarded as defining the boundaries of what constituted scientific inquiry. It is deeply ironic, therefore, that apart from its own incapacity to address the complexities of language, its metaphysical determination of truth and its implicit assumption that beings with the systems studied 'are held in some kind of unity – each with its own assigned place' [Niall 2004: 18] in what it views as the natural world – are simply forms of metaphysics that inform the will-to-power in the production of knowledge. What is given in positivism, therefore, constitutes a reiteration of the will-to-power-as-knowledge. Its precise locus is the outside face of any identity; its biopolitics simply dissimulates and sweeps aside the interiority of the world of any identity, and bare life remains without discourse. A measure of its currency and its movement away from justice can be seen in the following examples: Crotty [1997]; Menassa et al., [2009]; Neuman [2007].

- ***Post-positivism/positivism*** both retain the metaphysical thesis that there remain ultimate and universal valid and reliable truths about *the* world that can be obtained only by empirical means. The language of these paradigms speaks only to the present-at-hand world of identities.

  What is given in both the positivist and post-positivist paradigms for social science [vide Popper, 2002a,b; Kuhn, 1970], without which it would not be possible to practice such science of *the* world, is the presence of theories, other extant forms of knowledge and a priori, a paradigmatic ground plan. Ironically, their very methodology precludes any possibility of self-critical reflexivity on the metaphysical foundations for this form of hegemony in the social sciences.

  Particularly, problematic is the transparency of language that is taken as a given. Perhaps, most tellingly, too, these paradigms work with the presupposition of *the* world as external to the self. Such elision of the particularity of being-in-the-world of the self is a measure of moves away from justice to come. Such moves are obvious in Philips and Burbules [2000] study in educational research, along with Onwuegbuzie and Teddlie's [2003] mixed methods research.

- ***Critical Theory*** will be examined a little more fully in connection with what is given in education. Critical theory in the narrow sense referring to Adorno and Horkheimer can easily be stretched to include Marcuse and Habermas. In a broader sense any philosophical project with practical aims could be identified in terms of critical theory – including, for example, feminism and post-colonialism.

- ***Feminism***: Almost 10 years ago Randall [2004] posed a challenge for feminist qualitative research: 'our mission . . . must be nothing short of rethinking and reworking the future' [ibid: 23]. Virginia Olesen's [2011] review of innovations in 'Feminist Qualitative Research in the Millennium's First Decade' suggests that much has already been achieved in terms of a continued and determined direction of travel towards justice to come.

  But, there are critical questions that emerge from Olesen's review. What is given here in feminist qualitative research is the metaphysics of being as presence that largely presents once more the outer granular face of that identity, the self. In Olesen's [2011: 134–36] review of feminist research there are challenges made in this discourse, including:

  - 'enduring concerns' directed towards 'othering';
  - 'subjectivities';

- 'complications' and 'contradictions' arising from 'globalization';
- 'deconstruction of data' [to which we will return much later];
- 'difference';
- understanding the significance of silence [Mazzei, 2003, 2004]; and
- 'how to avoid exploiting and distorting women's voices' [Hertz, 1997].

But in Olesen's writing there remain certain conformities with the full force of being as presence – and all that implies for the exile and alienation of the self. Such conformity emerges from the placement of these discourses within paradigmatic structures.

But, it was Olesen's [2011: 136] observation regarding Lather's [1993a] notion of 'transgressive data' as offering 'the most worked out feminist model' that created the possibility of space outside dominant metaphysical determinations. This calls for a subversive move, 'retaining the term to circulate and break with the signs that code it' [ibid: 674]. Along with Irigaray and Green's [2008] teachings, these inspired the exploration here of opening space for research away from the production of paradigms. Feminist discourse opens spacing for disputation within the extant order. But, it still remains located within the horizon of being as presence constituted by the projection of paradigms that provide preliminary outline sketches constituting ground plans in a region of being for all current forms of research.

Another more subversive move in the spirit of Lather's 'transgression' is that of opening spacing for research that no longer conforms to the ground plan of the paradigms, by taking away the grounds for the full force of being as presence at work in such a pre-supposed plan of research. At issue, surely, is the opening of spacing for the interiority of identities concerned with the self. Much of the feminist discourse points in this direction before it is continually closed down by forces of being as presence driving enframing in the space opened by the paradigms. What remains is largely the outer present-at-hand face of 'the self' consonant with patriarchal projections of '*the* world', rather than the interiorities and the particularities of a multiplicity of unique worlds in which people live their lives.

- ***Post-colonialism***: there have been many leads taken in this field, too, in challenging aspects of the extant social order. Not least is the lead taken by Julia Kristeva [1977, 1984 {1974}, 1994{1991}] in her exploration of foreignness, particularly her latter study in Paris, *Strangers to Ourselves*, that contributed to debates on immigration. Really exciting had been the discovery that for Ôrît Îchîlôv [2004],

Kristeva has made a significant contribution to an original *technē* of practice [ibid: 150–59]. However, ironically, once more, it is an index of the powers of ontotheological structuring driving enframing that her challenges to the language of research have remained within a distinctly specialized disciplinary domain. Here we should also keep in mind the sovereign powers at work in the *language* of paradigms. Its biopolitics includes by exception aspects of the Other that does not conform to the structuring of the law inscribed in enframing.

Post-colonialism constitutes a rich field of inquiry with many resources that have the potential to open questioning and to take away the grounds from the ontotheological structuring of being as presence driving enframing, but, ironically, at the time of writing, any explicit language concerned with this latter issue is notable for its absence [*vide* Homi Bhabha 1990, 2004; Edward Said, 1994, 2003, 2005, 2012; Franz Fanon, 1965, 2006, 2008a,b; and Gayatri Spivak 1993, 1998]. These various studies have all contributed in their own different ways to open languages of exploration for the complex interplay of identities 'in which the coloniser and colonised are dependent upon one another'. But, the biopolitics of this particular disciplinary practice renders the interiority of the self as hidden behind such agency.

Perhaps the most exciting developments in this field of research in the past decade reflect the lead taken by feminists in their 'endarkening' of the space for research [Olesen, 2011: 131,134]. In Olesen's [2011: 130] review of 'postcolonial feminist thought' the play of *différance*, along with Cynthia Dillard and Chinwe Okpalaoka's [2011: 147–62] questions and concerns about unfolding 'temporality' structuring relationships among 'Black women' [ibid: 157] and the 'spiritual nature of . . . feminist praxis' [ibid: 147] constitutive of a post-metaphysical order, comes close to the surface.

At issue remains, however, the production of spacing for paradigms in which the full force of being as presence tends to reduce this discourse so that we come to see only the outer face of the self. We simply get rich hints of the interiority of the inner worlds constituting the identities of the self before they are closed down by the force of being in the spacing opened by the paradigms for research.

- ***Trans-disciplinarity***, too, as an emergent and growing force in the practice of research, identified within Gibbs' [2013] review, tacitly reflects the play of *différance*, albeit within an extant order privileging the gnostic structuring of the world within a number of leading contributions in the field [*vide* Pohl and Hadorn, 2006; Lawrence, 2010; Nicolescu, 2010a,b, 2011]. The direction of travel advocated in Gibbs' [2013] paper towards the 'specific, local and uncertain . . . the complex and heterogeneous' is consonant with moves towards justice to come. In the context of his interest in pragmatist /neopragmatist discourse Gibbs [2013] generates what appears to be a compelling argument for what he calls a 'catalytic' approach to trans-disciplinary research that is critically dependent upon choosing an appropriate 'abductive case', drawing on the work of Thomas [2010]. Gibbs [2013] locates such abductive cases within what might be regarded as the liminal space between 'nomothetic explanation and ideographic understanding' that for him are 'reflected in practical judgment'. His direction of travel is towards *phronesis* and is dependent, he suggests, upon 'systematic agency'. Such abduction, then, for Gibbs [ibid] is directed towards the opening and 'liberation of reason from formality', requiring nothing less than what is given in 'contextualisation, collaboration and reflection' [ibid].

In critical terms, however, and in accord with the metaphysics of presence at work in this discourse, it could also be read as another iteration of Nietzsche's [1973] 'eternal return of the same' in the 'will-to-power' constituted here as a re-presentation of aspects of the practice of research. Although such iterations will undoubtedly generate new insights, understandings and knowledges of practices that historically have been 'concealed through the disciplinary lens', it remains stubbornly locked up within the ontotheological structuring of practice. It does not have to be that way.

In the biopolitics of this form of practice it is a mark of the disguise created in enframing that each of the following studies of trans-disciplinary research is distinguished by the absence of any critical reflection on both what is given in the ontotheological structuring of such practices or, indeed, of the significance of bare life: Hadorn et al., [2008]; Brown et al., [2010]; and Norrie et al., [2012].

In summary, therefore, despite the many protestations from within critical, feminist, post-colonialist, and trans-disciplinary forms of discourse, the full force of the ontotheological structuring of being as presence driving enframing means that with few exceptions what emerges from research in the spacing generated by the paradigms is the outer granular face of the self. In the biopolitics of paradigmatic research, the sovereign powers at work in such languages simply constitute as exceptions those aspects of the inner worlds of the self that does not conform to its laws of inclusion. In this way in reflecting critically upon *what is given* in the paradigms, each of them has revealed its own forms of 'metaphysical exigency' [Derrida, 1988a: 93]. Continually, this presses in on the self to reveal only the outer face of its identity in what is represented as *the* largely present-at-hand-world-of-practice. Enframing and the familiar guardrails of being as presence, too, each constitutes its own locus of security and seduction. As Shakespeare's character, Macbeth[9], observed:

> *. . .He shall spurn fate, scorn death, and bear*
> *His hopes 'bove wisdom, grace, and fear.*
> *And you all know, security*
> *Is mortals' chiefest enemy.*

Delimiting education: The biopolitics of security

In reflecting upon *what is given* in the paradigms one should not forget the effects of the spacing they generate for what Raymond Williams [1966] calls 'permanent education' [ibid: 14]. It invites reflection upon what the 'whole environment' of research, 'its institutions and relationships, actively and profoundly teaches' [ibid: 15]. Though the term 'permanent' suggests an enduring and stable form of education in research, consonant with its effects upon the 'docile body', it gives no indication of its function or nature. The gerund 'delimiting',[10] in contrast, names the action of determining the visible limits and boundaries of the education emerging from cultures of research. Here it is the issue of delimiting education, therefore, that will be of primary concern. Its nature arises from researchers' enculturation within *the* world of research. In biopolitical terms it makes secure such practices, in which bare life is included by means of its exception. Its locus is the 'at hand' dimensions of practice. As in all forms of education, there are within the forces of 'delimiting education' both a training component, *educare*, and a development component, *educere*. The locus of both is the 'at hand' dimensions of *the* world of practice. Delimiting education, therefore, is an education in the conditional, calculable and possible dimensions of integrative practices, including those of research.

'Delimiting education' stands alongside authentic forms of education, but how these forms emerge within the endless drift of the 'empire of signs' will have to wait until the concluding chapters. Movements of the latter cultivate space for the impossible/possible, unconditional/conditional and incalculable/calculable dimensions of practice. Authentic education cultivates the particular and unique dimensions of practice, and with the interiority of worlds of the multiplicity of selves, consonant with moves towards justice. Authenticity for Heidegger [1962] emerges from 'the non-relational character of death, as understood in anticipation' that 'individualises *Dasein* down to itself' [ibid: 308]. This is a good starting point for thinking about 'authentic education', but in the course of the final chapters we will move towards a Derridean reading of this phenomenon, avoiding the possible trap created by its theology that gives the appearance of transcending and somehow standing above practice. In what follows we are going to focus largely upon the further elaboration of 'delimiting education'. We will return to the radical disputations posed by authentic education. What connects the two forms of education is their complex movement in the flux of time. The question of just how each form is constituted within cultures of research and their complex interplay within the constitution of *différance* will have to wait until the final chapters.

Delimiting education: The stages set for research

In Europe, for example, the EU Association for Higher Education has a Council for Doctoral Education concerned with the 'development, advancement and improvement of doctoral education and research training'.[11] In such strategizing 'education' and 'training' are already in danger of becoming essential modalities of technology as the very means to such advancement.

Being concerned with *what is given* in research, therefore, it is also important to take account of 'delimiting education' and authentic forms of education. In the context of Heidegger's phenomenology it is helpful to examine the 'naming force' of the German term for education, *Bildung*, at work in all forms of education. Heidegger tells us this process moves in two directions. What *Bildung* expresses is twofold:

> First, *Bildung* means forming [*Bilden*] in the sense of impressing a character that unfolds. But at the same time this forming [*Bilden*] forms [*bildet*] [or impresses a character] by antecedently taking its measure from some measure-giving paradigmatic image, which for that reason is called the pre-conception. [*Vor-bild*, Heidegger, 1998b: 166]

Heidegger concludes that *Bildung*[12] means 'impressing a character on someone' that unfolds, especially in being guided by a pre-conception or vision of education's ontology [ibid: 167]. It alerts us here to the metaphysical direction given by forces delimiting education in research, antecedently taking their measure from its paradigmatic ground plan, and from *the* world constituting the granular outer face of identities of the self. It is delimiting education that constitutes one of the boundaries for biopolitics as the outer granular face of the self. But in the biopolitics such education does not serve to uncover its own boundaries.

Thomson [2005] reminds us, 'the English *education* harbours a similar ambiguity' [ibid: 161] to that of '*Bildung*'. The modern term, education, echoes both the Latin *educare* – 'to rear or bring up' 'in the sense of training' and *educere* – 'to lead forth' – 'in the sense of developing meanings' about *the* world. *What is given* in education, as in *Bildung*, is an antecedent understanding of what is gained by delimiting education in research. Its teaching is foregrounded by the privileging of the outer granular face of the self.

It is the full force of the metaphysics of being as presence continually unfolding and pressing itself into the present in the tiny word *is* that constitutes grounds for the training and development of researchers. In this movement there is no prospect of justice because 'bare life' always falls short of its futural horizon. In its focus upon the transparency of delimiting education in research, both its movement of *educare* and *educere* focus attention upon the production and what are seen as developments of 'at hand' forms of knowledge. The metaphysical precedence of the sublime naming force and gathering powers delimiting education in research, its being as presence, elides almost completely the 'to-handed' interiority of bare life, and in so doing is always in danger of exiling the self from itself.

It is, perhaps, a measure of its dominion, that this circular economy of what is given in such delimiting education fails, it would seem, to ever open the possibility of breaking the circle: that is, in conceiving education not as something antecedent, but as something consequent that emerges without pre-conception. Here is the possibility of authentic education emerging from Husserl's radical side where *what is given* in conducting research is nothing. At issue is the possibility of a language and space for research that is not predicated upon paradigms for such inquiries. But, we have much work to do in approaching such transformative space, not least in opening thinking and questioning concerning delimiting education emerging from critical theory.

The silent possibility of generating spacing for the transformation of society was at the heart of their inspired critique of Marxist Utopian philosophy in the work of Adorno and Horkheimer. Their radical critique of Utopianism was in full swing with the publication of *The Dialectic of Enlightenment* [Adorno and Horkheimer, 2002]. They saw humanity being reduced to new forms of barbarism. In concert with Marx and Hegel their modus operandi was dialectical thinking that moves from extant forms of alienation through to the hope of emancipation. They argued that the 'Enlightenment, understood as advancing thought, directed towards the liberation of human beings and installing them as masters', became 'the sign of a disaster triumphant' [ibid: 1]. What emerged from their critique was how fear-driven domination continues to drive the engine of capitalism.

Such a locus of fear continues to press into delimiting education in research. In naming the action of the verb, to delimit, the gerund form 'delimiting' is used here to indicate an enduring and active process of education demarcating and defining borders. These arise from the antecedent movement of being as presence creating limits for the social world as a visible *spectacle*. As a performative, such a visible *spectacle* carries with it the possible fear of failure that practice may fall short of the demands made by such a performative. It would appear to be such a locus of fear that it is behind the moves in the Roberts Report [2002] and in the Vitae RDS agendas as means of improving doctoral education – the fear of failure to ensure that all researchers complete their studies, the fear that some research may not meet the standards required, the fear that persons so engaged may not gain employment, the fear of not providing value for money invested by sponsors, all of which can be seen at work in moving to gain greater mastery and control delimiting education available in research.

What is given in such mythologies of mastery and control will undoubtedly be augmented and reinforced, almost certainly, though unconsciously, by categorical divisions in the Vitae RDS that are now constituted as space for commoditization, and as a powerful locus of 'commodity fetishism' [Adorno, 1991] within the Roberts'-inspired [2002] improvement agenda: not only for researchers and employers, but also for universities that wish to implement such 'systems' and so meet their own professional obligations in a competitive world. Paradoxically, while certainly never intended as such, Giddens' [1990: 131] 'phenomenological juggernaut' in the late modern world, sweeping everything away in its path, will have been given much more fuel in the Roberts [2002] agenda and in the Vitae [2010] project.

In some ways it could be argued that the development of RDS is not far removed from the given presuppositions that Gur-Ze'ev [1999] indicates informed Horkheimer's project in developing their initial positive Utopian version of Critical Theory. This constituted grounds for beliefs concerning what is given in terms of:

1. a human essence, where reason, solidarity and quest for freedom are central. Here is the foundation of the Enlightenment's conception of unlimited human potential for emancipation and elevation. In this sense it is a moral imperative as well as a political need to struggle for progress in the realization of unfulfilled human potential.
2. critical theory, offering a liberating concept of knowledge that is capable of dividing 'emancipatory' from 'oppressive' representations of knowledge and its legitimization apparatuses [Gur-Ze've, 1999].[13]

However, in its foregrounding of 'at hand' knowledge production there is no consideration given to 'bare life' and the hidden interiority of the multiplicity of worlds of the self. In its biopolitics this critical theory foregrounds *the* world and in so doing by its inclusion, constitutes as an exception the particularity and interiority of each unique 'world' of the self and the many possibilities of 'bare life'. It is a mark of the sovereign powers of the language of delimiting education cultivated in such cultures of critical theory that such powers are rarely questioned. But, similarly to the discursive practices of feminism, and of neo-colonialism, there are sometimes strong glimmers illuminating aspects of the interiority of the multiplicity of unique worlds hidden behind human agency.

In reflecting upon the issue of 'becoming better human beings' in a European context, for example, Stein Wivestad [2006] helpfully distinguishes four stories that variously create pictures on the backdrop to those stage acts identified as research. The details need not concern us here. What is particularly revealing is the biopolitics, again foregrounding *the* world of such stories, so that as a locus of delimiting education we are taught repeatedly about the granular external face of the self. Wivestad reminds us that within our traditions there remain the 'Aristotlean story about happiness, the biblical story about salvation, Plato's story in *The Republic* about liberation from the cave, and the modern story about freedom from all authorities and traditions' [the M story] [ibid: 2–3]. But, despite exploring the difficulties and complexities of each story, and in drawing upon the work of Nigel Tubbs [2005], who presents 'a refined M story' centring upon the individual experiencing and thinking subject – the "I" – there remains what is brought into the present in *the* world once more, namely, the granular external face of the self. Though, interestingly, there is a glimmer of the hidden interiority of bare life behind the agency of the self, with Tubbs' realization of 'the subject's ability to stay patiently in doubt' as its 'main condition for improvement', ironically *the* metaphysical world of the granular self' and its economies prevail. In terms of delimiting education, do these many different examples not give us a measure of the powers at work in the ontotheological structuring driving the naming force of being as presence in enframing? The biopolitics delimiting education, in focusing upon matters of the transparent aspects of *the spectacle* of research in terms of 'quality' and of the veracity of truth claims, and upon measures of the 'outcomes' of research – however each of these terms may be defined – serves to provide an almost perfect disguise for its ontotheology.

Powers delimiting education

Though never intended in this way there is another possible strategy that can emerge from the ontotheological structuring, one that awakens us to the possibility of the forces of delimiting education running counter to the nihilism of enframing. Such a strategy is suggested in a move to Israel, where Gur Ze'ev's [1999] reading of Horkheimer and Adorno's later development of what they called 'negative Utopianism'. It promotes a 'call' from Gur Ze'ev [2010a] 'to overcome meaninglessness in a Godless world' [ibid]. Any reading privileging power, Gur Ze'ev rejects completely. His 'negative theology' refuses to recognize the strategizing of truth as a power. For him in such theology the Diasporic nomad makes possible transcendence from the nihilism of enframing. Its religiosity and improvisations are expressed through the eroticism of being as love that is generally not found in the foregoing neo-Marxist or capitalist discourses and practices. Agamben [1993] arrives at not a dissimilar position. He considers love is never directed at this or that property of the loved one [being blonde, being small etc.] but neither does it neglect the properties in favour of an insipid generality [universal love]. As we noted earlier, the lover wants the loved one with all its predicates, its being as it is' [ibid: I]. For Gur-Ze've, one express form of such love is a refusal to accept 'the present process of subjectification' – it carries with it the moral imperative to resist what Gur-Ze've [2010a: 314] identifies as 'the reality of constructing the dehumanised agent – the subject'.

But, in the discursive practices that variously reflect the struggles and constructions of the nomadic Diaspora, Gur Ze'ev, like Horkheimer and Adorno, retains the politics of plenitude and the privileging of the metaphysics of being as presence as an axis around which he organizes his vision. Here, too, we could move with Gur Ze'ev [2010b] in his detailed review of groups of 'pedagogic thinkers' that have emerged in critical theory – including 'McLaren, Gruschka, Mason, De Olivera, Zeichner, Roth, Weiler' who Gur Ze'ev [2010b] sees as 'insisting on the humanist modernist project'; 'Peters, Lather, Biesta' who are considered to 'emphasise new possibilities within the framework of postmodern discourses and postmodern conditions' [ibid: 17]; and 'Lankshear, Kohly, Burbules, Moraes, Olssen, Helman, Duarte, Giroux' who, according to Gur Ze've, variously search for a 'creative synthesis between postmodern and modern sensibilities, conceptions, practices' [ibid: 17]. But, once again the details are much less interesting than the fact that many of these thinkers would appear not yet to have thematized any concerns that are to do with 'bare life' or 'enframing'. And, certainly none of these thinkers has taken a Derridean reading of the latter two phenomena.

More interesting, too, are the forces, delimiting education, shaping *what is given* in the practices of research. The economy of the gift would appear to be inescapable. Yet, the very possibility of exploring Husserl's radical side requires nothing less than a decisive movement away from *what is given* in practice.

The everyday activity of giving and receiving gifts is familiar to everyone, and there are times, perhaps, for many people where there has been a desire to give something unconditionally with no expectation of receiving anything in return. According to Derrida's readings of Husserl, however, there can be no unconditional gift. Even in a gift that is given – "with no strings attached," such as here, the possibility of nothing mediating the researcher in their practice – as Dooley and Kavanagh [2007] have observed, 'as soon as it is recognised by the recipient as a gift, it is immediately drawn in an economy of exchange' [ibid: 9]. It is important to keep in mind, too, that in any such economy the fulfilment of any identity is also an illusion. In exploring some of the consequences of this position, in *Given Time* Derrida [1991] argues not only that 'the pure gift can never be presented' [Dooley and Kavanagh, 2007: 9] but also:

> If the gift is annulled in the economic odyssey of the circle as soon as it appears as a gift or as soon as it signifies itself as a gift, there is no longer any logic of the gift and one may safely say that a consistent discourse on the gift becomes impossible: it misses its object and always speaks, finally of something else. [Derrida, 1991: 24]

This is the logic of the odyssey of the circular economy where the gift leaves only its 'trace' behind. The many archives of research all provide testimony, if this were needed, of just how much in each of the foregoing economies of research people 'are impassioned to push against the limits of those conditional economies' of *what is given* 'in attempts to open them to improvement' [Dooley and Kavanagh, 2007: 10]. In research such drives have been manifest in the continual reiteration of the will-to-power-as-knowledge; in systems of formal education such passion is manifest in formal measures driving the improvement agenda [Flint and Peim, 2012; Flint, in preparation, iii].

But, 'unlike Odysseus[14] who 'is always searching for home, and finds his way back' in being broken this Derridean reading of the Odyssean circle always leaves researchers who may wish to explore such a possibility wandering, and who, as Dooley and Kavanagh [2007] suggest, 'like Abraham [may become] exiled from the place of birth, endlessly *destin-errant*, wandering the desert' [ibid: 6]. The past can never be seen in 'its purity or presence' [Dooley and Kavanagh, 2007: 6]. Derrida [1995a] reminds us, what is concealed from view is 'not a thing, some information that I am hiding or that one has to hide or dissimulate, it is rather an experience that does not make itself available to information and knowledge, and that immediately encrypts itself' [ibid: 201]. What is hidden from view, then, is irretrievably lost in the catastrophe of memory. Derrida likens this to the 'experience of death' [Dooley and Kavanagh, 2007: 7]. Herein lies the existential basis connecting with Derrida's *différance*, opening spacing for a relationship with the possibility of death, and the nothing. What this means for moves towards justice in the practice of research will be taken up in concluding this book. We still have much work to do, first in uncovering the extent to which methodological thinking turns us away from questions concerned with *what is given* in the ontotheology of research and its inclusion of bare life.

In moving to uncover such methodological thinking in the next step of this thesis we should also be mindful of the antecedent structuring of delimiting education manifest in what Gadamer's [2004: 354] analysis of the 'historical consciousness' revealed '*vis-a-tergo*' [ibid] as pre-judice; that is, of those pre-judicial structures of law that precede and structure all inquiries [Table 2.1]. As we have seen the structuring of laws involving their bond of inclusion/exception constitute grounds for the sovereign powers of the languages of research. It is such pre-judicial structuring of the languages of research that constitutes grounds for the driving force delimiting education in research. Ironically, it leaves bare life in a 'state of exception'.

CHAPTER SEVEN

Transformations-in research methodologies: Moving beyond enframing

The world of research would seem to have become consumed with the matter of making secure [*Sicherstellen*] and improving the quality of its 'outcomes'. The ontotheology of research would appear to remain a pivotal issue in safeguarding the continued development of professional standards. It is no surprise, therefore, to find that the express forms of the organization of practices – in terms of paradigms, methodologies, methods, and so on – that appears to make secure truth claims to knowledge – however these various terms may be defined – gives no ground for questioning such ontotheology. Consequently, research has simply not developed a language of critique for enframing [*das Ge-stell*]. Such moves towards what is represented as 'quality research' tend to distract attention almost completely from the significance of those pivotal moments of the impossible, incalculable and unconditional dimensions of *practice* that emerge from 'bare life' at the point where new insights, understandings, connections and possibilities emerge from research. But, there are some researchers at the leading edge of practices who are beginning to open thinking upon these pivotal moments. Although there are currently no express languages for bare life and enframing in research, some of the issues connected with these phenomena are beginning to emerge from concerns with methodology.

Perhaps one of the most spirited and inspirational forms of sustained critical engagement with the extant methodological order in research comes from Patti Lather [1991, 1993a,b, 2004, 2006, 2007a,b]. In 'Fertile Obsession: Validity after Poststructuralism', Lather [1993a] spoke of 'the human sciences' being 'in search of a discourse to help chart the journey from the present to the future'. Her expressions could be read as figuring a movement towards justice. It is there in her sense of the 'loss of certainties and absolute frames of reference' [Lather, 1993a: 673]. Space for such movement Lather opened with deconstruction 'anticipat[ing] a generative methodology that registers a possibility' [ibid: 673] where the 'space' she had created was 'marked as provisional'. It opened the possibility of a new science 'to take form' [ibid: 673], where she was concerned with 'the complexities of language and the world' [ibid: 673]. The particular direction for her paper was given in response to Lyotard's [1984: xxv] question concerning the locus of 'legitimacy' emerging from the movement of post-modernism. The latter had been informed by its 'incredulity towards metanarratives' [ibid: xxiv].

We are going to move in a different direction. Lather's [1993a] question concerning the human sciences like this thesis is located 'outside the limits of normative framings of validity'. In response, however, she continues to hold on to the guardrails created by metaphysical determinations of *what is given* in practice – even though what had been given in this case was conceived in its 'antifoundational possibilities' [ibid: 673]. It suggested more work was required in uncovering the nature of methodological practice in research.

In response once more to Lyotard, at issue here is another question concerning the possibilities of moves towards justice in research. At issue in such moves is a form of research where nothing is given. Before we can arrive at that point, however, we *have* yet to uncover the nature of the hidden forces at work shaping methodologies. A good starting point is the emerging debates.

In being in the throw of history, as Marx [1852: 1] had indicated, the full force of the naming powers of our little word, 'is' – being – that drives enframing emerges from any cursory examination of what Denzin and Lincoln [2011b: 3] have identified as 'historical moments' of qualitative research. For these leaders in the international field such moments and the many traditions given in the name of research define its practice. Although there is for Denzin and Lincoln a felicitous, albeit unconscious, play of *différance,* in their express representation of 'the overlap' of 'these [historical] moments' that they note 'simultaneously operate in the present' [ibid: 3], the implications of such play are not explored.

Such moments provide headline indications of the debates concerned with *what has been giv*en in research over the past century or more – debates [ibid: 3] concerned with 'traditional research' [1900–1950], 'the modernist or golden age' [1950–1970], 'blurred genres' [1970–1986], 'the crisis of representation' [located in the mid-1980s–early 1990s], 'postmodernism' [early–mid-1990s], 'post-experimental inquiry' [1995–2000], the 'methodologically contested present' [2000–2008] and 'the future'. In these various debates, in accord with the movement of being as presence, the metaphysical directions given in their economies of signs remain, ironically, located within Debord's [1977] *The Society of the Spectacle*. At the point of writing there remains only very limited language in research giving expression to the critique of such a possibility and its relationship with enframing. In our examination of *practice* it suggested a form of biopolitics encompassing research and *the spectacle*.

The biopolitics of *the spectacle*

In the paradigms such economies of signs arise from the strategizing and foregrounding of truth claims concerning whatever *is*, as objects of our economies. Here, as we have seen before, being as presence, the mighty *is*, remains the locus of the gathering powers of enframing driving such knowledge production. *The spectacle* is the 'social relation among people' mediated by such economies of signs [Debord, 1977: 5–8]. The latter economies more familiarly appear as images on our 'TVs', 'computers', 'tablets', 'laptops', 'ipads' and so on, in specific forms, 'as information or propaganda, as advertisement or direct entertainment consumption'. Such economies ground the 'the model of socially dominant life' that still remains at the time of writing [ibid: 8]. Some 30 years after the original publication of *The Spectacle*, it is continually brought into 'the present' by paradigmatic forms of research in accord with the gathering powers of being as presence [ibid: 5–8]. This is, perhaps, a mark of the hegemony of *The Spectacle*. Its very 'language . . . consists of signs of the ruling production, which at the same time are the ultimate goal of this production' [ibid: 7]. The sovereign power of such language, we should perhaps remind ourselves, lies in the inclusive bonding of beings with bare life rendered in a state of exception. The current biopolitics of research in concert with the forces delimiting education in research tends to foreground the conditional, calculable and possible dimensions of human existence. This conflation of politics and education focuses attention upon the production of what in hegemonic cultures is represented as its ever-improving quality, benchmarked upon the fantasy of 'transparency'.

Such metaphysical determinations are generated within the ontotheology of research, creating the space for the continued expansion of rather than questioning Debord's 'Spectacle'. Denzin and Lincoln's [2011b: 3] final two movements concerned with the technological application of 'qualitative data analysis software' QDAS [Davidson and di Gregorio, 2011: 637–38] more obviously reflect the unfolding of such enframing as an essentially technological phenomenon. As technologies the paradigms of research in their metaphysical structuring of existence constitute only one way of revealing *the* world, on grounds of reason connecting objects of consciousness with their subjects.

Such economies of signs, as we have seen, are also gathered on grounds of the politics of plenitude. In the hegemony of completing the circle [that is always broken] the locus of these gatherings are truth claims produced as objects of consciousness, uncovered in research. Here we return once more to the strategizing of truth claims. Paradoxically, the biopolitics in generating a 'state of exception' for bare life is based upon its own continual fuelling of drives to improve the 'good life' in accord with the sovereign powers of its very language.

The most obvious manifestation of the sublime range of powers at work in research directed towards the 'good life' lies in the reproduction of *The Society of the Spectacle*. Consequently, it is important here to take time for meditation on the grounding of such powers, so that in the spirit of moves towards justice this deconstruction can open space for the possibility of balancing localized and centralized powers.

Within the ontotheology it is easy to miss its significance for the reproduction of *The Spectacle* in the Western world. For researchers what is done largely constitutes the ontological grounds for their inquiries. The organization [or form] of their research in terms of paradigms and specialist disciplinary structures [including multi-disciplinary forms of inquiry] constitute its theological structuring. The theological structuring, we should recall, constitutes the boundaries for research along with the opening space for the highest beings that can be revealed within a particular organization. This form of structuring is by no means fixed. As indicated by Lather [1993a,b, 1994, 2004, 2006 2007a,b], the paradigmatic organization of the human sciences continues to change. But, the ontotheology along with the state of exception remains untouched by such innovative thinking.

In accord with the biopolitics of research, its structuring does not ordinarily invite questioning its grounding presuppositions. The professionalism of researchers placing great significance upon the quality of truth claims, along with the hegemony of training regimes, simply reproduces this biopolitics shaping bare life and once more eliding almost completely the issues of ontotheology and enframing. Paradoxically, what is so easily elided in the hegemony of such regimes is the violence being done in the name of ethical research. Such violence, as we have seen, imputes the selection of particular aspects of practice to the exclusion of the 'spectral-other', consonant with the sovereign powers of such language.

It is, perhaps, helpful at this point to remind oneself of the issues emerging from the ontotheology in research methodology.

Biopolitics: the ontotheology of research

There is an assumption built into the way paradigmatic research is grounded that is not beyond question. It is an assumption based upon the metaphysical principle of being, imputing that 'something' – that is, the complex mapping of a region of being identified earlier [Table 2.1] – *is* repeatable to the extent it *is*. But as we have seen, this is a falsehood based on 'being as presence' – the 'is' – that always comes into being in the repetition and reiteration of signs. And such reiterations are always open to contingency and failure. *What is given* in 'data' or in a particular methodology are *not* some elemental building blocks for research. What a methodology is, or its 'whatness', therefore, is not a matter of some essential quality but rather reflects the reiteration of signs in the name of methodology. Here once more we need to challenge the politics of plenitude.

What has to be disputed with great resolve, therefore, is both the ontological grounding of the ideas used in research as universal and the theological structuring of the idea in its paradigmatic form. The latter culminates in the many specialist disciplinary structures located within paradigms, where the theological structuring of such specialist form of organization is entirely consonant with the strategizing and foregrounding of truth claims.

Within the paradigms it is a measure of the sovereign powers at work in such language that the 'crisis of representation' [Denzin and Lincoln, 2011b: 3] concerning the adequate means of representing society remains locked up in the nomothetic structuring of modern forms of writing that are represented to have occurred in the period between 1985 and 1995. But, the ontotheological structuring driving enframing is not a product of any one particular paradigm or of any specific time period; it works to shape each of them – being nascent in the world of Ancient Greeks, where, for Heidegger [1977, 1991 {1957}], it enjoyed a lengthy embryonic period that finally gave birth to the full force of technological enframing in the twentieth century. At the time of writing, in the biopolitics of qualitative research the issue of representation remains as topical as ever: not least because in a post-9/11 world much of the representations within the paradigms of research continue to silence bare life.

For qualitative research Agamben's focus upon bare life opens space for a multiplicity of possibilities, whereas Heidegger's enframing simply conceives all forms of bare life in terms of a collective excess of energy ['standing reserve']. The latter critique of enframing, we should remind ourselves, emerged from the nostalgia of Heidegger's eschatological thinking. Bare life, our very humanity, does not have to be reduced in this way. It has a future. Opening space for the future of bare life requires a re-conception of research as an event [*événement*] as something to come [*venir*]. But there is more work to be done before we arrive at what this means for research.

It is important first to uncover how the biopolitics of representation within research deals with the issue of representation and its relationship with bare life. The deconstruction that follows, therefore, emerged from a number of distinctive methodological acts on the stage set for research. It sought to examine the biopolitics of methodology that silences bare life and the issues arising from enframing.

Biopolitics: methodological acts

In concerning himself with the issue of 'representation', in terms of 'how the qualitative research process can be visualised', in *Social Research Methods,* in Alan Bryman's [2008: 370ff] ground plan, there is simply no mention of any 'state of exception'. Ironically, a measure of the full force of Bryman's biopolitics is given by his numerous references to 'reflexivity' [ibid: 426, 427, 441, 682–83, 698] that make no reference to the ontotheology at work.

Here, perhaps, the violence charged to Bryman's ground plan is better understood when it is appreciated that the axis of understanding around which the understandability of research organizes itself is that of quantitative research [ibid: 141]. In biopolitical terms, the latter is based upon the strategizing of truth claims once more as the basis for knowledge production. This simply excludes those aspects of *the* social world that exceed and do not fit with the conditional and possible dimensions of *the* world of *the* self, and of identities more generally, in accord with what in this fantasy world is re-presented as the movement of research towards calculation and quantification. His underlying suppositions concerning qualitative research are apparent in what is represented as its 'critique'. It underlines such research as being 'too subjective'. His 'critique' puts a spotlight on how qualitative research creates difficulties for replication, 'problems of generalisation' along with issues of 'transparency' concerned with what qualitative researchers 'actually *did* and how she or he arrived at the study's conclusions' [ibid: 392; emphasis as in the original]. Paradoxically, however, Bryman's critique is being selective in its reflexivity, and in serving to secure only its own regime, eliding completely bare life within his conception of research. Its biopolitical violence is now palpable. The very same violence continues to be reiterated in his more recent edition [Bryman, 2012: 380ff].

A similar violence is at work in Keith Punch's [2009] *Research Methods in Education,* where he draws his readers' attention to a 'hierarchy of concepts' and questions concerning the objects and subjects of research, rendering [*Zustellen*] human beings in a state of exception. Ironically, as long as researchers consider only the ethics of methodological questions concerning how to generate truth claims for knowledge gathered in *the present*, there is no reason given in this logic for considering the wider issue of the effects of such ethics upon bare life. Ironically, with the 'state of exception' exorcised from the internal logics of research, Punch's [2009] schema is entirely sound. Even more revisionist forms of research [Sulkunen, 2008] still remain locked within the horizon of being as presence, and the possibilities opened by bare life and the ontotheology driving enframing simply have no language of expression in such research.

Biopolitics: the criterionology of methodology

Another move in the development of methodologies of research that may possibly anticipate challenges to the existing structuring of research is that concerned with the criteria upon which the quality of such research may be evaluated. In biopolitical terms the traditional criteria of validity, reliability and so on presuppose a single truth that research aims to uncover – consonant with remaining within Plato's Pharmacy [Derrida, 1981b; Flint, 2013a,b,c]. Herein constitutes a ground for the production of truth claims to knowledge, once more silencing bare life. Even the alternative criteria for the trustworthiness of claims to knowledge based upon their 'credibility', 'transferability', 'dependability' and 'confirmability', first suggested by Lincoln and Guba [1985], tend to favour the reproduction of the ontotheological structuring driving enframing. They do so because the locus of such evaluation remains matters of the veracity and fidelity of the methodologies used to produce particular objects [and subjects] of knowledge on grounds of reason. Such objects [and subjects] are also evaluated upon grounds of the principle of assessment used within the paradigmatic structures of research, constituting another dimension of enframing [Flint and Peim, 2012; Peim and Flint, 2009]. At issue remains a basis for the evaluation of research constituted in *différance* that not only provides the basis for evaluating standards but also opens spacing for the possible regeneration of bare life for better or worse [Flint, in preparation, iv].

As we have seen earlier, the hegemonic cultures of training in research are also focused upon the methodologies used to generate truthful claims to knowledge. At the point of writing the biopolitics reproduced within such cultures, too, elides any reflexivity concerned with the state of exception. What is becoming apparent, therefore, is that there is a requirement and a responsibility to inaugurate a critical examination of the issue of enframing in research that is foregrounded by possibilities opened by qualitative research for 'bare life' that brings this notion into public use.

What is augured and expected is talk within languages opening both formal space for critical engagement with the issue of enframing and for possibilities of bare life being regenerated within the event of research.

Again one may anticipate that moves directed towards refiguring how validity is conceived, may open spacing for bare life and consideration of enframing within methodologies. In recent years there have been a number of different projections of understandings of how validity may be understood [Lincoln et al., 2011: 120–23], including the possibility of new criteria for the practice of social inquiry conceived as 'practical philosophy' [Schwandt 1996]. Lincoln and her colleagues [2011] also provide an authoritative review of a number of ways of understanding validity as authenticity. Although these open spacing for 'non-foundational' criteria, the basis for understanding such criteria used by this group remains located on the axis of 'objectivity' and 'subjectivity' [ibid: 121–22]. Though this remains located in *what is given* in the practice of research and within its ontotheology, the question remains concerning the spacing generated by such modalities of transgression in research and any possible implications it may have for the biopolitics of the state of exception.

A case in point is what Lincoln and her colleagues [2011: 122–23] have called 'transgressive validities'. They provide a useful summary of the issues concerned with 'transgressive validity' following the work of both Richardson [1994, 1997] and Lather [1993a]. Here we should keep in mind Richardson's [1997] work on the crystallization as a radical alternative to the triangulation of 'data' used in methodologies, generating space for what she describes as a *transgressive* form of validity. For her 'to see how transgression looks and how it feels' it is necessary to 'find and deploy methods that allow us to uncover the hidden assumptions and the life-denying repressions of sociology; resee/refeel sociology. Reseeing and retelling are inseparable' [ibid: 167; Lincoln et al., 2011: 123]. Here, in the possibility of the 'refeeling' and in the 'retelling' there is always the opportunity for opening space for the movement of those beings that are not conditional, calculable or possible that do not readily 'fit' within any ontotheological structuring driving enframing. Here too, there is the possibility in such retelling of opening thinking concerned with the hidden particularities of the unique worlds that ordinarily remain at best in a state of exception: currently such issues simply do not exist in the biopolitics of research. It has no language for them. These possibilities *have* yet to be given a re-constituted language of research, as 'event' [*événement*], opening scope for the regeneration of life.

Lincoln and her colleagues [2011: 123] also draw their readers' attention to another attempted radical interpretation of validity by Lather [1993a]. Lather's move towards justice is reflected in her attempts to rupture 'validity as a regime of truth' [ibid: 674]. It was her move towards the impossibility of displacing 'its historical inscription. . . via a dispersion, circulation and proliferation of counter-practices of authority that take the crisis of representation into account [ibid: 674]. In Lather's own 'simulacrum' posing as a 'transgressive validity checklist' she creates a helpful summary of what she calls 'ironic validity', 'paralogical validity', 'rhizomatic validity' and 'voluptuous validity' [Lather 2007a: 128–29]. The headlines from each of these criteria show that the direction of her thinking is closely aligned to moves towards emancipatory justice *in* research, for example:

Ironic validity

- Foregrounds the insufficiencies of language and the production of meaning-effects, produces truth as a problem. . .

- Disperses, circulates and proliferates forms, including the generation of research practices that take the crisis of representation into account.
- Creates analytical practices that are doubled without being paralysed. [Ibid: 128; emphasis as in the original]

Her text bears witness to the space opened for practice by ironic validity that is unconditional, impossible and incalculable [though she does not use these terms], consonant with silent moves towards justice. In Lather's moves towards the 'problematics of representation' in the context of the 'insufficiencies of language' there is also a nod in the direction of the uniqueness of each experience, again indicating a latent force in her work directed towards justice.

However, within Lather's practice lies another possible index of the hegemonic powers at work in training regimes for researchers. She would appear to remain wedded to the foregrounding of the production of truth claims to knowledge as if, somehow, truth exists as a building block for research in accord with the falsehood of the principle of being. Lather indicates that her work may be located within the specialist discipline of 'post-structuralism' [ibid: 120]. Lincoln and her colleagues [2011] arrive at the same interpretation – they locate both Richardson's [1994, 1997] and Lather's [1993a] explorations of 'transgressive validities' within a 'poststructural' order [ibid: 122–23]. Lather's [2007a] more recent writings remain within the same specialist disciplinary structure and appears to have been accepted without further question. But, these paradigms, disciplinary structures, data, truths are *not* building blocks for research located in the present – they come into being only to the extent that we continue to reiterate and regenerate these patterns. This requires as we showed earlier the interplay of present and futural horizons for the event of research.

Biopolitics: Technologies of research

Both Richardson and Lather in their own particular ways appear to miss completely the relationship of their 'transgressive criteria' with the unfolding of technology or bare life. Their own individual standpoints are each located within an extant disciplinary structure for research and so run the risk of their potentially radical conceptions being displaced and removed from any possible critique of such structure.

Three issues that emerge as a consequence of thinking about the relationship between the naming force and gathering powers of being and research will illuminate the significance of such a relationship for bare life that is in need of its formal inauguration in all fields of research.

Bare life – futural horizons

Neither Laurel Richardson nor Patti Lather would appear to thematize the language of temporality. But, in her exploration of 'writing as a method of inquiry', Richardson [2000] speaks about 'how we write affects what we write about' [ibid: 927] and she provokes her readers to explore different genres in their writing [ibid: 931]. In such a challenge, therefore, there is always the possibility of researchers working with the constitution of *différance*. However, in placing their transgressive validities within the present – in locating them within a poststructuralist paradigm – ironically both Lather and Richardson serve to reproduce *the* world of research. There is always then the danger of their discourses being reiterated in the 'eternal return of the same will-to-power' manifest in conflicting, contested and sometimes contradictory forms of intelligibility.

But, if their transgressive validities were to be reformulated within a futural horizon in the constitution of *différance* then there is every possibility of opening spacing for thinking, too, concerned with enframing and the possibilities open to bare life [Flint, in preparation, iv]. Deconstructive language, constituted as *différance*, opens spacing for the possibilities of bare life.

Bare life: Constitution in *différance*

In order to make sense of Derrida's approach to deconstruction it is important to really dig down and find out more about what is meant by his term *différance* and just why *the gathering of beings no longer makes sense* and how it cuts through the metaphysical directions given by a multiplicity of other phenomenological terms. This is a move in the direction of justice because the horizon of *différance* is futural and in its play in all identities it awakens us to the unique particularities of experience, of history and of the symbolism of the 'spectral-other' at play in each identity. But, let us remove all of these connecting ideas and imagery in the metonymy of methodological research and return once more to the issue of the constitution of *différance* and its opening of spacing for possibilities in bare life.

Strictly speaking *différance* surpasses any identity – truth, knowledge, paradigm, data – because its movement is what makes any identity in research possible. What makes this movement possible is that any such identity's 'present' elements are 'related to something other than' themselves' [ibid: 142] – that is, each element is already unconditionally positioned by historic narratives – such as those inscribed within paradigms – that fold over and press in on any present identity found in research. This movement of spacing already marks the present with past elements. Equally, the movement of such identity is always related to the future, and without this relationship there would be no possibility of change. So, 'this movement [of *différance*] keeps the mark of past elements reflecting such qualities' [Derrida, 1973a: 142]: those moods, dispositions, fragments that appear in the memory of the identities. What is represented in 'the present', then, is always corrupted by the imperfection of its relationship with the future of such an identity that is always unknowable. Those idle dreams, partly formed visions, thoughts, ideas that point towards the possibilities suggested by this identity found in research are all likely to render it imperfect. This is the movement of '*différance*' [Derrida 1976: 142–43]. Its movement is unconditional and always already exceeds its disciplinary apparatus. This movement of *différance*' is already there cultivating research as an event [*événement*]. As something coming [*venir*] its spacing is not only opened by the deconstruction of research, it awakens thinking to the possibilities of something 'to come' [*á-venir*] in bare life.

But, in accord with the foregrounding of truth claims to knowledge, in the economies of signs reiterated within research such a play of '*différance*' is completely elided by the viral fantasy of objective language emerging from quantification that is also coming to infect qualitative research. The training [*educare*] in *the* world of research and dimensions of *educere* currently leading researchers out in the name of delimiting education [that is cultivating and being cultivated within the pre-judicial paradigmatic structures of research, Table 2.1] serve only to refine and to develop quantification as *the* logic of truth claims. The *aporia* of authentic education, therefore, constituted in the play of *différance* in any identity then reveals the 'undecidables'[1] that have been swept aside in the language of the marketization and aligned objectification and quantification of research.

In educational and political terms there is good reason why there should be much more critical debate concerned with quantification and objectification in the language of formal systems of research. Not least within every identity found in research the play of *différance* that makes signification possible in the first place is itself *incalculable*. For example, there can be no movement and transformation of the logics of quantification without the incalculable. As we have indicated already, 'there is an interval that must separate any identity represented in the present from what it is not – those marks of the past and the future' [ibid: 143] – for this identity re-presented in the present, to be itself. As Derrida [1973a] points out 'this interval that constitutes it as present must, by the same token, divide the present in and of itself' [ibid: 143]. Any re-presented identity in research – and here quantification is not somehow excluded – is always fissured and haunted by the double play of its past and any visions it points towards in the unknowable future. Quantification has no answer to this issue, except by recourse to the logics grounding its own regime of truth.

For many possible critics this consideration of *différance* may all seem to be matters of purely academic interest. Certainly, from the experience of the IAPD and ICPD conferences though there is much interest in *practice* per se, it would seem that the forces delimiting education absorb participants back into paradigmatic forms of compartmentalization as soon as the conferences have been concluded. But, in our everyday world every one of us continually draws upon the play of *différance*. Without it we could not make sense of existence. Its very play, always dividing and fissuring the present, makes *impossible* any objective presence.

The real struggle to which Agamben [2009] had referred earlier, concerning the movements to create the identity of a subject in the play between the apparatus of research and the beings working here arises from the biopolitics of bare life. But, the impossible, incalculable and unconditional elements of the play of *différance,* constituting vital dimensions at play in all our identities and in the lived world of human beings, are easily brushed aside in the name of objectivity and the transparency of truth claims. Tacitly, however, in the on-going flow of everyday life these dimensions are all inimitable to the particular ways in which each of our identities and our life-worlds unfolds in such practice. The *aporia* of authentic education emerging from the constitution of *différance* does not mean that such apparatuses are somehow to be swept aside. In ethical terms it returns us once more to the moves towards justice and its relationship with extant research. Such moves towards justice work with deconstruction in order to exceed and to open dispute in aspects of extant laws of research.

Authentic education constituted in the play of *différance,* therefore, continually opens spacing for critical reflection upon the expansion of ethics in research. It embraces the pivotal issue of moves towards justice. At issue once more is the naming force and gathering powers of being as presence at work in research. In the inauguration and initiation of the public use [Heidegger's '*das Man*] of the *aporia* of authentic education emerging from the play of *différance,* there is a third and pivotal issue concerning the significance of the relationship between being as presence and extant research that deserves to be considered.

Bare life: Value positing

All research in some ways reflects the particular value positions adopted by researchers. At issue is the 'idea' in research [Table 2.1]. It has become so common to express values that it becomes almost impossible to understand the powers at work in this language. But, if we are serious about making sense of bare life, then we need to take the plunge and think back to our earlier deconstruction of values. Ironically, in the context of the governance of research, particularly in the United States and in the United Kingdom, with moves towards more positivistic measures of research, where 'being is reduced to an object, values are made the issue of the subject' [Caputo, 1987: 236]. Such agencies, therefore, are in danger of being entrapped as instruments of ontotheology. This does not mean that somehow values should be eschewed; it simply alerts readers to the sublime powers at work in such an everyday phenomenon.

In more familiar terms of contemporary *Society of the Spectacle*, such enframing and the capital it produces is manifest in neo-liberalist agendas with their drives towards competition in the marketplace that are currently being continually re-fuelled by research [Flint, in preparation, ii]. It further underlines the need for authentic education in research. This is an education balancing the ever-enhancing intensity and extensity of the powers at work in contemporary research in this age of information [Flint, 2013a].

Here one is almost shocked by the pedagogic force delimiting education in research and its effects upon bare life.

Bare life: Pedagogic reconstruction of research

Consideration of the foregoing three issues makes apparent almost unconsciously in much everyday practice that research serves to re-contextualize bare life as objects of consciousness within Aristotle's 'good life'. Each of the paradigms constitutes its own particular ways of understanding the latter. Herein lies a pedagogical dimension to the forces delimiting education at work in research. In pedagogical terms the work of such 'delimiting education' is, according to Bernstein [2000], a matter of applying the principle of 're-contextualisation' [ibid: 33], so that new knowledge becomes re-packaged in an understandable form for a public audience. Thematization, outcomes, findings, pivotal ideas from authoritative theorists and so on are all used as familiar pedagogic devices. Re-packaged, the complexities of practice are often re-presented as apparently familiar generic processes of research.

Placing emphases upon truth claims and knowledge production, such pedagogy delimiting education in research serves to fulfil a biopolitical function. This is easily missed because it has become so familiar. Both the forces delimiting education and the biopolitics of research serve to ground truth claims concerned with bare life upon the principle of reason connecting subject with object, or upon the basis of one of its contemporary progeny [Flint and Peim 2012; Flint, in preparation, ii]. Such truth claims are then packaged and neatly compartmentalized within specialist domains of paradigmatic research.

In radicalizing Bernstein's [2000] principle of pedagogy as a cultural phenomenon rather than in terms foregrounding the agency of individuals, essentially the way research re-contextualizes bare life, is by formal means of the ontotheological structuring driving enframing [Table 2.1]. It points to a pedagogic function for all research that deserves to be challenged because of its silencing of bare life. But, bare life constitutes our future. Ordinarily, in placing an emphasis upon the quality of knowledge production and truth claims arising from research, both the forces delimiting education and the biopolitics of bare life dissimulate completely any issues arising from its ontotheology. And bare life remains without any express discourse.

Authentic education alerts researchers to the hidden forces at work delimiting education and the biopolitics of bare life. Authentic education in *the* world of practice makes plain the pedagogic significance of the ontotheology that finds its culmination in paradigmatic forms of research. Authentic education continually sounds a warning bell to researchers, therefore, reminding them that such hidden forces serve only to drive the self from itself. The *aporia* of authentic education, therefore, has much work to do in opening space for the critical examination of the ways in which the contemporary 'meaning makers' for beings in research – namely, the principles of reason, of assessment [Flint and Peim, 2012] and of the market [Flint, in preparation, ii] – are always in danger of moving humanity into the simulacra of a 'matrix'[2]-like existence.

The driving force of such authentic education is justice to come. It is constituted as we have seen in the play of *différance*. More tangibly for research, perhaps, although Lather [2007b] does not foreground *différance* in her paper, what could be called her bare act of methodology begins to uncover some of the issues at stake in authentic education in research.

Bare acts of methodology

The case in point in Lather's work arises from a discussion with three other colleagues that she identifies as an 'interlude' and as 'naked methodology', carrying with it a brilliant [though unintended] play on bare life and its pedagogical re-contextualization in research methodology, expressed in her own understandings of a 'double[d] science'. More concretely, Lather [2007b] herself also chose to be 'naked in the Jacuzzi, surrounded by women, all dressed, as they asked questions' [ibid: 49] about her early conceptualizations of a 'project on writing the lives of women with HIV/AIDS' [ibid: 49]. She also chose to identify herself informally as 'Patti' as another sign of her double play that was there questioning the extant order.

In the context of her project, *Standing with Angels: Women and HIV/AIDS*, 'Patti' and her colleagues recorded their discussions emerging from her express interest in matters of what she calls 'double science, double gestures, double writing' [ibid: 49] that related in some way with two of her colleagues' dissertations. She had been concerned that their research would somehow do the women 'injustice' [ibid: 51]. She had been 'so struck by' the 'generosity' of the women to 'one another' [ibid: 51]. In reflecting critically upon her own practice 'Patti' went on to raise a question: 'what does it mean to use other people's lives as data?' [ibid: 52].

As Agamben [2009] has made plain, such reductions of people into data arises in the process of 'de-subjectification', out of which, in their struggle and those of the researchers, there is the possibility of becoming active subjects. But, here is to be found a tacit requirement for authentic education constituted in the play of *différance*, which is given greater poignancy in this case. It finds expression in another question raised by 'Patti': 'Why do I want them [the women with HIV/Aids] to be data, rather than my teachers?' [ibid: 51]. At issue in her silent appeal here to authentic education are moves towards justice.

In many senses of their unspoken direction of travel towards justice, Lather and her colleagues were struggling for a form of inquiry and a way of writing with the women that would respect the uniqueness of the lives and experiences of each of the women with HIV/AIDS. Part of that struggle was located in the realization of the violence inscribed in extant cultures of research and 'Patti's' express very real concern that she would 'kill them' with her 'high theory' [ibid: 51].

Ironically, however, the real issue remains the absence of any express language concerned with enframing that many critics are likely to regard mistakenly as more 'high theory'. Enframing is one such form of language. As we have seen it gives expression to the complex ever-unfolding relationship of researchers and others with the naming force and gathering powers of being as presence. Bare life is Janus faced. For Heidegger in looking back enframing provided a rationale for generating what he saw as a new beginning in philosophy. In looking to the future in research, the other side of this Janus face reveals bare life. In this way the discussions concerned with 'naked methodology' for Patti and her colleagues then give expression to the play of *différance* making concrete the possibilities of bare life for the women in their research.

Such terminology can be easily placed on the sidelines as 'high theory' because it is initially unfamiliar. Although Lather did not share the technical languages of enframing, of bare life, she had recognized the contradictions at work in her study. In her research, aspects of the women's lives had been significantly reduced to 'data' – that which is given and available for use. The violence of the logic inscribed in this pedagogical re-contextualization of aspects of the lives of these women with HIV/Aids in the name of research opened for her the real anxiety that she would 'kill them' in her own writing. The possibility of death was never far away. In this context Lather and her colleagues' research can be seen as a work of mourning that is directed towards keeping alive beings and their possibilities – opening space for bare life.

After working with these women, it was apparent from her writing, Lather's moves towards justice for this group had arisen from her deeply held respect for the courage, vitality and the unique voices of each of these women as beings whose express sense of being went far beyond any 'data' that the group of researchers may collect from them. Paradoxically, however, as another aspect of the double play, at the time 'Patti' and her colleagues did not have the language to express precisely the violence being done to the lives of those women in the name of ethically legitimated research. Yet, the bare life of each of the women gave expression to a wellspring of energy and vitality that currently appears to remain largely beyond the capacity of current hegemonic forms of research to make any formal sense of it.

In this reading of Lather and her colleagues' [2007b] writings, their concerns could be seen as being directed towards resolving the ways in which formal research, in its pedagogical re-contextualization of aspects of the lives of the women with HIV/AIDS, had served to generate another constitution for these women in a 'state of exception' [Agamben, 1998, 2005]. Here is another locus for authentic education in *différance*, opening spacing for bare life. Another dimension of any such authentic education involves uncovering the significance of bare life where it is swept to the side as an exception in those fantasies of objectivity and truth.

Here methodology opened in the name of bricolage underlines some of the issues at stake in drawing upon an authentic education in *différance* for research.

Acts of methodology

The case in point here is Kincheloe's [2008a] own research act in his reading of 'Critical Pedagogy and the Knowledge Wars of the Twenty-First Century'. For two decades the Canadian professor of research at McGill, Kincheloe had emerged as the international leader in this field until his death in December 2008. In examining critically Kincheloe's methodology it is important to keep in mind that his research act constitutes another gathering of identities in the name of bricolage. It therefore remains within the existing traditions and the paradigm constituted by critical theory, in its politics of plenitude and in its continued extension of regimes of power. But, as a rigorous methodological approach to uncovering the multiplicity of dimensions of complexity in the social world, bricolage in the hands of Kincheloe is there to expose and to make real what he sees as the elision and dissimulation of such complexity by the 'crypto-positivists' who in their re-presentations of 'evidence'-based practice closely align themselves with the powers of governmentality.

In the words of Kincheloe [2008a: 4] 'our critical pedagogical effort to thwart these power plays involves engaging in a transformative multilogicality'. This may appear to be a move towards justice, and undoubtedly this was Kincheloe's intention. But, ironically, in remaining located within the politics of plenitude, he sought to gather other signs in an attempt to transform the extant order in research, amounting to a reiteration of the same social order, along with the continued intensification and extension of its powers. Unfortunately, his discursive practice remains stubbornly locked up within the very same 'will-to-power' expressed in his projected understandings of bricolage.

Understandably, at issue for Kincheloe was always the 'corporatist powers' of governmental agencies in their alignment with what he calls the 'protopositivists' in their endless moves towards enlarging stocks of capital. The networking [Castells 2009] on a globalized stage set for what are ironically mostly conceived as technological developments in our contemporary world serves only to ensure that the goliath of the corporatist and governmental empires at work on this particular stage enjoy a continued and unabated freedom to move above and on the surface of our 'liquid modern' world [Bauman 2011]. But, this is not a matter for Kincheloe, or possibly one of his fellow critical pedagogues, such as Giroux, appearing in the guise of the character David, symbolizing the operation of the bricolage, in a re-run of the Ancient parable on a stage set by bricolage. In assuming the identity of 'David' in accord with the Ancient parable, the politics of plenitude adopted by Kincheloe, Giroux and others within the critical theory tradition will always fall short of slaying the goliath of all those corporate and governmental bodies. Its language is much more likely to be located within a state of exception by such powers. Nor is it simply a matter of engaging the interests of a whole possible army of such David-characters, all in their own way working with what is at hand in their various bricolages.

The failure of critical theorists is not just a matter of the sociology of the liquid modern world, although that remains an issue. The issue is the locus of Kincheloe and his critical theorists' standpoint within the politics of plenitude and its presuppositions. Until now, it would seem little consideration has been given in research to the sublime powers of the ontotheology driving enframing.

This is not a matter of somehow using the powers of imagination associated with other forms of language that may have been indicated by earlier references to poesy, or even of writing stories of research using different genres as Laurel Richardson [2000] suggested. For example, in another genre William Wordsworth's poetic exploration of the powers of imagination in *The Prelude*[3] is also based upon the plenitude and fulfilment of identity:

Imagination – here the Power so called
Through sad incompetence of human speech,
That awful Power rose from the mind's abyss. . .

Poesy is not a panacea; the poetic imagination can still remain caught up in the gathering powers of being as presence just as research. What is demanded is the kick-starting of radically different ways of practicing research drawing from the constitution of *différance*. At issue are moves towards justice through a radicalized form of bricolage, identified here in terms of deconstruction, that work on the presupposition that what is at hand in research is the nothing. It has been argued that this demands nothing less than the *aporia* of an authentic education in *différance*, directed towards a critical examination of all principal dimensions of research activity, not the least of which are the following:

- The corporatist funding agencies for research;
- Governmental agencies and agencies of higher education involved with research;
- Methodologies, paradigms and epistemes currently used in research along with their analysis and evaluation;
- Dissemination of research activity on the public stage within a range of media illuminating beautifully the play of *différance*;
- Quality assurance agencies currently shaping how research is conducted

The training arising from this authentic education in *différance* should be directed towards removing grounds for the ever-enhancing powers of the corporatists whose interests in research serve to retain versions of *The Society of the Spectacle* [Debord, 1977]. The training would be concerned with opening critical dialogue, opening reflection upon the extant structuring of the laws of research and its language. Its moral compass is directed towards both balancing the hubristic powers inscribed in traditional forms of research and opening resources in bare life for those dispossessed, marginalized and crushed in so many ways by the forces delimiting education within '*the society of the spectacle*'. Qualitative research and practice-based forms of inquiry both provide many rich and challenging examples of such events, but at the point of writing there remains no discourse that connects these various events in ways that question the sovereign powers at work in '*the spectacle*'.

Authentic education in *différance* opens spacing for moves towards justice. But, here it is vital to keep in mind the *aporia* of the 'non-way' that 'we have to face constantly' [Derrida, 1999: 73]. As Derrida suggests, in research 'pathbreaking implies *aporia*' [ibid: 73]. From this perspective it is suggested that 'the impossibility to find one's way is the condition of ethics' [ibid: 73] in research. Certainly, at the point of writing any biopolitical concerns directed towards uncovering both the particularities of the unique worlds in which each of us as human beings live, do not carry with them any methodological way-markers. As we have seen methodology currently remains largely silent on the matter of uncovering bare life. But, deconstruction at least reveals the cinders of what remains from bare life.

Finding a way in the *aporia* of authentic education means taking on the responsibility of working with the existing pre-judicial structures [Table 2.1] inscribed within the many traditions of research. It means deconstructing those pre-judicial structures in research constituting the *trompe-l'œil* of 'transparency' currently 'delimiting education' in research. The locus of the latter lies in the gathering powers and naming force of being as presence. The challenge of authentic education, therefore, is to alert us, as we are here, to the ways in which being as presence is shaping research and in so doing silencing bare life.

But, there still remains the issue of the methods used in research.

CHAPTER EIGHT

Transformations-in methods: Opening space for beings

Ordinarily methods provide a focus for what needs to be done by the researcher in order to collect data in response to [a] particular question [s] or hypothesis [es]. But, such moves rarely, if ever, take account of the biopolitics involved, or, the deconstruction of *what is given* in the practice of using methods, as distinct from their representation within the literature. Let us first open thinking, therefore, on the issue of what is given in methods, where the direction of travel once more is moves towards justice.

Such moves generate spacing for methods constituted by *différance*, exceeding the coded space generated within current cultures of research. As we have seen this can be achieved through deconstruction, continually alerting us to the double play and the fissuring of the presence of any representation of identity concerned with methods. Already, in biopolitical terms, our earlier deconstructions have awakened us to a multiplicity of beings emerging in the world of identities revealed by existing methods of qualitative inquiry. At issue remains just how methods may help in uncovering rather than dissimulating the often hidden and unique worlds of human beings, of bare life and of the play of *différance* in identities that often become lost behind representations of 'evidence,' 'outcomes' and 'findings' from research.

In this matter the question remains as to the extent to which methods are enacted in ways that reveal the play of *différance* before its reduction to subjects and objects of research.

At issue in the deconstruction that follows, therefore, are the ways in which existing methods are already revealing the play of *différance*, exceeding their possible reduction to economies of signs constituted on grounds of reason. We are attempting to uncover from the writings of research beings constituted in the play of *différance* that do not readily fit into the ontotheology of research. In moving to explore this issue what will emerge is much more detail concerned with the biopolitical violence of methods used in the human sciences.

The writing is divided into two steps. The opening step will focus upon the biopolitical violence inscribed in research methods. The final step is presented as a series of case studies, illuminating a number of challenges to the ways in which methods are organized and conducted. As we found before with both the paradigms and the methodologies, while such challenges point to various possibilities for bare life, once again the language of biopolitics, of authentic education and of delimiting education, along with enframing and bare life, are notable for their absence.

In the Janus face of bare life we now see the biopolitics of research renders one side in a state of exception with all its potential and possibilities. Viewed from the other side it reveals a sublime reservoir of capital and the locus of commodification in the form of lakes of energy and possibilities constituted in enframing. For example, one such reservoir is identified as the knowledge economy. The question of the nature of the relationship between these two sides will have to wait until the final chapters. The question also remains as to whether extant methods serve to open space and possibilities for bare life. In part this is a matter of styling our methods.

Styling methods

In concerning ourselves with what is given in research during the course of the methods used, it is helpful to introduce the language of the 'styles' of practice employed in *Disclosing New Worlds* by Charles Spinosa and his colleagues [1997]. In being concerned once more with the issue of the transformation of research as an event, the question remains concerning the extent to which the metaphysical spaces constituted by current methods open possibilities for change in our relationship with such methods. Here the focus upon their possible transformation will centre not upon any possible metaphysical determination of 'style', but upon their styling. The latter term already recognizes that any possible 'style' is already marked by past elements and is continually open to corruptions by its relationship with the future.

In remaining with the metaphysics, Charles Spinoza and his colleagues [1997: 19] suggest that style is the way that practices fit together – they see style, not as one aspect among many, but rather that 'style constitutes' things 'as what they are' [ibid: 19]. It is a style of practice, according to their argument, that opens 'disclosive space' [ibid: 20]. It does so in a threefold manner by:

- coordinating actions;
- determining how things and people matter; and,
- being what is transferred from situation to situation. [Ibid: 20]

Although these authors' formulation of style and space provide us with metaphysical determinations of practice, in moves towards justice such understandings can now enjoy a deconstructive reading of styling [rather than style] constituted in the play of *différance*. In such play the identity, method, is not a simple given. As Derrida suggests in *Positions* [1981a], 'each allegedly simple term' such as 'method' 'is marked by the trace of another term' – not least, methodologies, practices, what is done, holding apart the researcher and her objects and so on. Thus, 'the presumed interiority of meaning is always worked upon by its exteriority' [ibid: 33], and in *practice* the meanings of methods change with the traces of the spectral-other.

In moves towards justice in this deconstructive reading of the styling of methods that follows we will be concerned, therefore, with deconstructing these three functions of style emerging in the traces of research and in particular its biopolitics. At issue in considering the styling of methods is the regeneration of spacing for bare life. Such moves towards the re-conception of research as an event are consonant with the *aporia* of authentic education emerging from the constitution of *différance*.

Authentic education emerging from the cultures of research demands nothing less than the responsibility to uncover from deconstruction the unconditional, impossible and incalculable dimensions of the practices arising from using methods of research, opening spacing for bare life. In being concerned with the styling of methods there remain questions concerning the relationship between metaphysical representations of practice and the unfolding dynamics of *practice* itself constituted in the play of *différance*, that is, by 'the systematic play of differences, of the traces of differences, of the spacing by means of which elements are related to each other' [Derrida, 1981a: 27].

Practising research

In adopting standpoints derived from critical theory, in their *Student's Guide to Methodology,* there is a hint of such play of difference for Peter Clough and Cathy Nutbrown [2012] in their observation that 'the job of method is only to hold apart the researcher and her objects so that we can tell the difference between them' [ibid: 31]. In this matter these authors hold on to the notion of method as 'procedures and techniques for gathering data'. They advise their readers that methods do not constitute what *is* or 'even describe it'. Rather they suggest that method reveals the 'circumstances in which the researcher' constitutes a particular object, and it 'normally seek[s] to provide a guarantee that researcher and object are distinct from each other' [ibid: 31]. Once again it is apparent that the strategizing of truth claims provides this telic focus upon objects of consciousness.

The styling of methods in the traditions of research, therefore, opens a deconstructive reading of the axis of understanding connecting subjects with objects, around which understandability organizes itself. Particular styles are each constituted on grounds of Husserl's [1960, 1970, [1973{1939}, 1983] phenomenology. Their biopolitics then renders the 'desubjectification' [Agamben, 2009: 20] of human beings and other identities – the subjects of research – that are reduced to 'data'. Its albeit unannounced violence in silencing bare life, it has become so much part of everyday practice it is unlikely to shock readers into becoming conscious of whether bare life may at least emerge from research as its active subject.

In practising methods of research such violence also determines that people and other identities it features are all subjects of the politics of plenitude. As we have seen in such politics there is a complete elision of what we are working with in research, namely, the 'cinders' and 'traces' of identities. Ironically, in this form of politics lies one of the principal drivers for re-working, re-fining and re-developing aspects of the methodological practices of research; but such practices will never become perfectly complete despite such drivers. Social practice is always necessarily incomplete. The biopolitical violence imparted in accord with the politics of plenitude lies in its complete elision of the traces of existence. But, human beings are unconditionally incomplete, not least in virtue of our relationship with the possibility of death, with the mystery of earth, the unknowable Other, the undecidable. Ironically, the politics of plenitude shaping identities will always necessarily fall short of bringing them to fulfilment.

The driving force of such violence in the politics of plenitude, however, is not so much the methodological and philosophical considerations given here, as the strategizing of truth claims to objects of knowledge becoming commodities within the capitalist world. Such thinking is often dissimulated below the mirage created from headline representations of the knowledge economy that appear on our screens.

T.S. Eliot's poesy in The Waste Land[1] evokes the imagery of:

> *Unreal City*
> . . .
> *A crowd flowed over London Bridge, so many,*
> *I had not thought death had undone so many,*

The question remains, then, as to the nature of the silent voice of bare life calling from the language of research and just whether the styling of methods used may reveal more concerning bare life.

With regard to the matter of methods used in research Margo Alastalo's [2008: 26–41] *History of Social Research Methods* lays emphasis upon both the methods of data collection and of analyzing data. These are echoes from the Greek, *μέθοδος* [methodos], connoting the pursuit of knowledge and the Latin, *methodos*, meaning a mode of proceeding [OED]. But, she makes no reference to the play of *différance*. Indeed,

Clough and Nutbrown's [2012] silent ontotheology structuring method as ways of writing and speaking about research that determine the basis *upon which* there is a complex inter-relationship between researcher and the beings of concern to her remains without deconstruction. And, once again the significance of such modalities of research for bare life in our relationship with essential forms of technology would not appear to have been examined in these terms.

In silently drawing from the meaning maker of reason, in their writings Denzin and Lincoln [2005, 2011] continue to open spacing for significant innovations and advances in the methods and methodologies of qualitative forms of research. Their silent biopolitics, however, remains in foregrounding bare life. For example, in Lincoln and her colleagues [2011: 101–15] analytical summary of 'constructivism' [or interpretivism], they open space for manifold realities that 'exist in the form of multiple mental constructions' that are 'socially and experientially based', being 'local and specific [and] dependent for their form and content on the persons who hold them' [Guba, 1990: 27]. Once more bare life remains in a 'state of exception', and the biopolitical significance of the disclosive spacing of such beings, however, is not yet regarded as an issue.

Lincoln and her colleagues' [2011: 101–15] idiom for ontology in remaining structured around the foregrounding of knowledge generates a space reducing down the possibilities of being to those objects of consciousness that focus the subjectivity of the researcher – in terms of the multiple mental constructions, social experience and so on. In accord with their own projected understandings of the 'relativism' inscribed within this ontology for research, they cite Guba and Lincoln [2005: 193], for whom 'local and specific constructed realities and co-constructed realities' constitute such 'relativism' [Lincoln et al., 2011: 102]. In conclusion Lincoln and her colleagues [2011] reflect:

> *we construct knowledge through our lived experiences and through interactions with other members of society. As such, as researchers, we must participate in the research process with our subjects to ensure we are producing knowledge that is reflective of their reality.* [Ibid: 102; emphasis as in the original]

Here there is a strong but unspoken sense of a move towards uncovering the uniqueness of the interiority of the self in each case consonant with moves towards justice, opening spacing for bare life. But, in their metaphysical production of knowledge there is constituted a means–ends structuring, connecting the researcher as 'subject' with 'knowledge' as the object of consciousness consonant with enframing. Although ontologically their grounds for such research are the rigorous *actions* undertaken by researchers, and their theology is implicit in the *organization* of this particular form of research, Lincoln and her colleagues would appear not yet to have deconstructed the problematic implications of such ontotheology.

It might be anticipated that a 'postmodern', 'participatory' heuristic used in inquiry [Lincoln et al., 2011: 102] constitutes a provocation to the ontotheology of enframing. But, no such challenge is on the table. Though in Lincoln and her colleagues' [2011] current idiom there are many implicit spaces opened for beings in such 'participative reality', its constitution remains located upon Husserl's axis of ontology connecting 'subjectivity' with the 'objectivity' of consciousness [ibid: 102]. The production of such spaces for the unfolding of bare life is already presupposed by their citations from a number of works that exemplify the 'participatory' heuristic in the production of knowledge. They include Heshusius' 'freedom from objectivity' arising from 'a new understanding of the relation of the self and other' [Heshusius, 1994: 15 cited by Lincoln et al., 2011: 102] and Kilgore's [2001] reflection that social construction 'does not assume that rationality is a means to better knowledge' [ibid: 54; cited by Lincoln et al., 2011: 102]. Again, and significantly, the spaces wordlessly produced for 'freedom', for the self's relationship with 'the other', point to the constitution of beings in the play of *différance*, thus opening to disputation our relationship with essential forms of technology. Although Lincoln and her colleagues' [2011] citation from Kilgore [2001] illuminates questions raised about means–ends structuring, its consequences in terms of enframing fall short of generating any current language of expression within research.

At issue is the closing down of the unspoken spacing for beings to that of space for a specified relationship between what are re-presented as forms of 'subjective and objective reality' [Lincoln et al., 2011: 102]. In the space produced within Lincoln and her colleagues' current idiom, although it points towards possibilities for bare life, such possibilities are continually closed down, according to Heron and Reason [1997; cited by Lincoln et al., 2011: 102] to relationships between 'knowers who can only be known by other knowers'. The hegemonic culture of the hermeneutical means–ends structured circular logic generating these heuristics is self-sustaining and is predicated on assumptions concerned with the privileging of knowledge, deferred from signs drawn from Newton and Bacon and their contemporaries in the seventeenth century. The repetition and reiteration of the ideological circular logic of what is given in practice serves only to drive enframing within its ontotheological structures, here constituted in terms of what is done in practice [ontological grounds] within paradigmatic and disciplinary structures of research [its theological structuring].

It was interesting to find out, therefore, to what extent feminist forms of research might question the reiteration of signs in such circular logics [which are always broken].

Practising critical theory

Pertti Alasuutari and her colleagues [2009: 265–67] present radical feminist perspectives on data collection and research against the backdrop created by a paper concerned with 'modern measurement in social sciences' [Bovaird and Embretson, 2008: 269–89]. The latter paper reflects on the logics of 'meaningful metrics'. However, any understandings of the 'meaning maker' of reason, of metaphysics more generally, at work, as examples of technological enframing, are notable for their absence. Currently, the forces delimiting education in research emerging from its cultures, as we have suggested earlier, are conceived only in terms of performativity, reflecting drives towards the perfectibility of research in its desire for truth. This is one of the ironies of the forces delimiting education, because in relation to the traces of identities [in which there is always already the play of the spectral-other] there is always an inexorable and almost ineluctable rationale to improve their quality.

In Susan Speer's [2008] review of 'Natural and Contrived Data' she cites 'C. Kitzinger's [2000: 170] observation that 'little feminist research is conducted using naturalistic data where gender and sexuality just "happen" to be present' [Speer, 2008: 292]. In presenting 'gender as an interesting case for an analysis of the relative virtues of natural and contrived data' she also agrees with Kitzinger's position. One might expect that what Speer's identifies as natural data may open space for methods that challenge the biopolitical order within research. But, her review concentrates on the technical matter of identifying the variety of different naturalistic data collection techniques employed, including 'natural conversation' [Sacks et al., 1974: 698], 'natural conversational materials' [Schlegoff and Sacks, 1973: 291], 'actual utterances in ordinary conversations' [Schlegoff, 1988: 61], 'actual occurring data' [Heritage and Atkinson, 1984: 18] and 'actual, empirical, naturally occurring garden variety actions [Schlegoff, 1996a: 166]. In all cases cited, ironically, the focus remains upon the methods used in order to make truth claims to knowledge from such naturalistic data, rather than the implications for the biopolitics of research and its silencing of 'bare life'.

In Speer's [2008] own terms, when she reflects upon 'three reasons feminist researchers have been reluctant to stray from the use of contrived materials' [ibid: 292–3], the focus remains upon knowledge production. Although in her review she speaks of 'feminist researchers' who 'deal with topics they deem too sensitive, private or delicate to be accessed in their home environments [e.g., talk about sex, infidelity, sexual harassment, rape, incest and so on]' Speer makes no explicit mention of the significance of the unique 'worlds' of the women involved [ibid: 293]. In her concluding 'discussion' Speer indicates that 'the use of naturalistic material will become more common' [ibid: 307]. It remains an open question as to whether in the name of justice to come some thought might also be given to the biopolitics of research and the ways in which naturalistic forms of inquiry might be employed in moves towards questioning the ontotheology of research.

In recognizing that Speer has been caught up by the gathering powers and the full force of being as presence, one understands the urgency arising wordlessly from the drives of enframing, concentrating attention upon actions taken in the name of 'methods'. It is such actions that constitute the very grounds for enframing in virtue of the 'meaning maker' at work in her research, namely, reason. Her study also reveals that it is structured in theological terms by reflecting upon what is considered to be real in this method – namely, the fact of participants talking and through their talk giving examples of 'sexist talk'. Here is the precise locus of the highest order of beings arising from this particular specialist area of research. Some measure of the silent force constituted by enframing is given by Speer's idiomatic use of 'capturing' data, such as that identified as 'sexist talk' [ibid: 293].

Speer's [2008] idiom for social research is not considered to be universal for feminists by any means, although it is entirely consonant with the prejudicial structuring of a number of leading archives of research,[2[Introduction]] wherein demands are made upon researchers to address their research in this invented world of 'objectivity'.

Once more the strategizing of truth claims to knowledge is at the heart of such practices. In terms of styling the locus of coordination and what determines how things and people matter, it is not the actions of particular individuals, but rather the 'meaning maker' of reason grounding enframing that remains an issue [Heidegger, 1962, 1977, 1991]. Moves towards justice, therefore, require nothing less than taking on the responsibility of deconstructing such forms of practice.

In the cases that follow each of the researchers has taken on the responsibility of attempting to confront aspects of methods employed. In each case the disputations they present in their writings currently remain with the extant paradigmatic and epistemic structuring of research. Consequently, in this deconstructive reading of their work we will be exploring the unique particularities of traces of the worlds of each of the researchers, the meaning makers they each employ and the forces at work in the very practices themselves, rather than their representations.

St Pierre [2011: 611–26, who provides the basis for the first of these cases, was concerned with the language of 'post-'. In her writings there is another possible axis of understanding around which understandability organizes itself suggested by her challenges for qualitative research. Her writings indicate a concern for practising research. They owe their radical constitution to the play of *différance*. In working silently with the constitution of *différance*, on the presupposition that nothing is given it was particularly exciting to discover that St Pierre comes very close to using this constitution as a basis for her creative interplay with the paradigms.

Challenging the biopolitics: Silence speaks

In this deconstructive reading of St Pierre's [2011, 2006; St Pierre and Roulston 2006] writings the force of the logic employed suggests that the inspiration and the challenges of her discursive practice are post-paradigmatic. Let us join St Pierre [2011] in one of her recent chapters, 'post qualitative research: the critique and coming after' [ibid: 611–25]. In this paper she opens further questions concerned with what she calls 'transgressive data' [ibid: 621]. St Pierre arrives at her critical reflections upon such data on a stage set for research where 'deconstruction happens' [ibid: 620]. Here we should pause for a moment. Deconstruction owes its radical constitution to the play of *différance*. Herein lies the basis for suggesting that the logic of St Pierre's writings open a disclosive space that is extra-paradigmatic.

At first glance her writing, however, can easily suggest an ethic of practice that in part remains caught up within the albeit broken circular economy constituted by the ontotheological structuring of paradigms. St Pierre [2011: 620] speaks of 'each researcher who puts 'posts' to their work [post-structuralist, post-humanist, postmodernist, etc.] and indicates they will each create a different *articulation* [Hall, 1986/1996; Laclau and Mouffe, 2014{1985}], *remix, mash up, assemblage, a becoming* of inquiry that is not a priori, inevitable, stable or repeatable, but is rather created spontaneously in the middle of the task at hand' [ibid: 620]. At issue in St Pierre's writings, therefore, is a concern for *language* in which there is space for different articulations, and for the remixing of 'a becoming of inquiry'. In such language what is given is the nothing; St Pierre speaks of the absence of an a priori [ibid: 620], but this, like the nothing, is generative and creates something: in Derrida's terms, the constitution of *différance*.

Unconsciously, too, her writing brings into the open the sovereign powers at work in such language. Sovereign powers that are continually and silently challenged within her writings by the play of the spectral-other, the play of *différance*, are continually working against the possible reduction of beings to subjects and objects of reason or other metaphysical exigencies.

The problem arises, however, in generating such powers through language, in that the extant ontotheology of the paradigms constitutes its own locus of sovereign power, already serving to locate St Pierre's contribution within a categorical form in the same structure. The powers of St Pierre's language are then, in effect, placed against the powers emerging from the economy of exchange of signs within the existing paradigms. Within the hermeneutic circular logic of such ontotheology, its hegemony cultivates delimiting forms of education and training of researchers, which are directed solely towards the production of truth claims to knowledge. This drives the methods, methodologies and quality assurance procedures currently employed in research.

St Pierre's [2011] assertion – 'I don't believe in the rigorous inquiry I desire can be taught in a sequence of research courses or described in textbooks' [ibid: 620] – appears to reflect a *cri de coeur* for authentic education: the opening of spacing for the impossible, incalculable, indeterminate dimensions of practice without which such practices of inquiry could never become transformed. Herein lies an inspiration for this study – the reorientation towards justice to come constituted in the play of *différance* as a feature driving a newly expanded ethics of research that takes seriously, as St Pierre has indicated, the issue of 'deconstructive work and the transformations it can enable' [ibid: 620].

Such a drive towards justice remains unspoken in St Pierre's writings. In part it is revealed within the 'field of play' in which she places her doctoral study [ibid: 621]. Although she does not appear to use the language of 'world', St Pierre's writings begin to reveal traces and particularities of her own unique 'world' as a researcher consonant with moves towards justice. She reflects that her writing opened and became 'a space' for her. Here she is careful to add that such space is 'not just textual'. In her unique world her readers get an indication of the importance of her place of birth and her geographical home in 'Essex County' [ibid: 621]. Similarly, Edward S. Casey's [1997] 'philosophical history' of *The Fate of Place* opens reflection upon the unique and particular significance place has for each of us as human beings [Flint, 2012a]: its significance for the very 'practice' of 'action research' is explored by Stephen Kemmis and his colleagues [2014], drawing from Schatzki's notion of 'regional ontologies', though this latter group does not yet make explicit use of the constitution of *différance*.

In St Pierre's own experience of writing her doctoral dissertation, the traces in her paper begin to disclose for her how in her world she had studied diligently two literatures. She had been concerned with the particular idioms of 'theory' and of 'qualitative research methodology'. In being reflexive, St Pierre reveals that although in the earlier phase of her study these had 'mostly remained separate', it also became clear qualitative methodology had been 'grounded in humanism [and positivism]' she 'no longer believed', and it 'ruptured' [ibid: 621].

There is also a possible double play here, because St Pierre's writings constituted in the play of *différance* and the uniqueness of her world as a researcher also reveal the spectral-other at play in her voice that has its own spacing outside the ontotheology of paradigms. Her writings open the possibility of another rupture, where one is no longer working with the gathering powers of identities in their assumed plenitude, but within the radical constitution of *différance* and deconstruction. Such rupture opens disclosive space for 'bare life' and its express possibilities.

In St Pierre's terms 'theory' became a 'powerful personal tool' that she 'needed to study for her own good'. She describes how, following her readings of 'Derrida's rich, complex, and perfectly formed sentences' and 'Deleuze and Guattari's new concepts – *bodies without organs, becoming animal, smooth space*' [ibid: 620, emphasis as in the original]– she had come to see there may be 'another sentence in another book that might shatter' her 'life again'. In this sense of the textuality of her temporal relationship with past literature and future possibilities, her writing seems to make real her own life-world in the play of *différance*, which St Pierre calls 'theory'. The name, in this case, '*theory*', as a performative carries with it the possibility of its own death, the nothing that opens spacing for regeneration. In St Pierre's understanding, it '*produces people*' [ibid: 620; emphasis as in the original]. Here one also keeps in mind the play of mask and voice in the identity, 'person'.

In returning to the issue of the styling of practice adopted by St Pierre in her writings, we find that it does not 'fit' within the extant ontotheology of research. The fact that her practice of writing is not suited to its paradigmatic structures arises quite simply because unconsciously her textuality works with the constitution of *différance.* It is this radical constitution where no gatherings of signs are possible that opens a particular place for St Pierre's writings.

Her own writing about data reflects a continual play in the flux of *différance* in lived time, making concrete how it may be possible to understand what deconstruction brings in the drive for justice in research. In particular St Pierre [2011: 621] identifies "transgressive data" that she appreciates is 'clearly at work' in her 'study' – *emotional data, dream data, sensual data, memory data* and *response data.* For her such data is not visible. In one stroke her writing opens the possibility of research, no longer premised upon the strategizing of truth claims that continually appear not to be able to work without the visibility of 'data'. St Pierre's transgressive data also disrupts linearity, consciousness and the mind/body dichotomy characteristic of Cartesian ways of thinking, in the context of more traditional forms of data collection and analysis. Once again her writing appears to be cultivated by authentic education in *différance*, silently alerting researchers to the hidden pre-judicial structures that are shaping the styles of practice in research.

Despite her obvious concern for the unique worlds of people with whom she works, however, St Pierre's practice involving methods and methodologies remains coordinated within the terms of reference of the extant paradigms of research. Rather than following the logic of her own transgressive *practice* in terms of its relationship with the technology of research, St Pierre continues to hold on to the familiar metaphysical guardrails constituted by paradigmatic structuring. She *has* also yet to bring into sharper focus the disclosive spacing her writing is beginning to uncover for bare life. Undoubtedly, part of the difficulty is that the current practices of research would appear to be in denial concerning our relationship with the technology of research. Not, as we have seen repeatedly, is there any express language for bare life in research.

The next case concerns the writings of Laurel Richardson [1992, 1993, 1994, 1997, 2000] reflecting her practice of post-modern sociology.

Challenging the biopolitics: postmodern sociological research

Richardson's [1993, 1997] explorations of writing as a method of sociological inquiry, of using poetry and drama in her research as 'deliberately transgressive forms', have proven to be influential over the past 20 years. In rationalizing her use of such forms she cites Robert Frost, for whom "poetry provides the shortest emotional distance between two points, the speaker and the listener/reader' [Richardson, 1993: 696]. In the words of Lincoln and her colleagues [2011]:

> In writing experimental [non-authoritative, non-positivist] texts, particularly poems and plays, Richardson [1997] has sought to 'problematize reliability, validity, and truth' [ibid: 165] in an effort to create new relationships: to her research participants, to her work, to other women, to herself. [Ibid: 122; emphasis as in the original]

Of particular interest in Richardson's [1997] idiom is the point where, in being deconstructive, transgressive forms of practice open spaces for social scientists to 'conjure a different kind of social science . . . [which] means changing one's relationship to one's work, how one tells about the sociological' [ibid: 167]. Richardson's [1994] writings suggest that one of the pivotal forms of practice is language itself that she sees as a 'constitutive force' writers and speakers alike use 'to create a particular view of reality and the self' [ibid: 518]. In this particular paper she identifies a number of genres of writing, of which 'experimental representation' is of particular interest because it opens space as what she sees as an 'emergent transgressive phenomenon' [ibid: 520].

Particularly exciting is her experimental approach to writing and the way she is engaging with other researchers; unconsciously Richardson, like St Pierre, moves close to the reconceptualization of research as an event opening spacing for the regeneration of life. This is a key point to which we will return in the concluding chapter.

But, while in concert with such experimental forms of writing, where 'conventions are difficult to specify', Richardson [1994: 520] encourages her readers to write in their own particular ways, her own practice as a sociologist would appear to delimit the scope of such practices. Working with researchers on professional doctorate programmes it is apparent that governmental practices reproduced in institutions outside the disciplinary apparatus of academia tend to rely upon positivistic groundings for their work [Fell et al., 2012]. This is why the interest in the styles of writing concerned with *practice* per se, constituted in the play of *différance* as a deconstructive force operative within a multiplicity of practices.

In the biopolitics of such practice, however, moves towards justice in the deconstruction of the particularity and uniqueness of each world of the self are always easy to elide, for example, in Richardson's [1992] study of unmarried mothers, represented as 'consciously self-revelatory', reflecting the lived experience of the researcher [ibid: 125] in 'venturing beyond' what may be regarded as 'improper' in 'breach[ing] sociological writing expectations by writing socio-logy as poetry' [ibid: 126]. However, Richardson is not presenting the interiority of the world of her-self here. Rather she represents a trace of its external granulated face. The biopolitical violence done in such dissimulation can be glossed in her particular language game as a questioning of the extant order cast by sociology.

In being reflexive, while Richardson [1992, 1993, 1994, 1997, 2000] structures her writings about language in the context of content and form, like St Pierre there would appear to be no language available within Richardson's particular brand of post-modern discourse that opens critical reflection upon the ontotheological structuring driving enframing. In Richardson's [1992, 1993, 1994, 1997, 2000] writings the theological structuring of the highest order beings arises from the forms of writing used. Its ontological grounds are constituted by what is done in the name of writing. In the absence of any consideration by Richardson [1992, 1993, 1994, 1997, 2000] of the 'meaning maker' at work in any writings there remains also the question of just how much enframing is underlined and reinforced – by the principles of reason, of assessment, of the market – as meaning makers in particular forms of writing. There remains also the question of the extent to which the grounds for the ontotheological structuring driving enframing are removed in practices drawing from the constituting powers of *différance* and deconstruction.

The next case based upon Lather's writings takes as its headline her particular phrase concerned with 'an incitement to discourse'.

Challenging the biopolitics: 'Incitement to discourse'

This case illuminates the subtleties of the biopolitical disguise [*verstellen*] involving both enframing [*das Ge-stell*] and possibilities open to bare life. In seeking 'an incitement to discourse' Lather's [1993a] express intention had been to 'rupture validity as a regime of truth, to displace its historical inscription'. Here Lather [1993a] moves directly to re-form the heart of power within the apparatus of research. Her approach involves moves towards 'dispersion, circulation, and proliferation of counterpractices of authority that take the crisis of representation into account' [ibid: 674]. She invoked a playful exploration of a number of transgressive forms of validity. Each of the cases, as Lather identifies in her paper, is distinguished by the gathering of signs, providing a counter-locus of power. Each case that follows, therefore, is distinguished by the further enhancement of powers in the social world directed against the ruling positivity within paradigms.

Lather's *Ironic validity* arises from *simulacra* – signs developed from other signs, 'copies without originals' found in the 'Disneyland' of research [ibid: 677]. It is interesting that she delimited the simulacra to research, and there is no mention of the trace or of the politics of plenitude at work here. In considering *practice* per se her deconstruction would appear to work with any form of practice constituted from the economy of signs identified earlier in terms of the society of *the spectacle*.[2] Lather also explores *Lyotardian paralogy/neopragmatic validity*. For her it 'foster[s] heterogeneity', represented in her practice as "refin[ing] our sensitivity to differences and reinforces our ability to tolerate the incommensurable" via 'the constant search for new ideas and concepts that introduces dissensus into consensus' [Fritzman, 1990: 371–72]. Again the gathering of signs on grounds of the politics of plenitude is palpable. In fact, one of her frames for questioning validity, which Lather identifies in terms of 'Derridean rigour/rhizomatic validity', the radical constitution of difference is reduced once more to the gathering of signs in the form of 'a vocation and a response to the call of otherness in any system' [Lather, 1993a: 680]. It is deeply ironic, therefore, that she chooses to identify her responses in terms of 'four "framings" of validity that take antifoundational discourse theory into account' [ibid: 676; emphasis as in the original]. Although in this paper Lather undoubtedly opens space for a number of ways of understanding validity, ironically her approach serves only to continue to reproduce the ontotheological structuring driving enframing by means of her 'incitement to discourse'. The ontological grounds for her anti-foundational discourse is, in fact, what is represented in such discourse – in accord with the will-to-power and the will-to-will opening space for alternative forms of representation. The theological delimitation of her discourses is the postmodern and post-structuralist paradigm in which her representations are placed. Her meaning maker remains reasons connecting subject with object, albeit opening space for understanding non-standard ways of conceiving validity, with the consequent possibilities this opens for researching truth claims to knowledge in a postmodern paradigm.

Lather's [1993a] paper, therefore, though I suspect is not intended this way, provides an index of the subtleties and complexities involved in the biopolitics of practising research. Given the foregrounding of transgressive validity one might anticipate that the paper would open space for a radical probing of enframing in research. Instead, it simply expands the horizons of such enframing, albeit in directions, creating anti-foundationalist powers countering those powers that presuppose foundations. Also, there is no critically reflexive discourse directed towards such enframing or the politics of plenitude. Such practice, then, is delimited to a postmodern form of research within the paradigms. It does not provide any rationale for taking away the powers inscribed within enframing in practices outside this compartmentalized field of research. It simply invokes its own postmodern form of biopolitics, ironically continuing to silence bare life.

It is not difficult to find other cases of researchers who are beginning to question aspects of the extant order within methods of research – not least Ann Nilsen and Kathy Charmaz – but as in the foregoing three cases there is no further challenge given to the issues of enframing and bare life in research.

Challenging the biopolitics: Practising methods

From this deconstruction of a number of leading archives of research,[2[Introduction]] ironically, with the notable exception of St Pierre's [2011] and to some extent Lather's [1991, 1993a,b, 1994, 2004, 2006, 2007a,b] and Richardson's [1992, 1993, 1994, 1997, 2000] discourses, we have uncovered a multiplicity of forms of ontotheological structuring driving enframing. The biopolitics of such research, however, makes no mention of such ontotheology; rather, it is concerned almost exclusively with moves towards perfection in research reflecting a number of ways in such performativity have been conceived. Again the implications for 'bare life' also finds no disclosive space within this particular discourse. In this way the biopolitics concentrates attention upon the granular visible outer face of the self. In this biopolitics the particularity and uniqueness of the interiority of the self and the possibilities for bare life are dissimulated almost completely.

Such biopolitics is also further reinforced by forces delimiting education and the training of researchers in ways that focus attention upon the agency of the ego. In this biopolitical world of research the Husserlian–Cartesian axis of understanding is egological: its hegemony foregrounds ideologies of the self and the ego as the centres of control, dissimulating almost completely their phenomenological reduction that reveals them as marionettes of enframing. What is being transferred between various practices, then, is the biopolitics of enframing and its ontotheological structuring, constituting its own sublimely effective disguises within research.

In reflecting critically upon the practising of education, the question remains concerning the extent to which such education emerging from the engagement of practitioners within research serves to open disputation with such orthodoxy. At issue, therefore, is both a characterization of 'delimiting education' that emerges from engagement in the methods of research along with an indication of any authentic education in which practitioners become immersed.

Biopolitics of practising education in research

The forces delimiting education arise from its biopolitics, reflecting the pre-judicial structuring [Table 2.1] of research. The latter, as we have seen, is constituted on the basis of sovereign powers inscribed within the multiplicity of its languages – and its laws – that are all characterized by their bonding of inclusion with states of exception. It is such bonds and the sublime sovereign powers of the languages of research that silence bare life. In such an *aporia* bare life finds itself driven by the forces delimiting education, although in some cases there are challenging questions that arise independently from authentic education. The naming force and the gathering powers of delimiting education generate an almost perfect disguise [*verstellen*] of the ontotheological structuring driving enframing [*das Ge-stell*]. The essential locus of delimiting education, then, is our relationship with the visual manifestations of being – what it makes possible as calculable and conditional aspects of such practice. It is such delimiting education that provides researchers with way markers in which any *aporia* in the methods of research for many researchers no longer remains an issue.

Paradoxically, such delimiting education cultivated within the metonymic 'Disneyland of research' masquerades as securing grounds for the development of objective findings, quality methods and clearly defined 'evidence' or 'outcomes' from such methods. For the docile body it becomes a delimiting education in the seeming inexorability of the intensity and extensity of the biopolitical violence inflicted upon the uniqueness of the particular worlds of human beings. Such bare life is easily swept aside rendering for human beings a state of alienation in *the* modern world. Paradoxically, delimiting education is the locus of cultivation and expansion of such forces of violence in almost all dimensions of research. Despite the multiplicity and range of research methods employed, what seems to be a common factor emerging from among the great majority of studies represented in the literature is a focus upon the external granular face of the self. The almost complete elision of the uniqueness and particularity of the interiority of the worlds of human beings in research and the more general elision of bare life are a deeply shocking and completely unexpected outcome from this study.

In hermeneutical terms, given the ideological circularity of the stages within the apparatus of research, provisionally it would also appear that at the time of writing the forces delimiting education in the sense of *educare*, that is, training in research, are directed towards re-fining, implementing and developing aspects of the extant circular economy of signs generated from research. There is a double irony at work here, because even in the sense of *educere*, within the hermeneutical circular logic of research any leading out from delimiting education into new possibilities tends to remain locked within the circularity of *what is given* in concert with the visibility of such practice. But, this circularity is always necessarily broken, as we have seen before, thereby creating a rationale for its own continual development that is always impossible. Herein, therefore, lies one of the driving forces of enframing. Within such cultures, therefore, there remain ever-greater forces at work ensuring that bare life remains locked in its state of exception.

Within such cultures delimiting education in research, too, the visual dimensions of being – the conditional, calculable aspects of what is deemed possible on the basis of research 'evidence' – the order of domination ensures that all forms of *educere* remains within the same order. This is why there is a need to radicalize the constitution of practices of research and of education. One step towards such radicalization is at least the realization of the effects of delimiting education within cultures of research.

Ironically, too, where one might imagine that postmodernist methods may contribute to a form of education that opens space for people to think differently about aspects of the practice, the ontotheological structuring of paradigmatic research locates such methods in the same space as that of '*the society of the spectacle*'. Its default form of education is delimiting in accord with its ontotheology and its biopolitics silencing bare life. However, we have uncovered a handful of exceptional examples, including St Pierre, Richardson, Lather and others, whose writings silently open spacing for bare life through their own largely unspoken immersion in the play of *différance* that in *practice* is not delimited by paradigmatic structuring. In this way unconsciously their writings begin to open spacing for authentic education in research.

Authentic education in research, therefore, in opening spacing for research raises a number of questions that could have a bearing on the possible transformation of research methods. Not the least are questions concerned with the effects of the pre-judicial structures [Table 2.1] that are shaping agency involving methods, methodologies and paradigmatic structures of research in accord with the 'juggernaut'[3] of enframing. In moving the ethics of research out of its current deontological structuring, is it not time for researchers to be concerned with the extent to which thinking generated on grounds delimiting education within the visible 'spectacle' of society currently serves only to contribute to the ever-expanding calculus of sublime powers it continues to generate on this planet? The question remains, too, concerning the styling of authentic education, because in the *aporia* of everyday practice it would seem that the forces delimiting education and its powerful connection with the visual aspects of the world seem to provide a ready pathway in the world of so many researchers. Such pathways are always made obvious for the analysis of research.

CHAPTER NINE

Transformations-in the analytics of research: Generating spacing for thinking

Our various analyses of research so far have revealed the biopolitics closing down the space and the world hidden behind the visible granular face of identities. It is a biopolitics that has remained stubbornly silent and seemingly without any word on the issue of bare life. It constitutes a structural accord with the laws and sovereign powers inscribed in the many *languages* of research. Despite the earlier pragmatic, existential and temporal readings of being-in-the-world it leaves us still in danger of reproducing what many critics understand as an Apollinarian style that true to the mythology of this sun god and its associated folklore of transparency nonetheless inspires an egological Cartesian/Husserlian worldview of the practices of research.

We *have* yet to examine any possible thinking arising from the forces of analysis at work in the *language* of research, beyond what could be seen as the meta-analyses of enframing and the state of exception. Of particular interest are the forms of thinking and analysis emerging from the biopolitics of displacement of bare life in the different dimensions of its practices.

In order to open a language for the collective body involved in research, we will draw from the works of Deleuze and Guattari [2004{1987}]. They pair the metaphors of 'molecular' and 'molar' drawn from discourses of chemistry and geology, to create a picture of sub-microscopic particles – the statements of the granular selves as their molecular arrangement – and their molar composition as a body. Following the work of the Italian scientist Amedeo Avogadro, who became professor of physics at the University of Turin in 1820, chemists, pharmacists, geologists and others use the adjective, molar, to count extremely large aggregates of particles.

In *A Thousand Plateaus* Deleuze and Guattari [2004 {1987}] use the terms molar and molecular to describe political bodies. As a molar entity research in its multiplicities belongs to the state or the civic world. It is affiliated with governmental apparatuses.

The molecular counterpart to the molar in Deleuze's discourse refers to the individual responses to phenomena – the analytical statements, possibilities, reflections, suggestions and evaluations made by people. The metaphors of molecularity and of molecular action reflect the dynamism of chemical and geological worlds and the social processes of transformation that move beyond the scope of planning within the apparatus of research. Biopolitics, in this sense, is understood to involve both molar and molecular orders that each generates, with bare life remaining in its state of exception in both social orders.

In opening the space for analysis and thinking Deleuze and Guattari introduce the horizontal and contingent geometry of the rhizome in radical contrast to what we have seen as the growth of the predictable hierarchical structuring of architectural space of tree-like geometries shaping the ontotheology of many forms of organization.[1] As Felicity J. Coleman [2005: 232] suggests, the rhizome is 'Deleuze's apparatus for describing' such contingent transformations – its use as a biological metaphor was introduced by Deleuze and Guattari [2004 {1987}] in *A Thousand Plateaus*. Rhizome is 'a form of plant that can extend itself through its underground horizontal tuber-like root system and develop new plants' [Colman, 2005: 231]. In the social world of research Colman suggests that it may be thought of as 'any network of things brought in contact with one another, functioning as an assemblage machine for new affects, new concepts, new bodies, new thoughts; the rhizomatic network is a mapping of forces that move and/or immobilise bodies' [ibid: 231]. One such rhizomatic network for qualitative research has been identified by Judith Davidson and Silvana di Gregorio [2011] as being 'in the midst of a revolution', to which we will return shortly. The very locus of such a revolution in this case is the possible transformation of the complex relationship between 'qualitative research and technology' [ibid: 627]. Deleuze and Guattari's thinking suggests that rather than understanding technology as providing the basis for a meta-analysis of research, one seeks to examine the unique cultural formations that emerge from specific rhizomatic structuring of thought around, for example, aspects of enframing, including the logics of inductive analysis, the production of information technologies for use as research tools and the arts of practices used in research and in the issue of narrativity.

At issue remains an examination of the multiplicity of forms of contingency, arising from iterations of gathering of powers at work mediating the assemblages and apparatuses in which researchers' are located. Viewed in this way the unique place from which each research emerges onto the public stage is heterogeneous, opening a multiplicity of connections within any emerging rhizomatic plateau of thought. But, it still remains to be uncovered to what extent disclosive space is opened for thinking that begins to question the extant ontotheological structuring of research.

In Deleuze's language an assemblage is any number of 'things' or pieces of 'things' found in a single context. An assemblage can bring about any number of 'effects' – as expressed in aesthetic, machinic, productive, destructive, consumptive, informatic, and so on forms.[2] Rather than being a more tightly organized form, as one might find in an apparatus, an 'assemblage' involves a jumbling together of discrete pieces within a molar body, and producing any number of effects from the interactions of the 'molecules' within such a body. Within the assemblages of research Deleuze and Guattari [2004{1987}] suggest that a rhizome contributes to the formation of plateaus, through its lines of thought.

Within the biopolitics of paradigmatic research we *have* yet to uncover just how such thinking begins to point towards what ordinarily remains silenced as bare life. The loci of such biopolitics in this study is six books[2[Introduction]] that together constitute what may be considered as leading archives of research. Unspoken in each of these books there remains the adoption of particular biopolitical standpoints concerned with the understanding of the complex relationship between research and bare life. These have bearings upon the various ways in which bare life may be understood. As Derrida [1999] notes, 'there is no politics without the book in our culture' [ibid: 66]. As assemblages we *have* yet to find out the effects of these specific books in terms of the forces at work in their particular modalities of analysis. Of particular interest are the 'analytical frames' [Kincheloe, 2001: 685] used by researchers to generate understandings and knowledges of the social world.

Plateaus of thought generated by inductive analysis

One of the common analytical frames used by researchers is that of inductive analysis. In being grounded upon the principle of reason, this provides another dimension of enframing. In *Social Research Methods* Bryman [2008] speaks of 'general strategies of qualitative data analysis' being presented as a matter of 'analytical induction'. Herein lies the basis for a rhizomatic plateau for qualitative research that may emerge from this particular book; itself in Deleuze and Guattari's tems regarded as an 'assemblage'. The same approach is evident in Cohen and his colleagues' [2007] account of grounded theory and content analysis [ibid: 472–87]. Here can be found an approach 'to the analysis of data in which the researcher seeks universal explanations of phenomena by pursuing the collection of data until no cases that are inconsistent with a hypothetical explanation [deviant or negative cases] of a phenomenon are found' [ibid: 539]. The extensity of this particular rhizomatic plateau of thought can be gauged by its application by other leading researchers in the field [*vide* Hammersley and Atkinson, 1995: 234–35; Bloor, 1978; Cressey, 1950; Lindesmith, 1947; Punch, 2009: 172–73]. Once more in the moves towards generalization the biopolitics focuses the attention of researchers upon the visibility of the external granular face of identity, sweeping away understandings of bare life.

Such inductive logic also finds expression in qualitative research as 'grounded theory' [*vide* Glaser and Strauss 1967]. The term 'grounded theory' might suggest a process that connects directly with the issue of being human. Glaser [1992] now adopts a distinctly different standpoint from that of Strauss and Corbin [1990]. The purpose of 'grounded theory' is to constitute theoretical 'codes', existing in a fluid state, being continually open to revision in the light of new forms of data. Once again the analysis is located within an economy of exchange of what is given by the data that is driven by the principle of reason. As Charmaz [2006] puts it 'focused coding requires decisions about which initial codes make the most analytical sense to categorise your data incisively and completely' [ibid: 56–7]. The theological structuring of this assemblage is constituted in the paradigms. Its ontology remains what is done in practice. Once more in the biopolitics of such analytical framing [Bryman, 2008: 538–56] concern is directed towards analysis on the basis of the strategizing of truth claims.

Again, within the formation of this particular rhizomatic plateau, in Cohen and his colleagues' [2007: 178] discussions concerning the so-called constant comparative method devised by Glaser and Strauss [1967], using the same analytical induction, the biopolitics remains the same. Enframing and the state of exception never become raised to the status of consciousness, even as non-issues. The drives delimiting education in this culture are all currently directed towards the production of what are considered to generate the best quality outcomes in terms of the production of knowledge. Together with its theological structuring in the paradigms the biopolitics simply forecloses on any possibility of opening reflection upon enframing and bare life. It does so in not providing any possible language that researchers can draw upon to explore such issues. This is another reason why the case has been made for the expansion of research ethics to include consideration of moves towards justice. In democratic terms such expansion is considered a necessary requirement for opening space in research with a new language, assemblages, and moves towards other plateaus. It opens the democratic prospect of researchers examining the implications of the biopolitics for themselves and to arrive at their own positions.

In the more recent archive titled *Research Methods and Methodologies in Education* [Arthur et al., 2012], Robert Thornberg [2012a: 85–93; 2012b] opens space for reflection on the inductive logic of traditional forms of ground theory, GT. He argues that such traditional logic is predicated on assumptions concerned with the 'discovery' of extant forms of data and theories [Thornberg, 2012a: 91]. Implicit in this logic, it would appear, is an assumption concerned with the repetition of the principle of being 'something is repeatable to the extent that it *is*' [Caputo, 1987: 123; emphasis added], so that in this tradition it has always been simply a matter of discovering being, of revealing what *is,* in this case through classical forms of GT. Here, once more, it would seem the biopolitics turns attention away from consideration being given to the exigencies of repetition and reiteration of signs, or more accurately, traces of signs from research.

Plateaus of thought generated by Kincheloe's bricolage

'Critical Pedagogy and the Knowledge Wars of the Twenty-First Century', Kincheloe's [2008] paper, at least promised the possibility of opening space for another rhizomatic plateau involving different forms of thinking. Written within the tradition of critical theory as a rhizomatic plateau that emerged from the work of Adorno and Horkheimer earlier in the twentieth century that had sought a radical challenge to the extant order of Enlightenment thinking, it promised the possibility of opening space for new thinking. Kincheloe spoke of 'the politics of knowledge and the contemporary knowledge wars' that we have also seen, 'cannot be separated from the relationship between the epistemological, ontological, the political economic, and the ideological' [ibid: 2]. Kincheloe indicates that the full scope of practices located at the interstices of 'these four domains' of such a relationship 'constantly interact in a synergistic manner to shape the nature of the knowledge produced by Western power wielders in the contemporary era'. In Kincheloe's [2008a] terms:

> utilizing a crypto-positivistic, evidence-based science . . . excludes complexity; context; power; multiple modes of research design; the ever-changing, in-process nature of the phenomena of the social world; subjugated and indigenous knowledges from diverse social and geographical locales; and the multiple realities perceived and constructed by different peoples at divergent historical times and cultural places, dominant power brokers attempt with a great deal of success to regulate what people view as legitimate knowledge. [Ibid: 2]

We can now add to this list of excluded elements with the important and almost always hidden interiority of the world of the self, together with bare life, and the more general particularity and uniqueness of the places in which people live their lives [Flint, 2012a]. This move by Kincheloe gestures towards justice in its focus upon place and a sense of the unique cultures of the people involved. And, although he does not use the language of justice there is a strong dimension of deconstruction at work in his discursive practice.

An index of the magnitude of the issue confronting research till just five years ago is given in Kincheloe's [2008a] standpoint that 'in the last years of the first decade of the twenty-first century, the hegemonic politics of knowledge and the crypto-positivistic epistemology that is its conjoined twin are destroying the world' [ibid: 3]. Though not implied in the same way as here, silently and ironically it would seem his express epistemological terms here reflect the gathering powers and the naming force of being driving enframing; the very same force at work shaping the very agencies open to his critique.

His particular strategy, drawing upon bricolage, was to 'use critical pedagogical effort to thwart these power plays' that for him 'involve[d] engaging in a transformative multilogicality' [ibid: 4]. This employed a wide range of theories, including 'critical theory, feminist theory, social theory, anti-racist theory, poststructuralism, complexity and chaos theory queer theory, and post/anti-colonial theories' [ibid: 5]. The object of this bricolage had been to expose the multiple harms done by power [ibid: 5]. The thought structuring this particular and emergent rhizomatic plateau was that of utilizing 'multilogicality' as a means of countering the monological thinking that Kincheloe had seen dominating what for him was regarded as the politics of knowledge production. Working from a neo-pragmatist standpoint Paul Gibbs [2013] is continuing to explore a similar approach based upon an axis of understanding concerned with trans-disciplinarity. At this point it should also be clear that there are dimensions of such practices concerned with maintaining bare life in silence that make the production of knowledges the very matter of concern for biopolitics. But, it is, perhaps, an index of the powers at work in the biopolitical orders constituted in research that a leading researcher of Kincheloe's standing had not been made explicitly conscious of such an issue. Our concern are the sovereign powers of language. At the time of Kincheloe's paper there would appear not to have been a language opening reflection upon the issue of 'bare life' [*zēn*] in research.

At issue in Kincheloe's approach is a battle concerned with the politics of knowledge production. Kincheloe's [2008a] bricolage concerns itself with marginalized groups from 'Asia, Africa, Latin America, the Islamic World, the oppressed in North America, Australia, New Zealand, and Europe, and indigenous communities around the world' [ibid: 6]. It is important not to lose sight of this vision. In his particular politics of research he aimed to 'construct a political economic ecology of knowledges that lead to new ways of seeing and being' [ibid: 6]. His study illuminates the way 'episto-power operates to exclude diversality from the curricula and public knowledge'. In its moves towards exposing the uniqueness of people's experiences there is a gesture towards justice. Bricolage for Kincheloe refused to be 'content' with 'monological and monocultural perspectives' [ibid: 8].

One has much sympathy with this form of bricolage because it connects the reader with the 'under-dog,' in its rhetorical and moral appeal made to help those whose lives and cultures are in danger of being swept aside by emerging dominant hegemonies of research. However, in Kincheloe's own research act, in attempting to counter the powers of 'crypto-positivism' he employs a strategy of developing antithetical powers that still remain within the ontotheology driving enframing. This is why here we have put forward the alternative strategy of enhancing the scope of ethics to incorporate moves towards justice. At issue is the attempt to move towards the exploration of languages opening space for critical examination of the biopolitics involved in research.

Plateaus of thought generated by the unconscious

Ironically, in the continual reiteration of the biopolitics of research there remains the possibility that we are continually blinded, caught in the headlights of its concern for what is visible. What has generally elided attention in almost all contemporary debates is not what is done in practice, of which readers are variously conscious. Borrowing a metaphor from Freud, if for one moment the world of research can be regarded as an iceberg, what has so far remained hidden from view has been the great mass of the iceberg, some 90 per cent of it that remains concealed beneath the surface in the unconscious. Yet, for a number of psychoanalysts following Freud, including Lacan and Žižek, the unconscious is seen to structure our very existence. It suggested the possibility of another assemblage and of rhizomatic plateaus of thought in research emerging from its concerns with the unconscious.

From a Lacanian perspective on the unconscious at work in assemblages of research, at issue remains the question of what connects and drives the reiteration of aspirations, rhetorics, identities and practices of professionals. It carries with it the aligned question concerned with desire, and the role it plays in drives towards the improvement of the quality of research, and drives towards ever more sophisticated, complex and differentiated knowledges of the social world [Lacan 2006].

In his readings of Freud, Lacan distinguishes three orders of the unconscious that he considered were analogous to language: 'the real', 'the imaginary' and 'the symbolic'. In Fink's [1995: 1–31] thesis the unconscious is language. Identifying the subject as constituted by the symbolic order, Lacan followed Heidegger in arguing that 'language speaks the subject'. So, rather than placing the individual at the centre of debate, Lacan's decentring of his analysis suggests a way of examining how the continually shifting symbolic order of research affects the subjective experience of individuals. Lacan identifies and capitalizes the symbolic order as 'the Other' that in its totality can never be assimilated into one's subjectivity. Lacan distinguishes 'the Other' from 'the other'. For him, imaginary others have their roots in the 'mirror stage', when the infant sees an 'other' it thinks will fulfil its desires.

Consequently, desire in Lacan's way of thinking originates from something lacking in the subject and 'the Other' [Fink, 1995: 3–70]. As Fink [1995: xi] notes, 'otherness runs the unlikely gamut from the unconscious, the Other as language, and the Other as desire [ego ideal] to the Freudian superego [Other as *jouissance*]'.

From this perspective the drives towards analysis used in the assemblages of research is predicated upon desires to overcome what are conceived to be current lacuna along with any incompleteness and limitations in what is already known within a specified field of knowledge. There is the desire, as we have seen repeatedly, to gain objective forms of knowledge in accord, tacitly at least, with Husserl's [1970{1954}; 1973{1939}, 1983] ontology. There is in this sense a presumption of such a lack identified by Lacan and here uncovered within the symbolic orders located in Lacanian terms as 'the Other'. Desire, Lacan suggests, 'moves from one signifier to another' in discursive practices in its continual attempts to satisfy itself; desire's purpose is insatiably directed towards desire. Unconscious desire becomes manifest through fantasy, of which we have already identified in quite a number in research. Another particular fantasy has set the scene in the United States for the governmental engineering of evidence-based practices within research [Denzin 2011: 645–57].

The structuring and drives behind desires are for Lacan constituted by *jouissance* [Fink, 1995: 98–122; Lacan, 2006]. Misleadingly, *jouissance* is ordinarily translated as 'enjoyment', but, in Lacanian discourse it carries the certainty of pleasure in pain and, in the original French, has obvious resonances with sexuality and sexual pleasure in orgasm. *Eros,* like the moves of *educare* and *educere* in education, comes to fill the gap left by our own essential incompleteness.

What is real in the unconscious, for Lacan, can become manifest only through trauma; it is the unknowable *objet a* – Lacan's unobtainable object of desire – that is implicated in each of his three orders and cannot be absorbed into symbolic reality. In Lacanian terms, fantasy defines a subject's impossible relation to the *objet a*. It has always been there from the earliest writings of the Ancient Greeks. In Homer's *Odyssey* [2003: 88], for example, it is constituted as excess beyond words. Here, the *objet a*, as the object cause of desire for on-going activity in research, is a void, a lacuna, the lack around which such discursive practices are structured. Viewed through a Lacanian lens, the unconscious imperative for the principle of reason [Heidegger, 1977, 1991], the principle of assessment [Flint and

Peim, 2012] and the 'principle of the market' [Flint, *in preparation ii*] as grounds for the unfolding drives of enframing in research now becomes obvious. It is the ever-unfailing *jouissance* that structures our desires and the impossibility of our encounter with the real – as we have seen, all of these discourses generated in the analysis of research are based only upon traces of the real. But, as Fink [1995] realizes:

> [*Jouissance*] insists as an ideal, an idea, a possibility thought permits us to envision. In [Lacan's] terminology, it ex-ists: it persists and makes its claim felt with a certain insistence from the outside, as it were. Outside in the sense that it is not a wish [desire], 'Let's do that again!' but, rather, '*Isn't there something else that you could do, something else that you could try*?' [ibid: 35; emphasis added]

Such an ideal, too, shapes bare life. The manifold expressions of such *jouissance* can be found in almost all research. As a structure for desire, *jouissance* does not exist; it is sustained through fantasies, including those in the sociology of this liquid modern world that increasingly drive the violence of the elite corporate neo-liberalist market agendas [vide Giroux, 2008], where the fantasy of so-called evidence-based research becomes an adjunct in the hegemony of management and the control of large bodies. For such bodies, forever in the throw[3] of the continually changing and slippery liquid modern world, where intelligibility becomes defined by the crude ethics constituted from the principles of reason, of assessment and of the market, life both inside and outside the obvious elites that exist on the surface is an endless struggle in the biopolitics of a performative world. Ironically, in the biopolitics of this nihilistic order, one's standing in its molecularity, as a valued agent, provides an index of bare life's contribution within the liquid modern forms of the molar body concerned with research.

In the micropolitics of the everyday world of researchers, there is always a danger that these larger questions concerning the molar body are dissimulated. Standard ethical procedures for research tend to focus upon the molecular order of practices within a particular place and defined organization, involving specified other people, rather than the molar bodies in which such molecular orders are continually in play. One is reminded of the approach used in calculus. In focusing upon the infinitesimally small elements of molecularity in the assemblages and the apparatus of research it is easy not to appreciate or to be able to gain some measure of the effects on the molar body of seemingly imperceptibly small changes at the molecular level. It is hard to distinguish significant patterns from random noise when presented with infinitely small changes on a molecular level. For example, in experiments in radioastronomy at Jodrell Bank in Cheshire, astronomers arrange sensitive receivers to pick up imperceptibly small signals from objects emitting radiofrequency signals that are light years away from earth. Ordinarily, their signals are lost in the random background haze of signals here on earth. In integrating such signals over long periods of time the effects of these infinitesimally small and non-random signals can be found to add up to produce measurable effects that show up as peaks on the monitors and can be analyzed, whereas the background random signals simply cancel each other out.

So, on a molecular level in the social world, when viewed from its molar scale, once the effects of imperceptibly small changes in the world of each self is integrated in order to understand their effects upon the molar body, each of the imperceptibly small changes becomes sublime lakes of excess energy hidden in the many assemblages, rhizomatic plateaus of thought and the apparatuses of state. From a Heideggerian perspective such lakes constitute a measure of the excess energy and possibilities that are reflected in those small contributions of bare life at the molecular level. Unlike radioastronomy, however, for bare life, as we have seen, there are significant dimensions that necessarily remain beyond the bounds of any calculation.

The proposed expansion of the ethics of research to incorporate moves towards justice in relation to its extant laws deserves, therefore, to be organized at both the molar and molecular levels of such practices. Here, too, it is apparent that any deconstruction in the name of justice to come will make obvious the granular face of the self, found in both molecular and molar forms of practices, and how it conceals the uniqueness of its own interiority, its own world. At issue remains an ethics concerned with justice to come that focuses upon the particularities and uniqueness of bare life, opening space for its possible regeneration for better or worse.

Deleuze would undoubtedly take issue with the foregoing reading of psychoanalysis. In Deleuze's discourse the psychoanalytical premising of desire upon an insatiable 'lack' or in being regulated by an Oedipal 'law' is contested [Ross 2005: 63]. As Alison Ross [ibid] observes, for Deleuze, who tries to correct such 'inaccuracies', desire is defined as 'a process of experimentation on a plane of immanence' [ibid: 63]. In her reading of Deleuze, psychoanalytical theory constitutes desire as 'impotent force'. However, in accord with Deleuze, our earlier reading of psychoanalytic theory also suggests that though 'impotent', such desire may be viewed as opening positive and productive spacing, so that Deleuze may be seen as creating further refinements of that earlier reading: Not least from this reinterpreted perspective, where 'desire is viewed not just as an experimental and productive force, but also a force able to form connections and enhance the power of bodies in their connection' [Ross, 2005: 63]. Here the term 'experimental' is used in the sense explored by Paul Feyerabend [2010] in his celebrated work, *Against Method*, where everything is possible.

On reflection, therefore, the capillary powers at work within the apparatus of research and its assemblages are perhaps even stronger than had been suggested from the earlier reading of Lacan. It is the immanence of this productive desire in practice that can generate a vocabulary for explaining the hold of what Kincheloe had identified earlier as 'crypto-positivistic, evidence-based science' that makes 'profoundly complex' and powerful demands in 'our proto-fascist era' [ibid: 2]. Tellingly, in terms of the biopolitics of research, as Ross [2005] notes, in 'Deleuze's writing with Guattari productive and positive desire works . . . as an operative vocabulary through which they explain fascism in politics as the desire for the repression of desire' [ibid: 64]. Here it opens space for the examination of such forms of repression at work within research. At issue remains the biopolitics constituting bare life.

In moves towards justice arising from the deconstruction in the cases that follow, what becomes more obvious are the ways in which biopolitics works in practice.

Plateaus of thought generated from technological languages

This desire to make sense of our complex world through qualitative social research is perhaps nowhere more strongly felt than in Davidson and di Gregorio's [2011: 627] explorations of the application of 'qualitative research and technology'. In reproducing the hegemony of data constituting the founding elements of research within its molecular order, one of their desires is devoted to offering 'qualitative researchers' the following:

1. A convenient digital location in which to organize all materials related to a study
2. A suite of digital tools that could be applied to those materials, including the ability to store and organize data as well as fragment, juxtapose, interpret and recompose that same material
3. Easy portability; and
4. A remarkable new form of transparency that allowed the researcher, and others, the opportunity to view and reflect upon the materials [di Gregorio and Davidson, 2008; Davidson and di Gregorio, 2011: 627].

Again it is easy to be taken in by the metaphysics. Once more the biopolitics elides completely the issues of enframing and of the possibilities open to bare life. Here we return once more to the strategizing of truth claims. In the biopolitics this particular approach to analysis in qualitative research provides an index of the calculus of control directed towards perfectibility. Such calculus reflects moves towards evidence, and objective outcomes, that is, the findings from research. Its outcomes are now being wrought within their late modern furnace using quanta, logics and electronics. In this way their calculus creates an architectural space for thinking concerned with qualitative research identified in terms of 'Quality Data Analysis Software, QDAS' [Davidson and di Gregorio, 2011: 627].

In using what is presented as a 'revolutionary' technology, the authors' obvious sense of *jouissance* and their desires are directed towards using this technology in order to accommodate the perceived needs of 'qualitative researchers from diverse disciplinary and methodological perspectives' [ibid: 627]. Paradoxically, such *jouissance*, combined with the absence of any language of ontotheology or discourse giving expression to bare life, deflects almost completely any critical examination of enframing. In their moves as trainers [the movement of *educare*], in delimiting the education of other researchers, their paper makes plain their desires for creating a sophisticated, fast and powerful tool that can be used by qualitative researchers to make analytical connections with their often-complex multi-layered forms of data. There is simply no consideration given to the immobilizing effects of QDAS on this emerging assemblage arising from its multiplicity of metaphysical exigencies.

The ontological ground in this particular schema is constituted by the agency and the on-going activity of researchers that utilize one of the QDAS packages. The hierarchically structured architecture of disclosive space created for thinking by this software constitutes its theological structuring. It is represented as a two-dimensional space centring upon the interrogation of data, viewed in terms of its:

- exploration,
- organization,
- interpretation; and
- integration [ibid: 628].

But, despite the obvious ontotheological structuring of the space created for analysis and thinking within QDAS, in accord with the biopolitics that sustains bare life there remains no critical examination given to the effects of enframing generated by the architecture of such disclosive space. Instead, within their own silent biopolitics of displacement of bare life in this assemblage, each of these actions then opens the researcher to a number of 'dispersed practices' [Schatzki, 1996: 91–8] that create a platform for the foregoing dimensions of the interrogation of data. They include searching for content, comparing subsets, retrieving, annotating, linking, coding, grouping, rethinking, writing, connecting, combining, incorporating and identifying aspects of *what is always already given* in the data [Davidson and di Gregorio, 2011: 628].

The biopolitics of the QDAS assemblage in opening rhizomatic plateaus of thought also gathers other researchers to itself. A number of these pivotal 'others' raise questions concerning QDAS, opening space for reflections concerned with the worlds of the researchers and others involved. For example, Udo Kelle's [1997] paper sets forth reflection on the 'New Prometheus' to be found in the 'monster computer' [Lee and Fielding, 1996]. Kelle argues that from an anthropological standpoint such arguments 'overemphasize' the problems in the use of computer technology in the analysis of data. From the perspectives of Kelle, along with Lee and Fielding, the new version of QDAS, now available, 'web 2.0, QDAS', is itself 'challenged on many fronts as researchers seek out easier to learn, more widely available and less expensive, increasingly multi-modal, visually attractive, and more socially connected technologies to support their qualitative research endeavours' [Davidson and di Gregorio, 2011: 627]. Despite the unspoken references to the unique worlds and places in which research may be situated, the biopolitics foregrounding truth claims to knowledge remains seemingly untouched. The assemblages created around QDAS would appear untroubled. They remain so because no one is yet dealing with the issue of the biopolitics of displacement of bare life in such research and with the aligned naming force and the gathering powers of being as presence drawn upon by each of these groups.

As suggested in the use of Deleuze's term assemblage, created here on the basis of QDAS, there has been considerable jumbling of the molecular dimensions from the 'moment' where this technology was first developed. In speaking of 'moments in qualitative research' Lincoln and Denzin [2011: 629] observed, it should be recalled, how QDAS emerged from an earlier 'moment', identified in terms of a 'crisis of representation', when it 'was quickly drawn into the fray' [ibid: 631]. From Davidson and di Gregorio's [2011] perspective, 'many universities have proven resistant to QDAS', and they contrast such loci of resistance with the 'significant expansion of QDAS in governmental, commercial and other non-profit settings' [ibid: 635; di Gregorio 2006; di Gregorio and Davidson, 2008].

The latter agencies are undoubtedly duped by the claims made within the QDAS assemblage that continues to be shaped by a desire for its folklore of performativity of perfection, based upon what is made visible within its hierarchically structured architecture of disclosive space for thinking. Herein bare life, whose inclusion within such architecture for research remains a matter of exception, reaches its culmination. Herein the fantasy of desire for perfection fails to uncover pivotal aspects of the existence of bare life that necessarily remain unconditionally impossible and incalculable as loci for the cultivation of knowledge – not least, the relationship of bare life with death, with earth, and with the Other. In the biopolitics of performativity, however, both the possible reshaping and the loss of humanity in such technology is not even elevated to being a non-issue; currently it remains without any language of expression.

In their biopolitics of performativity, taking no account of bare life within their language of research, Davidson and di Gregorio [2011] speak of QDAS opening a 'remarkable new form of transparency' [ibid: 627]. Ironically, what is particularly 'remarkable' is the astonishing lack of understanding concerned with the architectural space required for the cultivation of bare life itself, without which such QDAS analysis would be quite impossible.

In accord with such biopolitics of performativity and their 'crypto-positivistic epistemology', their desires would appear to be strongly shaped by the calculus of control. Such an axis of understanding then generates its own displacement activities, ensuring the hidden issues of the gathering powers of being as presence, and the ontotheological structuring driving enframing remains a non-issue without language. In the biopolitics of displacement, where understandability is located around the axis of understanding created by the calculus of control there are obvious concerns expressed in terms of 'the challenge of the internet' [ibid: 636–37]. For Davidson and di Gregorio [2011] and the developers of QDAS software this constitutes a problem not concerned with our relationship with technology or with the biopolitics of displacement of bare life. Rather their concerns centre upon 'an avalanche of unstructured data' from the internet [ibid: 636]. In most of what remains in their paper they devote to opening reflections on the developments of new tools that serve to integrate internet use with QDAS.

In the world of this particular assemblage, in their moves to expand 'the conversation' in 'addressing ethical concerns' [ibid: 638–39] the authors, not surprisingly, open further reflections upon the ethical dilemma facing researchers using QDAS 2.0 with the internet. In drawing from an earlier study of 'The Ethics of Internet Research' [Bassett and O'Riordan, 2002] in which 'in navigating the complex terrain of Internet research', Davidson and di Gregorio [2011] agree with Bassett and O'Riordan [2002], who argue that Internet should be viewed as the 'cultural production of texts' [ibid: 233]. The desire, therefore, and their intention to improve qualitative analysis through the continued development of QDAS remain insatiable, it seems. Paradoxically, such desire arises, as we have seen, from attempts to use such technology to overcome the necessary lacuna at the heart of human existence. What does this mean for the biopolitics shaping practice?

Paradoxically, the supposed 'revolutionary' biopolitics of QDAS lies in providing a mapping of the molecularity within any molar body that it maintains in a state of exception without, it would seem, becoming aware of the vital significance of such exception for its own existence as a form of analysis. With the quantum transitions over the past decades in the information technologies the authors talk with obvious excitement concerning the analytical techniques that are now available for qualitative researchers. Such biopolitics lays emphasis upon the multiplicity of subjects and objects that can now be analyzed using the latest 'QDAS' [ibid: 627–43] and upon the various innovations leading to 'networked tools' [ibid: 634–36]. But, while these are innovative tools for qualitative research it is also important to understand that the biopolitics involved serves to render 'bare life' as standing reserve in the ontotheological structuring driving enframing in such technologies. Though this particular assemblage generated by QDAS cuts through much analysis in its theorizing of the world of research – in its metaphysical determinations of entities and events [based on being as presence], and its ontotheology – paradoxically the significance for its analysis of the gathering powers and the naming force of being as presence currently remain a non-issue. It fails to give any consideration to the state of exception in which its biopolitics places bare life. Instead, and in accord with the biopolitics of displacement and the forces delimiting education, QDAS focuses upon the effectiveness of this technology in generating a wide range of outcomes now available for qualitative data analysis. In focusing upon the outer granular face of the self its violence upon bare life reaches its acme. In the absence of any language and with it the laws and sovereign powers that might give expression to such biopolitics, and, in particular, what it means for the complex relationship between research and bare life, at the time of writing there remains no space in which to conceive such a relationship.

The biopolitics of the assemblages based upon QDAS also makes plain the ideological hermeneutic circularity of the logics that as simulacra delimit and circumscribe the architectural space for what is done in the practices of research. The phantom of this economy of exchange ironically purports to be grounded upon the principle of reason that in remaining completely unable to find any independent grounding in the lives of human beings, simply grounds itself. Each of the different assemblages is then formed on the ghost of grounds reiterating what is done in practice – what amounts to a mere simulation of such grounds. And, their own particular organization of such practice is no more than a meagre shadow that returns us to Plato's cave allegory where its prisoner is held under the same illusion of reality by the shadows on the wall – with the ironic hubris of their theological structuring delimiting in each case the highest forms of beings possible within such a prison.

Within this assemblage humanity always remains in danger of becoming imprisoned in its simulacra. The reason is simple. It has taken largely no account of bare life; no account of the aspects of bare life that necessarily remain beyond knowledge; and no account of the paradox of the principle of reason that in the absence of grounds supplies its very own grounding. Such analysis is without basis. Its hubris deserves to be exposed in qualitative research. Provisionally, therefore, the rhizomatic plateau of thinking within the biopolitics of these particular assemblages, focusing solely upon the transparent *spectacle* of what may be determined as possible on the basis of calculation, would therefore seem to index demarcations limiting the scope for thinking. Once again in the *trompe-l'œil* of transparency 'bare life' and the ontotheology structuring enframing are completely lost.

Given that the arts opens contrasting languages to the sciences, at issue remains, therefore, what scope is there for new thinking within assemblages concerned with languages of art in research. There remains the question of the extent to which art opens 'smooth space'[4] for bare life in radical contrast with the striated space generated by QDAS with its many divisions and categorizations. Here, T.S. Eliot's poesy presented in Little Gidding[5] also springs to mind:

> *. . . History may be servitude,*
> *History may be freedom. See, now they vanish,*
> *The faces and places . . .*
> *. . . to become renewed, transfigured, in another pattern*

In historical terms the question remains as to how much for each of us as unique beings does the work of art open reflection upon other patterns of the incalculable, unconditional and impossible dimensions of the facticity of practice: to what extent does art open disclosive space for the analysis of bare life?

Plateaus of thought generated from languages of art

In opening reflection on 'analysis and representation across the curriculum' Laura L. Ellingson [2011: 595] introduces her readers to what she calls a 'qualitative research continuum', opening space for a multiplicity of assemblages. She uses this notion in 'mapping' the 'field of qualitative methodology' constituted as a 'broad spectrum of possibilities' that in the tradition have tended to be constructed in terms of binary divisions of 'art/science, hard/soft and qualitative/quantitative' [Potter, 1996; Ellingson, 2011: 596]. For Ellingson, in the 'analytical mapping' of practice most research occupies the middle ground in her continuum, reflecting the interplay of both the languages of art and science.

At issue in this case is the possibility of new thinking emerging from assemblages formed at one 'extreme' of her continuum, concerned with the art of practice, as the language of art is usually placed in binary opposition to scientific/technological language. In thinking in terms of assemblages one is also conscious that each re-iterates its own language, each with its own unique language game.

However, provisionally it would seem, Ellingson's desire directs her towards maintaining a grip on the metaphysical guardrails of being as presence. Such desire shapes her practice. For example, Ellingson [2011: 595] foregrounds the exposition of her 'qualitative continuum' with a conception of data that remains within the extant exchange economies of objects and subjects given in qualitative research. In her terms in the analytical framing of research 'data or other assembled empirical materials will be understood' in terms of 'the process of separating aggregated texts [oral or visual] into smaller segments of meaning for close consideration, reflection and interpretation' [ibid: 595]. In radical contrast, therefore, remain the question of the extent to which the artistic left-hand side of her continuum opens radically contrasting 'smooth space' for assemblages and the rhizomatic plateaus of thinking, so opening disclosive spacing for bare life and taking away grounds for enframing.

In conceiving the art-based left end of Ellingson's spectrum there is a seemingly unconscious reiteration from Husserl's work, however, in express forms of desire for 'openly subjective knowledge' that is located within a distinctly feminist [rather than Cartesian] space. Within her assemblage she reveals 'embodied . . . stories, poetry, photography and painting', drawing from Carolyne Ellis' [2004] work concerned with *The Ethnographic I*. But, although Ellingson [2011: 599] recognizes 'among artistic/interpretivists, truths are multiple, fluctuating and ambiguous' [ibid: 599], her 'analytical framing' remains largely directed, it would appear, by her desire for the safety and security provided by the gathering powers and naming force of being as presence. It is this desire and with it the intention to be comprehensive in her review, it would seem, that drives Ellingson to gather together a wealth of studies that light up aspects of the assemblages emerging from her continuum, not least art-based research situated on the left-hand side of her spectrum [vide, Richardson, 2000; Spry, 2001; Ellis, 2004; McAllister et al., 2005; Lee, 2006; Parry, 2006; Ellingson, 2011: 599].

As Tami Spry's [2001] autoethnographic studies are located here, it is interesting to uncover to what extent her biopolitics opens space for reflection upon aspects of 'bare life'. This is not a Cartesian-based assemblage. In her 'embodied methodological praxis' Spry's [2001: 706] approach to 'analytical framing' challenges critical reflection on many aspects inscribed within the traditions of qualitative research. She speaks of the *'personal/professional/political emancipatory potential of autoethnographic performance as a method of inquiry'* [ibid: 706, emphasis as in the original]. In staging her research act she locates *'autoethnographic performance'* at *'the convergence of the "autobiographic impulse" and the "ethnographic moment"'* [ibid: 706, emphasis as in the original]. For Spry such a location is never fixed, it is *'represented through movement and critical self-reflexive discourse in performance'* [ibid: 706, emphasis as in the original]. The temporal unfolding of such movement is manifest in *'articulating the intersections of peoples and culture through the inner sanctions of the always migratory identity'* [ibid: 706, emphasis as in the original].

Her poetic form of writing opens space for a multiplicity of readings of her paper symbolizing a distinct break from the traditions of research. Paradoxically, however, while reflecting a strong but silent gesture in moves towards justice, her language still remains imprisoned within the metaphysical exigencies constituted by being as presence. Her study opens with the statement:

> 'BEING THERE'

In 'being there' her metaphysical language opens space for a great variety of possibilities. BEING HERE follows. Readers find themselves in a liminal space. Spry [2001] then continues in a playful dialogue with an imagined reader:

> '"Threshold"
> Strange
> right,
> wrong,
> odd
> . . .
> where I am to begin ethnographic fieldwork
> with Chilean shaman.
> *I am not there,*
> *but I am not here either.*
> . . ..
> Clifford Geertz [1988] writes of fieldwork,
> "Being *There is a postcard experience.*
> It is Being Here, a scholar among scholars
> that gets your anthropology read . . ."
> Mih-ha Trihn [1991] writes, "*Knowledge is no knowledge*
> *until it bears the seal*[6]
> *of the Master's approval*"'. [ibid: 85; emphasis added]

This liminal space Spry creates in her assemblage is filled with tensions, contradictions and the interplay of possibilities. The architecture of the coded space it has generated would appear to reflect a strong desire to open subjectivity to a multiple of discourses, generating a play of possible subjectivities. One is not sure from this introduction where the self is located. There is a double play with representation in the possibility of 'being there' located on a 'postcard'. One gets little hints, too, of the anxieties, moral dilemmas and feelings experienced in a unique place constructed by 'the other' – 'I am at NCA1' – located for this particular world of the self, and given staccato expression in her poesy: 'strange/ right/ wrong/ odd/ tensive/ dialectical/ liminal. . .'. In this liminal space one also uncovers numerous references to a performative world of practicing ethnography 'among scholars': 'report back', 'evaluation', 'reviewed'. . . and the aligned suggestion of possible demands for authenticity, Spry's 'verisimilitude'. The issue of knowledge and its acknowledgement within relations of power foregrounds her work.

Later one reads the silent traces of some of the feelings, tensions and concerns that surface from being there/being here within formal ethnographic research. Spry cites Goodall [1998][7] for whom '[o]ne of the most "disturbing" characteristics of autoethnography is that its prose style or poetic is at odds with the clear scholarly preference for an impersonal, nonemotional, unrhetorically charming, idiom of representation' [ibid: 6]. Her reflection on this issue is unequivocal. It 'was something [she] was glad to be rid of' [Spry, 2001: 723].

Silently, then, her assemblages open space for the interiority of the self and the possibilities of bare life. In 'An Eating Outing' [2001], she, for example, opens another liminal space in her exploration of the experience of 'anorexia nervosa'. She writes: 'In much of my early life I often felt like I was calling to myself. Speaking from subject "I" to a disembodied "you-self".' In the performance of autoethnography Spry began to find herself, as that trace of 'someone, someone from inside my body, finally, gingerly, began to call back' [ibid: 715]. In this matter she notes how:

> Theory helps me name the experiences interred in the body, whereas performance helps me to reinhabit my body, immersing myself into those scary spaces—introducing me to myself—so that the semantic expression of autoethnographic practice reflects the somatic experience of the sociocultured body. [ibid: 715–16]

In this way the assemblages from her writing are, in the words of Denzin [1997],[8] 'not just subjective accounts of experience', rather 'they attempt to reflexively map multiple discourses that occur in a given social space' [ibid: xvii].

However, in the biopolitics of research presented within her paper the absent presence of 'bare life' remains. In this particular reading of her paper the architecture of space created remains structured around the metaphysical exigencies of being as presence. Ironically, however, Spry's [2001] ethnography does take seriously Geertz's [1988] challenge that 'like quantum mechanics or the Italian opera, it is a work of the imagination' [ibid: 140]. But, the wellspring of such imagination still remains in the grip of being as presence. Herein lies the 'meaning maker' shaping the disclosive space for her poesy; the very same meaning maker we had uncovered from the earlier technological assemblages.

Her paper highlights that in order to cultivate such imagination what is demanded is more than simply multiples of other discourses, suggesting silently another constitution of language in *différance*. In practice, however, the question also remains concerning just how other languages/meaning makers may affect the movement of desire. The question remains, how does narration per se affect the space for thinking within its assemblages.

Plateaus of thought generated from narration

The case of Matti Hyvarinen's [2008: 447] assemblage, 'analysing narratives and story-telling', similarly reveals the practice of much play of possibilities unfolding in narratives. She, too, gives no consideration to bare life, but although unspoken her analysis appears to open considerable space for it.

If we look once more at the locus of desire emerging from Hyvarinen's [2008] writings its intention is directed towards examining the many possibilities for agency involving writing and its associated subjectivity. The ubiquity of narratives is one of the emergent themes in her writing. To cite Roland Barthes's [1977] well-known passage, the omnipresence of narrative is characterized in terms of its being:

> able to be carried by articulated language, spoken or written, fixed or moving images, gestures, and the ordered mixture of all these substances; narrative is present in myth, legend, fable, tale, novella, epic, history, tragedy, drama, comedy, mime, painting. . . . Stained glass windows, comics, news item, conversation. [ibid: 19]

But, within such rich multiplicities Hyvarinen's desire appears to be directed towards uncovering just how 'stories theorize the particular' by comparison with the quantitative forms of analysis that for her 'represent general trends' [ibid: 450]. Most exciting here is what Hyvarinen [2011] draws from the work of Ochs and Capps [2001], concerning the exploration of 'narrative activity [as] a sense-making process rather than a finished product' [ibid: 15]. It suggests the possibility of using narrativity within the particularities of unique worlds.

Her focus upon the particular is as close as she gets to bare life, reflecting unspoken moves towards justice. She also speaks of the ways in which 'life stories exhibit thickness of expectation and the strong presence of the "I"' [ibid: 456]. Here she is particularly mindful of Bakhtin's [1986] thesis concerning the role expectation plays within everyday discursive practices. For Bakhtin utterances are 'constructed, as it were, in anticipation of encountering' expectations from others involved in such practices [ibid: 94; Hyvarinen, 2011: 456].

The complex interplay of expectation Hyvarinen [2011] then constructs in terms of the relationship between dominant cultural canons focuses upon Communism [ibid: 457]. Here, of course, we are concerned with the Capitalist canon and expressions of bare life. Moreover, in practice the metaphysical exigencies that displace bare life make no distinction between arbitrary boundaries distinguishing capitalist and communist societies. It is revealing that Hyvarinen [2011] returns to individual expression, consonant with her axis of understanding concerned with the subjectivity of agency. Silently, within this biopolitics the principle of reason is there in the background structuring the grammars of expression for this invention, the 'individual.' Like Gibbs [2013] and Kincheloe [2008a,b] and others, who use the language of trans-disciplinarity, her desire is finally directed towards the exploration of 'interdisciplinary mission'. But, as we have seen each of these groups remains located with the politics of plenitude and the constitution of objects and subjects on grounds of reason and other metaphysical exigencies, ironically silencing bare life.

Surely, the fantasy of reason and the metaphysical exigency of being as presence needs to be exposed in qualitative research – its faculty purports to create a transparent world that is ever in danger of remaining imprisoned by the fetishism of shadows created within Plato's cave. At least *différance* provides a basis for understanding the composition of traces of narratives found in research, opening disclosive space for bare life.

Différance has been in play throughout this examination of analytical techniques used in research. It continually opens possibilities for bare life in the 'event' [*événement*] of research as something coming, as something that continually opens us to the interplay of the unknowable future and to the hubristic powers that paradoxically maintain a grip on the present they re-present as 'transformation'. These powers are in danger of blinding so many from the simulacra with which they are working for much of the time. The biopolitics of desire driving such powers, with its fantasy of the transparency of strategizing of truth claims, reflects once again the paradox of the sublime powers at work still turning shadows in Plato's allegorical cave into the naming force and gathering powers of being driving enframing. Much remains to be learned, therefore, from the effects of unconscious desires in shaping practices. In *practice* this is a matter for both research and authentic education concerned with the effects upon bare life.

Such illusory powers continue to fuel the forces delimiting education in research. The radical challenge to the force, therefore, must come from the constitution of *différance* and the many traces of nomadic diaspora that emerge from it. It means subjecting 'delimiting education' to the on-going deconstruction in the name of justice to come.

In examining research through the lens of philosophical discourse the elaborations of the *practice* from the perspective of bare life has created numerous possibilities for further research. But, a significant weakness of the current study is that it remains paper-based – it is important to understand more about *practice* in its opening stages before it is reduced to official forms of documentation given the name 'research'. Provisionally, it was surprising, too, to find that art's smooth space for eclectic forms of practice still appears to remain within limits constituted by striations of paradigmatic space generated in enframing.

Given the general absence of languages giving expression to 'bare life', there remains the question of the implications of this analysis for the development of policy concerned with research.

* * *

Epilogue

In deconstructing the paradigmatic organization of research we began with the question: *Is it not possible to step beyond learning?*

The following theses, emerging from the deconstruction of paradigmatic research, indicate that its ontotheology is currently delimiting education in, and so what may be learned from, research:

1. *Paradoxically, the fantasy generated from forces delimiting education cultivated within enframing remains located within continued moves towards the metonymic perfection of the ontotheological structuring of research in its own simulacra. In this Disneyworld of research such simulacra are foregrounded in their very own language as objects of consciousness. But, this objective language of the ruling production, as we have uncovered repeatedly in the absent–present laws of research remains, as Debord has shown, 'at the same time its ultimate goal'. Whereas, in largely unspoken ways, in moves towards justice in qualitative research, in art-based and practice-led forms of research, in the event of such formal means of inquiry its spacing opens possibilities for the regeneration of bare life, disputing space created within 'the society of the spectacle', for better or worse.*
2. *Any transformations in the world of research have remained located almost exclusively with concerns directed towards the 'at-hand' outer granular face of the self. The unique qualities, particularities and experiences revealed of bare life in its 'to-handed' immersion in its worlds of practice remain almost completely elided within current forms of social and educational research.*

* * *

Qualitative research is in an excellent position to take the lead in opening debate on these matters. At issue remains the possible transformation of policy in research. It is to this issue that we now turn.

PART FOUR

The politics of practice

CHAPTER TEN

The politics of evidence: Challenging forces 'delimiting education' in this liquid modern world

Issues of methodology are always intimately connected with matters of policy governing research. It is policy that largely determines priorities, the basis upon which funding is allocated, and not least the loci of interest for research at particular times and in particular places. For the molar body in Lather's [2006] terms policy is put in place in order to 'regulate behaviour and render populations productive' [ibid: 787]. Part of the issue is a matter of biopolitics. As she suggests, this 'entails state intervention in and regulation of the everyday lives of citizens in a "liberal" enough manner to minimize resistance and maximize wealth stabilization' [ibid: 787]. But here we have to keep in mind 'bare life'. In Lather's unspoken conception of biopolitics, this remains without any language of expression.

The particular difficulty with any possible reformulation of a biopolitics that foregrounds rather than displaces bare life is that historically modern research has taken the lead given by classical philosophy. The Romans, with their focus upon knowledge, reinforced this way of understanding *the* world – bare life seemingly remaining without language. This was pivotal in opening space for gaining control of *the* world through knowledge. Our modern Western social world, its traditions, languages, cultures, institutions, organizations and practices – including many of our approaches to research – all reflect this earlier history that still continues to press itself upon us in this new millennium.

Consequently, for policy makers, politicians, administrators and other governmental agencies, silently, bare life has never been raised even to the point of being a non-issue. It was this very same power that President Bush had used in presiding over the Patriot Act issued by the US Senate on 26 October 2001. It followed the act of terrorism now identified as '9/11' that saw the loss of 2,996 lives[1] and the demolition of the Twin Towers in Manhatten. The act allowed the attorney general to 'take into custody' any alien suspected of activities that 'endangered the national security of the United States'. Though it carried with it the caveat that 'within seven days the alien had to be released or charged with violation of immigration laws or some other criminal offence' [Agamben, 2005: 3], it served as a basis for the 'radical erasure of any legal status for the individual, thus producing a legally un-namable and unclassifiable being' [ibid: 3]. In fact, in legal terms Agamben's study reveals that in Europe the 'suspension of the constitution' has often been employed as a matter of law at times of war.

The biopolitics: The state of exception and policy

We all now live in a 'state of exception' [although most of us do retain a legal status]. In being encultured, socialized and formally educated within Western forms of education into this way of living it is now difficult to appreciate the violence being done in the name of delimiting education in the mythology of research for the 'good life' [Flint and Peim, 2012]. Almost a century and a half ago, poet Walt Whitman wrote *Song of Myself*, 'an American epic' that for Bloom [2004] 'defines the ethos of a nation' [ibid: 530], but unlike many practices of research at least Whitman was intimately aware of his own mythology. His poesy is clear on this matter:

> *Sure as the most certain sure, plumb in the uprights, well entretied,*
> *braced in the beams,*
> *Stout as a horse, affectionate, haughty, electrical,*
> *I and this mystery here we stand*

There remains mystery, too, in bare life, constituted as it is in the play of *différance* whose language is ordinarily silenced and at best made an exception by the sovereign powers of the language of research. It is also possible to change radically our ways of doing research concerned with the social world that has challenging implications for the biopolitics of bare life and the way we understand the interplay of education with practices of research and just how this plays out in policy. What follows, therefore, in concluding this book, is a preliminary exploration of this standpoint as a way of opening further debate on these issues.

There are other hidden powerful forces at work in the biopolitics of research. In its focus upon what are represented as 'evidence' and upon 'evidence-based-practice', as we uncovered earlier, there are always already a number of sublimely powerful forces at work shaping how we see things and what is seen. In this study the general absence of concern for both such hidden forces and the biopolitics of bare life is demonstrable. Ironically, it arises from the absence of language within specific fields of practice to express the violence being done in the name of ethical research.

The absence of languages to express such forces delimiting education is not a matter of omission, nor does it imply some form of languor. Nor is it a new phenomenon. For example, in the psychologist David Smail's [1993] account of unhappiness that arose for many casualties of the 1980s business culture there is no mention of delimiting education, too, but he speaks of how people 'were being robbed of the linguistic tools to express the violence being done to their understanding' [ibid: 106] in managerialist discourses. In research such violence arises from the strategizing of truth claims, requiring compartmentalization and specialization in order to maintain the integrity of such claims. Such foregrounding of truth claims constitutes the base for the current biopolitical and performative focus upon production, productivity, with bare life rendered without a language of expression. Have we not reached a time, therefore, where more consideration should be given to languages that begin from the express privileging of bare life rather than knowledge production? This deconstruction of the forces delimiting education in research has begun to lift the veil of ignorance.

Here, in approaching the issue of policy-making in research, therefore, it is helpful to examine the loci of such ignorance enjoyed by policymakers and others. The object of this approach is to create a backdrop for the stage set by a significant authority within the international field of qualitative research, in Norman Denzin's [2011], ground-breaking paper on 'The Politics of Evidence'. It also suggests a number of other lines of critique and of resistance that can be in energizing the movement of research policy that currently constitutes an obvious and significant threat to qualitative research.

The biopolitics of quality: An egregious disguise

In revealing the forces 'delimiting education' our deconstruction provides a basis for understanding what amounts to a profound locus of ignorance hidden behind an egregious disguise created by the current Disneyland figures of transparency and audit, shaping the work of many policymakers and others. As the Latin expression, *egregi-us* – literally, towering above the flock – suggests, such disguise has proved to remain powerfully effective.

But, before returning to this matter a brief exegesis is perhaps helpful, in order to critically examine first how such forces have been understood within discourses of research.

Historically, policymakers' unfamiliarity with matters of research is much more than might be suggested by their policy analysis being situated within doctrinaire forms of positivism [Rist, 2000]. Their unawareness is not a matter that will ever be fully corrected by any appeal to 'applied cultural work and [the] ethnography of policy', not even to appeals for 'quality policy analysis that can engage strategically with the uses of research for social policy [in moves] towards the improvement of practice' as suggested by Lather [2006: 783]. While opening a significant question for policymakers, Lather's [2006] understanding of the 'human sciences' as the 'unconscious of the sciences', and her exploration, based on her reading of Foucault, of 'undoing and recomposing' the very ground on which the human sciences stand, serves only to open reflection upon both powers delimiting education in research and the *aporia* – the non-way confronting researchers in their practice.

Although Lather's work in concert with Foucault [1970 {1966}, 1972] makes no mention of the forces delimiting education or of authentic education, there is within its compass a dimension of *educere*. What provokes such a movement, it would appear, is her sense of 'reflexive scientization' that she draws from Ulrich Beck [2000]. This has the advantage of awakening us to the possible institutionalization of self-doubt, self-interrogation, and self-reflexivity [Backstrand, 2003: 33, cited by Lather, 2006: 788]. At this point of self-doubt Lather meets Derrida's *aporia* – the non-way that for him is a condition of walking. However, the question remains within the movement of *educere*, that is, which direction will be taken. Lather's citation of Foucault, for whom the human sciences constitute a locus of 'counter-science' of knowledges that serve to "unmake' that very man who is creating and re-creating his positivity in the human sciences' [Foucault, 1970 {1966}: 379; Lather, 2006: 785], suggest a movement in the direction of authentic education. But, in the absence of any expression of the powers hidden within politics delimiting education, not least the sublime powers of being manifest in enframing and its grounding ontotheology and the possibilities open to bare life, there remains some doubt about the direction Lather has taken. At issue remain forces delimiting education in research. These simply constitute a locus of almost perfect disguise; distracting agency with their foregrounding of issues of 'transparency' and 'quality' [whatever these terms mean], maintaining the hidden forces shaping research in a state of exception. Therefore, while there may be hope for a 'sea change in the conceptualization in accountability' as Weber [1999: 453, cited by Lather, 2006: 788] suggested, it will not come from using Foucault in 'rethinking the research-policy-practice nexus' [Lather, 2006: 788].

Ironically, as a possible counter-science, in its present form, in being constituted largely upon grounds of the politics of plenitude, as we have seen, qualitative research serves to generate ever-enhanced powers in opposition to those produced within positivistic sciences further expanding the powers of enframing. What is demanded in policy terms is a radically contrasting constitution for the sciences consonant with the futural horizon of bare life – namely, that of *différance*. This comes with the incorporation of moves towards justice and authentic education in an expanded ethic of such an event. Given the sublime intensity and extensity of the forces delimiting education in all forms of research, there remains much work to do in such an expanded ethic.

As an index of the powers of disguise and displacement used in the biopolitics of research it was difficult to find any reference to this issue within the archive of leading textbooks used to ground this study.[2[Introduction]] But, the biopolitics of displacement foregrounding evidence, truth, and the issues of knowledge production, as we have seen, can now be understood in the way it serves to create a state of exception for bare life.

The biopolitics of displacement

We have indications of the forces delimiting education in research from the deconstructive analyses of Heidegger, Foucault, Agamben, Derrida, Lacan and many others. These philosophers have opened spacing for thinking regarding bare life on the basis of their discourses concerned with a number of obvious figures, not least death, the nothing, anxiety, guilt, being, temporality, language, power, the Other, the trace, the supplement, the unconscious, undecidability and so on. But, in research many of these matters remain at best selectively expropriated but largely silenced. Herein lies a profound locus of ignorance concerned with bare life for policymakers and others. Such ignorance and the sidelining of pivotal discourses concerned with bare life results from the forces delimiting education in research. The latter forces of demarcation serve to partition and separate such issues within specialist discourses of philosophy, the arts, history, anthropology and so on.

The work of Heidegger – in the everydayness of *Dasein*'s experience of the dominion of *das Man* and its powerful effects upon what 'one' does – reveals one dimension of the forces delimiting education in research. Here the biopolitics lays emphasis upon the norms of particular forms of organization, delimiting education in aspects of such sociology [Giddens, 1984, 1990, 1991, 1993; Parsons, 1967a,b]. Thus while these sociologies are insightful in terms of the complex interplay of norms and values in social practices, at best in terms of the 'structuration' of agency, they tend to sweep aside any consideration of the particularity and uniqueness of the interiority of the world of the self and of bare life. And, although, as Giddens [1993] has claimed, analytic to the concept of agency is the possibility of doing otherwise, such agency is itself grounded in the principle of reason and so reproduces another aspect of enframing, leaving bare life without discourse.

In Heidegger's [1977, 1991] later work, too, concerned with the gathering powers and naming force of being that constitutes grounds delimiting education within *das Ge-stell*, enframing has become strongly evident in our deconstruction of methodological thinking in research. In biopolitical terms enframing is usually experienced in terms of performativity: moves towards efficiency, quality assurance, requirements made for evaluation or other forms of assessment of 'evidence' in technocratic regimes. It is such drives that are delimiting education in research. What becomes hidden and the locus of pre-judice, *vis-a-tergo*, as Gadamer [2004] has suggested, are the forces at work behind such drives that unconsciously dominate human beings [ibid: 354] [Table 2.1]. Delimiting education currently remains the driving force behind the biopolitical violence visited upon bare life. What is taught [albeit unconsciously] from working in research, and becomes the very basis of professionalism, is the imperative always to surpass current 'standards' identified on the basis of the forces delimiting education. Ironically, therefore, bare life is never even given an express language.

Ordinarily, in the biopolitics of research its formal training directs researchers towards identifying or generating new paradigmatic, methodological, methodical and analytical categories in which to situate their studies. But, again we have uncovered what amounts to a largely unconscious dimension to these familiar processes of research – *all such movements towards new categories reflect the naming force and gathering powers of being and its manifest forms of enframing.* Much earlier it was noted how Gadamer's [2004: 354] hermeneutic of historical consciousness in his analysis of *Truth and Method* had uncovered in research the 'power of the prejudices that unconsciously dominate' experiences of undertaking research. In this deconstructive reading of such pre-judicial structures it is clear that this is not a matter for the individual, but rather a question of such structures always already in place before undertaking any research [Table 2.1]. In adopting an approach to analysis suggested by Husserl's philosophy, so far we have identified the 'pre-' constituted before the 'judicial' in terms of '*what is given in practice*'. Such judicial structures arise, then, from the ontotheological structuring driving enframing within a multiplicity of rhizomatic networks, assemblages and apparatus connecting practices. Such pre-judicial structures delimit education in research and constitute laws retained by the sovereign powers of its languages.

Such judicial structures, like those of language, as we have seen, bond together a force of inclusion/exception. Within the biopolitics of 'bare life' coupled with drives delimiting education, bare life in its multiplicity of possibilities is always in danger of becoming available for use. The collective body of bare life is thereby rendered as a sublime lake of energy, thoughts and possibilities that are available for use within the languages, laws and the ontotheological structuring of research. Herein lie the forces at the heart of contemporary capitalism [and communism]. The awe-inspiring arrays of unique worlds constituting the interiority of the self are simply located in a state of exception. Traces of those very worlds sometimes become sucked into the unconscious driving force behind those unique qualities that are sought after within particular dimensions of professional practices.

In lifting the veil of ignorance and in approaching Denzin's [2011: 645–57] much-needed paper concerned with 'The Politics of Evidence', as an index of the sovereign powers at work in the judicial forms of the languages of research, it is also scandalous to find that there is simply no mention of bare life; ironically its state of exception remains a gift of the politics of evidence. In moving to understand the arguments propounded within debates – Kincheloe's [2008a] 'knowledge wars' – it is important to keep in mind that we are in danger of approaching these debates with a view of *practice* being circumscribed and delimited as solely the province of research.

Practices involving the doings and sayings of people, we should remind ourselves, are teleoaffective phenomena affecting the molar dimensions of the social body. They are not delimited in any way by research per se. The ontotheology driving enframing is not somehow delimited to practices of research alone. As we have seen earlier such enframing is shaping *The Society of the Spectacle* [Debord, 1977] in what now emerges as the sociology of our 'liquid modern' world [Bauman, 2011].

In its current 'molar' [Conley, 2005a: 171–72] structuring the surface of those lakes of excess energy is dominated by the 'molecular' [Conley, 2005b: 172–74] interactions of elites, including policymakers. In this sociology the worlds of policymakers and other elites are privileged and radically disconnected from those others who inhabit the endless molecular encounters and struggles in the flows, eddies and counter-flows within the bulk of the liquid. The powerful dominion of this sociology for ethics and for policy-making in research deserves to be addressed more fully.

Biopolitics in a liquid modern world

Denzin's [2011: 645–57] critical examination of *The Politics of Evidence* helpfully gathers together much literature in moving to inform and to open debate concerned with the place of qualitative research within the production of evidence for governmental agencies and other powerful and globally networked corporations, which variously make use of 'findings' from such research. In reflecting upon the 'research act'[2] Denzin opens his paper with the proposition, foregrounded by his reading of St Pierre [2006], that 'qualitative researchers are caught in the middle of a global conversation concerned with emerging standards and guidelines for conducting and evaluating qualitative research' [ibid: 645].

On the surface of our liquid modern world, as suggested by Denzin [2011: 647], such gathering powers of being are manifest in a multiplicity of reiterations of the will-to-power, reflecting ever-more powerful globalized institutionalized apparatuses, assemblages and rhizomatic networks, mediating plateaus of thinking, representing a multiplicity of interest groups within research. 'Evidence' would appear to constitute grounds consonant with this multiplicity of interest groups. Both the biopolitics and the sublime forces experienced in delimiting education serve to reinforce the hegemony of 'grounds'. The ethic delimiting education in research structures three dimensions of activity in *the* world of practice on grounds of evidence; namely, in securing the basis for the conditional, calculable and possible dimensions of such activity, placing bare life without express language. This is the 'dialectical illusion that historical consciousness' [Gadamer, 2004: 354] of *the* world of practice appears to create. The judicial structures and the aligned sovereign powers that are already in place, delimiting kinesis of its molecular interactions within such forms of practice, do so within the horizon of being as presence. In ethical terms such structures delimit the transparency of research to the conditional, calculable and possible dimensions of performativity within the technological dimensions of *practice*.

But, the horizons structuring the unique worlds of human beings are futural. In such horizons lies the background understanding of being delimiting education and shaping the capitalist world; it generates the desire for change. Such horizons unconditionally open bare life to impossible and incalculable dimensions of practices that will always necessarily remain beyond our capacity to know. In the molar body of the modern world futural horizons are there as largely hidden forces driving those molecular inter-relationships in practices grounded in the hegemony of being as presence, reason, assessment, the market, policy, theory, performativity, values, identities and so on. It is at the interface of these two radically contrasting forms of horizons of practice that subjects are cultivated, being seeded from the logics of economies of signs that initially exist in forms of desubjectification consonant with the horizon of being as presence. Here in practice, then, we have the meeting of two horizons for the biopolitics of bare life.

Biopolitical horizons

Policy-making is located at the interstices of these two horizons of being – the horizon of being as presence and the horizon of being to come – though the biopolitics silencing bare life and its aligned forces delimiting education have created the illusion that only the conditional, calculable and possible dimensions of practice matter. The dominant horizon of being as presence, of course, has enjoyed a long history from the Ancient Greek philosophers. Within this dominant horizon it is these three dimensions that constitute the tangible aspects of all technologies of production in *the* modern world.[3] Policymakers can be forgiven for adopting such a standpoint as it is entirely consonant with dominant current forms of ethic of practice, remaining delimited by the very same horizon of being as presence.

In the 'politics of evidence', therefore, ironically, the desires and drives arising from our futural horizons, constituting grounds for the cultivation of 'evidence', are continually elided. Herein lies the basis for the ignorance displayed by policymakers and others, in holding onto extant forms of ethics. In the *bio*politics of the production of 'evidence' the futural horizons of bare life remain located within a state of exception. The forces delimiting education continually reinforce this position by focusing the attention of policymakers only upon those conditional, calculable and possible dimensions of practices.

One prominent and much vaunted official version of the institutional machinery of 'scientifically based research [SBR]' or the 'evidence-based movement', can be found, for example, in the National Research Council's [NRC], 'new gold standard' for measuring research taken from 'medical science' [ibid: 647; NRC, 2002, 2005]. However, is it not deeply ironic that such a gold standard is constituted on the basis of ignorance?

In such institutional apparatuses and their associated rhizomatic networks of thought, as Denzin [2011: 647] notes, 'quality research' represents its logics for 'scientific' and 'empirical' forms of inquiry as being 'linked to theory'. Its methods, in accord with such governing logics, purport to 'direct investigation' and to produce 'coherent chains of causal reasoning based upon experimental or quasi-experimental findings, offering generalizations that can be replicated and used to test and refine theory' [ibid: 647]. But, leaving aside the complex issue of the metaphysical determination of these various subjects, it has been shown they come to life only when they are cultivated in futural horizons.

Ironically, in the molar body in the throw of such logics, research is deemed to be 'high quality' in accord with its identity as 'scientific' [Denzin, 2011: 647; NRC, 2005]. Given the forces delimiting education at work behind the cultivation of such subjects it is not surprising that there are sublime powers directed towards maintaining the illusion of control over such subjects through their conception of 'scientific inquiry'.

In the United States, Denzin [2011: 647] reminds his readers, 'such research must conform to the Office of Human Subject Research definition of scientific inquiry' and it is in their definition of 'scientific research' that the continued reiteration and the cultural reproduction of the profoundly delimiting seventeenth-century, Newtonian, Baconian and Plato-inspired view of reality can be seen. According to this Office, science is:

> any activity designed to test an hypothesis, permit conclusions to be drawn, and thereby to develop or contribute to generalizable knowledge, expressed in theories, principles and statements of relationships. [U.S. Code of Federal Regulations, Title 45, Part 46, cited by Denzin, 2011: 648]

Herein lies its conception of all scientific research. Once again the violent and flagrant biopolitical dissimulation of bare life does not even enjoy a language of expression. Hence, the continued ignorance of policymakers concerning the forces at work behind their own productions might be expected, but remains deeply outrageous, especially given the hubris involved. Not only do policymakers remain without language and associated space for thinking concerned with the violence done to bare life, ironically, in holding on to the metaphysical exigencies of 'scientific research', they also remain imprisoned within its ontotheological structuring. For example, for one of the highest authorities in the United States:

> 'Research is described in a formal protocol' [*the ontological ground*] '[so prescribing all forms of such on-going activity] that sets forth an objective and a set of procedures designed to reach that objective' [*theological structuring*] [cited by Denzin, 2011: 648; U. S. Code of Federal Regulations, Title 45, Part 46 as quoted in American Association of University Professors AAUP, 2001: 55; see also AAUP, 1981, 2002, 2006]. [emphasis added with the insertions of ontological and theological structuring]

In such 'research' enframing cultivated within such ontotheological structuring is simply not recognized by these authorities – yet paradoxically it is always in danger of reducing bare life to a standing reserve of excess available energy.

This is why it is so important to open a language for the ethics of research that keeps in play any pre-judicial structures inscribed in the traditions of research [Table 2.1] with directions of travel towards justice. The earlier deconstruction indicates that a number of significant researchers are beginning to uncover a range of issues concerned with biopolitics and forces delimiting education in research. There are at least three inter-related outstanding issues:

1. Currently, there are no languages within research giving expression to the biopolitics of bare life. Rather, primacy is given to delimiting forms of education in research [although this specific terminology is not currently employed], placing emphasis upon the performativity

of knowledge production in accord with enframing, constituting a basis for professionalism.[2[Introduction]]

2 And, much paradigmatic/epistemic-structured research would appear to be constituted within its epistemologies on grounds of the politics of plenitude,[2[Introduction]] reproducing the hegemony that in research nothing lies beyond its scope.
3 Ethical systems of research appear to remain located within the horizon of being as presence, rather than futural horizons consonant with the temporal structuring of the unique worlds of human beings.[2[Introduction]]

These issues can be addressed by opening research to its reconstitution in *différance*. This can be achieved straightforwardly from the deconstruction of extant forms of practice. Before arriving at the point there remains the complex issue of extant forms of ethics grounding both qualitative research and policy.

Biopolitics – towards an expanded ethic of research

The foregoing study has underlined the increasing range of concerns directed towards questions of justice in research. However, as we have seen within the traditions these remain located within horizons of 'being as presence', leaving bare life without express language. At issue, therefore, in this policy debate is any indication of moves towards justice. The complication arrives when 'ethics and models of science flow into one another' [Denzin, 2011: 648], because as we have shown almost all traditional understandings of justice remain also within the horizon of being as presence. Contra Denzin [2011], therefore, the 'hand in glove' relationship of ethics and models of science, with 'IRB panels . . . simultaneously rul[ing] on research that is ethically sound *and*' is assumed to be 'of high quality' [ibid: 648], constitutes a significant locus of error.

Provisionally, this study has shown the need for a radical rethinking of the ethics of research that needs to be expanded and to become restructured [moving away from its current deontological structuring] to incorporate moves towards justice. It is a reconstituted ethics that begins not with moves towards the production of knowledge, but with the foregrounding of bare life. As this radically reconstituted ethics it would certainly no longer work 'hand in glove' with science because in deconstructing the latter a number of languages emerge opening space for critical examination of enframing, bare life and the forces delimiting education within research.

A pivotal issue is not only the absence of any language that gives expression to enframing and its related issues, but also, and ironically in the forces delimiting education constituted in enframing, the drive towards the production of truth claims continues to render the self's possible alienation. Ordinarily, hegemonic moves to generate so-called evidence in research are aligned with a critical evaluation of the methods, methodologies and analytical techniques used and any claims to knowledge. This epistemologically grounded hegemony delimiting education in research teaches researchers what is considered to be important – namely, the quality of data, evidence, methodology, methods and so on. Such teaching, however, simply makes no mention of any matters concerned with the hidden drives from any 'pre-judicial' structures of research that generate a locus 'delimiting education' in the production of evidence, where the issues of 'enframing', '*das Man*', 'bare life' simply do not feature. The forces delimiting education tend to give no grounds, therefore, for any significant questions for the extant order within paradigmatic forms of research. Of course, there are continual challenges made by researchers within all of its specialist practices, but provisionally, within the governmental apparatus of paradigmatic structures for research such loci of contestation tend to remain delimited within the metaphysical exigencies of specialized structures.

Given the sublime intensity and extensity of the hidden social forces involved one may initially and mistakenly empathize with Denzin [2011], for whom the real danger is that 'we have lost the argument even before it gets started' [ibid: 648]. [Denzin's 'we' refers to the community of qualitative researchers]. However, while the languages are not currently in place that give expression to such hidden social forces, as we have seen, many dimensions of qualitative research have begun to open space for significant questioning of aspects of the extant order both within research and within specific societies and communities of practice. For example, Cannella and Lincoln [2004] make the point:

> The NRC Report is a U.S. government-requested project designed to clearly define the nature of research that is to be labelled as representing quality . . . accurately referred to as methodological fundamentalism . . . contemporary conservative research discourses . . . have ignored critical theory, race/ethic studies, and feminist theories and silenced the voices and life conditions of the traditionally marginalised. [Ibid: 165; cited by Denzin, 2011: 648; see also Feuer, 2006; Freeman et al., 2007; Hammersley, 2005; St Pierre, 2006; St Pierre and Roulston, 2006]

Although there is here no specific mention of issues concerned with delimiting education, bare life and so on, or the provocation of authentic education in research, these issues are substantially implicated in this very discourse concerned with those 'marginalized' within society, where the effects delimiting education are always so acutely felt.

It is agreed, too, as Denzin [2011] has indicated, 'the politics and the political economy of evidence is not a question of evidence or no evidence' [ibid: 647]. In the everyday micropolitics of undertaking research one also agrees that such politics is 'a question of who has the power to control the definition of evidence, who defines the kinds of materials that count as evidence, whose criteria and standards are used to evaluate the quality of evidence' [ibid: 647]. But, ironically, what is missing in this focus upon agency is that it contributes to another dimension of the forces delimiting education that continues to blind us from examining those hidden forces at work shaping the 'juggernaut'[4] of contemporary research.

The pivotal question is not 'who' but '*what* is the locus of power controlling the production of evidence', namely, the '*what*' concerning those matters hidden by the forces delimiting education that are shaping and driving the very means of the production of research. Ironically, the forces delimiting education serve to reinforce the ego-logy of centralized and hierarchically structured forms of leadership and management [Flint, 2012a,b, 2013c]. In cultivating grounds for such ego-logy, reinforcing the dialectical mirage of historical consciousness of practice that is so consumed by beliefs in 'hard evidence' driving its thinking, there remains, ironically, the forces delimiting education placing the ego in denial of any possible pre-judice.

In this matter qualitative research has a pivotal role to play in both challenging and in providing a much-needed balance to the centralized build-up of powers in the late modern world. This demands languages for the expression of thinking concerned with such hidden powers. Ordinarily, as we have witnessed earlier, the forces delimiting education in research create their own form of blinkers, ironically demarcating what can be seen in accord with the authority invested in delimiting forms of education. Therefore, in response to Denzin's [2011] challenge, in opening space for a discussion around what he calls 'chart[ing] a path to resistance' [ibid: 645], deconstruction and its moves towards justice within an expanded ethic of research would seem a good starting point.

Biopolitics – the forces delimiting education

In preparing the way for such deconstruction there are three other dimensions of the forces delimiting education in research that are pertinent to the issue of policy. These concern the process of desubjectification / re-subjectification from data analysis, the manipulation of the morality of research and the quantification of research and its relationship as a practice with the social world. Herein lies another locus for the deconstruction of policy-making.

Delimiting education, of course, represents how data analysis works within 'standardized modes of knowledge production' [Kincheloe, 2015a:

325]. It also provides one point of focus for Denzin's [2011: 648–49] critique of the NRC recommendations for policy. He draws upon an earlier study by Maxwell [2004], raising questions concerning 'rigorous, quantitative and [frequently] experimental designs' that 'have become the accepted modes of investigation' [Denzin, 2011: 648]. He notes that in Maxwell's terms this standpoint opens further questions concerned with 'meaning, context and process' [ibid: 649] of any data analysis.

At issue remains Denzin's summary of points not mentioned by Maxwell [ibid: 649]. These include Denzin's observations that 'amazingly . . . there is little attention given to the process by which evidence is turned into data. . . .', 'there are no detailed discussions of how data are to be used to produce good generalisations, test and refine theory, and permit causal reasoning . . .', nor how 'data carries the weight of scientific process . . .', nor how 'data can easily be shared . . .' and, finally, 'money and concerns for auditing from the audit culture seem to drive the process' [ibid: 649].

But, here Denzin remains focused upon the visual aspects of quantitative data analysis. The forces delimiting education in research place particular emphasis upon what is re-presented as 'transparency': herein lies the basis for the strategizing of truth claims and the powers enacted within research. Ironically, what Denzin and others in research do not yet see, it seems, is the violence wrought upon bare life by these standard processes deemed as ethical. His statements enact further powers uncovering some of the limitations of Maxwell's earlier critique. But, the forces delimiting education block consideration of the unconscious hidden forces at work in this process of data analysis.

From the perspective of bare life, however, the issue concerned with data amounts to its de-subjectification. Here, at the interface between possible futural horizons and horizons of being as presence, there is the possibility of re-subjectification and becoming an active subject. But, the process of analysis represented by Maxwell [2004] and by Denzin [2011] constitutes data only within the horizon of being as presence. It is not surprising, therefore, that policymakers, too, see only the visible aspects of such data analysis. What is called for once more, therefore, is a critical examination of such delimiting education in order to uncover and to expose its hidden and largely unconscious forces shaping research.

There remains, also, the moral question of how delimiting education affects the conduct of research. Until now it has been assumed on the basis of Schatzki's [1996] discourse that practices are constituted as a teleoaffective structures, with defined end points. The latter idea of Schatzki can be traced back to Kant. Such 'telos' in practices is predicated upon assumptions of a Kantian ethic governing their moral conduct. In MacIntyre's [1984] terms 'the difference between a human relationship uninformed by morality and one so informed is precisely the difference between one in which each person treats the other primarily as means to his or her ends and one in which each treats the other as an end' [ibid: 23].

But, in many institutional and organizational practices 'ends become means'. In biopolitical terms here we will focus for the moment upon only the visible dimensions of integrative practices. For example, in the implementation of the NRC model 13 recommendations are made concerning what 'research agencies should' do [Denzin, 2011: 648]. These recommendations are 'directed to federal funding agencies, professional associations and journals, and schools of education' [ibid: 648]. It is here that the manipulation of ends–means logics is found in the continued imperative of the modal verb 'should'. The NRC has recommended that 'research agencies *should*' 'define and enforce better quality criteria for peer reviews. . .' where 'publishers and professionals' *should* 'develop explicit standards for data sharing. . .' and 'schools of education and universities' *should* 'enable research competencies. . .' and so on [Denzin, 2011: 648].

On the question of the morality of such conduct Alistair MacIntyre [1984] cites the work of Philip Rieff [1977] for whom 'ends, the causes there to be served, are means of acting; they cannot escape service to power' [ibid: 22]. As we have seen they involve the 'obliteration of any genuine distinction between manipulative and non-manipulative social relations' [ibid: 23]. Though emotivist cultures are so deeply ingrained within research and its associated institutions, the point here is to raise the question of the extent to which policymakers 'treat the other as an end'. At issue, too, remains bare life. In all of the policy pronouncements by the NRC, SREE, AERA and other agencies in the United States and in the United Kingdom this is notable for its absence. The forces delimiting education in the biopolitics remains as strong as ever.

Biopolitics – delimiting education in *practice*

In biopolitical terms, in remaining with the visible dimensions of practice, there remains, too, the issues delimiting education in the quantification in the practices of research. It is here that such forces reach their acme [ακμή] in what Debord [1977] calls *The Society of the Spectacle*. It is here, too, that concern will be directed towards *practice* per se, rather than simply the practice of research. Passing reference has already been made much earlier to '*the spectacle*', but it is in the matter of the quantitative representation of *the* world that one is reminded by Debord that the 'commodity form is through and through equal to itself, the category of the quantitative' [ibid: para 38]. This is one consequence emerging from the logic of '*the spectacle*' where 'everything that was directly lived has moved away into representation' [ibid: para 1]. It may be helpful, therefore, to examine critically moves towards the privileging of quantitative analysis in research, on the basis that it is 'the quantitative . . . the commodity-form develops'; this form can develop only 'within the quantitative' [ibid: 38].

One should note in passing that once again forces delimiting education in research provide a direct focus upon the fantasy of transparent aspects of the struggles between policymakers and researchers; blocking, *vis-a-tergo*, completely any consideration given to the pre-judicial categorization of paradigmatic and epistemic forms of research that serve the generation of significant partitions within dialectic consciousness of practice per se. Delimiting education is driven by pragmatism. It does not concern itself with any consideration of hidden social forces at work in such partitioning. As a locus for *educare* it simply reinforces what is seen in practice. It largely blocks any consideration being given to the effects upon the smooth surface of practice being striated with such categorical partitioning. Once again the evidence produced by policymakers indicates their profound ignorance on this matter of delimiting education [Denzin, 2011].

The question remains, therefore, concerning the probing of delimiting education within paradigmatic forms of research. At issue, too, remains the question of what particular issues, questions and problems arise for policymakers and others from rhizomatic thinking that knows no such partitioning and works alongside the smooth surface of practice itself.

The privileging of quantitative analysis also reflects the deferral of signs from Bacon, Newton, Hulme, Berkeley and others in the early Enlightenment, continually folding over and pressing into practices of research [Flint, 2012b: 246–76]. This is not, however, any concern for delimiting education, itself directed towards only the visible aspects of what is seen in hegemonic cultures of research leaving open the question of what may be visualized in practice. Teaching only the ways in which rigorous quantitative research must be undertaken, delimiting education is in danger of remaining imprisoned within the striated surface of its own logics of researching practice. It thus blocks almost completely any consideration given to the place of history in shaping the privileging of quantitative analysis. Delimiting education remains obsessed with the fantasy of what quantitative analysis makes transparent; its language is grounded in the conditional, possible and calculable aspects of what can be learned about aspects of practice, so apparently obviating any imperative for trust.

In his reflections on 'standards for empirical social science research', for example, Denzin [2011: 650–51] notes how, for the American Education Research Association [AERA] [2006: 6–10] 'there is extensive discussion of quantitative procedures', and 'trust' is never an 'issue' [ibid: 651].

Biopolitics – the ethics of trust

As long as the biopolitics of policy-making correlates quantitative objectivity with trust, bare life, too, must remain without a home in language. Ordinarily, of course, the forces delimiting education serve to distract attention from these very issues.

But, what exactly is trust? AERA [2006] seems to be confused on this matter, too. In making a connection between trust and warranty of claims made by researchers they appear to be closing down the need for any trust, giving it ground within the horizon of being as presence. The horizon in which trust is located is futural, trust being a mark of one's confident expectation of something that is about to happen, making it impossible to ground. Herein lies the imperative for authentic [not delimiting] forms of education within both qualitative and quantitative research. The locus of AERA's confusion appears to lie in their conflation of warranty being given to *both* the procedural basis for knowledge claims and the truth of the claims themselves. Warranty is required only for the procedural basis of any given research: it calculates and defines what is possible under particular conditions that are made public.

This is not surprising. In developing what were then new criteria for evaluating truth claims in 'naturalistic inquiry' Lincoln and Guba [1985] spoke of 'credibility', 'applicability', 'consistency' and 'neutrality' of truth claims [ibid: 296–301] and in so doing similarly clouded the distinction between the futural horizons for trust/'trustworthiness' [ibid: 289–331] located within the horizon of being as presence governing their means of evaluation of research [Flint, in preparation, i, v]. Such clouding is not intended to impute some form of error made by the authors; rather it reflects their own albeit unconscious sensitivity to the vitalizing forces of bare life that remains the elephant in the room created by their 'naturalistic paradigm' [ibid: 36–8]. In part what is missing from their account is authentic education and its relationship with all forms of research. Research that is credible on this count challenges and is challenged by authentic education, opening languages and spacing for thinking that is awake to both the visible and hidden dimensions that can be visualized within such research.

Truth claims to knowledge, therefore, make demands upon trust connecting all stakeholders with authentic education at work in research. What connects trust and authentic education is that unconditionally they cannot be reduced to calculation; they are both incalculable. In foregrounding both visible and invisible aspects of such a process authentic education in research cultivates trust in the spacing challenging the existing social order. Trust and its correlative forms of risk are opened within the spacing between the present and futural horizons of the event of research. Trust opens and is opened by the disclosive spacing for authentic education in the language of *différance*. This is another reason for the need to rethink and revise the conception of credibility and so on used in evaluating research [Flint, in preparation iv].

Trust cultivated by authentic education literally vitalizes research and is, therefore, impossible to ground, remaining unconditionally incalculable. In the space opened by authentic education, there is always a *risk* that any former truth claims will be questioned, refined, changed in some way. Is this not the provocation that fresh, exciting and innovative researchers bring to the public stage? Trust cultivated in authentic education in research keeps alive that very risk. It opens space for research as an event [*événement*] as something futural that in its democratic moves towards justice it opens possibilities for the regeneration of humanity and of societies.

Without such interplay between trust, risk and authentic education there is always a significant danger of research becoming moribund. It is this vital interplay that is essential to research that would appear to remain absent from policymakers' thinking, at least those policymakers represented within Denzin's [2011] article. It is also quite a shock to discover at this point the extent of policymakers' ignorance on all of these matters: the very same policy-makers, filled with their own hubris once more, who are continually making almost impossible demands upon qualitative forms of research in order to reduce it to becoming another form of quantitative research. This also provides an indexical measure of the biopolitics in concert with forces delimiting education in research, serving to distract attention being given to such issues with their continual drives towards performativity and quality issues at the heart of researchers' professionalism.

On the basis of moves towards a revised understanding of 'credibility', in relation to the interplay of trust, risk and authentic education, most quantitative research has no credibility. What Denzin [2011: 649] calls 'hardcore SBR: evidence-based inquiry' falls at the first hurdle – in being captured within its own ego-logy, and in being consumed by the mythology of empiricism, it completely elides giving any consideration to the forces *vis-a-tergo* that always already shape and delimit its functioning [Flint, in preparation vi].

The purpose of quantitative forms of inquiry is to provide us with conditional and calculable dimensions of trends in any social phenomena. Such research depends upon the possibility of translating aspects of social phenomena into measurable qualities, constituting grounds for calculation. But, such quantitative forms of research operate within the horizon of being as presence, and are yet to address the challenge of its ontotheology driving enframing, rendering bare life in its state of alienation. Clearly, on this count quantitative research has much to do in order to gain credibility.

There is certainly no room for complacency in qualitative research. It provides credible means of generating knowledge concerned with the interplay between the possible, conditional and calculable dimensions of phenomena and practices, and the impossible, unconditional and incalculable aspects of the very same. This interplay gives qualitative research a structure that is moving towards spacing, no longer alienating the self, and even silently awakening researchers to bare life. Like quantitative inquiry, for qualitative research to gain credibility on this new measure, it, too, has much work to do in uncovering the hidden dimensions of its practices that constitute grounds for the sovereign powers of its many languages.

On this basis the Society for Research on Educational Effectiveness [SREE], having no place for qualitative research [Denzin, 2011: 649], is yet to address just how quantitative research alone can be employed in generating credible evidence, given that its grounds are merely simulacra that become lost within its hubristic presumptions concerning its own logics.

Biopolitics – the challenge of authentic education

On the basis of the foregoing exploration of credibility, risk, trust and authentic education in research, what is also called for is a re-examination of 'two global standards . . . offered for reporting empirical research': 'warrantability' and 'transparency' [AERA, 2006; Denzin, 2011: 650]. Warrantability deserves to be re-examined and opened to new thinking connecting it with the foregoing revised measure of the credibility of adequate evidence provided to justify conclusions. Similarly, the locus of transparency needs to be re-thought in ways that connect the precise logic of inquiry used in research with the forms of education involved in such practice [Flint, in preparation, v].

It is also important to move with thinking about *practice* into the smooth space before it became striated with a multiplicity of categorical forms of structuring. Returning to Debord [1977] the SREE and others consumed by the hegemonic illusory efficacy of quantitative research are immediately confronted with the challenge posed by commoditization that, as mentioned earlier, is cultivated by quantitative measures of phenomena and events in the world alone.

Indeed, there are a number of obvious questions that are yet to be addressed that provide the basis for questioning both quantitative and qualitative forms of research:

- what measures are in place that serve to equilibrate the forces at work in enframing, and also to balance the forces upon bare life?
- what measures are in place within research that ensure moves towards justice?
- what measures are in place to ensure that research is not reduced to being solely a commodity?

Debord's [1977] thesis now stands in relation to debates concerned with *The Terror of Neo-liberalist* market-driven economies [Giroux, 2008], along with the mind-numbing sameness of bureaucratic forms of organization found in George Ritzer's [2012] *Macdonaldization of Society*, and the anxieties created by on-going drives towards consumption in Oliver James's [2007] *Affluenza*. Each of them in their own unique ways reflects some of the manifestations of enframing in society. What connects each of them is the sublime naming force and gathering powers of being as presence and its impact upon bare life. They each in their own different ways reflect *the spectacle* that in Debord's understanding is striking in its connections with the hegemonic circularity of its repetitions of signs, those objects of consciousness generated from research.

Debord [1977] notes how 'the language of *the spectacle* consists of signs of the ruling production' [ibid: para 7] that arises from a 'world vision', here constituted in the name of delimiting education, 'which has become objectified' [ibid: para 5]. In this *spectacle* reproduced within the apparatus of modern research, therefore, 'everything that was directly lived has moved away into a representation' [ibid: para 1]. The forces delimiting education that we have identified as emerging from the unconscious experience of research provides a focus solely upon the mythological transparency of signs represented in *the spectacle*. Ironically, as Debord's critique suggests, 'the truth of *the spectacle* exposes it as the visible negation of life', as 'a negation of life that has become visible' [ibid: para 11], consonant with bare life's 'state of exception'. The great body of human beings, then, are simply reduced to being available for use within the capitalist canon [Flint and Peim, 2012]. As Debord [1977] has suggested the success of those economies of signs lies in 'the proletarianization of *the* world' [ibid: para 26; emphasis added] that has always been external to the self, corresponding to the 'concrete manufacture of alienation' [ibid: para 32].

Here paradigmatic research, as we have begun to witness, bases itself in the sovereign powers of the economies of signs in its apparatus, consonant with a biopolitics displacing bare life, creating a world that is both present and absent. As we saw earlier, *the spectacle* not only makes visible, but is also constituted in such visibility. Debord [1977] suggests in such a movement that the spectacle makes visible 'the world of the commodity', coming to dominate 'all that is lived' [ibid: para 37]. Provisionally we have shown that the forces delimiting education in the experience of research is an education constituted in commoditization. Consequently, the movement of such commoditization that research continually draws upon has been shown by Debord to be 'identical to the estrangement' of human beings 'among themselves and in their relation to their global product' [ibid]. It hardly constitutes a recipe for justice.

We might enquire, too, as to where 'the self' finds its home. But, in the context of 'research as a power-driven act', as Kincheloe [2005a: 324] reminds his readers, this is not a straightforward issue, requiring 'clarification of her or his position in the web of reality and the social relations of other researchers and the ways they shape the production and interpretation of knowledge' [ibid: 324]. Feminists, for example, continually open space for new thinking with incisive challenges concerned with the gendering of such acts of research [Lather, 1991; Hughes, 2002; Roseneil and Frosh, 2012]. In the apparatus of research the intentionality delimiting education directs the docile body towards 'becoming', as the feminists Luce Irigaray with Mary Green [2008] have suggested, manifest 'in objects, things, and their representations or mental reduplications'. The suggestion is made that in this apparatus, man continues to reproduce signs of where 'he search[es] for himself outside the self, while intending to appropriate this outside, notably through representations' [ibid: 221].

In enframing and its manifestation in '*the spectacle*' there is much high-octane fuel pumped into the engine of neo-liberalist cultures in which the market becomes 'the organising principle for all political, social and economic decisions' [Giroux, 2008: 2]. In the emerging market economies, education leaders and their organizations are driven along within hegemonic cultures that foreground performance, know-how and mastery. In taking a global view of neo-liberalism at the heart of capitalism, Henry Giroux [2008] suggests that it has to be understood within a larger crisis concerned with 'meaning, vision, education and political agency' [ibid: 3]. But, given that the apparatus of paradigmatic research and its assemblages are always in danger of being reduced to *the spectacle*, there is surely a need for new forms of leadership. Leadership creating spacing for bare life, where 'individuals can be educated as political agents equipped with the skills, capacities and knowledge they need to perform as political agents' [ibid: 3].

One possible starting point for policymakers, therefore, suggested by Hargreaves and Fink [2006], is the summons generated in cultivating cultures that foreground 'being-with others' and 'speaking-with others' [Irigaray, 2008a: 221]. But, if the foregoing analysis is correct, and the eternal return of the same that Heidegger [1977d] saw as pivotal to enframing is apposite, what is required is far more than simply defining what might be demanded of policy-making in any instrumental form. It is also much easier to undertake deconstruction in philosophical terms than to implement it in practice. On reflection, therefore, the provocations of authentic education in research are considerable and far-reaching.

CHAPTER ELEVEN

The politics of practice: Challenging spacing for play in delimiting forms of education

In research many work with the presupposition that what can be learned can be based only upon cognition of, or an embodied experience of, *what is given* in *practice* – data, epistemes/paradigms, methodologies, methods, analysis. . . . Moreover, the forces delimiting education in research continue to serve such practices by focusing with ever-greater acuity, it would seem, on matters of the conditional and calculable aspects of what is possible in the name of research. This as we have seen has now become a matter of policy in the leading nations around the world. This way of conducting research has only one event horizon – being as presence – restricting the outcomes of research to truth claims concerning objects of consciousness. Consequently, at every turn 'bare life' is ever in danger of being reduced to a sublime excess of energy driving the 'juggernaut of modernity' that continually threatens to run out of control.

Paradoxically, however, without the *inter-play* of the vitalizing forces of bare life with practices of research there could be no regeneration and transformation of *practice*. At issue, therefore, remains the question of the structuring of the event [*événement*] of research as something to come [*á-venir*] involving the *inter-play* of unconditional/conditional, incalculable/calculable aspects of what may become impossible/possible in the future. It is in this inter-play that subjects are generated from beings in the apparatus and assemblages of research. At issue, then, remains the question of how the *inter-play* of the event horizons for research may be structured – that is, the inter-play of the horizon of being as presence delimiting education in research along with the horizon to come of bare life, opening spacing for authentic education in research as a re-generative event.

The problem arises with the introduction of play in the apparatus of research. Our institutional apparatuses have largely been developed in order to create strict delimitations on the possibility of play. It is no accident there is no mention of play in either Foucault's or Agamben's readings of 'apparatus'. Within the apparatus of education, for example, it is assumed by many that play should be reserved for young children before more serious activities of learning about the world take place [Flint, 2009]. Many in research[2[Introduction]] assume, erroneously, that play correlates only with chaos, the absence of control and the absence of any structure. As we have witnessed earlier, practices of research do not recognize not only the vitalizing aspect of the inter-play with the forces of bare life, but also every aspect of the apparatus and its assemblages of research works assiduously to displace such bare life, closing down any such inter-*play*. It is the sovereign powers of the existing languages of research that affect such closure. But, such languages and their inscribed laws are always open to transformation.

In the mosaic of snapshots concerned with the inter-play of horizons in research that follows in this final step of the argument we sought to examine the rigour of the claim that such practice opens spacing for research as a regenerative event. The argument is divided into two aspects. Pivotal to this initial aspect remains what may be understood by 'play' and just how play is often closed down in research in the traces of that inter-*play* of researchers with signs. In the concluding aspect the deconstruction sought to develop a radicalized reading of Kincheloe's bricolage.

Play in research – challenging delimiting education

It is ironic that play is generally not thematized as an issue within research, because its field of language is 'in effect that of play' [Derrida, 1978: 289]. This is the field of the 'infinite substitutions' of signs. So, as the Dutch historian, and one of the founders of modern cultural history, Johan Huizinga [2008{1938}] forcefully demonstrated, play is the very seed corn for the cultivation of new cultures. Silently, and at least temporally, for example, over the past five years participants' involvement at IAPD and ICPD conferences where *practice* is the issue take on the challenge of keeping in play other possibilities for their research that are not ordinarily found within their own specialist forms of practice. Ordinarily, however, the forces delimiting education and the biopolitics serve to keep secure the extant ontotheology.

At issue, therefore, remains just how play that was regarded by the founder of Russian cultural-historical psychology, Lev Vygotsky, as a 'leading activity', generates space for the possibility of radically transforming cultures in the practices of research, not least, its ontotheology. Ordinarily, as we have seen the latter is elided almost completely [Flint, 2009]. It is, perhaps, helpful to be reminded of the ways in which the ontotheology becomes manifest, and how it positions bare life.

The pre-judicial structuring of the ontotheology is inscribed within research as law. It is there:

- In projections of beings *as such* [ontology] and *as a whole* [theology] of entities, bodies, objects, data found/used in the apparatus of research or its outcomes; and,
- In the idea as universal [ontology] and the idea as paradigm [theology] used to structure research;

Within paradigmatic structures their ontolo-*theology* is ordinarily further strengthened in binary expressions concerned with the separations of whatness –*thatness*; of subjectivity – *the subject*; of substantiality – *the substance*; of action –*organization*; and, of content – *form* [Table 2.1]. But, in each case in the repetition and reiteration of signs we have shown that in practice there is always considerable space generated for unexpected contingency. We should keep in mind, too, each of these terms is but cinders of identities. While this results in seemingly endless on-going activity involving the re-visioning, refining and developing of earlier standpoints in research in order to overcome such shortcomings, there are also limits to this process. It is such events that open possibilities for reinventing our lives through such practice or in which lives become reinvented in such experience, for better or worse.

In ethical terms bare life always requires space to play, space *to be*; otherwise it is in danger of becoming reduced to a machine-like puppet of enframing. In Heidegger's thinking, enframing constitutes grounds for only one way of revealing the world; that is, on grounds of reason [or one of its progeny in terms of the principle of assessment, Flint, 2012c: 63, and the principle of the market, Flint in preparation, ii]. As we have seen a pivotal dimension of enframing is the action of value positing. Such value positing is manifest and has been already uncovered in:

- the representation and metaphysical determination of entities;
- the production of theories;
- the reproduction of the forces delimiting education in research; and
- the paradigmatic structuring of research.

Play and in particular the inter-*play* of 'bare life' within the apparatus and assemblages of research opens disclosive spacing, cutting through all such metaphysical constraints. It opens spacing in moves towards justice.

At play in the apparatus of research

In Huizinga's [2008 {1938}: 1] seminal work *Homo Ludens*, literally, man playing, his intention had been to characterize the 'nature and significance of play' in a variety of cultural contexts: civilization, law, war, poetry . . . [ibid: 46–135]. His writings had, in fact, recognized that 'in play there is something "*at* play"' [ibid: 1; emphasis added]. But, his 'foreword', particularly, had contained a warning that readers should not fall too easily into 'a metaphysical conclusion' that all 'human activity' might be called 'play'.

In thinking through what is *at play* mediating the actions of researchers and others, one is reminded in reflecting upon Huizinga's [2008 {1938}] analysis of the great divide that separates *Natürwissenschaften* [life sciences/physical sciences], on the one hand, and the *Geisteswissenschaften* [cultural sciences], on the other. In examining the effects of play in cultivating cultural transformation within different forms of integrative practice, not once does Huizinga reflect upon the ways in which aspects of the natural history of human beings over much longer time-scales than those usually considered within the *Geisteswissenschaften* may be *at play* in shaping the actions of bare life.

We should keep in mind, too, one of the leading neuroscientists of the twentieth century, Paul Maclean, whose seminal work on play in the context of evolutionary neuroethology has also been much overlooked [Cory and Gardner, 2002]. In his *magnum opus* in this field, *The Triune Brain in Evolution,* Maclean [1990] provided a theoretical structure of the brain that in effect is three brains in one – a 'triune' brain incorporating a 'reptilian brain' that is surrounded by a 'paleomammalian limbic system', itself covered with 'neomammalian outer cortex'.

In evolutionary terms Maclean himself [1985] observed 'three outward manifestations' that for him 'clearly distinguish the transformation from reptiles to mammals' of which 'play' [ibid: 405] was regarded by him as particularly significant. His concerns regarding play served to ensure that his work was overlooked by many within the neuorethology community, who tend towards the foregrounding of cognitive grounds for understanding behaviours. But, Maclean [ibid: 413] draws the reader's attention to 'the peace keeping function of play'. His detailed investigations reveal that 'play behaviour in mammals might be construed as promoting harmony within the nest, and later, social affiliation' [ibid: 413]. He notes how 'a playful chimpanzee mother, described in the work of Jane Goodall, that would take to playing with her son, Frodo, almost always when he got too rough with his smaller sister' [ibid: 413]. Play, then, from this evolutionary perspective serves to maintain harmony within the home. The essential 'nest' in which 'bare life' dwells, of course, is language. In opening us to new possibilities play serves continually to open us to new understandings of the world that are surely required elements within any peacekeeping function.

Fortunately, there is at least one writer, Camille Paglia, who does not subscribe readily to the language divide between the arts/cultural sciences on one side and the life sciences/physical sciences on the other. In opening space for such *inter-play* her work suggests possibilities for further research. In her exploration of *Sexual Personae* in literature Paglia [2001], who is professor of humanities at the University of the Arts in Philadelphia, makes an important contribution in opening space for concerned with 'intricate intersection between nature and culture', where she locates those powerful forces of 'sexuality and eroticism' [ibid: 1] that until now have barely featured in this account of *practice*. For Paglia [ibid: 12] feminist discourse 'has been simplistic in arguing that female archetypes were politically motivated falsehoods by men'. For her 'sexuality is a murky realm of contradiction and ambivalence' that 'cannot always be understood by social models that feminism, as heir to nineteenth century utilitarianism, insists on imposing upon it' [ibid: 13]. In making sense of nature and art in literature Paglia draws confidently from biology and the life sciences as she does from Freud's psychoanalysis and her love of poetry, and so opens space for considerable challenge to male dominance in Western societies. For example, she notes that

> an erection is a hope for objectivity, for power to act as a free agent. But at the climax of his success, woman is pulling the male back to her bosom, drinking and quelling his energy. Freud says 'Man fears that his strength will be taken from him by woman, dreads becoming infected with her femininity and then proving himself a weakling.' [ibid: 27]

From this observation Paglia concludes that 'Masculinity must fight off effeminacy day by day. Woman and nature stand ever ready to reduce the male to boy and infant' [ibid: 27]. Her observations suggest a productive area for multi-disciplinary forms of research concerned with the dominant Apollinarian 'life-force' and how such struggles are enacted in order to gain control in *practice* through enframing. But, despite Paglia's radical opening of play between the cultural and life sciences and the possibilities this creates for further study, her writings still remain locked within the metaphysical exigencies of ontotheological structuring, albeit without the traditional barrier dividing the sciences.

The play of signs

Within the archival record created by the textbooks on research that were used to inform this study[2[Introduction]] at the time of writing there have been simply no references made to any play of signs. For example, there is no thematization of play within Richardson's [1994, 1997] explorations of 'crystallization'; Lather's [1994, 2007a,b] and Richardson's [1993] 'transgressive validity'; and St Pierre's [2011: 621] and Denzin and Lincoln's [2011: 565] 'transgressive data'. Denzin and Lincoln [2011] speak about 'transforming pure presence into a disturbing, fluid, partial and problematic presence' [ibid: 123]. Here is a radical moment for Denzin and Lincoln. Almost immediately it becomes withdrawn into the metaphysics of specialist dimension of extant paradigmatic research. In a final remark following her critical reflections upon 'Performance Ethnography', Judith Hamera [2011: 317–29], too, opens consideration of our hospitality given to 'acts of poiesis' that she hopes 'will productively intervene in our understanding of the world, and in the world itself' [ibid: 327]. Here, as in Denzin and Lincoln's writings, there is no mention of the play of signs.

So, what exactly is the issue, and what is indicated by the play of signs? In response what follows is a deconstructive reading of Denzin and Lincoln's radical thinking before its metaphysical compartmentalization.

Earlier we made a distinction between 'Rabbinical' and 'Joycean' critical forms of repetition. However, even though we have continually sought to expose the naming force and gathering powers of being as presence, in effect we have remained secure in research, it would seem, by assiduously holding on to the metaphysical guardrails of being as presence. It has been assumed until now that the motifs of presence represented at every layer within the 'apparatus' of research, a priori, provide the only secure grammar and grounds upon which to undertake meaningful research. Researchers are anxious, it would seem, that if play is introduced then there is a significant risk the apparatus of research or its associated assemblages would simply become reduced to the rubble of meaninglessness [Flint, 2009]. This is why there is so much anxiety with play and the flux of time. This is why there are so many deeply entrenched powers at work that seek to take away such play – there is a built-in silent assumption that unless the play in the flux of time is controlled in research we will be left with nothing.

Within the apparatus of research we have uncovered already the motifs of presence, *a priori*, in the pre-judicial ontotheology structuring of the actions of what is done in practice and the organizational structures of such practices constituted within the apparatus of research. Though we have passed over this point, it is apparent that the motif of being as presence is also to be found in forms of 'subjectivity' expressed in research, along with 'truth' and 'knowledge'. These, too, are effects constituted within the metaphysics of being as presence.

Much earlier before Derrida [1973a] it was clear that the present is derived from repetition and not the reverse [ibid: 52]; 'something is' takes on the unity of a subject/object to the extent that it is brought forth by repetition. Being, therefore, we should remind ourselves, is proportionate to repetition – 'repetition does not come second, as in re-presenting a prior presence', but rather in coming first 'repetition is an enabling condition of any prior presence' [Caputo, 1987: 139]. In research, therefore, its formality arises *not* from an *a priori* ontotheological structuring of grammar, *but from the repeatability of its various patterns of signs*, of repeatable traces that, as Caputo observes, lies deeper than this rational grammar and indeed 'conditions its possibility' [ibid: 142].

Initially, however, to many researchers, in moving with the logic of repetition, there is already a source of anxiety produced. To repeat, for example, is both to produce and to alter, and so make and remake something in research. Repetition, therefore, is 'the principle of irrepressible creativity and novelty'. It would be impossible to repeat without making anew and without altering what is already made. While most researchers, undoubtedly, will recognize the difference between generic formulations of methodologies, methods and so on, what happens in the practice of research with experienced researchers, such differences become localized within specific applications, without ever questioning, it would appear, the presence of the metaphysical structuring of research.

But, let us look again at the way play can cut through such metaphysical determinations of practice. We have now reached the radical side of Husserl's phenomenological reduction where as researchers we still remain immersed in the great empire of signs, but before any metaphysical determinations of practice in the apparatus of research. In this particular *epoché* the language in which we have arrived is constituted in the play of *différance*.

Let us look carefully at the logic of repetition. Any repetition of signs that alters is always already bound to *that which is to be repeated* [its *repetendum*], both more generally in so far as the repetition requires a *repetendum* – a recurring phrase or note – and in the particular sense of the 'constraints imposed by the *repetendum*' [ibid: 142]. This is another reason why there is the need for an expanded and reformulated ethic of research that is directed towards justice.

In radicalizing Denzin and Lincoln's point, therefore, where they speak of 'transforming pure presence', it is the essential freedom of signifiers to transform presence. With this freedom to play they have the power to create beyond them, 'to produce in ways that are no longer bound by being and presence' [Caputo, 1987: 142]. The backdrop to this reading is Derrida's [1973a] critical reading of Husserl in *Speech and Phenomena*. In research, for example, silently in their critical repetition of signs, as indicated by the earlier examples cultivated by Lather, Richardson, St Pierre, Hamera, Denzin and Lincoln, Spry, Hyvarinen . . . and many others, individuals have begun to exploit the latent connections and associative bonds, semiotic links [graphic and phonic links are also possible] and 'every relation of whatever sort, existing among signifiers' within research and other associated practices 'in order to set forth the power of repetition' [Caputo, 1987: 142].

The particular examples reflect both the inventiveness of the individuals concerned *and* their capacity to engage with the play of signs. Rather than the more common position of being located within the polysemy of meanings [Kincheloe, 2005a, 2008], in the play of signs we have moved away from the high ground of meaning to find ourselves located within the disseminative drift of signs. But, formally, what remains and provides structure within this drift are the differential chains of signs as traces that distinguish particular forms of its practice in terms of methodologies, methods and modes of analysis. Even within the drift these localized chains remain in place as loci for reiteration and repetition. Even within the drift, therefore, there remains a structuring – the continued reiteration of various grammars of research bear witness to such a position. With deconstruction and the moves towards justice the apparatus of research is not going to become reduced to meaninglessness, leaving researchers with nothing. In practice, too, as Nietzsche suggested, it is possible within such drift to work pragmatically with various fictions, not least concerning truth and knowledge. But, in working within the disseminative drift there is a rationale for researchers to become open to a continually humbling reminder of the fact that their data, theories, methods, methodologies and apparatus are all incomplete contingent effects that are continually open to repetition and reiteration, and provide us at best with just traces of knowledge. Herein lies a rationale for opening disclosive space for bare life and so confronting and disputing the continued expansion of powers in research.

The examples chosen earlier might suggest that *only* those aspects of research that reflect manifest forms of inventiveness involve the critical and Joycean forms of repetition of signs: this is a falsehood. The development of all forms of science essentially involve critical forms of repetition of signs, where researchers have sought to use new terms, new theories, or to change in some way the context of their studies, so generating new traces of knowledge from their work. That is how science makes progress. There is at some point in the development of all forms of research some play of signs in the repetition of the discourses mediating particular forms of research. Without such a possibility there could be no progress made in science.

Formally and informally, too, as we have suggested earlier, there are a number of ways in which concerns with play serve to challenge aspects of research, not least in removing the naming force and gathering powers of being as presence. The ways in which play works in practice for researchers within different settings and its effects, however, along with its effectiveness in generating inventive forms of research would appear to deserve much further study.

The play of the supplement in research

Within the disseminative drift the standard protocols concerned with citing authorities within a field or with forms of knowledge used become open to question. At issue is the notion of the so-called origin itself. An earlier study of Vygotsky's thesis concerned with what he called 'the zone of proximal development' [Flint, 2009] illustrates the point. Flint [2009] had experienced that many people cite Vygotsky as an authoritative figure within the field as the origin of particular ideas, of knowledge and so on, but in practice Vygotsky's understanding of play as 'more memory in action,' for example, was shown to reflect ideas that can be found in Hegel's and in Husserl's philosophies [Flint, 2009]. In this way Vygotsky is not the originator of 'play' as 'more memory in action', and, therefore, any power derived from citing Vygotsky as the originator is immediately diminished. Within the disseminative drift over time ideas get passed along and iterated in different ways by individuals and groups, reflecting the play of signs.

There is another side to this story concerned with the possible origins of research. It brings into play the supplement. Having undone the notion of origin that was intended to mean 'something purely present which then gets copied in more or less adequate reproductions' [Caputo, 1987: 139], one asks what else remains in play in the flux of time. In response it is repetition as the non-originary origin that passes forward.

As Caputo observes, 'Derrida deals with this somewhat elusive state of affairs by speaking of the supplement of the origin' [ibid: 139]. It means that the origin, what phenomenologists consider, is given along with first-hand experience, is in fact deficient and in need of help. Objects, subjects and persons in research are not fully given in practice: 'they do not fall from the sky' [ibid: 139]. Rather they stand in need of generative, productive work supplied by *différance*. And, as Derrida [1978] suggests, 'one could say' that this 'movement of supplementarity' unfolds in the 'movement of play' [ibid: 289]. 'The supplement', the sign, 'instead of being added on as an extra, is in fact productive of presence in the first place'. The supplement, then, as we noticed much earlier, 'is both a surplus, a plenitude enriching another plenitude, and it makes up for something missing' in research, 'as if there were a void there to be filled up'. It is 'not simply added to the positivity of presence . . . its place is assigned in the structure by the mark of emptiness' [Derrida, 1976: 144–5].

Given the concerns regarding both delimiting and authentic forms of education emergent in research in this study, it is interesting that in Derrida's [1976] reading of Rousseau, 'all education . . . [is] described or presented as a system of substitution [*suppléance*]' [ibid: 145]: all education is 'originally' supply or substitute education. In cultural terms herein with the logic of the supplement lies another basis for the forces delimiting education and of authentic education in research. 'In Rousseau's writing', as Royle [2003] observes, 'education is consistently figured as standing in for or making up for – 'Nature'. Nature itself, for Rousseau, 'does not supplement itself at all' [Derrida, 1976: 145; Royle, 2003: 51]. For Derrida [1976], however, there is always 'a supplement at the source' [ibid: 304].

Identification and identities found in research, therefore, are always inextricably and interminably bound up with the play of supplementarity. Identifying always entails logic of adding on, making up, being in place of, inviting the logic of playful inventiveness that was manifest earlier in the examples taken from research. It has the character, therefore, of being phantasmatic or imaginary.

'For Derrida the supplement is not a secondary prosthesis that is added to identity; rather it is already *within* identity' [Dooley and Kavanagh, 2007: 24]. Spoken words and memory, which are often in research taken to be the primary loci of 'data', are themselves always contaminated by writing. 'This contamination is an example of what Derrida calls "the logic of supplementarity"' [ibid: 24]. Contra Lincoln and her colleagues [2011: 115], there are, therefore, no discrete voices of the 'author', of the 'researcher', of the 'participant' in research that constitute the supposed origin of 'data' used in analysis. This standpoint concerned with the separateness of voice can be traced back to Plato [amongst others], whose 'attempt to banish writing from the pure interiority of speech and living memory, and to maintain a strict outside-inside distinction, is structurally impossible' [Dooley and Kavanagh, 2007: 24]: 'the outside is already within the work of memory' [Derrida, 1981b: 109][1]. 'Speech requires writing in order to be what it is' [Dooley and Kavanagh, 2007: 24]. There is a movement and a play linking them, emerging from the strange logic of the supplement.

What interests me about the supplement, and about play in language, as our essential dwelling place on this earth, therefore, is that play, including the viral play of the supplement, opens possibilities and generates space in language where humanity is no longer conceivable in terms of programmable information that is made visible within the forces delimiting education in research [Flint and Peim, 2012]. Play opens us to the flux of time [Flint, 2013a]. It opens spacing for bare life.

The play of signs and the forces delimiting education

In the play of the supplement within identity, one source of inventiveness that has been much explored in terms of the artistic 'energies' and 'impulses' that burst forth from nature itself is that deferred from the inter-play between Dionysian and Apollonian 'tendencies' or 'drives' that gain expression within what Paglia identifies as 'sexual personae'. In Paglia's [2001] theory concerned with these two 'principles', 'Dionysius is identification, Apollo objectification' [ibid: 96]. For her

> Dionysius is the empathic, the sympathetic emotion transporting us into other people, other places, other times. Apollo is the hard, cold separatism of western personality and categorical thought. Dionysius is energy, ecstasy, hysteria, promiscuity, emotionalism – heedless indiscriminateness of idea or practice. Apollo is obsessiveness, voyeurism, idolatry, fascism – frigidity and aggression of the eye, petrifaction of objects. [ibid: 96]

For the young Nietzsche [1995], too, in *The Birth of Tragedy*, 'these two very different tendencies walk side by side, usually in violent opposition to one another, inciting one another to ever more powerful births' until they seem 'at last to generate the work of art that is as Dionysiac as it is Apollonian – Attic tragedy' [ibid: 1]. For Keith Pearson and Duncan Large [2006] in its presentation of 'the Dionysian and Apollonian as "tendencies," "drives" but also artistic "energies" and "impulses" that burst forth from nature itself' [ibid: 36], *The Birth of Tragedy* 'is appreciated as one of the most important attempts within European modernism to acknowledge the destructive forces and energies of life and subject them to philosophical work' [ibid: 36]. For Pearson and Large, Nietzsche's writing in *The Birth of Tragedy* anticipates Freud's focus on the play between Eros and Thanatos that has been there in the background from the very opening of this book.

Interestingly in *Knowledge and Critical Pedagogy*, Kincheloe [2008b] explores the challenge of offsetting thanatos – the death drive – with eros – the life impulse – in writings about research, and in our learning within everyday practices. In Kincheloe's [2008b] writing, 'a critical pedagogy that constructs knowledge and formulates action based on eros with its drives to alleviate human suffering serves as a counterpoise to the empire's positivistic thanatos' [ibid: 100]. It is also interesting to note that despite the possible extreme manifestations of thanatopolitics in the concentration camps, the texts on research used as a basis for this study[2[Introduction]] simply make no reference to either eros or thanatos. This also may explain why the exploration of such forces was one of Kincheloe's [2005a] ways of creating a space for reassessing the nature of knowledge . . . and the modes of research that have created it' – so moving into what he called 'the fourth dimension of research' [ibid: 21].[2]

Such futural orientation of bricolage was evident in much of Kincheloe's [2005a, 2008a,b; Kincheloe and Berry, 2004] writings concerned with the bricolage. He, too, had recognized that 'procedure-bound science' falls short of questioning 'what it means to be human, what it might mean to live in a good and just society, and the worthiness of those who live in cultures and locales different from the West' [Kincheloe, 2005a: 348]. But, although Kincheloe [2005a] had called almost decade ago for a philosophical study of research – he used 'the phrase *philosophical research* to denote the use of various philosophical tools to help clarify the process of inquiry and provide insight into the assumptions on which it conceptually rests' [ibid: 336] – he had not considered that this may take us into an examination of the play of signs in research. Indeed, although Kincheloe had argued at the time that 'the education of researchers demands that everyone take a step back from the process of learning research methods' [ibid: 325], and he had foreseen the danger that what he called the epistemology of 'crypto-positivist evidence based science' [ibid: 2] aligned with 'hegemonics politics of knowledge' [ibid: 3] was destroying the world, he had not at that time considered the ironic possibility that forces delimiting education in research are cultivating such thanatopolitics.

The forces delimiting education first came to light in this study from the fantasy of the transparency of phenomena within research that are revealed through 'standardized modes of knowledge-production' [Kincheloe, 2005a: 325] in the current Disneyland of research. Yet, ironically, consonant with the ontology of the latter these forces maintain bare life without home in the language of research. Kincheloe's 'education of researchers' as a 'step back' from learning research methods we have now uncovered as the phenomena of authentic education is cultivated and grows within practices of research, so challenging, in its inter-play with the forces delimiting education in research, spacing for bare life. As a supplement 'delimiting education' serves both to add to the research by alerting researchers to the significance of its visible outcomes, and it also appears, in the hegemony, to make up for what is missing in providing what in biopolitical terms is represented as a precise focus upon the methodologies, methods and modalities of analysis required in each case. In the focus upon the polysemy of meanings in research it is easy to miss the play of this supplement, 'delimiting education', that continually unfolds in the disseminative drift, even within specialist discourses of research.

In biopolitical terms, as we have uncovered, both the foregoing dimensions of the supplement, delimiting education, work in concert and *aim* to help researchers focus upon issues of what is represented as quality research in terms of purportedly rigorously defined methodologies, methods and modes of analysis. So, in the *trompe l'oeil* of yet another dimension of '*the society of the spectacle*', in its commoditization of agency, ironically, it conforms to the benchmarks created for ethical research. In this way the biopolitics delimiting education obviates the need for any language expressing the ontotheology driving enframing.

What is missing in the flux of the disseminative drift is the basis for the control of any possible play in the flux of time: by demarcating the scope of any play of signs – delimiting education – therefore, takes the place of what is missing in research by fulfilling such a role. In doing their work the signs now accord with the grounding ontotheology that is ordinarily represented in epistemological terms of 'procedure-bound science' [Kincheloe, 2005a: 348]. In so doing the supplement, delimiting education, also adds to research in opening dialogue concerned with the issue of quality. In accord with its very nature it also blocks any consideration being given to the difficult questions concerned with bare life and the facticity of human existence. The supplement, therefore, acts as a virus, filling in any gaps where they appear.

Consequently, in response to the forces delimiting education the free play of signs is replaced by their work that is delimited by a multiplicity of metaphysical exigencies uncovered earlier – and grounded in being as presence represented within a multiplicity of epistemologies for knowledge production.[2] But, it would be a falsehood to suggest that the forces delimiting education are restricted to practices of research – this virus is cultivated in the drift of signs before they become discernable as *practice* in the social world. The sublime naming force, delimiting education, presses itself in upon the transparent aspects of the social world in fields of research, so shaping and restricting the production of knowledge. The vector of this sublime force delimiting education is directed towards 'the *subject* of history'; none other than living beings, who, in 'becoming master and possessor of their world which is history', and in producing themselves, as Debord [1977] suggests, 'exist' as objects of 'consciousness of his game' [ibid: para 74]. Such fantasy of mastery becomes possible only within a Disneyland form of existence. This is one possible outcome from the interplay explored earlier between living beings and Western forms of practice, including the apparatus of research [Agamben, 2009]. It is by no means the only one possible.

There remains, too, as suggested by Debord, a distinctly gendered aspect concerning the work of signs in the reproduction of current forms of '*the spectacle*' [vide Irigaray, 2008; Butler, 1990]. Research, too, provides an obvious locus of questioning from neo-colonialist and feminist discourses concerning many aspects of *the spectacle*, especially its more recent progeny, neo-liberalist market driven economies. But, here it is important to keep in mind that each of these challenges themselves constitutes loci for the further enhancement of powers – albeit in the form of powers that open space for disputation within the existing order.

It is important to keep in mind, too, and to open critical reflection in practice upon the extent to which within particular practices of research the methodological structures serve to ensure that it remains independent of the structuring of *The Society of the Spectacle* in which it is located. At issue is the possibility of moving out of *the spectacle*, questioning its on-going reiteration.

In the play of signs, constituted in *différance*, however, their spacing continually forecloses upon any gatherings of signs. Such play takes away the very metaphysical grounds for the continued enhancement of any localized powers generated in research. In reflecting upon the locus of cultivation for moves towards justice, play that is always already *at* play, one asks the question: is it not time that play finally awakens us to the possibility of at least taking localized actions in balancing the intensity/extensity of the seemingly inexorable global expansions of powers in this information age [Flint, 2013a,b,c]? At issue is the possibility of authentic education generated as a supplement within research. For Kincheloe [2005a] 'a central feature of this rigorous effort [in the bricolage] to identify what is absent involves excavating what has been lost in the naïveté of monological disciplinarity' [ibid: 346]. The supplement, authentic education, here challenges such excavation.

The play of signs and authentic education

Within the disseminative drift *authentic education* is not something that can somehow be added to the mix. This supplement is there in research; its viral actions are already at work almost un-noticed. For example, a hint of what is at stake was given by Kincheloe [2008b] in his deconstruction of 'normal consciousness' that for him not only provides a focus for 'Western society . . . as the only state of mind worth addressing and even then in the most narrow ways', but also constitutes 'a major impediment to the development of a critical complex epistemology and its understanding of multiple realities' [Goswami, 1993; Bridges, 1997; Varela, 1996, 1999; McLeod, 2000]. In the spirit of radicalizing this position there are at least two pivotal questions that emerge in examining the possible supplement – authentic education – manifestly at play within research.

1. What is currently missing within paradigmatic research?
2. What does 'authentic education' add to research?

In response to the first question this study has uncovered the irony of visibility pivotal to the forces delimiting education at work in 'normalis[ing] consciousness' and in addressing such consciousness in research. What is missing is an understanding of this paradox created by the *trompe-l'œil* for transparency in which there is an almost complete elision of the multiplicity of ways of the on-going activity of research, amounting to the *reiterations of the same* elision of bare life, which involve:

- Reiterations of the same paradigmatic research;
- Reiterations of the same ontotheology driving enframing;
- Reiterations of the same society of *the spectacle*; and
- Reiterations of the same hegemonic politics of plenitude and fulfilment of identities governing relationship with language.

Ironically, too, what is missing is the reiteration of the same delimiting education that has served to cultivate and remain cultivated by the metaphysical directions given by signs within '*the society of the spectacle*'. The latter continually attunes the normalized consciousness located within the Disneyworld of transparency to see endless new approaches, inventions, innovations created by research that in practice largely amount to reiterations of the same *spectacle*.

Absent, too, in these hegemonic regimes concerned with the fantasy of transparency is that the extant apparatus of research largely constitutes grounds for the production of 'at-hand' objects within *the world* of practice. Ironically, such forms of production that have met the current benchmarks for ethical research, we have uncovered, serve largely as the basis for alienation.

In being carried along by the juggernaut of on-going action what we have not fully grasped, it would seem, is just how such powers of enframing are in danger of reducing us down to its machine-like instruments. In bare life, with its seemingly insatiable capacity for adaptation and the wide range of natural variation, this latter point becomes almost impossible to measure with any certainty. One result from this study are the multiplicity of means human beings have adopted in their various moves towards making their own histories for better or worse, much of which emerge from contingency, and from informal connectivity and inventiveness. The many traces of authentic education that have begun to be uncovered point to a multiplicity of ways human beings keep things in play – through complex molar and molecular inter-play and connectivity involving assemblages, rhizomatic connections, plateaus of thinking and other contingencies emerging from practices that could never be planned within the apparatus of research.

Authentic education as a supplement fills in what is missing in alerting us to the forces delimiting education in research and adds to research in alerting us to the viral actions of supplements. As we have indicated in addition to questions concerned with what is missing in research, the supplement, authentic education, also carries with it the question of what more it adds to research.

This supplement is already at play in research. The pivotal issue here is what authentic education contributes to the complex relationship between trust and risk in research [Beck 2000; Giddens, 1990, 1991, 1993]. We have already uncovered how the forces delimiting education focus upon the calculable, conditional and possible dimensions of research and of our various practices. They are already in danger of reducing this relationship between trust and risk to a matter of calculation. Such reduction then forecloses any need for trust. 'Basically . . . trust', as Biesta [2005] indicates, 'is about those situations in which you *do not know* and *cannot know* what will happen' [ibid: 61; emphasis added]. This is the space opened for authentic education in research.

Authentic education continually adds to research in alerting and challenging researchers to opening play within what initially appear to be impossible, incalculable and unconditional dimensions of practice. This is the play cultivating the leading edge of developments in research. Without this kind of play there could be no significant transformations of practice. Authentic education is an education cultivated in *différance* and an education in *différance*.

In her exploration of 'qualitative futures', for example, Judith Preissle [2011] reflects on the work of Van Cleave [2008] 'who positions herself as a posthumanist scholar' [Preissle, 2011: 695], and who has critically examined the process of interviewing in qualitative research. Van Cleave is reported to cite 'many questionable assumptions about shared interviewer-respondent meanings and intentions that are 'so brilliantly' criticized by Sheurich [1997]. Preissle then notes how in an 'audacious move' Van Cleave opens reflection upon the issue of 'false memory' drawing from 'Schacter's [2001] cognitive and neuroimaging research' [cited by Preissle, 2011: 695].

But, there is nothing in this study to suggest that consideration be given to the overturning of the assumption in social theory concerned with the fulfilment and plenitude of identity arising from the impossibility, given sufficient time, of complete recollection of all matters grounding particular identities uncovered through research.

What remains to be added to research by authentic education are understandings of the relationship between trust and risk. Essentially and structurally our very humanity requires that bare life has space to be; its very being, *a priori,* is dependent upon the *repetendum* [that which is to be repeated], one does not know and one cannot know all that will happen in *practice.* In cultivating trust and helping us to understand and to work with the risks in the event of research, authentic education keeps open spacing for this *repetendum.*

However, the long-established grounds for the supplementary virus, delimiting education, seeks only to reduce down the space and the risk presented by such a *repetendum.* Within the virus, delimiting education, such repetendum has been given no language of expression in research. In the 'real world' constituted by delimiting education, apparently 'everyone knows' it is itself both securely grounded in reason and in the visibility of transparent forms of calculation. Any possible discussions emerging from authentic education in research concerned with threats to humanity are simply countered by empirical examples reflecting the considerable ethological variance within all dimensions of bare life, and bare life's seemingly almost infinite capacity for adaptation.

In speaking about 'Oral History' Linda Shopes [2011: 451–65] notes how memories are deeply implicated in oral history, in both its 'oral and social sense'. For her 'oral history records events about the past, but the recording takes place in the present; memory is the bridge between the two' [ibid: 459]. In working with this metaphor what follows suggests that any such possible 'bridge' is a product of the imagination structured by unconscious desires, opening significant questions within authentic education.

From a psychoanalytic perspective, as we mentioned earlier, *jouissance* structuring desire always tends to move such desire and its desire for more towards overcoming the impossible [Dooley and Kavanagh, 2007: 6]. It is this unconscious drive, lying at the heart of the fantasy of controlled calculation and perfection that is inscribed within the forces delimiting education. Its fetishism provides powerful distractions from humanity's requirement for a *space to be* that in its futural structuring is always already by definition unknown. Authentic education as a supplement, therefore, both fills in the lacuna created by the unknown in foregrounding discourses concerned with trust and risk and adds to research by opening critical reflection on the architectural and structural necessity of the trust-risk relationship governing the space open to bare life. Again qualitative research is ideally positioned to open further research on this matter.

This study has attempted to open reflection upon the requirement for a balance between the Apollonian spirit with is habitus set only on control and order and the Dionysian spirit at home in the play. At stake with the sublime powers at work in society with the emergence of this information age are the powers in the many technologies that have become part of our lives shaping humanity and bare life.

But, the *repetendum* remains in place, as an essential element of structure within the disseminative drift [Derrida, 1981b]. Pragmatically it gives a rationale for working with various fictions of truth, of knowledge, of learning . . . within practice. The use of the term 'fiction' is not intended to reduce 'research' in anyway. It is simply an indication of the provisionality of the stories told by researchers on the basis of their sophisticated, rigorous and exacting attempts to understand the social world. Authentic education as a viral supplement within research, therefore, adds to understandings of this complex process in opening researchers to the structural requirement for such fictions of research to remain within dynamic equilibrium with spacing for the incalculable, impossible and indeterminate dimensions of practices. In pragmatic terms, therefore, as we have seen already, the fictions constituted within the various *repetendi [ae]* serve as a basis for structuring research, and such structuring, rather than alienating the self, keeps opens spacing for it to be. What is demanded is disclosive space for bare life.

The movements of justice, therefore, in being based themselves upon the fiction of deconstruction open spacing in the essential dwelling place of language for bare life. Royle's [2000] writings suggest some helpful indications of the ways in which deconstruction that is always already at work in *practice* opens space and keeps in play the supplement, authentic education, through as we have witnessed earlier:

> the experience of the impossible; what remains to be thought: a logic of destabilisation always already on the move in 'things themselves': what makes every identity at once itself and different from itself: a logic of spectrality: . . . what is happening today in what is called society, politics, diplomacy, economics, historical reality and so on: the opening of the future itself. [ibid: 11]

In these various ways authentic education alerts researchers to the constitution of *différance*. The French term, *Jeu,* means gift as well as play. In this way authentic education is a gift both of the play of signs and of the viral actions of the supplement. Contra forces delimiting education, the horizon for the intentionality of deconstruction, like play, is futural; its spacing opens those involved in research to an authentic education in the unconditional, impossible and incalculable aspects of existence. Without this there could be no movement possible in any of its multiplicity of conditional and calculable dimensions involving the construction of 'persons', 'individuals', 'agents', 'subjects' and others in research that currently seem to consume researchers.[2[Introduction]]

In anticipation of the question of *how* one undertakes research in order to produce those fictions of knowledge, it is helpful to return once more to Agamben's [2009] understanding of the inter-relationship between the apparatus of research and beings.

The play of *différance*

One of the obvious consequences of the constitution of *différance* is that the apparatus becomes fissured in its spacing, separating a relationship between the past fictions generated within research from the unknown of its associated anxiety-producing 'monstrous arrivant', the future. Can we move beyond the standard ludic conceptions of play as manipulations of objects by subjects into the spacing within the 'apparatus'? The spacing of play opens possibilities 'for movement and articulation' within the apparatus and assemblages of research and for the making of history by researchers 'for better or worse' [Derrida 1992c: 64; Royle 2003: 33]. It is important, also, to keep in mind that the viral supplement delimiting education, and its counterpart, authentic education, always already mediate both sides of the temporally fissured inter-play between beings and the apparatus. Delimiting education in research has remained the dominant factor.

Such dominance deserves to be questioned within qualitative research. As suggested earlier the viral forces at play delimiting education are not well disposed to non-empirically based, immeasurable and incalculable philosophical assertions concerned with threats to bare life. The focus upon post-metaphysical practice constituted in *différance*, however, in opening inter-play with paradigmatic structures in the apparatus of research does open a way forward using radical bricolage. It also connects us back with the mysteries of earth.

Let us first briefly explore how authentic education is further expanded by philosophical consideration of our relationship with earth, before returning to questions concerned with the structuring of existence. With the growth of powers in this information age the argument here indicates strongly the need for heterogeneous spacing for bare life. Without this spacing being actively sought by means of authentic education in research, those more vulnerable members of society are likely to become more so. Our relationship with the mystery of the earth simply adds further to the need for an inauguration of research generating heterogeneous spacing for bare life.

In his later work on *The Origin of the Work of Art*, Heidegger [2002] challenges his readers with another dimension concerning our world, namely, 'earth'. Throughout the book we have been making reference to poetry, connecting directly with the mystery of earth. For some readers this may seem another distraction from the proper business of research. Perhaps one of the difficulties with poetry is that it does not work with concepts; it sustains within it mysteries and indeterminables about the world. Richardson [2012] observes: 'Heidegger's term for this aspect of the way art founds the world, is "earth"' [*Erde*]. Poetry, therefore, makes its words memorable in their 'earth' [ibid: 305], and in so doing opens spacing for authentic education. 'Poetry cannot give us concepts' precisely 'because their meaning depends upon their "earth"' [ibid: 306]. If we have been hearing the poetry cited earlier in this book right, it provides a powerful locus for reflection concerned with the structure of language more generally: 'it works by something it cannot express outright' [ibid: 307].

William Blake's poesy comes to mind; his metonymy reflecting the mythologies at work in our contemporary world is there in 'The Mental Traveller':[3]

I traveld thro' a Land of Men
A Land of Men & Women too
And heard & saw such dreadful things
As cold Earth wanderers never knew

But, the brilliance of such poesy and its hidden relationship with earth will do little to challenge the forces delimiting education.

Here we need to keep in play signs taken from the life sciences and literature opened earlier by Paglia [2001]. In speaking of the cultures of Apollo and his great opponent, Dionysius, Paglia prefers the latter, 'chthonian', meaning of the earth [ibid: 5]. In her terms in making sense of practice is the chthonian dimension of liquid nature that she views as a 'miasmic swamp whose prototype is the still pond of the womb' [ibid: 12]. Like Heidegger, from her study of literature she reveals numerous examples of the hidden and mysterious forces at work in the world of practice that for Paglia may be understood in our literature in terms of the forces generating a multiplicity of sexual personae.

What is in danger of being lost in Paglia's and others' writings is any consideration given to the illusion of self-presence – another product of the politics of plenitude – they each tend to generate especially when they are aligned with hegemonic assumptions concerned with pure memory and pure speech in research that we have been attempting to question. Earlier, for example, we passed over Lather's [1993a] disputation to the way writing is in danger of poisoning memory with a simulacrum, without even pausing for a moment to think about the pharmakon. Its several meanings for Plato in the *Phaedrus* ranged from 'poison' to 'remedy' or 'cure' [Lucy, 2004:

90]. In Niall Lucy's [ibid] reading of Derrida [1981b: 95–172] he alerts readers to the 'ambivalence of the pharmakon', 'constitut[ing] a medium in which opposites are opposed' and 'the movement and the play that links them, or makes one side cross over to another – . . . good /evil, inside / outside' [Lucy, 2004: 91], . . . and here we can add delimiting education/ authentic education. So, for example, one might say that in this pharmakon delimiting education provides a necessary focus upon standards and quality of research; delimiting education thus providing a much-needed 'cure' for the many loose ends created by authentic education. Equally it could be argued that delimiting education as a poison arises from ever expanding and enhancing the forces of the late modern juggernaut [enframing], poisoning authentic education by replacing it with simulacra. But, Derrida is not arguing that somehow the pharmakon exists prior to the constitution of difference between 'delimiting education'/ 'authentic education'. 'On the contrary', as Niall [ibid: 91–2] shows, Derrida's 'argument is that the pharmakon is the condition on which' such an oppositional difference 'is produced'. In Derrida's [1991b] terms 'the pharmakon is the movement, the locus, and the play [of the production of] difference. It is the *différance* of difference' [ibid: 127]. Here we should notice, particularly, the play of heterogeneity. Although not thematized in this way, it is such heterogeneity to which we will now turn with a deconstructive reading of the disclosive spacing opened by bricolage as a challenge to the traditions of research.

CHAPTER TWELVE

The politics of identity: Moving towards justice in the event of research

What proved to be particularly astonishing in developing this thesis was the sublime sovereign powers of language at work in research shaping 'bare life'. Apart from the absence of any discussions concerned with such powers[2[Introduction]] – itself one of the products of technology in disciplinary structures – the forces delimiting education in research continually cultivate these powers. Ironically, as we have seen in concentrating attention only upon the conditional, calculable and possible dimensions of the practices of research such forces disguise almost completely bare life.

But, here, in the drift of that empire of signs mediating *practice* we have also begun to understand the challenges created by authentic education in research. Constituted in the play of *différance* the latter is cultivated by deconstruction continually unfolding in such play. Deconstruction is never yet another technique of research that is somehow added to *practice*. As we have seen it is always already at work in *practice*; in virtue of its constitution in the play of *différance* and its moves towards justice, it seeks continually to exceed extant laws inscribed in the practices of research. As a supplement authentic education, then, constitutes an education in bare life – it both continually alerts us to what is missing in research on the basis of deconstruction, namely, the generative forces of bare life, and adds to research in challenging thinking concerned with generative possibilities – for better of worse – arising from spacing for bare life within such practices.

Cutting through any metaphysical determinations generated within '*the society of the spectacle*', or its machinery of paradigmatic research, such spacing for bare life constitutes extra-paradigmatic spacing – *extrā ordinem* – outside the ordinary understandings of *practice* presented earlier. Largely unconsciously this extra-paradigmatic spacing is already being used by the positivist as much as the post-modernist researcher and without it there could be no genuine transformations in all such paradigmatic practices; the forces delimiting education in research continually work to close down such spacing in accord with the sovereign powers inscribed within its languages and its laws.

One of the obvious manifestations of such forms of closure has been the monological thinking emerging from ever-more specialized fields within particular academic disciplines. Under Kincheloe's stewardship the delimitations of such thinking were continually exposed by a methodology identified as 'bricolage' that continually sought to question such specialization utilizing logic from multiple disciplines. The form of this particular discourse was characterized earlier as '*Rede*' – it seeks to look outward to the encompassing social practice, challenging and opening new epistemological horizons for social/educational research. But, though considered by some within the traditions to be daring and thought-provoking, even Kincheloe's bricolage remains to this day located largely within horizons of being as presence.

Like bricolage, deconstruction, too, works with what is at hand in practice. But, unlike bricolage within the current traditions, deconstruction is no longer delimited by the horizon of being as presence. Deconstruction, in its moves towards justice that seek to go beyond existing laws inscribed in research, always already emerges from within futural horizons of *practice*. Deconstruction, then, in radicalizing bricolage opens spacing that is extra-paradigmatic and no longer imprisoned within the metaphysical exigencies of paradigmatic/epistemic forms of research. It opens spacing for the vitalizing forces of bare life in research that ordinarily remain hidden and located in a state of exception consonant with the thanato-political and the biopolitical orientations of research.

In the spirit of bricolage in working with what is at hand, and in moving towards justice, at issue remains the cultivation of research as an event [*événement*] that is no longer continually imprisoned within the metaphysical exigencies of paradigmatic structures.

This deconstructive reading of research, therefore, has revealed the figure of research as an event that opens spacing for bare life and at the same time removes any grounds for the pre-judicial ontotheological structuring of paradigms. At issue, therefore, is the preliminary deconstruction of research as an event that in opening smooth spacing outside the paradigms maintains a critical relationship with the striated spacings located within them. This event is conceived as the interplay of the extant traditions, with a post-metaphysical extra-paradigmatic rationality opening spacing and possibilities for bare life in its complex relationship with earth.

It cultivates also a language of expression and spacing for thinking concerned with the ways in which both research and the '*Society of the*

Spectacle' are inexorably being driven and shaped by the forces of the late modern juggernaut, shaping bare life. But, such forces are not ineluctable. They have not fallen from the sky. They are constituted in the play of *différance* and its heterogeneous spacing, consonant with the structuring of bricolage. Though the latter, too, in working with what is at hand knows no boundaries, until now it has remained within the striated *space* located within the secure metaphysical guardrails generated in the name of critical theory. The grammatological reduction that follows, therefore, takes seriously the generative powers of the nothing in opening both *extra*- and *intra*-paradigmatic *spacing* for bricolage.

Consonant with the heterogeneous structuring of bricolage, and in concert with the opening preface, this chapter has been divided into two sections. This opening section sought to articulate a conclusion to this study by concentrating upon the possibilities opened for bare life within the extant traditions. The epilogue that follows opens spacing for thinking concerned with whatever comes to shore in the future.

The intention is to generate spacing for thinking concerned with how research may be developed for better or worse as an event. One that opens possibilities for the regeneration of bare life and societies, and the various ways in which bare life/societies can better understand through research how they are being reinvented. This event exposes the production of truth claims to knowledge to the '*monstrous arrivant*' of what comes to shore in future, over which we have very limited control. It is an event that takes seriously the post-metaphysical[1] challenge of justice to come; the reformulation of ethics; and the deconstruction of the methodological languages of research. A radicalized bricolage generates the language and approaches to research that begins to open spacing for the critical examination of bare life.

Bricolage: A post-metaphysical rationality

One obvious starting point is Kincheloe's work. In radicalizing bricolage this deconstructive reading is constituted in *différance*. Radical bricolage both stands outside the paradigmatic structures within futural horizons to come and is located within the paradigms, opening spacing balancing the powers generated from metaphysical determinations of research.

As the architect at the leading edge of developments in bricolage in qualitative research in the first decade of the new millennium, Kincheloe's project emerged from his work with Lincoln and Denzin [2000]. He notes how they had 'used the term', bricolage, 'in the spirit of Claude Levi-Strauss [1966] and in particular his lengthy discussion of it in *The Savage Mind*'. For Kincheloe [2001] the French word *bricoleur* describes a handyman or handywoman who makes use of the tools available to complete a task. The *bricoleur's* 'trickery and cunning' had reminded Kincheloe [2001] of 'the chicanery of Hermes, in particular his ambiguity concerning the messages of the gods'. For Kincheloe 'if hermeneutics came to connote the ambiguity and slipperiness of textual meaning, then bricolage can also imply the fictive and imaginative elements of the presentation of all formal research' [ibid: 680].

Moving towards a post-metaphysical rationality, therefore, carries with it a responsibility to locate Kincheloe's readings of hermeneutics within the constitution of *différance* as radical hermeneutics. This constitution opens bricoleurs to the figures of the 'trace' and 'textuality' denoting a 'differential network and fabric of [its] traces' [Royle, 2003: 64], with this network 'referring endlessly to something other than itself' [ibid: 64]. In an interview with Richard Kearney, Derrida [1999: 68] indicates that he 'would include what we call action, or praxis or politics within the general space of what I call the trace'. Here we have discussed the biopolitics as another issue to be included.

The praxis of radical bricolage involves, therefore, in the same way as bricolage [Kincheloe and Berry, 2004: 108–27], a point of entry into such textuality, rather than the metaphysical determinations of 'text' [the term used by Kincheloe and Berry]. There is for the radical bricoleur a continual challenge in working with the bricolage to be aware of its metaphysical determinations, opening spacing for thinking concerned with these fictions through deconstruction. In doing so there is an understanding that such textuality is caught up in the drift of dissemination; that hermeneutic circles are always broken, fragmented and incomplete. It opens bricoleurs to studying the implications of such movements, particularly for the most vulnerable groups in society, where the effects of the ontotheology are always more acutely felt.

For the bricoleur textuality opens spacing for questioning those many visible reiterations of the apparatus of research in *the society of the spectacle*. The Polish Nobel Laureate in literature, Wislawa Szymborska, whose poetry, crafted 'with ironic precision, allow[ing] the historical and biological context to come to light in fragments of human reality',[1] in some ways, too, in her poem, 'Nothing Twice',[2] captures the locus of anxieties emerging from the performativity of being involved in reiterations of *the spectacle*:

Nothing can ever happen twice.

In consequence the sorry fact is

that we arrive here improvised

and leave without the chance to practice.,

In the spirit of such poesy and in pragmatic terms, in her response to claims made by Kincheloe, more than a decade ago, Lincoln [2001] elaborates further upon the work of such a 'handyman' in bricolage. For her 'Kincheloe's bricoleur is far more skilled than merely a handyman': 'this bricoleur looks for not yet imagined tools, fashioning them with not yet imagined connections. This handyman is searching for the nodes, the nexuses, the linkages, the interconnections, the fragile bonds between disciplines, between bodies of knowledge, between knowing and understanding themselves' [ibid: 693]. To this we can now add she is always alert to deconstructing the metaphysical directions given within research and to its politics of plenitude. Continually moving in the direction of justice to come the radical bricoleur is attuned to the ways in which traditions of research in the paradigms constitute their own simulacra, their own 'at hand' understandings of *the* world, leaving hidden the unique particularity of the 'to hand' 'world' of bare life. The radical bricoleur is intimately aware of the metaphysical significance of being-in-the-world and uses this in deconstructive readings of research. The locus of the radical bricoleur's handy work is not to be found in most homes. As Lincoln had observed regarding bricolage, and this is also true for its radical associate, 'this is not your father's bricolage. It is "boundary-work" taken to the extreme, boundary-work beyond race, ethnicity, sexual orientation, class' [ibid: 694] and, we can add, boundary-work outside metaphysical determinations of presence. It is such boundary work that has informed the earlier explorations of the critical Joycean play of signs as seed corn for any possible cultural transformation in this process of rethinking the practice of research in its complex relationship with education.

The generative powers of radical bricolage arise from its smooth spacing for deconstruction in and beyond all of the sciences. The boundary work here is concerned with the driving force of enframing in practices – that silent force at the heart of Kincheloe's concerns regarding the 'crypto-positivists' and the 'knowledge wars', for example. At issue remains how the ontotheology driving enframing is affecting bare life, and also whether it is possible to re-think the current boundaries constituted within the deontological structuring of the ethics of research. What is demanded by radical bricolage is no less than an examination of the affects and effects of the ontotheological structuring driving enframing upon the most vulnerable groups in *the society of the spectacle*. It is here, as we have seen repeatedly, that enframing is experienced most acutely. In moves towards justice, therefore, this bricolage de-constructs the metaphysical structuring of research in order to exceed its current location in the present. In so doing it opens spacing for bare life within its horizons to come. It is a form of bricolage that can be used to address large complex and multi-dimensional problems and issues affecting the socially disadvantaged groups and individuals within this liquid modern world – collectives whose vulnerability is certainly not reduced by the continued explosion of powers. Equally, it is perfectly adapted to work with issues emerging from the unique and particular interiority of the worlds of individuals and groups within singular cultural settings. The latter are almost always dissimulated by the current focus in much research upon the outer granular face of the self [Flint, in preparation, vii].

My own interest in moving towards a post-metaphysical rationality in bricolage arises from the complex powers mediating the relationship of bare life with *das Gestell*. From the study it has emerged that bare life has been given a Janus face by the hidden powers at work in research – on one side of this face opening space for future possibilities there is bare life, on its other side can be read the story of *das Gestell*, driven by Heidegger's nostalgia.

Kincheloe, too, had been concerned with the powers at work in the production of knowledge. But in reflecting critically upon Kincheloe's standpoint and the approach he had taken in bricolage one comes to a point of departure in the way the radical bricolage here works in its moves towards a post-metaphysical rationality. It is helpful to cite Kincheloe [2008] in full in his exposition that moves to project an understanding of the context for bricoleurs from his paper, 'Critical Pedagogy and the Knowledge Wars of the Twenty First Century'. In Kincheloe's [2008a] words:

> Critical bricoleurs understand the diverse contexts in which any knowledge producer operates. Transformative researchers struggle to uncover the insidious ways that dominant power blocs work to shape the knowledge they produce, they begin to better understand the relationship between any researcher's ways of seeing and the social location of her personal history. As the bricoleur appreciates the ways that research is a power-inscribed activity, she abandons the quixotic quest for some naïve mode of realism. At this point, the bricoleur concentrates on the exposé of the multiple ways power harms individuals and groups and the way a knowledge producer's location in the web of reality helps shape the production, interpretation, and consumption of data. At every space, the critical bricoleur discerns new ways that a hegemonic epistemology in league with a dominant power-soaked politics of knowledge operates to privilege the privileged and further marginalize the marginalized. [ibid: 5]

Certainly, the same powerful message of polarization emerges from Manual Castells' [2009] sociology of 'The Network Society'. There is alignment here, too, on the concerns about both how 'power blocs' variously 'work to shape the knowledge' and about the 'way power can harm individuals and groups', and by the harmful effects of polarization in our societies. But, our deconstruction uncovers from Kincheloe's metaphysical determination of bricolage yet another repetition of the 'eternal return of the same' in the 'will-to-power' [Table 2.1]. The problem, it would appear, that many of the leading exponents of bricolage have simply not addressed is just how what amounts to a relatively minor power bloc of researchers aligned to bricolage constitutes a meaningful response to the powers inscribed within the ever-growing corporate power blocs that are being cultivated daily in the intensity and extensity of their inexorable growth within our many neo-liberal economies in the societies of *the spectacle*.

Certainly, one possibility is to see what Kincheloe [2008a] calls such 'knowledge wars' as a locus of morality, fighting for those who are marginalized in such neo-economies. There is no argument with this moral standpoint. But, it simply does not address the complex issues arising from the ontotheology. There is, however, agreement with Kincheloe [2008a] who notes that 'with the expansion of the power and concentration of capital over the last couple of decades, scholarship and social movements have not kept up with the ways that power frameworks insidiously inscribe knowledge coming from diverse social locations' [Weiler, 2004; Kincheloe, 2005b]. Indeed. But, though Kincheloe [2005b] makes references to 'state of being' and 'ways of being' and to the way 'powers shape our perspectives and insidiously mould our constructions' [ibid: 45], or 'power shapes the way we make meaning' [ibid: 132], our complex relationship with being seems to elide both Weiler's and Kincheloe's watchful eyes.

Ironically, *is it not the gathering force and the naming powers of being* as presence in forms of integrated practice, including research, that is the locus of much social power, not simply the elites in our society? And, such 'expansion of power' to which Kincheloe refers, is not a function of particular agencies; *is it not* a matter of the very essence of power – at least as long as we hold on to the dominant politics of plenitude? [Heidegger, 1977c: 71–82]. At the time of writing such a locus of power would appear not to have been addressed within the literature of the bricolage movement [Rogers, 2012; Kincheloe, 2001, 2003, 2004a, b, 2005a,b, 2006, 2008a,b; Kincheloe and Berry, 2004; Denzin and Lincoln, 2000]. On the basis of the thesis developed here, therefore, there is little prospect of bricolage as it is currently formulated, addressing the issue of justice to come in the power blocs cultivated within the neo-liberal forms of capitalism [Harvey, 1991, 2007; Giroux, 2008].

The radical bricolage developed here is informed by an ethic of dissemination generated from authentic education in research. It alerts bricoleurs to the ways in which imposed schemes are no more than fictions that in themselves can sometimes be helpful and sometimes open us to dangers. The ethic informing the work of this post-paradigmatic bricolage is 'bent on dispersing constellations of power, clusters of control and manipulation, grinding us all under in their actions directed towards 'systematic dominat[ion], regulat[ion] and exclus[ion]' [Caputo, 1987: 260]. Such actions, we have suggested, arise from moving too closely towards delimiting education – constituted on grounds of the metaphysics of being as presence – within the pharmakon between authentic and delimiting forms of education in research. Such movements generating space for forces that poison research tend to block spacing for its remediation.

Such forces delimiting education have been evident from the opening of this study. *Practice*, we have seen, knows no boundaries and divisions given in the striated space of paradigmatic research. It has become apparent that its ontotheology is also at work moulding transformations in our contemporary society of *the spectacle*. We have shown how the practices of research aligned with styles of organization found in *the spectacle* of Western societies [Debord, 1977] are shaped by the technologies of modern capitalism manifest as the 'juggernaut of modernity' [Giddens, 1990]. They are threatening to overrun us all.

What has been particularly alarming in undertaking this study is to discover the mighty powers 'delimiting education' within research that are operative within *the society of the spectacle*. These foreclose the possibility of generating language that gives expression to this latent sublimely powerful social force of enframing shaping our societies and spacing for possibilities open to bare life. Western societies, it has been observed, have generated education systems that largely serve to educate us into becoming 'docile bodies' [Foucault, 1977: 135–69] within enframing [Flint and Peim, 2012]. Here, too, the radical bricoleur recognizes that the forces delimiting education in its pharmakon with authentic education have become imbalanced and so generating space that is in danger of being a poison for research and, more generally, for society.

There is another issue arising from the heterogeneity between enframing and the possibilities open to bare life in research. The issue arises from much of the discourses highlighted in this study.

Within research, as we have seen, the language and issues arising from enframing simply do not feature within such practices that themselves have become largely dominated by a hegemonic focus upon the *trompe-l'œil* of the calculable, possible and conditional dimensions of what are re-presented as 'transparent' social concerns emerging within *the society of the spectacle*. Like almost all of the present approaches to such concerns that are available in research, one of the significant issues with Kincheloe's approach to bricolage is that its discourse [Kincheloe, 2005b, 2006, 2008c] serves to generate further powers. The intentionality of such powers is directed towards emancipation. But, such powers arise on the basis of the naming force and gathering powers of being as presence, our tiny word for which is 'is'. Once more the ontotheology carries with it the possibility of enframing. Although much of his work may be understood as a powerful and critical response to enframing in our Western societies, it remains unspoken within Kincheloe's discourse – hence the interest in radicalizing his work.

The radical bricoleur is intimately aware, too, of broader social and historical horizons of the forces mediating enframing and bare life. Adorno and Horkheimer [2002], in their more mature work as founders of modern critical theory, began to understand that the Enlightenment drives towards emancipation may result in what they called 'negative Utopianism' or a dystopian state. Environmental disasters such as 'global warming' and measurable reductions in biodiversity, along with totalitarian regimes, and forms of dehumanization are all symptomatic of dystopia. Although Adorno and Horkheimer do not speak in terms of enframing [Heidegger, 1977] their particular understandings of the complex ways in which counter-intuitively metaphysics and reason-grounding aspects of the social world may ultimately generate forms of dystopia is not far removed from Heidegger's thesis.

Any looking back at enframing for the radical bricoleur is always accompanied by moves towards what comes to shore in the monstrous *arrivant*; that always-unknowable future, opening spacing and possibilities for bare life. The latter move opens that moral question of what ought to be. Research as an event, as something coming, suggests that from what is known about the Enlightenment and its known historic moves towards dystopia, and from what is known about the constitution of *différance*, we now stand at a crossroads in history where it is time to reinvent and reconstruct Enlightenment thinking, as indicated earlier, with a nod towards emancipation. Is it not time, as Susan Neiman [2011] has suggested, for rethinking and 'reclaiming' [ibid: 22] moral concepts that have lost their force over the past decades in more radical post-modern and post-structuralist forms of discourse? The radical bricoleur is open to such a challenge.

In opening questions concerned with the moral force of moves towards justice to come, Hobbes would always indicate that we should remain focused upon the '*is*', because as we have seen *the* world of research is structured upon the politics of plenitude in identities. Historically, however, in moving to counter such powers the constitution of Western languages locating the 'is' serve largely, only to enhance the scope and range of such relations of power. *Différance*, by comparison, as the constitution of a post-metaphysical language, works in the opposite direction in balancing such powers. *Is it not possible*, therefore, in exploring, rethinking and regenerating Enlightenment ideals from a moral perspective, to open spacing for dialogue concerning such a process within the pharmakon of authentic and delimiting education in research? The foregoing analysis suggests that qualitative research aligned with philosophical discourse is in a strong position to take a lead in opening such dialogue [Flint, 2013c], creating spacing for the regeneration of bare life.

Bricolage: The constitution of *différance*

There has always been an anxiety among many researchers that in foregrounding the play of *différance*, or more simply, play, everything that we know in research is in danger of being reduced to the meaningless rubble of random signs. Such anxiety arises more from ignorance than any rational basis for such a claim. In taking away the gathering powers and naming force of being as presence, as we have seen, *différance* does not reduce research and humanity down to an empty wasteland. Within the drift of signs there is reiterated significant *repetendi[ae]*; that is, chains of traces coming to make sense to us, and in their repetition providing strong reminders of aspects of our practices. These *repetendi[ae]* are the fictions we variously use to make sense of our worlds and of *the* world. The many pre-judicial structures [Table 2.1] we have uncovered shaping research are examples of such fictions. They are humbling reminders that the knowledge we have of the world from research is only ever the best fiction available at the time.

Without a *repetendum* there is no possibility of *différance*. This constitution of language is always already at play. Our various grammars are based upon it. The social anthropologist Lave and the computer scientist Wenger [1991], for example, in their studies of communities of midwives, tailors, quartermasters, butchers and non-drinking alcoholics demonstrated how shared 'practices' emerge without any formal instruction, by peripheral participants informally learning to repeat particular patterns of behaviour that provided the basis for them becoming full participants in such communities. But, unfortunately, there is no explicit mention in Lave and Wenger's work of the constitution of *différance*.

In practice the constitution of *différance* too, like the force of enframing, remains largely hidden behind the theories and other forms of metaphysical structuring of practice, greatly reducing its play of possibilities. For the radical bricoleur, in reflecting upon paradigmatic forms of research, therefore, its role as discloser of space in research and the way signs mediate just how such disclosure takes place also becomes hidden as a matter of commonsense understandings of language and of how research works in practice. As Heidegger reminds his readers, things in research become invisible once 'one' [*das Man*] becomes habituated to particular everyday familiar styles of practice. The bricoleur appreciates that ordinarily because researchers do not cope with the styles of research used directly – they have no way of coming alive to them and transforming them. They only become a concern for researchers when something breaks down in working with their practices. Researchers, of course, would say that they are always making transformations in the kinds of data, theories, methods and the methodologies they use, because this is how research works. But, the style – coordinating how *the* world is disclosed through research, and what people and things matter in research – that constitutes the practices of paradigmatic research as what they are has largely remained the same. It is a style, we have shown, that largely opens disclosive *space* within the '*society of the spectacle*'. With the forces of enframing, of delimiting education ever closing down the *space* for bare life, the style is breaking down. It is just that we have not yet got a language that gives expression to such a possibility.

In opening spacing outside the paradigms radical bricolage pays attention to styling how the world is disclosed because it alerts researchers to the pre-judicial structures at work within research. For example, in Rogers's

[2012] critical idiom, positivist epistemology in which 'knowledge of the social world is obtainable only through the objective scientific examination of empirical facts' is predicated on hegemonic assumptions that such a process 'will lead to the development of an understanding of the world and human interaction in "concrete and universal terms"' [ibid: 9]. In moving to uncover the style shaping the disclosive spaces produced in such research radical bricolage understands such monological epistemologies in terms of their ontotheology.

The practice of post-paradigmatic bricolage begins to make sense, therefore, only when the style of current paradigmatic forms of research, including traditional forms of bricolage, breaks down and does not seem to work in some way. This study, for example, has uncovered the paradox of the viral actions of delimiting education that in simply maintaining researchers' focus upon the 'transparent' aspects of what is done in practice serve to create a poison that is always in danger of closing down bare life. On the other side of the pharmakon authentic education carries with it a responsibility, as we have suggested, to make the style of paradigmatic practice an issue and to examine and to reconfigure how the style of disclosing spacing in research works. What follows, therefore, in bringing to a close this study, is a brief examination of how and why a reconfiguration of the styling of bricolage in moving to a post-metaphysical rationality is demanded in response to the dystopian forces of enframing.

Let us return once more to the interplay between beings and the apparatus of research, in which its subjects are constituted, if at all, from their initial desubjectification [Agamben, 2009]. At issue remains just how 'spacing between the pieces of apparatus' in this interplay 'allows for particular movement, that is to say, for history, for better or worse' [Derrida, 1992c: 64; Royle, 2003: 33]. But, Agamben's [2009] discourse maintains the interplay of the apparatus and beings in the present. As we have seen in the spacing the present becomes fissured in terms of the interplay of the unknowable future and the cinders of research deposited from the past in terms of its archives, textbooks and other official records. Here the discourse of radical bricolage simply extends the horizons of inquiry into the future, radicalizing the spirit of bricolage developed by Kincheloe [2005a] for whom

> in its embrace of complexity, the bricolage constructs a far more active role for humans both in shaping reality and in creating the research process and narratives that represent it. Such an active agency rejects deterministic views of social reality that assume the effects of particular social, political, economic, and educational processes. At the same time and in the same conceptual context, this belief in active human agency refuses standardized modes of knowledge production. [ibid: 325]

At the heart of such active agency for the bricoleur is decision making. At issue remains, therefore, the basis for decisions in research: especially in view of the spacing in the complex relationship between the apparatus of research and the futural unfolding of beings from which subjects within research emerge.

Making decisions

Decision making is located at the interstices of that fissuring between past and future, in the interplay between beings and pieces of the apparatus and assemblages of research. For example, decisions concerning which paradigms are to be used in research, the methodologies and methods to be employed and what kinds of data will be required and how and on what basis such data will be obtained and analyzed. Such decision-making is now given the provocation of working both within and in the smooth space outside the specialized divisions. Largely unconsciously this happens every day in practices of research. In addressing this question we will also open thinking concerned with the necessity of heterogeneous spacing for decision making that is characteristic of radical bricolage.

But, what is the nature of decision making? As Royle [2003] notes, Derrida's 'work is an attempt to shift away from thinking the decision in terms of presence, a self-identical calculating 'person-who-decides', the decision as an active act' [ibid: 5–6]. In the words of Derrida [2001c], 'a decision has to be prepared by reflection and knowledge. . . one has to calculate as far as possible, but the incalculable happens' [ibid: 61; Royle, 2003: 6]. For Derrida [1988b], too, every decision is 'structured by the experience and experiment of the "undecidable"' [ibid: 116]. Undecidability, however, is not a tool, a method or an approach that can be employed in research. Rather it is a 'ghostliness that renders all totalization. . .impossible' [ibid: 116], and thus challenging, as we have seen, the politics of plenitude. The moment of decision making, for Derrida [2001c], is 'a moment of non-knowledge' [ibid: 61]. It is 'heterogeneous to knowing' [ibid: 61].

The moment of the decision within the apparatus of research is further complicated as we mentioned much earlier by the distinction made by the philosopher, J. A. Austin [1975], in his account of 'how to do things with words', between 'constative' statements of fact or descriptions of things and performative statements, in which one does something in making such utterances. In the spacing of the apparatus of research, 'constative' statements characterize the cinders of what remain from past experience in research. Authentic education continually alerts us to the ghostliness of undecidability in such statements.

Derrida [1999] suggests that 'far from opposing the undecideable to the decision' [ibid: 66], in the possible employment of one of the pieces of apparatus used in research, he argues that 'there would be no decision in the strong sense of the word in ethics, in politics; no decision, and thus no responsibility, without the experience of some undecidability' [ibid:

66]. Given the absence of any explicit reference to the undecideable within leading textbooks on qualitative research,[2[Introduction]] questions remain as to whether such decisions made within the apparatus of research are simply programmed responses to particular issues or genuine decisions. The radical bricoleur is alert to how such programming, for example, can arise from the forces delimiting education.

In terms of the radical bricoleur, therefore, and to put the case in stronger terms in working on border territory at the edge of what is deemed possible within ontotheological structuring, the decision to theorize must first go through a moment of impossibility, in this case the impossibility of critically examining all of the alternatives to such action before it can become a decision. Here, too, radical bricolage makes obvious the supplement, authentic education that is supplied to the spacing in research, making up for what had been missing, namely, any formal distinction between programmed responses and genuine decisions made within research. The supplement, authentic education, also adds to the radical bricolage by enhancing the rigour of this process. In practical terms it raises difficult questions for researchers concerned with what is not known before any decisions are made.

In this case in developing the radical bricolage if one knew what to do beforehand, if one were in possession of knowledge before the decision, then, as Derrida points out, the decision would not be a decision. It would be the application of a rule, the consequence of a premise, there would be no problem; there would be no decision [ibid: 66]. For radical bricolage in ethical and political terms the starting point is the ghost of undecidability. It constitutes *the* starting point, as suggested earlier for the 'point of entry into' textuality, rather than the text as suggested by Berry [2004: 108], in moves towards justice in bricolage that is heterogeneous to the politics of knowledge production.

It is interesting to note, therefore, that while no specific mention of the heterogeneous structuring of decision making within bricolage is made by either Rogers [2012] or by Kincheloe [2001, 2003, 2004a,b, 2005a,b, 2006, 2008a,b], silently it would appear that in the decisions made by bricoleurs they pay attention to such heterogeneity. Kincheloe [2008a], for example, positioned himself as a 'critical pedagogue' when others were being driven by ideologies of the neo-liberal market [ibid: 1–3]. In an earlier paper he opened a heterogeneous space with 'critical ontology' [Kincheloe, 2003] in relation to the ethics of teacher education in higher education, reflecting moves towards a 'more just and interconnected ways of being human' [ibid: 48].

In each of these cases there are moves towards what we call justice in opening reflection upon the particularities of each case and in illuminating the differences. In deconstructing Kincheloe's discourse, his particular cases do not fit the standard patterns of behaviour projected within the ontotheology driving enframing. Such heterogeneity, Derrida [1999] suggests, arises because 'on the one side the field of politics, ethics and rhetoric', here coordinated by the forces delimiting education in research, requires what is on 'the other side, "justice"' [ibid: 73] – constituted in authentic education. For him what is 'foreign to the strategy requires the strategy' [ibid: 73]. He goes on to explain that in taking a 'decision', reflecting an 'ethical or a political responsibility' is absolutely heterogeneous to knowledge. Nevertheless we have to know as much as possible in order to ground our decision. But even if it is grounded in knowledge, 'the moment I take the decision it is a leap, I enter a heterogeneous space and that is the condition of responsibility' [ibid: 73].

In moving into heterogeneous spacing again, Rogers [2012] illuminates how, for Kincheloe [2008a], in political terms monological research examines the issue of objects as things-in-themselves, whereas tacitly justice to come begins to become possible when such research is no longer detached from the socio-historical contexts in which they are constituted. Once again, silently there is acknowledgement from Rogers that in Kincheloe's discourse knowledge production stands in heterogeneous relationship with justice to come.

In matters of decision-making in radical bricolage, therefore, as suggested by Derrida [1999], the two sides of the heterogeneous relationship are 'indissociable', which is a consequence of their 'heterogeneity, and because of this one calls for the other' [ibid: 73]. Ethical and political decisions concerned with bricolage are, as Derrida indicates, 'absolutely heterogeneous to knowledge' [ibid: 73]. That is why the heterogeneity of space generated by Kincheloe in his work with the bricolage is so important. Without it there could be no ethical or political decision made in shaping the bricolage. It does not mean that knowledge is unimportant, we need to know as much as possible in order to make decisions about bricolage.

Interestingly, Rogers [2012] draws attention to Kincheloe's [2004b] moves towards 'justice and new levels of understanding' [ibid: 69] that, in fact, stands in relation to 'demands that relationships at all levels be respected and engaged' [ibid: 69]. For Rogers this amounts to ethical moves in adopting what Kincheloe calls 'symbiotic hermeneutics'. But, Rogers's idiom remains locked within the metaphysics of being as presence giving expression to ethically grounded responsibilities to respect and engage relationships and to tacit expressions of the norms of such research, without becoming conscious of its pre-judicial structuring or to the irony of its metonymy that elides almost completely the simulacrum of respectful relationships in which, ironically, bare life appears to remain without language.

In examining how the approach of radical bricolage differs from Kincheloe's and Rogers's conceptions, there remain further questions concerned with the style of path breaking that continually alert the radical bricoleur to such pre-judicial structuring. Once more we are returning to the issues of the style/styling and how disclosive spacing is generated within radical bricolage because it is the style that opens questioning concerning the shaping of research.

In doing boundary work in radical bricolage, and in reflecting upon the style of practice employed, radical bricoleurs open questions on the precise basis for breaking new ground; being alerted already to the metaphysical directions given by any such 'ground'. Part of the difficulty raised by Derrida [1999] at this point arises from being confronted with a non-way, an *aporia*, emerging from the figures of undecidability, the performative, the constative, the trace, textuality and from our lack of knowledge of aspects of practice. But, in the foregoing paradigms/epistemes of research the powers delimiting education in such acts tend to dissimulate any *aporia*, drawing from the politics of plenitude and the naming force and gathering powers of being as presence.

The '*aporia*' in radical bricolage, therefore, 'we have to face constantly' [Derrida, 1999: 73]. As we noted earlier the *aporia* or non-way of walking is the condition of walking in a particular direction. As Derrida observes, 'path-breaking implies *aporia*. This impossibility to find one's way is the condition of ethics' [ibid: 73]. Authentic education, then, in its movement as a supplement in *practice*, continually alerts bricoleurs to the heterogeneity of the incalculable, impossible and unconditional dimensions of *practice* without boundaries. Authentic education, therefore, cannot be specified in positivistic terms. Its own *aporia* opens spacing for path breaking that is characteristic of the inventiveness of research on its border territories.

The intentionality of this radical bricolage is to keep play *at play*, in pushing ahead, in the repetition of signs, and, as we have seen, in disrupting attempts within research to arrest the play. For example, in reflecting upon the openness to mystery created by radical bricolage, one is reminded by Caputo [1987] of 'an old word . . . that has the advantage of being coined before the advent of the metaphysics of subjectivity and that is not as "logo-centric" as it seems: the old word is *per-sona*, *per-sonare*, the person as sounding-through, resonating' [ibid: 289]. For the radical bricolage, it opens possibilities for keeping play *at play* in all identities. As Caputo explains, 'this pre-Cartesian word does not name a seat of self-identity and has nothing to do with ego-logical metaphysics. On the contrary it means to name a difference, to pick up the interplay of mask and voice, face and speech, look and language. . .' [ibid: 289]. It suggests that radical bricolage in returning us once more to the issue of 'bare life' has much scope to disarm any pretensions to presence, and in opening spacing for research as an 'event', it has much to do in regenerating bare life and societies within the most vulnerable locales in this world.

Epilogue

We began this philosophical inquiry concerned with rethinking the practices of social and educational research by drawing a distinction between 'learning', as a metaphysical determination of something in research that *is* already presupposed to exist, and the challenge 'to let learn'. The latter reflecting moves towards experiences generated from immersion within the futural horizons of the languages of research constitute learning as an event unfolding from the experience of working within the flux of the spacing created within the molecular/molar dynamics of such idioms. Spacing for thinking concerned with possible moves towards something coming [*venir*] and something to come [*a'venir*] in the name of understanding research as a dynamic *event* [*événement*] that continually takes us by surprise in its futural [*l'avenir*] orientation is here constituted by 17 theses that have unfolded from this deconstructive reading of the complex interplay between practice, research and education:

1. *The emergence and continued expansion of the knowledge economy signifies a change in the relationship between the state and commodity production. Research with its focus upon truth claims to knowledge as a commodity is at the centre of such transformations of what are re-presented as the good life. This historical transformation is still in the process of being worked through.*
2. *The practice of research constitutes an instrument of governance for the production of truth claims to knowledge that variously become the subject of commodification.*
3. *Historically, such governance has always remained its dominant function, superseding all other functions.*
4. *Research may be seen as developing a technology for the management of knowledge production, constituting a complex and multi-layered apparatus in the revised sense used by Agamben for a range of functions – a police function, a socialization function, a social reproduction function and an educative function. This apparatus also constitutes grounds for assemblages and opens space for rhizomatic networks of thinking.*
5. *As a practice ontotheology drives enframing; being directed towards commodification of knowledge products within the economy, paradigmatic forms of research serve also to reproduce the society of the spectacle.*
6. *Technologies of research mould, order and define identities in accord with the will-to-improvement, the principle of assessment and the principle of the market.*
7. *The naming force and the gathering powers, at work and hidden behind such technologies, is being as presence, or enframing. Paradoxically, the will-to-improvement in enframing arises from the traces of identity mediating its various practices that are always necessarily incomplete and so constitute grounds for a sublime driving force in moves towards the fulfilment of identity.*

8 *The metaphysical languages of paradigmatic and epistemic forms of research constitute sublime sovereign powers. Such powers include bare life by means of its bonding in a state of exception within all forms of research.*

9 *The metaphysical practices of research stand in a triangular relationship with two emergent viruses – delimiting education and authentic education – that owe their constitution to a pharmakon. The virus delimiting education arises as a medium used to shape and define the production of knowledge as a commodity that always necessitates the trompe-l'œil of transparency, obviating the need for any remedial actions taken in defining precisely the basis of any claims to knowledge. But, in the pharmakon, this closes down the disclosive space for bare life that always remains in danger of becoming poisoned by such actions. Authentic education within the pharmakon is constituted in the play of* différance. *Though herein lies the locus for transformation in research, with its dominant focus upon commodification any such play becomes disparate, localized and hidden; ironically, despite the fact that without such play there could be no transformation in all forms of paradigmatic research, it tends to remain un-thematized.*

10 *Radical forms of language constituted by* différance *in the event of research remain without gathering powers and any naming force. The constitution of* différance *manifest in authentic education opens disclosive spacing for bare life. Herein lies the basis, too, for the balancing of powers generated from knowledge production.*

11 *The horizon of bare life is futural, consonant with the horizon of justice to come in research whereas in its metaphysical determinations of phenomena and events, research locates everything within the horizon of being as presence, alienating the self from itself.*

12 *From the perspective of bare life and the forces of enframing in research the deontological structuring of such practices requires radical re-examination and revision.*

13 *In the traditions of research disclosive space is generated within the horizon of being as presence in accord with technological enframing. This creates one side of a Janus face for bare life that looks back and is simply re-presented as a quantity of excess energy or 'standing reserve' that is available for use within the society of the spectacle. The other side looks forward and is continually open to possibilities unfolding in the future.*

14 *Justice to come in the event of research always exceeds its laws and the sovereign powers inscribed within its languages. As an*

event research opens disclosive space for bare life, seeking the particular, singular and the hidden interiority of 'to hand' aspects of the unique world of bare life. There is, therefore, no event of research without the singularity of the monstrous arrivant.

15 *Research as an event constituted in the deconstruction of knowledge production opens disclosive spacing for the regeneration of bare life/societies for better or worse.*

16 *In its relationship with bare life the extensity and intensity of experience and knowledge generated through the event of qualitative research places it in an excellent position to make concrete how and on what basis such events unfold within particular communities of practice. This process remains in its infancy.*

17 *The event of qualitative research [incorporating quantitative studies] is ideally suited to open spacing for thinking and the elaboration of possibilities for the continued regeneration of bare life/societies while bringing into focus and making concrete both the affects and effects of drives towards enframing.*

In moving towards justice at the border between the seemingly endless metaphysical determinations of identities in research and those aspects of experience that do not yet have a name, the study has also opened spacing for thinking concerned with the *arrivant*, hospitality itself, being given to bare life at the threshold of a wealth of different homes made within the idioms of research. This opens heterogeneous spacing for the radical bricoleur. She exists on the border territory at the interstices of practice between, on the one side, the ethics [*ethikos*] of paradigmatic research, its laws and customs with:

- the structuring of inclusion forging bare life;
- the telos of at-hand knowledge-power games that favour only the most powerful, eliding bare life; and,
- the rhetoric of research in its metonymic picturing of *the* world that creates metaphysical bridges over the flux.

On the other side, in the *aporia* of generative spacing of the nothing outside the paradigms, the radical bricoleur is ever alert to the possibilities of deconstruction in the endless drift of signs and the possibilities of their play:

- continually taking responsibility for moves towards justice;
- exposing the ontotheology of the power plays of integrated practices within *the society of the spectacle* while taking away their groundings;

- opening spacing for the regeneration of bare life in its particularity made ever-more vulnerable in such plays; and,
- opening spacing and thinking for authentic education constituted within the pharmakon of research as an event that in its orientation *vis-a-tergo* continually works to expose the structuring of rhetorics within '*the spectacle*'.

Whether such an event takes us by surprise, a matter of hospitality and any possible take-up of ideas within communities of research concerning the issue of bare life that has remained for millennia in a state of exception. We should also keep in mind in seeking to address this issue, too, the dynamic rationalities of 'bare life's spirit in *practice* without boundaries. Being cultivated within authentic education produced from the play of *différance*, although 'bare life's memory is deeply embodied it has remained almost completely below the radar of all forms of modern research. In facing the unknowable future and in moving towards justice, therefore, this preliminary study has shown there remains much to play for. Not least in moving to understand more about the complex relationship between bare life, '*practice*', research and education, exploring and characterizing how such practice opens space for the possible regeneration of community.

NOTES

Introduction

1 Terms borrowed from Caputo, J. D [2013] *Truth: Philosophy in Transit*, London: Penguin Books.

2 Alasuutari et al., 2009; Arthur et al., 2012; Bryman, 2012, 2008; Cohen et al., 2012, 2007; Denzin and Lincoln, 2011.

Chapter One

1 http://www.eua.be/cde/Home.aspx.

2 Cited by Professor Winckler – EUA President 2005–2009.

3 Heidegger [1992: 149–50] recognized that *paideia* [education] 'is not limited to a determinate realm of objects', nor can it be defined by content, it opens space for 'questioning and research' [ibid: 150].

4 *cogito ergo sum*.

5 Dreyfus in conversation with McGee, URL: http://www.youtube.com/watch?v=aaGk6S1qhz0, accessed 2 January 2014.

6 This translation is by Caputo.

7 *Stimmung* – atmosphere, tuning.

8 'The Open' is taken from Joan Stambaugh's [1992ff] *Finitude of Being*. It has connections with 'smooth space' and with 'unconcealment'.

Chapter Two

1 *The world* represents a theorized external world that is contradictorily shared by everyone. All other references to world, unless otherwise stated, presuppose one's being-in-the-world that is always a being-with and so shared with others (see also chapter 1).

2 Stambaugh's [1992] translation of *das Ge-stell*.

3 'The existentiell/existential distinction corresponds to that between ontic and ontological. In fact, it is the ontic–ontological distinction as applied to the entity Heidegger calls *Dasein*. My choosing to face up to death, for example, constitutes an existentiell, whereas that *being of Dasein* – hence *my being* – is being towards death, constitutes an existential' [Gorner, 2007, 110, fn. 9; emphasis added].

4 Calarcom, M. and Atterton, P. [eds] [2003: 102] *The Continental Ethics Reader*, New York: Routledge.

5 St. Thomas Aquinas' *Summa Theologica.*

6 te Velde, R.A. [1995] *Participation and Substantiality in Thomas Aquinas*, Leiden, Netherlands: Brill Publishers.

7 For Arendt [1998{1958}] the 'human condition of action' is basic to human existence: it being etymologically rooted in Aristotle's '*bios politikos*', denoting 'explicitly only the realm of human affairs, and stressing the action, praxis, needed to sustain it'.

8 Bloom [2004] admits that 'from 1911 – 1925, Eliot was a great poet, publishing his masterpiece in 1922, *The Waste Land*' [ibid: 896–97]. For Bloom *The Wasteland* connects with Walt Whitman's majestic elegy, *When the Lilacs in the Dooryard Bloom'd.*

9 *θέσις.*

10 *θέ.*

11 *Vorstellung.*

12 *Sicherstellen.*

13 *Das Ge-stell.*

14 *Zustellen.*

Chapter Three

1 Latin, *posse*, to be able, to be possible, to have power [OED].

2 https://www.vitae.ac.uk/ accessed 10th March, 2014.

3 *Warum, wenn es angeht, also die Frist des Daseins/ hinzubringen, als Lorbeer . . .*

4 http://quod.lib.umich.edu/o/ohp/10803281.0001.001/1:11/--impasses-of-the-post-global-theory-in-the-era-of-climate?rgn=div1;view=fulltext

Chapter Four

1 SRA [2003] uses terms: 'responsibility to pursue objectivity' without compromising 'ethical and methodological standards'.

2 Bloom [2004] – 'The situation in which the poem begins is that difficult moment in myth when the old gods are departing and the new are not yet securely themselves' [ibid: 468].

Chapter Five

1 Trans. A. S. Kline [2001]. Available at: http://poetryintranslation.com/PITBR/German/Rilke.htm

2 'Castle Duino', we learn from Edward Snow's translation of these elegies, is an ancient fortress-like structure set high atop cliffs overlooking the Adriatic near Trieste and the place where Rilke had been inspired to write these poems.

3 See URL: http://www.daimon.ch/3856305416_2I.htm accessed 20th February 2013.

Chapter Six

1 *λέγειν*.

2 *νόμος*.

3 '*Grundriss*' connotes a sketch, a foundation, a reason grounding the building of such research.

4 *Σοφία*.

5 *Logische Untersuchung*.

6 From the German, '*unter*' meaning under, found in his title, *Logische Untersuchen*.

7 *suchen*.

8 *nach etwas suchen*.

9 **Act 3, Scene V: line 30.**

10 Flint's term arising from informal discussions with A. P. Dougherty and C. L. Dougherty.

11 http://www.eua.be/cde/Home.aspx

12 *Bildung*: Hegel, 1977 {1807} [Sec. 28 for perhaps Hegel's best definition of *Bildung*]; Masschelein and Ricken, 2003; Stojanov, 2012.

13 Pagination was not given.

14 Homer's, *Ulysses*: 'deathless ones', i.e., the gods, are always on the side of Odysseus in this epic tale.

Chapter Seven

1 Derrida.

2 The *Matrix* trilogy of films makes reference to Baudrillard's *Simulacra and Simulation*, Plato's cave allegory, and Descartes' ontology.

3 *from* the Sixth Book. . .*from* The Prelude or Growth of a Poet's Mind, An Autobiographical Poem.

Chapter Eight

1 For Eliot his poem 'was a vision of a world stricken by the absence of Christian culture'. Bloom [2004: 904] points out, Eliotic critics always interpreted the poem as a voice in the wilderness, crying out for the return to Christian, classical and conservative idea of order'.

2 Berleant's [2004] deconstruction of Disneyworld arrived at a similar conclusion.

3 Giddens, 1990: 133.

Chapter Nine

1 Tree metaphor structuring research [Preissle, 2011: 690].

2 http://www.rhizomes.net/issue5/poke/glossary.html

3 Heidegger, 1962: 135, 179, 221].

4 Deleuze and Guattari [2004{1987}: 419].

5 The Four Quartets.

6 Spry's poetry does not disclose who Professor Mih-ha Trihn is – one is either expected to know or to research this veiled reference to a film made by the professor entitled 'Shoot for the contents' that refers in part to a Chinese guessing game and takes us into a unique maze of allegorical identities and storytelling in China.

7 Goodall, Jr., H. L. [1998, November]. *Notes for the autoethnography and autobiography panel NCA*. A paper presented at the National Communication Association Conventionin New York City.

8 Denzin, N. K. [1997]. *Interpretive ethnography: Ethnographic practices for the 21st century*, London: Sage.

Chapter Ten

1 'Lost lives remembered during 9/11 ceremony', 'The Online Rocket' September 12, 2008: http://web.archive.org/web/20100916051327/http://media.www.theonlinerocket.com/media/storage/paper601/news/2008/09/12/News/Lost-Lives.Remembered.During.911.Ceremony-3427598.shtml: Retrieved from Internet Archive, 10 March 2014.

2 Kincheloe [2001: 679].

3 Not withstanding its own contradiction, in *the* modern world everything would be appear to be re-presented as calculable, the possible, the conditional.

4 Giddens [1990]: Etymologically 'juggernaut' derives from the Hindi word *Jagannath*, 'lord of the world'. 'It is the title of Krishna, an idol of the deity was taken each year on a huge car, which followers are said to have thrown themselves under, to be crushed beneath the wheels' [ibid: 139].

Chapter Eleven

1 Derrida, 1981.

2 Kincheloe's website following his death: 'Joe Kincheloe's Critical Complex Epistemology/Pedagogy & Multidimensional Critical Complex Bricolage' URL: http://www.joekincheloe.us/

3 Bloom [2004]: 'The Mental Traveller' – a 'highly finished, economical, complex ballad. . .[that] seem[s] to deliberate experiences at telling versions of Blake's myths without using the technical vocabulary of private personages' [ibid: 311].

Chapter Twelve

1 Phrasing used to describe the basis for her Nobel Prize in Literature. Available at http://www.nobelprize.org/nobel_prizes/literature/laureates/1996/

2 Translated by Stanislaw Baranczak and Clare Cavanagh.

BIBLIOGRAPHY

Adorno, T. W. [1991] *The Culture Industry: Selected Essays on Mass Culture*, Bernstein, J. M. [ed.] London: Routledge.

Adorno, T. W. and Horkheimer, M. [2002] *Dialectic of Enlightenment: Philosophical Fragments*, trans. Jephcote, E. Stanford, CA: Stanford University Press.

Agamben, G. [1993] *The Coming Community: Theory Out of Bounds, Volume 1*, trans. Hardt, M., Minneapolis and London: University of Minnesota Press.

— [1998] *Homo Sacer: Sovereign Power and Bare Life*, trans. Heller-Roazen, D. Stanford, CA: Stanford University Press.

— [2002] 'Difference and Repetition: On Guy Debord's Films', trans. Holmes, B. in, McDonough, T. [ed.] *Guy Debord and the Situationist International*, Cambridge, Masachussets: MIT Press.

— [2005] *State of Exception*, trans. Attell, K. Chicago and London: University of Chicago Press.

— [2007] *Profanations*, trans. Fort, J., New York: Zone Books.

— [2009] *What Is an Apparatus and Other Essays*, trans. Kishik, D. and Pedatella, S., Stanford, CA: Stanford University Press.

Alastalo, M. [2008] 'The History of Social Research Methods', in Alasuutari, P., Bickman, L. and Brannen, J. [eds] *The Sage Handbook of Social Research Methods*, London: Sage, 26–41.

Alasuutari, P., Bickman, L. and Brannen, J. [eds] [2009] *The Sage Handbook of Social Research Methods*, London: Sage.

Altheide, D. and Johnson, J. M. [2011] 'Reflections on Interpretative Adequacy in Qualitative Research', in Denzin, N. K. and Lincoln, Y. S. [eds] *The Sage Handbook of Qualitative Research* [4th Edition], London: Sage, 581–94.

American Association of University Professors, AAUP [1981] 'Regulations governing research on human subjects: Academic freedom and the institutional review board', *Academe*, 67, 358–70.

—[2001] 'Protecting human beings: Institutional review boards and social science research', *Academe*, 87[3], 55–67.

—[2002] 'Should all disciplines be subject to the common rule? Human subjects of social science research', *Academe*, 88[1], 1–15.

—[2006] Committee A: Report on human subjects: Academic freedom and the institutional review boards. Available at: http://www.aaup.org/AAUP/About/committees/committee+repts/CommA/

American Education Research Association, AERA [2006] Standards for reporting on empirical social science research in AERA publications. Available at http://www.aera.net/opportunities/?id=1480

Arendt, H. [1998{1958}] *The Human Condition*, Chicago, IL: Chicago University Press.

Aristotle [2000] *Nicomachean Ethics* [2nd Edition], trans. Irwin, L. Indianapolis, IN: Hackett Publishing Company.

Armstrong, K. [2008] 'Ethnography and Audience' in Alasuutari, P., Bickman, L. and Brannen, J. [eds] *The Sage Handbook of Social Research Methods*, London: Sage: 54–67.

Arthur, J., Waring, J., Coe, R. and Hedges, L. V. [2012] *Research Methods & Methodologies in Education*, London: Sage.

Austin, D. A. [1996] 'Kaleidoscope: The Same and Different' in, Ellis, C. and Bochner, A. P. [eds] *Composing Ethnography*, Walnut Creek, CA: AltaMira Press: 206–30.

Austin, J. L. [1975] *How to Do Things with Words*. Cambridge, MA Harvard University Press.

Backstrand, K. [2003] 'Civic science for sustainability: reframing the role of experts, policy-makers and citizens in environmental governance', *Global Environmental Politics*, 3[4], 24–41.

Bacon, F. [1996 {1854]] Francis Bacon [1561–1626] *The Great Instauration*, Philadelphia, PA: The Works, available at: http://history.hanover.edu/courses/excerpts/111bac.html, accessed on 30 September 2010.

Bakhtin, M. M. [1986] *Speech Genres and Other Late Essays*, trans. McGee, V. W., Texas: University of Texas Press.

Barthes, R. [2005] *The Empire of Signs*, trans. Howard, R., New York: Anchor Books.

Bassett, E. and O'Riordan, K. [2002] 'Ethics of internet research: contesting the human subjects research model', *Ethics and Information Technology*, 4[3], 233–47.

Bauman, Z. [2011] *Culture in a Liquid Modern World*, Cambridge: Polity Press.

Beardsworth, R. [1996] *Derrida and the Political*, London and New York: Routledge.

Beck, U. [1992] *Risk Society: Towards a New Modernity*, London: Sage Publications.

Bentham, J. [2005{1843}] The *Works of Jeremy Bentham*, Bowring, J. [ed.], Edinburgh: WilliamTate, available at http://oll.libertyfund.org/index.php?option=com_staticxt&staticfile=show.php%3Ftitle=2234&Itemid=27, accessed 20 November 2010.

Berleant, A. [2004] The critical aesthetics of Disney World, *Journal of Applied Philosophy*, 11[2], 171–80.

Bernstein, B. [2000] *Pedagogy, Symbolic Control, and Identity* [2nd Edition], Plymouth: Rowman & Littlefield Publisher.

Berry, K. S. [2004] 'Structures of bricolage and complexity' in, J. L. Kincheloe and Berry, K. S. [eds], *Rigour and Complexity in Educational Research: Conceptualizing the Bricolage* Maidenhead: Open University Press, 103–27.

Bhabha, H. [1990] *Nation and Narration*, London: Routledge.

— [2004] *The Location of Culture*, London and New York: Routledge Classics.

Bhatti, G. [2012] 'Ethnography and representational styles' in Arthur, J., Waring, J., Coe, R. and Hedges, L. V. [eds] *Research Methods & Methodologies in Education*, London: Sage, 80–84.

Biesta, G. [2005] 'Against learning: Reclaiming a language for education in an age of learning', *Nordisk Pedagogik*, 25: 54–66, Oslo.
Bloom, H. [2004] *The Best Poems of the English Language: From Chaucer through to Robert Frost, Selected with Commentary by Harold Bloom*, New York: Harper Perennial.
Bloor, M. [1978] 'On the analysis of observational data: a discussion of the worth and uses of inductive techniques and respondent validation', *Sociology*, 12[3], 545–5.
Boal, A. [2008{1974}] *Theatre of the Oppressed*, McBride, C. A., McBride, M.-O. L. and Fryer, E. [eds] London: Pluto Press.
Bourdieu, P. [1968] 'Intellectual field and creative project', *Social Science Information* 8, 89–119.
— [1977] *Outline of a Theory of Practice*, Cambridge: Cambridge University Press.
— [1996] *The Political Ontology of Martin Heidegger*, trans. Collier, P., Cambridge, UK and Malden, MA: Polity Press.
— [2000] 'For a scholarship with commitment' in Franklin, P. [ed.] *Profession*, New York: Modern Languages Association, 42.
Bovaird, J. A. and Embretson, S. E. [2008] 'Modern measurement in the social sciences', in Alasuutari, P., Bickman, L. and Brannen, J. [eds] *The Sage Handbook of Social Research Methods*, London: Sage, 269–89.
Bridges, D. [1997] Philosophy and educational research: A reconsideration of epistemological boundaries. *Cambridge Journal of Education*, 27[2], 177–190.
British Educational Research Association, BERA [2011] *Ethical Guidelines for Educational Research*, London: BERA.
Brown,V. A., Harris, J. A. and Russell, J. Y. [2010] *Tackling Wicked Problems through the Transdisciplinary Imagination*, London: Earthscan.
Burgess, H., Weller, G. and Wellington, J. [2011] 'Tensions in the purpose and impact of professional doctorates', *Work Based Learning e-Journal*, 2[1], 1–2.
Butler, J. [1990] *Gender Trouble*, London: Routledge.
Brydon-Miller, M., Kral, M., Maguire, P., Noffke, S. and Sabhlok [2011] 'Jazz and the Banyan Tree', in Denzin, N. K. and Lincoln, Y. S. [eds] *The Sage Handbook of Qualitative Research* [4th Edition], London: Sage: 387–400.
Bryman, A. [2007] 'The end of the paradigm wars' in, Alasuutari, P., Bickman, L. and Brannen, J. [eds] [2008] *The Sage Handbook of Social Research Methods*, London: Sage: 13–25.
— [2008] *Social Research Methods* [3rd Edition], New York: Oxford University Press.
— [2012] *Social Research Methods* [4th Edition], New York: Oxford University Press.
Cannella, G. S. and Lincoln, Y. S. [2004] 'Dangerous discourses II: Comprehending and countering the deployment of discourses [and resources] in the generation of laboratory inquiry', *Qualitative Inquiry*, 10[2], 165–74.
Cannella, G. S. and Miller, L. L. [2008] 'Constructing corporatist science: Reconstituting the soul of American higher education'. *Cultural Studies – Critical Methodologies*, 8[1], 24–38.

Caputo, J. D. [1986] *The Mystical Element in Heidegger's Thought*, The Bronx, New York: Fordham University Press.

— [1987] *Radical Hermeneutics: Repetition, Deconstruction and the Hermeneutic Project*, Bloomington and Indianapolis: Indiana University Press.

— [2013] *Truth: Philosophy in Transit*, London: Penguin.

Casey, E. S. [1998] *The Fate of Place: A Philosophical History*, Berkeley: University of California Press.

Castells, M. [2009] *The Rise of the Network Society: Information Age: Economy, Society, and Culture v. 1: The Information Age: Economy, Society, and Culture Volume* [2nd Edition], Chichester, West Sussex and Oxford: Wiley-Blackwell.

Charmaz, K. [2005] 'Grounded theory in the 21st century', in Denzin, N. K. and Lincoln, Y. S. [eds] *The Sage Handbook of Qualitative Research* [3rd Edition], London: Sage, 507–35.

— [2011] 'Grounded theory methods in social justice research', in Denzin, N. K. and Lincoln, Y. S. [eds], *The Sage Handbook of Qualitative Research* [4th Edition], London: Sage, 359–80.

Chawla, D. [2006] 'The bangle seller of Meena Bazaar', *Qualitative Inquiry*, 12[6], 1135–38.

Clarke, J. and Newman, J. [1997], *The Managerial State: Power, Politics and Ideology in the Remaking of Social Welfare*, London: Sage.

Clough, P. and Nutbrown, C. [2012] *A Student's Guide to Methodology* [3rd Edition], London: Sage.

Coe, R. J. [2012] 'The Nature of Educational Research', in Aurthur, A., Warring, M., Coe, R. J. and Hedges, L. V. [eds], *Research Methods and Methodologies in Education*, London: Sage: 5–14.

Cogan, J. [2006] 'The phenomenological reduction', *The Internet Encyclopedia of Philosophy*, ISSN 2161–0002, http://www.iep.utm.edu/, 16 March 2014.

Cohen, L., Manion, L. and Morrison, K. [2007] *Research Methods in Education* [6th Edition], London and New York: Routledge.

— [2012] *Research Methods in Education* [7th Edition], London and New York: Routledge.

Coleman, F. J. [2005] 'Rhizome', in Parr, A. [ed.], *The Deleuze Dictionary*. Edinburgh: Edinburgh University Press.

Conley, T. [2005a] 'Molar', in Parr, A. [ed.], *The Deleuze Dictionary*, Edinburgh: Edinburgh University Press, 171–72.

— [2005b] 'Molecular', in Parr, A. [ed.], *The Deleuze Dictionary*, Edinburgh: Edinburgh University Press, 172–74.

Conquergood, D. [1991] 'Rethinking ethnography: towards a critical cultural poetics', *Communication Monographs*, 58, 179–94.

Cory, G. and Gardner, R. [2002] *The Evolutionary Neuroethology of Paul MacLean: Convergences and Frontiers*, London: Praeger.

Costley, C. and Gibbs, P. [2006] 'Researching others: care as an ethic for practitioner researchers', *Studies in Higher Education*, 31[1], 89–98.

Cressey, D. R. [1950] 'The criminal violation of financial trust', *American Sociological Review*, 15, 738–43.

Cronin, A., Alexander, V. D., Fielding, J. Moran-Ellis, J. and Thomas, H. [2008] 'The analytical integration of qualitative data sources', in Alasuutari, P.,

Bickman, L. and Brannen, J. [eds], *The Sage Handbook of Social Research Methods*, London: Sage: 572–84.

Crosier, D. and Parveva, T. [2013] 'The Bologna Process: Its Impact in Europe and Beyond', UNESCO: International Institute for Educational Planning, Paris: United Nations Educational, Scientific and Cultural Organization.

Crotty, M. [1997] *The Foundations of Social Research: Meaning and Perspective in the Research: Meaning and Perspectives in the Research Process*, St Leonards, New South Wales: Allen & Unwin.

Davidson, J. and Gregorio, S. [2011] 'Qualitative Research and Technology', in Denzin, N. K. and Lincoln, Y. S. [eds], *The Sage Handbook of Qualitative Research* [4th Edition], London: Sage, 627–43.

Debord, G. [1977] *Society of the Spectacle*, trans. Black & Red, Detroit, Michigan: Black & Red; Oakland, CA: AK Press.

Deleuze, G. and Guattari, F. [2004{1987}] *A Thousand Plateaus: Capitalism and Schizophrenia,* trans. Massumi, B. Minneapolis: University of Minnesota Press [original work published 1980].

de Man, P. [1989] 'Introduction to the poetry of John Keats', in Waters, L. [ed.], *Critical Writings 1953–1978*, Minneapolis: University of Minneapolis.

de Saussure, F. [2011 {1959}] *Course in General Linguistics*, Meisel, P. and Saussy, H. trans. Baskin, W. New York: Columbia University Press.

Denicolo, P. and Park, C. [2010] 'Doctorateness – an elusive concept?' Bohrer, J. and Clarke, J. [eds], *Southgate House*, Gloucester: The Quality Assurance Agency for Higher Education.

Denzin, N. K. [1997] *Interpretive ethnography: Ethnographic practices for the 21st century*. London: Sage.

— [2011] 'The politics of evidence', in Denzin, N. K. and Lincoln, Y. S. [eds], *The Sage Handbook of Qualitative Research* [4th Edition], London: Sage, 645–57.

Denzin, N. K. and Lincoln, Y. S. [eds] [2000] *Handbook of qualitative research.* [2nd edition] Thousand Oakes, CA: Sage.

Denzin, N. K. and Lincoln, Y. S. [eds] [2011] *The Sage Handbook of Qualitative Research* [4th Edition], London: Sage.

Denzin, N. K. and Lincoln, Y. S. [2005] 'Introduction: the discipline and practice of qualitative research' in *The Sage Handbook of Qualitative Research* [3rd Edition], London: Sage: 1–32.

Denzin, N. K. and Lincoln, Y. S. [2011a] 'The future of qualitative research', in Denzin, N. K. and Lincoln, Y. S. [eds], *The Sage Handbook of Qualitative Research* [4th Edition], London: Sage: 681–84.

— [2011b] 'Introduction: The Discipline and the Practice of Qualitative Research', in Denzin, N. K. and Lincoln, Y. S. [eds], *The Sage Handbook of Qualitative Research* [4th Edition], London: Sage, 1–20.

Derrida, J. [1973a] *Speech and Phenomena and Other Essays on Husserl's Theory of Signs*, trans. Allison, D., Evanston, IL: Northwestern University Press.

— [1973b] 'Difference' in *Speech and Phenomena and Other Essays on Husserl's Theory of Signs*, trans. Allison, D., Evanston, IL: Northwestern University Press, 129–60.

— [1976] *Of Grammatology*, trans, with a Preface by G. C. Spivak., Baltimore: Johns Hopkins.

— [1978] 'Structure, sign and play in the discourse of the human sciences', in *Writing and Difference*, trans. Bass, A., Chicago, IL: Chicago University Press, 278–93.
— [1981a] *Positions*, trans. Bass, A., Chicago: Chicago University Press.
— [1981b] *Dissemination*, trans. Johnson, B. London: Athlone Press.
— [1982a] 'Signature, event, context', in *Margins of philosophy* trans. Bass, A. Chicago: University of Chicago Press, 309–29.
— [1986] *Mémoires: For Paul de Man*, trans. Lindsay., Culler, J. and Cadava, E., New York: Columbia University Press.
— [1988a] *Limited Inc.*, trans. Weber, S. and Mehlman, J., Graff, G. [ed.], Evanston, IL: Northwestern University Press.
— [1988b] 'Afterword: Toward an Ethic of Discussion', trans. Weber, S. in *Limited Inc.* Evanston, IL: Northwestern University Press.
— [1989] ' Force of law: the 'mystical foundation of authority', trans. Quaintance, M. presented at the Cardozo Law School at a Colloquium entitled: 'Deconstruction and the Possibility of Justice'.
— [1989 {1962}] *Edmund Husserl's Origin of Geometry: An Introduction by Jacques Derrida*, trans. with preface and afterword by Leavey Jr. and J. P., Lincoln London: University of Nebraska Press.
— [1990] 'The force of law: The 'mystical' foundation of authority', *Cardozo Law Review* 11, 920–1045.
— [1991] *Given Time I Counterfeit Money*, trans. Kamuf, P. Chicago: University of Chicago Press.
— [1992a] Afterword: Towards an ethic of discussion. in *Limited Inc*, trans. S. Weber, Evanston, IL: Northwestern University Press, 111–60.
— [1992b] 'Afterwords: or, at least, less than a letter about a letter less' trans. Bennington, G. in, Royle, N. [ed.], *Afterwords*, Tampere, Finland: Outside Books, 197–203.
— [1992c] 'This strange institution called literature', trans Bennington, G. and Bowlby, R. in, Attridge, D. [ed.] *Acts of Literature*, London and New York: Routledge, 33–75.
— [1993] *Aporias: Dying – Awaiting [One Another at] the 'Limits of Truth'*, trans. Dutoit, T., Stanford: Stanford University Press.
— [1994] *Spectres of Marx: The State of the Debt, The Work of Mourning and the New International*, trans. Kamuf, P. London and New York: Routledge.
— [1995a] *Points. . .interviews, 1974–94.* [E. Weber, [ed.], trans: Kamuf, P. Chicago, IL: University of Chicago Press.
— [1995b] 'Passages – from Traumatism to Promise', trans. Kamuf, P., in Weber, E. [ed.] *Points. . . Interviews, 1974–94*, Stanford: Stanford University Press.
— [1995c] 'Force of law: the "mystical foundation of authority"', trans. Quaintance, M., *Cardoza Law Review*, 11[5/6], 921–1045.
— [1995d] *The Gift of Deat*h, trans. Willis, D. Chicago, IL: Chicago University Press.
— [1996] 'Remarks on deconstruction and pragmatism', in C. Mouffe, C. [ed.] *Deconstruction and Pragmatism*, London: Routledge: 77–88.
— [1997a] 'The Villanova Roundtable' in, Caputo, J. D. [ed] *Deconstruction in a Nutshell: A Conversation with Jacques Derrida*, Cambridge: Cambridge University Press: 3–28.

— [1997b] *Of Grammatology* [correct edition], trans. Spivak, G., Baltimore, MD: The John Hopkins University Press.

— [1999] 'Hospitality, justice and responsibility: a dialogue with Jacques Derrida' in, Kearney, R. and Dooley, M. [eds] *Questioning Ethics*, London: Routledge, 65–83.

— [2000] *Of Hospitality*, Anne Dufourmantelle invites Jacques Derrida to Respond, trans. Bowlby, R. Stanford, CA: Stanford University Press.

— [2001{1978}a] *Writing and Difference*, trans. and Introduction, Bass, A., London and New York: Routledge Classics.

— [2001{1978}b] 'Structure, sign and play', in *Writing and Difference,* trans. A. Bass, London: Routledge Classics. [Originally published in 1978 by Routledge & Kegan Paul], 351–70.

— [2001c] 'I have a taste for the Secret', Jacques Derrida in conversation with Maurizio Ferraris and Giorgio Vattimo in, Derrida, J. and Ferraris, M. *A Taste for a Secret*, trans. Donis, G. Cambridge, UK: Polity, 3–92.

— [2001{1978}d] 'Violence and Metaphysics', in *Writing and Difference,* trans. A. Bass, London: Routledge Classics. [Originally published in 1978 by Routledge & Kegan Paul], 97–192.

— [2005] *Rogues: Two Essays on Reason*, trans. Brault, P.-A. and Naas, M. Stanford: Stanford University Press.

di Gregorio, S. [2006, September 13–15] 'Research design issues for software users', Paper presented as the Seventh International Strategies in Qualitative Research Conference, University of Durham.

di Gregorio, S. and Davidson, J. [2008] *Qualitative research design issues for software users*, London: Open University Press.

Dillard, D. and Okpalaoka, C. [2011] 'The Sacred and the spiritual nature of endarkened transnational feminist praxis in qualitative research' in Denzin, N. K. and Lincoln, Y. S. [eds] *The Sage Handbook of Qualitative Research* [4th Edition], London: Sage, 147–62.

Dooley, M. and Kavanagh, L. [2007] *The Philosophy of Derrida*, Stocksfield: Acumen.

Ellingson, L. L. [2011] 'Analysis and representation across the continuum', in Denzin, N. K. and Lincoln, Y. S. [eds] *The Sage Handbook of Qualitative Research* [4th Edition], London: Sage, 595–610.

Ellis, C. [2004] *The Ethnographic Interview I: A Methodological Novel about Autoethnography*, Walnut Creek, CA: AltaMira.

Evans, T. and Hardy, M. [2010] *Evidence and Knowledge for Practice,* Cambridge: Polity Press.

Fanon, F. [1965] *The Wretched of the Earth*, Preface Sartre, J.-P., trans. Farrington, C. London: Penguin Books.

— [2006] *The Fanon Reader*, Haddour, A. [ed.], London: Pluto Press. The Fanon Reader.

— [2008a] *Black Skin, White Masks*, London: Pluto Press.

— [2008b] *Concerning Violence*, London: Penguin.

Fell, T., Flint, K. J. and Haines, I. [eds] [2011] *Professional Doctorates in the UK 2011*, Lichfield, Staffordshire: UK Council for Graduate Education.

Feuer, M. J. [2006] Response to Bettie St Pierre's 'scientifically based research in education: epistemology and ethics', *Adult Education Quarterly*, 56[3], 267–72.

Feyerabend, P. K. [2010] *Against Method* [4th Edition], London: Verso Books.

Fink, B. [1995] *The Lacanian Subject: Between Language and Jouissance, Princeton*, NJ: Princeton University Press.

Finley, S. [2011] 'Critical Arts-Based Inquiry: The Pedagogy and Performance of a Radical Ethical Aesthetic' in, Denzin, N. K. and Lincoln, Y. S. [eds] *The Sage Handbook of Qualitative Research* [4th Edition], London: Sage, 435–50.

Flint, K. J. [2009] 'A Derridaean reading of the zone of proximal development [ZPD]: the monster in the play of différance', *Educational Review*, 61[2], 211–27.

— [2011a] 'Some philosophical issues raised by the current development of the doctor of education in the UK', in Fell, T., Flint, K. J. and Haines, I. [eds] *Professional Doctorates in the UK 2011*, Lichfield, Staffordshire: UK Council for Graduate Education, 28–34.

— [2011b] 'Deconstructing workplace 'know how' and 'tacit knowledge': exploring the temporal play of being within professional practice, *Journal of Higher Education, Skills and Work-based Learning: The Journal of the University Vocational Awards Council*, 1[2], 128–46.

— [2012a] 'The importance of *place* in the improvement agenda', keynote lecture presented at the 'Brighton Conference for Educational Research', 23 June 2012.

— [2012b] 'The rhetoric of numbers', in Flint, K. J. and Peim, N. *Rethinking the Education Improvement Agenda*, London and New York: Continuum, 246–76.

— [2012c] 'Education, the language of improvement and governmentality: the enframing in practice', in *Rethinking the Education Improvement Agenda*, London and New York: Continuum, 42–68.

— [2013a] 'What's play got to do with the information age?', in Ryall, E., Russell, W. and Maclean, M. [eds] *The Philosophy of Play*, London: Routledge, 152–63.

— [2013b] 'There's no justice in education: Do recent improvements in education make a difference'? Paper presented at my Inaugural Lecture for Reader in Education at NTU, 26 June.

— [2013c] 'Where is 'justice to come' to be found in leadership?' Paper presented at: 'Educational Leadership: Four challenges for a new Educational Governance', 1st International Workshop of Research Group PSITIC [Pedagogy, Society and Innovation with ICT Support], Universitat Ramon Llull, Barcelona, Spain, 7 and 8 November.

— [*in preparation,* i] 'Bare life, doctorateness and the production of knowledge: towards a re-examination of standards'.

— [in preparation, ii] 'Education for Sale: Questions concerning bare life and the principle of the market'.

— [in preparation, iii] 'A Derridean reading of space for improvement: the monster in the field of play'.

— [*in preparation*, iv] 'Issues concerning bare life and the evaluation of the quality of research: validity, credibility and différance'.

— [*in preparation*, v] 'Issues concerning bare life and the evaluation of the quality of research: validity, credibility and *différance*'.

— [in preparation, vi] 'Bare life and research-based authentic education: a re-examination of the gold standards for reporting research'.
— [in preparation, vii] 'Bare Life in Radical Bricolage: Uncovering the inner-self within a post-metaphysical conception of methodology'.
— [in preparation, viii] 'Breaking the circle: enframing, bare life and polarisation in the society of the spectacle'.
Flint, K. J. and Barnard, A. [2010a] 'Space for personal development: an exploration of student experience involving one professional doctorate programme', *Work-based Learning e-Journal*, 1[2], 202–22.
— [2010b] 'The power of research: An exploration of critical dialogue as a model for the development of professionals', *Work Based Learning e-Journal*, 1[1], 125–41.
Flint, K. J. and Needham, D. [1997] 'Framing lifelong learning in the twenty-first century: towards a way of thinking', in Aspin, D. N. [ed.] *Philosophical Perspectives on Lifelong Learning*, Dordrecht, The Netherlands: Springer, 85–105.
Flint, K. J. and Peim, N. [2012] *Rethinking the Education Improvement Agenda*, London and New York: Continuum.
Flynn, T. [2003] 'Foucault's Mapping of History' in, Gutting, G. [ed.] *The Cambridge Companion to Foucault* [2nd Edition], Cambridge: Cambridge University Press, 29–48.
Foucault, M. [1970{1966}] *The Order of Things: An Archaeology of the Human Sciences*, trans. Tavistock/Routledge, London: Tavistock.
— [1972] *The Archaeology of Knowledge*, trans. Sheridan, A. M., London: Routledge.
— [1973{1966}] *The Order of Things: An Archaeology of the Human Sciences*, trans. Sheridan, A., London: Tavistock.
— [1977] *Discipline and Punish: The Birth of a Prison*, trans. Sheridan, A., London: Penguin Books.
— [1978] *History of Sexuality Volume 1: An Introduction*, trans. Hurley, R., New York: Pantheon.
— [1980a] *Knowledge/Power: Selected Interviews and Other Writings*, Gordon, C. [ed.], trans. Gordon, C., Marshall, L., Mepham, J. and Soper, K., New York and London: Prentice Hall.
— [1980b] 'Two lectures', in Gordon, C. [ed.] *Power/Knowledge*, Brighton: Harvester, 80–105.
— [1980a] 'Prison talk', in C. Gordon [ed.] *Power/knowledge: Selected interviews and other writings 1972–1977.* New York: Pantheon Books.
— [1982] 'The subject and power', in Dreyfus, H. L. and Rabinow, P. [eds] *Michel Foucault beyond Structuralism and Hermeneutics*, Brighton: Harvester, 208–26.
— [1985] *History of Sexuality Volume II: The Use of Pleasure*, trans. Hurley, R., New York: Pantheon.
— [1986] *History of Sexuality Volume III: Care of the Self*, trans. Hurley, R., New York: Pantheon.
— [1980b] 'Nietzsche, genealogy and history' in, Rabinow, P. [ed.] *The Foucault Reader*, Harmondsworth: Peregrine: 76–100.
— [1988a] *The History of Sexuality: The Will to Knowledge: The Will to Knowledge volume 1*, trans. Hurley, R., London: Penguin.

— [1994a] 'Truth and power', in Faubion, J. D. [ed.] *Power: Essential Works of Foucault: 1954–1984, Volume Three*, trans. Hurley and Others, New York: New York Press: 111–33.

— [1994b] 'Truth and juridical forms', in Faubion, J. D. [ed.] *Power: Essential Works of Foucault: 1954–1984, Volume Three*, trans. Hurley and Others, New York: New York Press, 1–89.

— [2002{1969}] *The Archaeology of Knowledge*. trans. Sheridan Smith, A. M. London and New York: Routledge.

Freeman, M., de Marrais, K., Preissle, J., Roulston, K. and St Pierre, E. A. [2007] Standards of evidence in qualitative research: An incitement to discourse, *Educational Researcher*, 36[1], 1–8.

Freire, P. [1972] *Pedagogy of the Oppressed*, London: Pelican.

— [1975] 'Pilgrims of the obvious', *Risk*, 11[1], 1–18.

Fritzman, J. M. [1990] 'Lyotard's paralogy and Rorty's pluralism: their differences and pedagogi-cal implications.' *Educational Theory*, 40[3], 371–80.

Gadamer, H.-G. [2004] *Truth and Method*, trans. Weinsheimer, J. and Marshall, D. G., London and New York: Continuum International Publishing.

Gardner, S. [1999] *Kant and the Critique of Pure Reason*, London and New York: Routledge.

Garfinkel, H. [1984{1967}] *Studies in Ethnomethodology*. Cambridge: Polity Press.

Geertz, C. [1988] *Works and lives: The anthropologist as author*. Stanford, CA: Stanford University Press.

Gibbons, M., Limoges, C., Nowotny, H., Schartzman, S., Scott, P. and Trow, M. [1994] *The Production of Knowledge: The Dynamics of Science and Research in Contemporary Societies*, London: Sage.

Gibbs, P. [2013] 'Research paradigms of practice, work and learning' in Billett, S. [ed.] *International Handbook of Professional Learning*, Dordrecht: Springer [reading based on an early draft].

Gibbs, P. and Barnett, R. [2014] *Thinking about Higher Education*, London: Springer.

Gibbs, P. and Costley, C. [2006] An ethics of community and care for practitioner researchers, *International Journal of Research & Method in Education*, London: Routledge, 239–49.

Giddens, A. [1979] *Central Problems in Social Theory: Action, Structure and Contradiction in Social Analysis*, Berkeley: University of California Press.

— [1984] *The Constitution of Society*. Cambridge: Polity.

— [1990] *The Consequences of Modernity*, Cambridge: Polity Press.

— [1991] *Modernity and Self-Identity: Self and Society in the Late Modern Age*, Cambridge: Polity.

— [1993] *New Rules of Sociological Method* [2nd Revised Edition], Cambridge: Polity Press.

Gilligan, J. [1998] 'Reflections from a life behind bars: build colleges, not prisons', *Chronicle of Higher Education*, B7: 9, 16th October.

Giroux, H. [1982] *Theory and Resistance in Education: A Pedagogy for the Opposition*, Boston: Bergin & Garvey.

— [2008] *Against the Terror of Neoliberalism: Politics Beyond the Age of Greed*, Boulder, Colorado and London: Paradigm Publishers.

Glaser B. G. [1992] *Basics of grounded theory analysis Emergence vs. forcing*, California: Sociology Press.

Glaser, B. G. and Strauss, A. L. [1967] *The Discovery of Grounded Theory: Strategies for Qualitative Research*, Chicago: Aldine Publishing Company.

Goodall, Jr., H. L. [1998, November] *Notes for the autoethnography and autobiography Panel NCA*. A paper presented at the National Communication Association Convention in New York City.

Gorner, P. [2007] *Heidegger's Being and Time: An Introduction*, Cambridge: Cambridge University Press.

Goswami, A. [1993] 'The Self-Aware Universe: How Consciousness Creates the Material World', New York: Tarcher/Putnam.

Guba, E. G. [1990] *The Paradigm Dialog*, Newbury Park, CA: Sage.

Guba, E. G. and Lincoln, Y. S. [1985] *Naturalistic Inquiry*, Newbury Park, CA: Sage.

— [2005] 'Paradigmatic controversies, contradictions, and emerging confluences', in Denzin, N. K. and Lincoln, Y. S. [eds] *The Sage Handbook for Qualitative Research* [3rd Edition], Thousand Oakes, CA: Sage Publications, 191–25.

Gur-Ze'ev, I. [1999] 'Max Horkheimer and Philosophy of Education' presented in *The Encyclopedia of Educational Philosophy and Theory* that was accessed at the following URL: http://www.ffst.hr/ENCYCLOPAEDIA/doku.php?id=horkheimer_and_philosophy_of_Education, accessed on 25th February 2013.

— [2010a] 'Adorno and Horkheimer: Diasporic philosophy, Negative Theology, and counter-education', *Policy Futures in Education*, 8[3,4]: 298–314 http://dx.doi.org/10.2304/pfie.2010.8.3.298

— [2010b] *The Possibility/Impossibility of a New Critical Language in Education*, Rotterdam, The Netherlands: Sense Publishers.

Hadorn, G. H., Hoffman-Riem, H., Biber-Klemm, S., Grossenbacher-Mansury, W., Joye, D., Pohl, C., Wiesmann, U., and Zemp, E. [eds] [2008] *Handbook of Transdisciplinary Research*, Dordrecht: Springer.

Hall, S. [1990] 'Cultural identity and diaspora', in Rutherford, J. [ed.] *Identity, Community, Culture, Difference*, London: Lawrence and Wishart.

— [1996] 'On postmodernism and articulation: An interview with Stuart Hall', in Morley, D. and Chen, K.-H. [eds], Stuart Hall: Critical dialogues in cultural studies, London: Routledge: 131–50. [Reprinted from *Journal of Communication Inquiry*, 10[2], 45–60, 1986].

Hamera, J. [2011] 'Performance ethnography', in Denzin, N. K. and Lincoln. Y. S. [eds] *The Sage Handbook of Qualitative Research* [4th Edition], Thousand Oakes, CA: Sage, 317–29.

Hammersley, M. [2005] 'Is the evidence-based practice movement doing more good than harm? Reflections on Iain Chalmers' case for research-based policy making and practice', *Evidence & Policy: A Journal of Research, Debate and Practice*, 1[1], 85–100.

Hammersley, M. and Atkinson, P. [1995] *Ethnography Principles in Practice*, [2nd Edition] London: Routledge.

Hargreaves, D. and Fink, D. [2006] *Sustainable Leadership*, San Francisco: Jossey-Bass.

Hartnett, J. [2003] *Incarceration Nation: Investigative Prison Poems of Hope and Terror,* Walnut Creek, CA: AltaMira Press.

Harvey, D. [1991] *The Condition of Postmodernity: An Enquiry into the Origins of Cultural Change*, Oxford: Wiley Blackwell.

— [2007] *A Brief History of Neoliberalism*, Oxford: Oxford University Press.

Hegel, G. W. F. [1977 {1807}] *Phenomenology Of Sprit*, Oxford: Oxford University Press.

Heidegger, M. [1962] *Being and Time*, trans. Macquarrie, J. and Robinson, E., Oxford: Blackwell Publishing [trans. of *Sein und Zeit* [7th Edition], Tubingen: Max Niemeyer Verlag].

— [1968 {1954}] *What Is Called Thinking*, trans. Wieck, F. D. and Gray, G. G., New York: Harper & Row Publishers [Originally published in [1954] *Was Heisst Denken*? Tuebingen: Max Niemeyer Verlag].

— [1969] *Identity and Difference*, trans., Stambaugh, J., New York: Harper & Row.

— [1971] *Poem, Language, Thought,* trans. Hofstadter, A., New York: Harper and Row.

— [1972 {1969}] *On Time and Being*, trans. Stambaugh, J. New York: Harper & Row [Originally published under the title: *Zur Sache des Denkens*[1] [Tubingen: Max Niemeyer Verlag, 1969].

— [1977] *The Question Concerning Technology and Other Essays,* trans. Lovitt, W., London and New York: Harper & Row.

— [1977a] 'The Question Concerning Technology' in, *The Question Concerning Technology and Other Essays,* trans. Lovitt, W., London and New York: Harper & Row, 1–35.

— [1977b] 'The Turning' in, *The Question Concerning Technology and Other Essays,* trans. Lovitt, W., London and New York: Harper & Row, 36–53.

— 1977c] 'The word of Nietzsche: "god is dead"', in *The Question Concerning Technology and Other Essays,* trans. Lovitt, W., London and New York: Harper & Row, 53–114.

— [1977d] 'The age of the world picture', in *The Question Concerning Technology and Other Essays,* trans. Lovitt, W., London and New York: Harper & Row, 115–54.

— [1977e] 'Science and reflection', in *The Question Concerning Technology and Other Essays,* trans. Lovitt, W., London and New York: Harper & Row, 155–83.

— [1982] *On the Way to Language*, trans. Harper & Row, New York: Harper & Row.

— [1985a] *Gesamptausgabe, Vol. 61: Phänomenologische Interpretationen zu Aristotles: Einführung in die Phänomenologische Forschung*, Frankfurt: Klostermann.

— [1985b] *Prolegomena to the History of the Concept of Time*, trans. Kisiel, T., Bloomington, IN: Indiana University Press.

— [1991] *The Principle of Reason*, trans. Lilly, R., Bloomington and Indianapolis: Indiana University Press [published in German as *Der Satz vom Grund*, 1957 by Verlag Gunther Neske, Pfullingen].

— [1992] *Plato's Sophist*, trans. Rojcewicz, R. and Schuwer, A., Bloomington, IN: Indiana University Press.

— [1998a] 'Letter on "Humanism"', in McNeill, W. [ed.], *Pathmarks*, Cambridge: Cambridge University Press, 239–76.
— [1998b] 'Plato's Doctrine of Truth' in McNeill, W. [ed.], *Pathmarks*, Cambridge: Cambridge University Press, 155–82.
— [2000] *Introduction to Metaphysics*, trans. Fried, G. and Polt, R., New Haven and London: Yale University Press.
— [2000b] 'The origin of the work of art', in Young, J. and Haynes, K., [ed. and trans.] *Off the Beaten Path*, Cambridge: Cambridge University Press, 1–52.
— [2002] *Identity and Difference*, trans. Stambaugh, J., Chicago, IL: University of Chicago Press.
Held, D., McGrew, A., Goldblatt, D. and Perraton, J. [1999] *Global Transformations: Politics, Economics and Culture*. Stanford, IL: Stanford University Press. Introduction, 32–86.
Hempel, C. G. [1969] 'Logical positivism and the social sciences', in Achinstein, P. and Barker, S. F. [eds] *The Legacy of Logical Positivism*, Baltimore: John Hopkins University Press: 163–94 [Also reproduced in Hempel, C. G. [2001] *The Philosophy of Carl G. Hempel*, Fetzer, J. H. [ed] Oxford: Oxford University Press].
Heritage, J. and Atkinson, J. M. [1984] 'Introduction', in Atkinson, J. M. and Heritage, J. [eds] *Structures of Social Action. Studies in Conversation Analysis*, Cambridge: Cambridge University Press, 1–15.
Heshusius, L. [1994] 'Freeing ourselves from objectivity: Managing subjectivity or turning toward a participatory mode of consciousness?', *Educational Researcher*, 23[3], 15–22.
Heron, J. and Reason, P. [1997] 'A participatory inquiry paradigm', *Qualitative Inquiry*, 3, 274–94.
Hobbes, T. [2012] 'Morality and self-interest', in Sher, G. [ed.] *Ethics: Essential Readings in Moral Theory*, New York: Routledge.
Homer [2003] *The Odyssey*, trans. Rieu, E. V., Introduction, Jones, P. London: Penguin Classics.
Hughes, C. [2002] *Key Concepts in Feminist Theory and Research*, London: Sage Publications.
Huizinga, J. [2008 {1938}] *Homo Ludens: A Study of the Play-Element in Culture*, Abingdon, Oxon: Routledge.
Hume, D. [2012] 'Morality and natural sentiments', in Sher, G. [ed] *Ethics: Essential Readings in Moral Theory*, New York: Routledge, 79.
Husserl, E. [1960] *Cartesian Meditat*ions, trans. Cairns, D., The Hague: Nijhoff.
— [1970] *Logical Investigations*, trans. Findlay, J., New York: Humanities Press.
— [1970{1954}] *The Crisis of the European Sciences and Transcendental Phenomenology*, trans. Carr, D. Evanston: Northwestern University Press.
— [1973{1939}] *Experience and Judgment*, trans. J. S. Churchill and K. Ameriks, London: Routledge.
— [1983] *Ideas Pertaining to a Pure Phenomenology and to a Phenomenological Philosophy: First Book: General Introduction to a Pure Phenomenology*, trans. Kerston, F. Dordrecht, The Netherlands: Kluwer Academic Publishers.
Hyvarinen, M. [2008] 'Analysing Narratives and Story Telling' in, Alasuutari, P., Bickman, L. and Brannen, J. [eds] *The Sage Handbook of Social Research Methods*, London: Sage, 447–60.

Îchîlôv, Ô. [2004] *Political Learning and Citizenship Education under Conflict: The Political Socialisation of Israel and Palestinian youngsters*, London: Routledge.
Inwood, M. [1999] *A Heidegger Dictionary*, Oxford: Blackwell Publishing.
Irigaray, L. with Green, M. [2008] *Luce Irigaray: Teaching*, London: Continuum.
James, O. [2007] *Affluenza,* Reading: Random House Group.
Kamberelis, G. and Dimitriadis, G. [2011] 'Contingent articulations of pedagogy, politics and inquiry', in Denzin, N. K. and Lincoln, Y. S. [eds] *The Sage Handbook of Qualitative Research* [4th Edition], London: Sage, 545–61.
Kant, I. [1997] *Critique of Practical Reaso*n, Gregor, M. [ed.], Reath, A. [Introduction], Cambridge: Cambridge University Press.
Kaplan, A. [1964] *The Conduct of Inquiry. Methodology for Behavioural Science*, Scranton: Chandler Publishing Company.
Kelle, U. [1997] 'Theory building in qualitative research and computer programmes for the management of contextual data', *Sociological Research Online*, 2[2].
Kemmis, S., Taggart, R. and Nixon, R. [2014] *The Action Research Planner: Doing Critical Participatory Action Research*, Dordrecht: Springer.
Kendall, G. and Wickham, G. [1999] *Using Foucault's Methods*, London: Sage.
Kilgore, D. W. [2001] 'Critical and postmodern perspectives in learning', in Mirriam, S. [ed.] *The New Update of Education Theory: New Directions in Adult and Continuing Education*, San Francisco: Jossey-Bass.
Kincheloe, J. L. [2001] 'Describing the bricolage: conceptualizing a new rigor a new rigor in qualitative research', *Qualitative Inquiry*, 7[6], 679–92.
— [2003] 'Critical ontology: Visions of selfhood and curriculum, *Journal of Curriculum Theorizing*, 19[1], 47–64.
— [2004a] 'Introduction: the power of the bricolage: expanding research methods', in J. L. Kincheloe and K. S. Berry [eds], *Rigour and complexity in educational research: Conceptualizing the bricolage*, Maidenhead: Open University Press, 1–22.
— [2004b] 'Questions of disciplinarity/interdisciplinarity in a changing world', in J. L. Kincheloe and K. S. Berry [eds], *Rigour and complexity in educational research: Conceptualizing the bricolage* Maidenhead: Open University Press, 50–81.
— [2005a] 'On to the next level: Continuing the conceptualization of the bricolage', *Qualitative Inquiry*, 11, [3], 323–50.
— [2005b] *Critical Constructivism Primer.* New York, New York: P. Lang.
— [2006] 'Critical Ontology and Indigenous Ways of Being: Forging a Postcolonial Curriculum', in Kanu, Y. [ed.] *Curriculum as Cultural Practice: Postcolonial Imaginations.* Toronto: University of Toronto Press.
— [2008a] 'Critical pedagogy and the knowledge wars of the twenty-first century', *International Journal of Critical Pedagogy*, 1[1], 1–22. Available at: http://freireproject.org/wp-content/journals/TIJCP/Vol1No1/48–38–1-PB.pdf
— [2008b] *Knowledge and Critical Pedagogy: An Introduction.* Dordrecht: Springer.
Kincheloe, J. L. and Berry, K. S. [2004] *Rigour* and *Complexity* in *Educational Research: Conceptualizing* the *bricolage*, Maidenhead, Berkshire: Open University Press [emphasis as in the original].

Kitzinger, J. [2000] 'Doing feminist conversation analysis', *Feminism and Psychology*, 10[2], 163–93.
Kögler, H. H. [1996] *The Power of Dialogue: Critical Hermeneutics after Gadamer and Foucault*, trans. Hendrickson, P., Cambridge, MA: MIT Press.
Kristeva, J. [1977] *About Chinese Women*. London: Boyars.
— [1984 {1974}] *Revolution in Poetic Language*, New York: Columbia University Press [this is an abridged version of: *La Révolution Du Langage Poétique: L'avant-Garde À La Fin Du Xixe Siècle, Lautréamont Et Mallarmé*. Paris: Éditions du Seuil.
— [1994 [1991}] Strangers to Ourselves, trans. Roudiez, L. S. New York: Columbia University Press [originally published in 1991 by Librarie Artheme Fayad as *Étrangers à nous-mémes*].
Kuhn, T. S. [1970] *The Structure of Scientific Revolutions* [2nd Edition], Chicago: Chicago University Press.
Lacan, J. [2006] *Écrits* [1st Edition], trans. Fink, B., New York: Norton & Co.
— [2007] *The Rise of the Network Society: Information Age: Economy, Society, and Culture v. 1 [Information Age Series]: The Information Age: Economy, Society, and Culture Volume*, New York: W.W. Norton & Co.
Laclau, E. and Mouffe, C. [2014{1985}] *Hegemony and Socialist Strategy: Towards a Radical Democratic Politics* [2nd Edition], London and New York: Verso.
Langer, S. [1953] *Feeling and Form: A Theory of Art Developed from Philosophy in a New Key*, London: Routledge and Keegan Paul.
Lather, P. [1991] *Getting Smart: Using Feminist Research and Pedagogy within/in the Postmodern*, New York: Routledge.
— [1993a] 'Fertile obsession: validity after poststructuralism', *Sociological Quarterly*, 34[4], 673–93.
— [1993b] 'Writing: A Method of Inquiry' in, Denzin, N. K. and Lincoln, Y. S. [eds] *Handbook of Qualitative Inquiry* [2nd Edition] Thousand Oakes, CA: Sage, 923–43.
— [1994] 'An Ache of Wings: Women, AIDS and Angels,' Curriculum Theorizing Conference; AERA, 'Validity After Poststructuralism: On [Not] Writing About the Lives of Women with HIV/AIDS' and 'Textuality as Praxis.' Stone-Society for the Study of Symbolic Interaction Annual Symposium, 'Interpretive and Textual Strategies: Toward Transgressive Validity: Researching the Lives of Women with HIV/AIDS.
— [2004] 'This is your father's paradigm: Government intrusion and the case of qualitative research in education', *Qualitative Inquiry*, 10[1], 15–34.
— [2006] 'Foucauldian scientificity: rethinking the nexus of qualitative research and educational policy analysis', *International Journal of Qualitative Studies in Education*, 19[6], 783–91.
— [2007a] *Getting Lost: Feminist Efforts towards a Double[d] Science*, New York: State University of New York Press.
— [2007b] 'Naked Methodology' in Lather, M. *Getting Lost: Feminist Efforts toward a Double[d] Science*, Albany, New York: State University of New York Press, 49–57.
Latour, B. [2007] *Reassembling the Social: An Introduction to Actor-Network-Theory*, Oxford: Oxford University Press.

Lave, J. and Wenger, E. [1991] *Situated Learning: Legitimate Peripheral Participation*, Cambridge: Cambridge University Press.

Lawrence R. [2010] 'Beyond disciplinary confinement to transdisciplinarity', in Brown, V. Harris, J. and Russell, J. [eds] *Tackling Wicked Problems through the Transdisciplinary Imagination*. London, Earthscan, 16–30.

Lee, A. [1992] 'Post-structuralism and educational research: some categories and issues', *Issues In Educational Re*search, 2[1], 1–11.

Lee, R. and Fielding, N. [1996] 'Qualitative data analysis: representations of a technology: a comment on Coffrey, Holbrook and Atkinson', *Sociological Research Online*, 1[4].

Lefebvre, H. [1996] *The Production of Space*, trans. Nicholson-Smith, D., Oxford: Blackwell Publishing.

Levi-Strauss, C. [1966] *Savage Mind*, trans. Weidenfeld, G and Nicholson Ltd., New York: Oxford University Press.

Lewis, M. [2008] *Derrida and Lacan: Another Writing*, Edinburgh: Edinburgh University Press

Lincoln, Y. S. [2001] 'An Emerging New *Bricoleur*: Promises and Possibilities—A Reaction to Joe Kincheloe's "Describing the Bricoleur"', *Qualitative Inquiry*, 7[6], 693–705.

Lincoln, Y. S. and Denzin, N. K. [2011] 'Toward a "Refunctioned Ethnography", in Denzin, N. K. and Lincoln, Y. S. [eds] *The Sage Handbook of Qualitative Research* [4th Edition], London: Sage, 715–18.

Lincoln, Y. S. and Guba, E. [1985] *Naturalistic Inquiry*, London: Sage Publications.

Lincoln, Y. S., Lynham, S. A. and Guba, E. G. [2011] 'Paradigmatic Controversies, contradictions, and emerging confluences, revisited', in Denzin, N. K. and Lincoln, Y. S. [eds] *The Sage Handbook of Qualitative Research* [4th Edition], London: Sage, 97–128.

Lindesmith, A. [1947] *Opiate Addiction*, Bloomington, Indiana: Principi.

Lovitt, W. [1977] Translator's footnote cited in Heidegger. [1977: 3].

Lucy, N. [2004] 'Pharmakon', in Lucy, N. [ed.] *A Derrida Dictionary*, Oxford: Blackwell Publishing, 90–92.

Lyotard, J.-F. [1984] *The Postmodern Condition*, Manchester: Manchester University Press.

Maddison, D. S. [1999] Performing theory/embodied writing, *Text and Performance Quarterly*, 19, 107–24.

— [2005] *Critical Ethnography, Method, Ethics and Performance*, Thousand Oakes, CA: Sage.

Maguire, K. and Gibbs, P. [2013] Exploring the notion of quality in quality higher education assessment in a collaborative future. *Quality in Higher Education*, 19[1], 41–55.

Masschelein, A. N. and Ricken, N. [2003] 'Do We [Still] Need *the Concept of Bildung', Educational Philosophy and Theory*, 35[2], 139–54.

May, S. [2011] *Love: A History*, New Haven and London: Yale University Press.

McWhorter, L. [2005] 'Episteme' in, Protevi, J. [ed.] *A Dictionary of Continental Philosophy*, Edinburgh: Edinburgh University Press, 176–77.

Menassa, E., Mima, S. and Chaar, B. [2009] A pilot study of university professors and students' perception regarding accreditation of business schools in Lebanon, *International Journal of Business Research*, 9[2], 129.

McLeod, J. [2000] The development of narrative-informed theory, research and practice in counselling and psychotherapy: European perspectives. *European Journal of Psychotherapy, Counselling and Health*, *3*[3], 331–33.

MacLeod, M. L. P. and Zimmer, L. V. [2005] 'Re-thinking emancipation and empowerment in action research: Lessons from small rural hospitals', *Canadian Journal of Nursing Research*, 37[1], 68–84.

MacIntyre, A. C. [1984] *After Virtue*, Notre Dame, Indiana: University of Notre Dame Press.

Maclean, P. D. [1985] 'Brain Evolution Relating to Family, Play, and the Separation Call', *Arch Gen Psychiatry*, 42, 405–17.

— [1990] *The Triune Brain in Evolution: Role in Paleocerebral Functions*, New York: Springer.

Macpherson, I., Brooker, R., Aspland, T., and Cuskelly, E. [2004] 'Constructing a territory for professional practice research: Some introductory considerations', *Action Research*, 2[1], 89–106.

Madison, D. S. [1999] Performing Theory/embodied writing, *Text and Performance Quarterly*, 19, 107–24.

— [2005] *Critical Ethnography: Methods, Ethics and Performance*, Thousand Oakes, CA: Sage.

Maguire, K. and Gibbs, P. [2013] 'Exploring the notion of quality in quality higher education assessment in a collaborative future'. *Quality in Higher Education*, 19[1], 41–55. ISSN 1353–8322.

Marx, K. [1852] *The Eighteenth Brumaire of Louis Bonaparte*. Karl Marx, available at: http://www.marxists.org/archive/marx/works/1852/18th-brumaire/ch01.htm, accessed 2 March 2013.

Maxwell, J. A. [2004] 'Using qualitative methods for causal explanation', *Field Methods*, 16[3], 243–64.

Maxwell, T. [2003] 'From first to second generation professional doctorate' *Studies in Higher Education*, 28[3], 279–91.

McAllister, C. L., Wilson, P. C., Green, B. L. and Baldwin, J. L. [2005] '"Come and take a walk:" Listening to early Head Start parents on school-readiness as a matter of child, family and community health', *American Journal of Public Health*, 95, 617–25.

Merleau-Ponty, M. [2002] *Phenomenology of Perception: An Introduction*, London: Routledge Classics.

Mezirow, J. [1997] 'Transformative learning: theory to practice', *New Directions for Adult and Continuing Education*, 74, 5–12 Summer.

Mazzei, L. A. [2004] 'Silent listenings. Deconstructive practices in discourse-based research', *Educational Researcher*, 33, 26–34.

— [2003] 'Inhabited Silences: In pursuit of muffled sub-text', *Qualitative Inquiry*, 9: 355–66.

Mills, J. S. [1869] *On Liberty*, London: Longman, Roberts and Green.

Mills, S. [2003] *Michel Foucault*, London and New York: Routledge Critical Thinkers.

Morgan, D. L. [2007] 'Paradigms lost and pragmatism regained: methodological implications of combining qualitative and quantitative methods', *Journal of Mixed Methods Research*, 1[1], 48–76.

Morse, J. M. [2006] The politics of evidence, *Qualitative Health Research*, 16[3], 395–404.

Mouffe, C. [2005{1993} *The Return of the Political*, London and New York: Verso.
Muijs, D., and D. Reynolds. [2005] *Effective teaching: Evidence in practice*. [2nd Edition]. London: Sage Publications.
Mulhall, S. [2003] *Inheritance and Originality: Wittgenstein, Heidegger, Kierkegaard*, New York: Oxford University Press.
Murray, A. [2010] *Giorgio Agamben*, Milton Park, Abingdon, Oxon: Routledge Critical Thinkers.
National Research Council, NRC [2002] *Scientific Research in Education. Committee on Scientific Principles for Education Research*, Shavleston, R. J. and Towne, I. [eds], Washington, DC: National Academic Press.
— [2005] Advancing scientific research in education. Committee on Scientific Principles for Education Research, Towne, I., Wise, L. and Winters, T. M. [eds], Washington, DC: National Academic Press.
Neiman, S. [2011] *Moral Clarity: A Guide for Grown-Up Idealists*, London: Random House Group.
Neuman, L. W. [2007] *Social Research Methods: Qualitative and Quantitative Approaches*, London: Pearson.
Niall, L. [2004] *A Derrida Dictionary*, Oxford: Blackwell Publishing.
Nietzsche, F. [1973] *The Will to Power: In Science, Nature, Society and Art*, trans. Kaufman, W. and Hollingdale, R. J. New York: Random House.
— [1995] *The Birth and Tragedy* trans. Fadimon, C. L., London: Dover Edition.
Nicolescu, B. [2010a] 'Disciplinary boundaries – What are they and how they can be transgressed?' Paper prepared for the 'International Symposium on Research Across Boundaries', Luxembourg: University of Luxembourg. Retrieved from http://dica- lab.org/rab/files/2010/06/Paper-Nicolescu-Special-Issue.pdf
—[2010b] 'Methodology of transdisciplinarity'. *Transdisciplinary Journal of Engineering and Science*, 1[1], 19–38.
— [2011] 'Transdisciplinarity: The Hidden Third, between the subject and the object', in Chirilă, I. and Bud, P. [eds], *atiinþă, Spiritualitate, Societate [Science, Spirituality, Society]*, Romania: Eikon, Cluj-Napoca, 11–34.
Nilsen, A. [2007] 'Great Expectations? Exploring Men's Biographies in Late Modernity' in Sigmund, G. and Henrichsen, B. [eds] *Society, University and World Community. Essays for Ǿrjar Oyan*, Oslo: Scandinavian Press, 111–35.
— [2008] 'From questions of methods to epistemological issues: the case of biographical research', in Alasuutari, P., Bickman, L. and Brannen, J. [eds] *The Sage Handbook of Social Research Methods*, London: Sage, 81–94.
Nonaka G. and Takeuchi, H. [1995] *The Knowledge-Creating Company: How Japanese Companies Create the Dynamics of Innovation*, Oxford: Oxford University Press.
Norrie, C., Hammond, J., D'Avray, L., Collington, V. and Fook, J. [2012] 'Doing it differently? A review of literature on teaching reflective practice across health and social care professions', *Journal of Reflective Practice*, 1–12.
Nowotny, H., Scott, P. and Gibbons, M. [2001] *Re-thinking Science: Knowledge and the Public in an Age of Uncertainty*, Cambridge: Polity Press and Oxford: Blackwell Publishers.
Ochs, E. and Capps, L. [2001] *Living Narrative. Creating Lives in Everyday Storytelling*, Cambridge, MA: Harvard University Press.

Olesen, V. [2011] 'Feminist qualitative research in the millenium's first decade', in Denzin, N. K. and Lincoln, Y. S. [eds] *The Sage Handbook of Qualitative Research* [4th Edition], London: Sage, 129–46.

Onwuegbuzie, A. J. and Teddlie, C. [2003] 'A framework for analyzing data in mixed methods research', in Tashakkori, A. and Teddlie, C. [eds] *Handbook of Mixed Methods in Social and Behavioral Research*, Thousand Oakes, CA: Sage, 351–85.

Oxford English Dictionary, OED [2013] Available at http://www.oed.com, accessed January – December, 2013.

Oxford Learning Institute, OLI [2013] 'Trends in doctoral education'. Available at http://www.learning.ox.ac.uk/supervision/context/trends/, accessed 2 January 2014.

Paglia, C. [2001] *Sexual Personae: Art and Decadence from Nefertiti to Emily Dickenson*, London and New Haven: Yale University Press.

Parry, D. C. [2006] 'Women's lived experiences with pregnancy and midwifery in a medicalised and fetocentric context: Six short stories', *Qualitative Inquiry*, 12, 459–71.

Parsons, T. [1967a] *The Structure of Social Action, Vol. 1: Marshall, Pareto, Durkheim: 001* [2nd Edition] Cambridge: Free Press.

— [1967b] *The Structure of Social Action, Vol. 2: 002*, Cambridge: Free Press.

Pearson, K. A. and Large, D. [2006] *The Nietzsche Reader*, Oxford: Blackwell Publishing.

Peim, N. A. and Flint, K. J. [2009] 'Testing Times: Questions concerning assessment for school improvement', *Educational Philosophy and Theory*, 41[3], 342–61.

Pelias, R. J. [2011] 'Writing into position: strategies for composition and evaluation', in Denzin, N. K. and Lincoln, Y. S. [eds] *The Sage Handbook of Qualitative Research* [4th Edition], London: Sage, 659–68.

Philips, D. C. and Burbules, N. C. [2000] *Postpositivism and Educational Research*. Lanham & Boulder: Rowman & Littlefield Publishers.

Peters, M. [2004] 'Poststructuralism and the aims of educational research', in Peter, M. P. and Burbules, N. C. [eds] *Poststructuralism and Educational Research*, Lanham, MD: Rowman and Littlefield.

Pieterse, J. N. [1992] 'Emancipations: modern and postmodern', *Development and Change*, 23[3], 5–41.

Pohl, C. and Hadorn, G. H. [2006] *Gestaltungsprinzipien für die Transdisziplinäre Forschung – ein Beitrag des td-net*, München: Oekom.

Popper, K. [2002a] *The Logic of Scientific Discovery*, London: Routledge Classics.

— [2002b] *Conjectures and Refutations: The Growth of Scientific Knowledge*, London: Routledge Classics.

Potter, W. J. [1996] *An analysis of thinking and research about qualitative methods*, Mahwah, NJ: Lawrence Erlbaum.

Preissle, J. [2011] 'Qualitative Futures: Where We Might Go From Where We've Been', in Denzin, N. K. and Lincoln, Y. S. [eds] *Sage Handbook for Qualitative Research* [4th Edition], London: Sage, 685–98.

Prendergast, M. [2007] 'Thinking narrative [on the Vancouver Island ferry]: A hybrid poem,' *Qualitative Inquiry*, 13: 747.

Punch, K. [2009] *Introduction to Research Methods in Education*, London: Sage Publications.
Rancière, J. [2010] *Dissensus: On Politics and Aesthetics*, trans. Corcoran, S. [ed.], London, New York, Sydney and New Dehli: Bloomsbury.
Randall, M. [2004] 'Know your place: The activist scholar in today's political culture', *SWS Network News*, 21: 20–23.
Rawls, J. [1972] *A Theory of Justice*, Oxford: Oxford University Press.
— [2012] 'A Theory of Justice' in, Sher, G. [ed.] *Ethics: Essential Readings in Moral Theory*, New York: Routledge, 387–402.
Reckwitz, A. [2002] 'Toward a theory of social practices: a development in culturalist theorizing', *European Journal of Social Theory*, 5[2], 243–63.
Richardson, L. [1992] 'The Consequences of Poetic Representation: Writing the Other, Rewriting the Self', in Ellis, C. and Flaherty, M. [eds] *Investigating Subjectivity: Research on Lived Experience*, Newbury Park, CA: Sage.
— [1993] 'Poetics, dramatics, and transgressive validity: the case of the skipped line', *The Sociological Quarterly*, 34[4], 695–710.
— [1994] 'Writing: A Method of Inquiry', in Denzin, N. K. and Lincoln, Y. S. [eds] *Handbook of Qualitative Research*, Thousand Oakes, CA: Sage, 516–29.
— [1997] *Fields of Play: Constructing an Academic* Life New Brunswick, NJ: Rutgers University Press.
— [2000] 'Writing: a method of inquiry', in Denzin, N. and Lincoln, Y. S. [eds] *Sage Handbook of Qualitative Research* [Second edition], London: Sage Publication.
Richardson, J. [2012] *Heidegger*, London and New York: Routledge.
Ricoeur, P. [1995] *Le concept de responsabilité*' in, *Le Juste*, Paris: Esprit.
— [1999] 'Memory and forgetting', in Kearney, R. and Dooley, M. [eds] *Questioning Ethics: Contemporary Debates in Philosophy*, London and New York: Routledge, 5–11.
Rieff, P. [1977] *Moral Choices in Contemporary Society*, London: Publishers Inc.
Rist, R. [2000] 'Influencing the policy process with qualitative research', in Denzin, N. K. and Lincoln, Y. S. [eds] *Handbook of Qualitative Research*, Thousand Oaks CA: Sage Publications.
Ritzer, G. [2012] *The McDonaldization of Society* [20th Anniversary Edition], Los Angeles: Sage Publications.
Roberts, G. [2002] SET for Success: 'the Report of Sir Gareth Roberts' Review'. Available at: http://webarchive.nationalarchives.gov.uk/+/http://www.hmtreasury.gov.uk/ent_res_roberts.htm
Rogers, M. [2012] Contextualizing theories and practices of bricolage research. *The Qualitative Report*, 17[T&L Art, 7], 1–17. Retrieved from http://www.nova.edu/ssss/QR/QR17/rogers.pdf
Rorty, R. [1998] *Truth and Progress: Philosophical Papers*, Volume 3, Cambridge: Cambridge University Press.
Rose, G. [1984] *Dialectic of Nihilism: Poststructuralism and the Law*, Oxford: Basil Blackwell.
Roseneil, S. and Frosh, S. [eds] [2012] *Social Research after the Cultural Turn*, Houndmills, Basingstoke: Palgrave MacMillan.
Ross, A. [2005] 'Desire', in Parr, A. [ed.] *The Deleuze Dictionary*, Edinburgh: Edinburgh University Press, 63–4.
— [2008] 'Introduction', *South Atlantic Quarterly*, 107[1], 1–1.

Royle, N. [2000] *After Derrida*, Manchester and New York: Manchester University Press and St Martin's Press.
— [2003] *Jacques Derrida*, Abingdon, Oxon: Routledge.
Sacks, H., Schlegoff, E. A. and Jefferson, G. [1974] 'A simplest dynamics for the organisation of turn-taking for conversation', *Language*, 50[4], 696–735.
Said, E. W. [1994] *Culture and Imperialism*, London: Vintage Books.
— [2003] *Orientalism* [25th Anniversary Edition], London: Penguin.
— [2005] *Power, Politics and Culture: Interviews with Edward W. Said*, Viswanathan, G. [ed.], London: Bloomsbury Publishing.
— [2012] *Reflections on Exile: And Other Literary and Cultural Essays*, London: Granta Books.
Schatzki, T. [1996] *Social Practices: A Wittgensteinian Approach to Human Activity and the Social*, Cambridge: Cambridge University Press.
Schatzki, T., Cetina, K. K. and von Savigny, E. [2001] *The Practice Turn in Contemporary Theory*, Abingdon, Oxon: Routledge.
Schmidt, C. [1985] *Political Theology: Four Chapters on the Concept of Sovereignty*, trans. Schwab, G. Cambridge, MA: MIT Press.
Scott D. and Morrison, M. [2010] 'New sites and agents for research education in the United Kingdom: Making and taking doctoral identities', *Work Based Learning e-Journal*, 1[1], 15–34.
Scott, D., Brown, A., Lunt, I. and Thorne, L. [2002] 'Integrating academic and professional knowledge: constructing the practitioner-researcher', paper presented at the 4th International Professional Doctorates Conference. Brisbane, University of Queensland.
Schacter, D. [2001] *The seven sins of memory: How the mind forgets and remembers*, Boston: Houghton Mifflin.
Schlegoff, E. A. [1988] 'Presequences and Indirection: applying speech act theory to ordinary conversation', *Journal of Pragmatics*, 12, 52–65.
— [1996] 'Confirming allusions: toward and empirical account of action', *American Journal of Sociology*, 104[1], 161–216.
Schlegoff, E. A. and Sacks, H. [1973] 'Opening up closings', *Semiotica* 8, 289–327.
Schwandt, T. A. [1996] 'Farewell to Criteriology', *Qualitative Inquiry*, 2, 58–72.
Seddon, T. [2000] What is doctoral in doctoral education? Paper presented at the *3rd International Professional Doctorates Conference*, 'Doctoral Education and Professional Practice: the next generation?', Armidale, 10–12 September.
Sepp, H. R. and Nenon, T. [ed.] [1986] *Husserliana – Edmund Husserl Gesamelte Werke: Band XXV: Aufsätz und Vorträge* 1911 – 1921, Dordrecht, The Netherlands: Martinus Nijhoff Publishers.
Sher, G. [ed.] [2012] *Ethics: Essential Readings in Moral Theory*, New York and London: Routledge.
Shopes, L. [2011] 'Oral history', in Denzin, N. K. and Lincoln, Y. S. [eds] *Sage Handbook for Qualitative Research* [4th Edition], London: Sage, 451–65.
Smail, D. [1993] *The Origins of Unhappiness*, London: Harper Collins.
Social Research Association, SRA [2003] *Ethical Guidelines*, UK: Social Research Association [printed copies available at: admin@the-sra.org.uk].
Speer, S. [2008] 'Natural and contrived data', in Alasuutari, P., Bickman, L. and Brannen, J. [eds] *The Sage Handbook of Social Research Methods*, London: Sage, 290–312.

Spinosa, C., Flores, F. and Dreyfus, H. L. [1997] *Disclosing New Worlds: Entrepreneurship, Democratic Action and the Cultivation of Solidarity*, Cambridge, MA: MIT Press.
Spivak, G. C. [1993] Outside in the Teaching Machine, New York: Routledge.
— [1998] *In Other Worlds: Essays In Cultural Politics*, Abingdon, Oxon: Routledge.
Spry, T. [2001] 'Performing Ethnography: An Embodied Methodological Praxis, *Qualitative Inquiry*, 7[6]: 706–32.
Stambaugh, J. [1986] *The Real is not the Rational*, New York: State University of New York Press.
— [1992] *The Finitude of Being*, New York: State University of New York Press.
Stein, P. [1966] *Regulae Iuris: From Juristic Rules to Legal Maxims*, Edinburgh: Edinburgh University Press.
St Pierre, E. A. [2006] 'Scientifically based research in education: Epistemology and Ethics, *Adult Education Quarterly*, 56[3], 239–66.
— [2011] 'Post qualitative research: the critique and the coming after', in Denzin, N. K. and Lincoln, Y. S. [eds] *The Sage Handbook of Qualitative Research* [4th Edition], London: Sage, 611–26.
St Pierre, E. A. and Roulston, K. [2006] 'The state of qualitative inquiry: A contested science', *International Journal of Qualitative Studies in Education,* 19[6], 723–28.
Stephenson, J., Malloch, M. and Cairns, L. [2006] 'Managing their own programme: a case study of the first graduates of a new kind of doctorate in professional practice' *Studies in Continuing Education*, 28[1], 17–32.
Strauss, A. and Corbin, J. [1990] *Basics of Qualitative Research: Grounded Theory Procedures and Techniques*. Newbury Park, CA: Sage.
Stojanov, K. [2012] 'The Concept of Bildung and its Moral Implications', Paper presented at New College, Oxford, at the Annual Conference of the Philosophy of Education Society of Great Britain, 30 March – 1 April.
Sulkunen, P. [2008] Social research and social practice in post-positivist society', in Alasuutari, P., Bickman, L. and Brannen, J. [eds] *The Sage Handbook of Social Research Methods*, London: Sage, 68–80.
Thomas, G. [2010] 'Doing Case Study: Abduction Not Induction, Phronesis Not Theory', *Qualitative Inquiry*, 16[7], 575–82.
Thomas, J. [1993] *Doing Critical Ethnography*, London: Sage.
Thomson, I. D. [2000] 'Ontotheology? Understanding Heidegger's *Destruktion* of Metaphysics', *Internationa l Journal of Philosophical Studies,* 8[3], 297–327.
— [2005] *Heidegger on Ontotheology: Technology and the Politics of Education*, Cambridge: Cambridge University Press.
Thornberg, R. [2012a] 'Grounded Theory'Authur, in Coe et al., [eds] *Research Methods and Methodologies in Education*, London: Sage, 85–93.
— [2012b] 'Informed grounded theory', *Scandinavian Journal of Educational Research*, 56: 243–259.
Tubbs, N. [2005] Special issue – philosophy of the teacher. *Journal of Philosophy of Education*, 39[2], 183–414.
Van Cleave, J. [2008] 'Deconstructing the conventional qualitative research interview'. Paper presented at the 2008 SQUIG Conference in Qualitative Inquiry, University of Illinois, Urbana-Champaign.

Varela, F. [1996] 'Neurophenomenology: A methodological remedy for the hard problem'. *Journal of Consciousness Studies*, 3, 330–50.
— [1999] *Ethical Know-How: Action, Wisdom, Cognition*. Palo Alto: Stanford University Press.
Vitae [2014] 'Researcher Development Framework', RDF. Available at: http://www.vitae.ac.uk/researchers/428241/Researcher-Development-Framework.html, accessed 10 January 2014.
Von Krogh, G., Ichijo, K. and Nonaka, I. [2000] *Enabling Knowledge Creation*, New York: Oxford University Press.
Weber, E. P. [1999] 'The question of accountability in historical perspective', *Administration and Society*, 31[4], 451–94.
Weiler, H. [2004] 'Challenging the orthodoxies of knowledge: Epistemological, structural, and political implications for higher education'. Available at http://www.stanford.edu/~weiler/unesco_paper_124.pdf
Wellington, J. J. [2013] 'Searching for Doctorateness', *Studies in Higher Education*, 38[10], 1490–1503, http://dx.doi.org/10.1080/03075079.2011.634901
Wenger, E. [1998] *Communities of Practice: Learning, Meaning, and Identity*, Cambridge: Cambridge University Press.
Williams, R. [1966] *Communications*, [Revised Edition] London: Chatto & Windus.
Willett, J. [1977] *The Theatre of Bertolt Brecht: A Study from Eight Aspects*, London: Methuen Drama.
Wisker, G., Morris, C., Cheng, M., Masika, R., Warnes, M., Trafford, V., Robinson, G. and Lilly, J. [2010] Doctoral Learning Journeys: Draft Report, Higher Education Academy National Teaching Fellowship Scheme Project 2007 – 2010, University of Brighton and Anglia Ruskin University.
Wittgenstein, L. [1969] *On Certainty*, Oxford: Blackwell.
Wivestad, S. [2006] 'On becoming better human beings': 1–15 [available as PDF on the internet though not URL given], accessed 2 March 2013.
Woodruff Smith, D. [2007] *Husserl*, London and New York: Routledge.
Woodard, F. and Weller, G. [2011] 'An action research study of clinical leadership,engagement and team effectiveness in working across boundaries', *Work Based Learning e-Journal*, 1[2], 80–114.
Wrathall, M. [2005] *How to Read Heidegger*, London: Granta Books.
Wright, J. [2003] 'Poststructural methodologies – The body, schooling and health', in Evans, J., Davies, B. and Wright, J. [eds] *Body Knowledge and Control. Studies in the Sociology of Physical Education and Health*, London: Routledge, 34–59.
Zimmerman, M. E. [1990] *Heidegger's Confrontation with Modernity: Technology, Politics, Art*, Bloomington and Indianapolis: Indiana University Press.
Ziarek, E. P. [2012] 'Bare Life', *Impasses of the Post-Global: Theory in the Era of Climate Change*, Vol. 2, http://dx.doi.org/10.3998/ohp.10803281.0001.001, Open Humanities Press.

INDEX